# ANNUAL EDITIONS

# World History
## Volume 2—1500 to Present
*Eleventh Edition*

**EDITORS**

**Joseph R. Mitchell**
*Retired History Instructor, Howard Community College*

Joseph R. Mitchell is a retired adjunct history instructor at Howard Community College in Columbia, Maryland, and a popular regional speaker. He received a MA in history from Loyola College in Maryland and a MA in African American History from Morgan State University, also in Maryland. He is the principal coeditor of *The Holocaust: Readings and Interpretations* (McGraw-Hill/Dushkin, 2001). He also co-authored (with David L. Stebenne) *New City Upon a Hill: A History of Columbia, Maryland* (The History Press, 2007).

**Helen Buss Mitchell**
*Professor of Philosophy, Howard Community College*

Helen Buss Mitchell is a professor of philosophy and director of the women's studies program at Howard Community College in Columbia, Maryland. She is the author of *Roots of Wisdom: A Tapestry of Philosophical Traditions* and *Readings From the Roots of Wisdom.* Both books were published by Wadsworh/Cengage and are now in their sixth and third editions respectively. She has also created, written, and hosted a philosophy telecourse, *For the Love of Wisdom,* which is distributed nationally by Dallas TeleLearning. She has earned several graduate degrees, including a PhD in intellectual and women's history from the University of Maryland.

ANNUAL EDITIONS: WORLD HISTORY, VOLUME 2—1500 TO THE PRESENT,
ELEVENTH EDITION

Annual Editions is published by the **Contemporary Learning Series** group within the
McGraw-Hill Higher Education division.

1 2 3 4 5 6 7 8 9 0 QDB/QDB 1 0 9 8 7 6 5 4 3 2 1

ISBN 978-0-07-805097-8
MHID 0-07-805097-9
ISSN 1054-2779 (print)
ISSN 2158-3560 (online)

Managing Editor: *Larry Loeppke*
Developmental Editor II: *Debra A. Henricks*
Permissions Coordinator: *DeAnna Dausener*
Marketing Specialist: *Alice Link*
Project Manager: *Robin A. Reed*
Design Coordinator: *Margarite Reynolds*
Cover Graphics: *Kristine Jubeck*
Buyer: *Susan K. Culbertson*
Media Project Manager: *Sridevi Palani*

Compositor: Laserwords Private Limited
Cover Images: inset, clockwise from top left: U.S. Air Force photo by Staff Sgt. Joseph Swafford;
USGS photo by Walter D. Mooney; U.S. Coast Guard photo by Petty Officer 3rd Class Patrick Kelley;
Stockbyte/Getty Images; background: Comstock Images/Jupiterimages

# Editors/Academic Advisory Board

Members of the Academic Advisory Board are instrumental in the final selection of articles for each edition of ANNUAL EDITIONS. Their review of articles for content, level, and appropriateness provides critical direction to the editors and staff. We think that you will find their careful consideration well reflected in this volume.

## ANNUAL EDITIONS: World History Vol 2
11th Edition

### EDITORS

**Joseph R. Mitchell**
*Retired History Instructor, Howard Community College*

**Helen Buss Mitchell**
*Professor of Philosophy, Howard Community College*

## ACADEMIC ADVISORY BOARD MEMBERS

# Preface

In publishing ANNUAL EDITIONS we recognize the enormous role played by the magazines, newspapers, and journals of the public press in providing current, first-rate educational information in a broad spectrum of interest areas. Many of these articles are appropriate for students, researchers, and professionals seeking accurate, current material to help bridge the gap between principles and theories and the real world. These articles, however, become more useful for study when those of lasting value are carefully collected, organized, indexed, and reproduced in a low-cost format, which provides easy and permanent access when the material is needed. That is the role played by ANNUAL EDITIONS.

History is a dialogue between the past and the present. As we respond to events in our own time and place, we bring the concerns of the present to our study of the past. It has been said that where you stand determines what you see. Those of us who stand within the Western world have sometimes been surprised to discover peoples and cultures long gone that seem quite "modern" and even a bit "Western." Other peoples and cultures in the complex narrative of World History can seem utterly "foreign."

At times, the West has felt that its power and dominance made only its own story worth telling. History, we are reminded, is written by the winners. For the Chinese, the Greeks, the Ottoman Turks, and many other victors from the past, the stories of other civilizations seemed irrelevant, and certainly less valuable than their own triumphal saga. From our perspective in the present, however, all these stories form a tapestry. No one thread or pattern tells the whole tale, and all seem to be equally necessary for assembling a complete picture of the past. As we are linked by capital, communications, and conflict with cultures whose histories, value systems, and goals challenge our own, World History can offer keys to understanding. As businesspeople and diplomats have always known, negotiations require a deep knowledge of the other's worldview. In an increasingly interconnected world, we ignore other civilizations at our own peril. As the dominant world power, we touch the lives of millions by decisions we make in the voting booth. Once powerful cultures that have fallen can offer cautionary advice. Those that survived longer than their neighbors offer hints.

When we read the newspaper or surf the Internet, we find confusing political, economic, religious, and military clashes that make sense only within the context of lived history and historical memory. The role of the United States in Afghanistan and Iraq, the perennial conflicts in the Middle East, China's and India's emerging roles as economic superpowers, the threat posed by religious fundamentalism, Africa's political future, the possibility of viral pandemics—these concerns of the global village have roots in the past. Understanding the origins of conflicts offers us the possibility of envisioning their solutions. Periodization, or the marking of turning points in history,

cannot be done universally. Cultures mature on different timetables and rise and fall independently. We have followed, in this volume, the periodization of the Western world, beginning with Exploration and Colonization, continuing through the Enlightenment and Industrial/Scientific Revolutions, examining the hot and cold wars of the Twentieth Century, and ending with Global Problems, Global Interdependence. Within this narrative of Western progress, one can find responses to imperialism and resistance to expansionism. Women emerge as citizens and even rulers. China's decision to abandon its exploration of the world as well as its competence in mechanization and mass production offers a parallel narrative to Europe's embracing of this path. And, we conclude with a survey of challenging new problems—nuclear weapons; religious zealotry and terrorism; the AIDS crisis; and global warming.

The articles have been selected for balance, readability, and interest. They are offered to the instructor to broaden and deepen material in the assigned text as well as to provide a variety of focuses and writing styles. The *Topic Guide* will help instructors navigate the volume and choose the readings that best complement a unit of study.

Our intention has been to offer the most current articles available. If you know of good articles that might be used in future editions, please use the prepaid *Article Rating Form* at the back of this book to make your suggestions.

*Joseph R. Mitchell*

Joseph R. Mitchell
*Editor*

*Helen Buss Mitchell*

Helen Buss Mitchell
*Editor*

# Contents

## UNIT 1
## The World and the West, 1500–1900

1. **Aztecs: A New Perspective,** John M. D. Pohl, *History Today,* December 2002
   Who were the Aztecs? What were their accomplishments? What caused their downfall? For centuries, the answers to these questions were shrouded in mystery and misinterpretation. John M. D. Pohl offers a fresh *interpretation* of the Aztecs and their *civilization,* by writing from the *perspective* of our twenty-first century world.                                                2

2. **The Mughal Dynasties,** Francis Robinson, *History Today,* June 2007
   Although originally viewed as *Islamic* conquerors, the *Mughals* established dynasties that practiced an inclusive tolerance and encouraged artistic endeavors. The *Taj Mahal* in Agra has become their most lasting legacy.                                6

3. **The Peopling of Canada,** Phillip Buckner, *History Today,* November 1993
   Canada was the creation of two *imperial powers*—France and England—during two distinct time periods. At first a French *colony* and later a British one, Canada experienced dramatically different *immigration* patterns. During the earlier French phase, *emigration* to Canada was painfully slow. However, during the later British phase, the emigration rate rose dramatically, creating a cultural dichotomy that still affects Canada today.                                                              10

4. **The *Real* First World War and the Making of America,** Fred Anderson, *American Heritage,* November/December 2005
   Known as the *French and Indian War* in the American colonies, the *Seven Years' War,* fought on three continents, was truly a world war. It had a profound impact on the colonies and a most detrimental one on the *Native Americans* who had inhabited the land for centuries.                                                            14

5. **The Ottomans in Europe,** Geoffrey Woodward, *History Today,* March 2001
   In its contacts with the *non-Western world,* Europe usually gained the upper hand. However, one non-Western power was able to fight *Western Europe* to a standstill and sometimes threatened its very existence. For a few centuries, the *Ottoman Turks* were a problem that Europe couldn't ignore.                                  19

6. **How American Slavery Led to the Birth of Liberia,** Sean Price, *The New York Times Upfront,* September 22, 2003
   Liberia was founded by African-Americans who *emigrated* from the United States in the 1820s. Their descendents dominated the politics of the region until a bloody coup by native Africans ended their rule.                                              23

7. **Fighting the Afghans in the 19th Century,** Bruce Collins, *History Today,* December 2001
   British involvement in nineteenth century *Afghanistan* produced troubles and eventually a brokered peace. The problems the British faced are similar to those facing the United States today.                                                               25

The concepts in bold italics are developed in the article. For further expansion, please refer to the Topic Guide.

# UNIT 2
## The Ferment of the West, 1500–1900

The concepts in bold italics are developed in the article. For further expansion, please refer to the Topic Guide.

# UNIT 3
## The Industrial and Scientific Revolutions

# UNIT 4
## The Twentieth Century to 1950

The concepts in bold italics are developed in the article. For further expansion, please refer to the Topic Guide.

# UNIT 5
## The Era of the Cold War, 1950–1990

The concepts in bold italics are developed in the article. For further expansion, please refer to the Topic Guide.

# UNIT 6
## Global Problems, Global Interdependence

The concepts in bold italics are developed in the article. For further expansion, please refer to the Topic Guide.

The concepts in bold italics are developed in the article. For further expansion, please refer to the Topic Guide.

# Correlation Guide

The *Annual Editions* series provides students with convenient, inexpensive access to current, carefully selected articles from the public press. **Annual Editions: World History, Volume 2—1500 to the Present, 11/e** is an easy-to-use reader that presents articles on important topics such as *immigration, the industrial and scientific revolutions, global interdependence,* and many more. For more information on *Annual Editions* and other *McGraw-Hill Contemporary Learning Series* titles, visit www.mhhe.com/cls.

This convenient guide matches the units in **Annual Editions: World History, Volume 2, 11/e** with the corresponding chapters in two of our best-selling McGraw-Hill World History textbooks by Bentley et al. and Bentley/Ziegler.

| Annual Editions: World History, Volume 2, 11/e | Traditions & Encounters: A Brief Global History, Volume 2—From 1500 to the Present, 2/e by Bentley et al. | Traditions & Encounters: A Global Perspective on the Past, Volume 2—From 1500 to the Present, 5/e by Bentley/Ziegler |
|---|---|---|
| **Unit 1:** The World and the West, 1500–1900 | **Chapter 19:** Transoceanic Encounters and Global Connections<br>**Chapter 20:** The Transformation of Europe<br>**Chapter 24:** The Islamic Empires<br>**Chapter 27:** The Americas in the Age of Independence<br>**Chapter 28:** The Building of Global Empires | **Chapter 23:** The Transformation of Europe<br>**Chapter 24:** New Worlds: The Americas and Oceania<br>**Chapter 27:** The Islamic Empires<br>**Chapter 30:** The Americas in the Age of Independence<br>**Chapter 32:** The Building of Global Empires |
| **Unit 2:** The Ferment of the West, 1500–1900 | **Chapter 19:** Transoceanic Encounters and Global Connections<br>**Chapter 20:** The Transformation of Europe<br>**Chapter 28:** The Building of Global Empires | **Chapter 23:** The Transformation of Europe<br>**Chapter 24:** New Worlds: The Americas and Oceania<br>**Chapter 28:** Revolutions and National States in the Atlantic World<br>**Chapter 31:** Societies at Crossroads<br>**Chapter 32:** The Building of Global Empires |
| **Unit 3:** The Industrial and Scientific Revolutions | **Chapter 26:** The Making of Industrial Society | **Chapter 29:** The Making of Industrial Society |
| **Unit 4:** The Twentieth Century to 1950 | **Chapter 29:** The Great War: The World in Upheaval<br>**Chapter 30:** An Age of Anxiety<br>**Chapter 31:** Nationalism and Political Identities in Asia, Africa, and Latin America<br>**Chapter 32:** New Conflagrations: World War II<br>**Chapter 33:** The Cold War and Decolonization | **Chapter 33:** The Great War: The World in Upheaval<br>**Chapter 35:** Nationalism and Political Identities in Asia, Africa, and Latin America<br>**Chapter 36:** New Conflagrations: World War II and the Cold War |
| **Unit 5:** The Era of the Cold War, 1950–1990 | **Chapter 33:** The Cold War and Decolonization | **Chapter 36:** New Conflagrations: World War II and the Cold War<br>**Chapter 37:** The End of Empire |
| **Unit 6:** Global Problems, Global Interdependence | **Chapter 35:** A World without Borders | **Chapter 38:** A World without Borders |

# Topic Guide

This topic guide suggests how the selections in this book relate to the subjects covered in your course. You may want to use the topics listed on these pages to search the Web more easily.

On the following pages a number of websites have been gathered specifically for this book. They are arranged to reflect the units of this Annual Editions reader. You can link to these sites by going to www.mhhe.com/cls

## All the articles that relate to each topic are listed below the bold-faced term.

### Africa
6. How American Slavery Led to the Birth of Liberia
8. New Light on the 'Heart of Darkness'
40. 10 Million Orphans
41. In God's Name: Genocide and Religion in the Twentieth Century

### Americas
1. Aztecs: A New Perspective
4. The *Real* First World War and the Making of America

### Asia
2. The Mughal Dynasties
21. Samurai, Shoguns and the Age of Steam
26. One Family's Tryst with Destiny
27. The Roots of Chinese Xenophobia
28. Exposing the Rape of Nanking
33. Korea: Echoes of a War
34. Mao Zedong: Liberator or Oppressor of China?
36. Remembering the War—Japanese Style
38. Coming to Terms with the Past: Cambodia
44. The Next Asian Miracle

### Business
19. The Workshop of a New Society
20. Slavery and the British
44. The Next Asian Miracle

### China
27. The Roots of Chinese Xenophobia
28. Exposing the Rape of Nanking
33. Korea: Echoes of a War
34. Mao Zedong: Liberator or Oppressor of China?
36. Remembering the War—Japanese Style
44. The Next Asian Miracle

### Cold war
23. Sputnik + 50: Remembering the Dawn of the Space Age
30. Starting the Cold War
32. The Plan and the Man
33. Korea: Echoes of a War
34. Mao Zedong: Liberator or Oppressor of China?
35. Iraq's Unruly Century

### Culture
1. Aztecs: A New Perspective
2. The Mughal Dynasties
3. The Peopling of Canada
12. The Return of Catherine the Great
14. A Woman Writ Large in Our History and Hearts

### Economics
13. From Mercantilism to the 'Wealth of Nations'
19. The Workshop of a New Society
32. The Plan and the Man
44. The Next Asian Miracle

### Environment
23. Sputnik + 50: Remembering the Dawn of the Space Age
39. The Weather Turns Wild
46. A User's Guide to the Century

### Europe
3. The Peopling of Canada
5. The Ottomans in Europe
9. The World, the Flesh and the Devil
10. The Luther Legacy
13. From Mercantilism to the 'Wealth of Nations'
19. The Workshop of a New Society
20. Slavery and the British
22. No Marx without Engels
25. Two Cheers for Versailles
29. Judgment at Nuremberg
30. Starting the Cold War
32. The Plan and the Man
37. Coming to Terms with the Past: Former Yugoslavia
41. In God's Name: Genocide and Religion in the Twentieth Century

### France
3. The Peopling of Canada
13. From Mercantilism to the 'Wealth of Nations'
14. A Woman Writ Large in Our History and Hearts
15. A Disquieting Sense of Deja Vu
16. The Paris Commune

### Geography
1. Aztecs: A New Perspective
4. The *Real* First World War and the Making of America
6. How American Slavery Led to the Birth of Liberia
46. A User's Guide to the Century

### Germany
10. The Luther Legacy
29. Judgment at Nuremberg
41. In God's Name: Genocide and Religion in the Twentieth Century

### Great Britain
3. The Peopling of Canada
4. The *Real* First World War and the Making of America
7. Fighting the Afghans in the 19th Century
8. New Light on the 'Heart of Darkness'
11. Elizabeth I: Gender, Power and Politics
13. From Mercantilism to the 'Wealth of Nations'
17. In God's Place
18. John Locke: Icon of Liberty
19. The Workshop of a New Society
20. Slavery and the British

### Human rights
8. New Light on the 'Heart of Darkness'
9. The World, the Flesh and the Devil
20. Slavery and the British

# Internet References

The following Internet sites have been selected to support the articles found in this reader. These sites were available at the time of publication. However, because websites often change their structure and content, the information listed may no longer be available. We invite you to visit www.mhhe.com/cls for easy access to these sites.

# Annual Editions: World History, Volume 2

## General Sources

### CNN on Line Page
www.cnn.com

This is a U.S. 24-hour video news channel. News, updated every few hours, includes text, pictures, and film. It has good external links.

### C-SPAN Online
www.c-span.org

See especially C-SPAN International on the Web for International Programming Highlights and archived C-SPAN programs.

### Echo Virtual Center
http://echo.gmu.edu/center

This database of information is for cataloguing, annotating, and reviewing sites on the History of Science, Technology and Medicine site.

### Historical Text Archive
http://historicaltextarchive.com

This award-winning site contains links to world history, regional or national, and topical history and resources. For speed, use the text version.

### Humanities Links
www-sul.stanford.edu/depts/hasrg

Philosophical, cultural, and historical worldwide links, including archives, history sites, and an electronic library of full texts and documents are include on this website. The resources are useful for research in history and the humanities.

### HyperHistory Online
www.hyperhistory.com

At this website, click on "hyperhistory" and navigate through 3,000 years of world history. There are links to important historical persons, events, and maps.

### International Network Information Systems at University of Texas
http://inic.utexas.edu

This gateway has pointers to international study sites for Africa, India, China, Japan, and many other countries.

### Military History
http://militaryhistory.about.com

Here is a good place to start exploring military history. The site includes a timeline of major wars and links to military history by period.

### United Nations System
www.unsystem.org

Everything is listed alphabetically at this official website for the United Nations system of organizations. Examples: UNICC; Food and Agriculture Organization.

### U.S. Department of State Home Page
www.state.gov/index.html

Organized by categories: Hot Topics (e.g. Country Reports on Human Rights Practices), International Policy, Business Services, and more.

## Unit 1: The World and the West, 1500–1900

### The Mughal Empire
www.bbc.co.uk/religion/religions/islam/history/mughalempire_1.shtml

Comprehensive website that offers glimpses of and information on the empire that controlled and contributed to India and the surrounding areas it conquered.

### The Ottoman Empire
www.ottomanempire.com

Covers the meteoric rise of The Ottoman Empire to its decline and fall. Includes information on the leading players in that process.

## Unit 2: The Ferment of the West, 1500–1900

### The Adam Smith Institute
www.adamsmith.org

This company and its website are dedicated to the economic principles and theories of Adam Smith. Visit here to explore those theories and Smith's original texts.

### Britannica.com: Mercantilism
www.britannica.com/eb/article?eu_53378

This entry from the online Encyclopedia Britannica explains the economic theory and practice of mercantilism. It also provides links to information and popular sites on mercantilism.

### Victorian Web
www.victorianweb.org

At this website, open up links to Victorian Times, which includes social context, visual arts, politics, and Victorianism. This is an expansive collection of links.

### The Witch Hunts Main Page
http://departments.kings.edu/womens_history/witch

Contains theories about the causes of the Witch Hunts, a timeline, common errors and myths, a review of torture, an annotated bibliography, and links to other related sites.

## Unit 3: The Industrial and Scientific Revolutions

### Center for Mars Exploration
http://cmex-www.arc.nasa.gov

A starting place for an exploration of the history of Mars, with links to the Whole Mars Catalog and Live from Mars information about Pathfinder and Global Surveyor.

### Sir Isaac Newton
www-gap.dcs.st-and.ac.uk/~history/Mathematicians/Newton.html

This website is a virtual museum about Isaac Newton and the history of science.

### Sputnik
www.history.nasa.gov/sputnik

This informative site provides a history of sputnik and the dawn of the space age.

# Internet References

## Unit 4: The Twentieth Century to 1950

### First World War.Com
www.firstworldwar.com

Fact based guide which covers all aspects of the war, including causes, major campaigns and battles, and how the war ended and how it changed the course of history.

### U.S. Holocaust Memorial Museum
www.ushmm.org

From this site you can access the official trial records, with photographs, of the Nuremberg trials, along with complete information about the Holocaust.

### World War 2 Timeline
www.worldwar2.net

Surveys all aspects of this global conflict that changed the World and still impacts on our world today.

## Unit 5: The Era of the Cold War, 1950–1990

### The Marshall Plan
www.marshallfoundation.org

Here is a brief overview concerning the Marshall Plan.

### Russia on the Web
www.valley.net/~transnat

Among other links at this very complete site, click on History for a virtual tour of the palace where Nicholas II and Alexandra lived, Mikhail Gorbachev's home page, or Russian Studies on the Internet, a listing of sites related to Russian history and culture.

### Vietnam Online
www.pbs.org/wgbh/amex/vietnam

Official website for the PBS series "Vietnam: A Television History," first broadcast in 1983 and repeated in 1998. It covers all phases of the war and its legacy.

### WWW Virtual Library: Russian and East European Studies
www.ucis.pitt.edu/reesweb

Through the NewsWeb at the University of Pittsburgh, there is a massive collection of links to both historic and contemporary information about Russia and Eastern Europe. At this website, there is everything from maps of the former Soviet Union to Bucharest's home page.

## Unit 6: Global Problems, Global Interdependence

### Africa News Website: Crisis in the Great Lakes Region
www.africanews.org/greatlakes.html

The African News webSite on the Great Lakes (i.e., Rwanda, Burundi), Zaire (now Democratic Republic of the Congo), Kenya, Tanzania, and Uganda is found here, with frequent updates plus good links to other sites.

### Africa Notes
www.csis.org/html/2africa.html

CSIS Africa Notes is published monthly. Check into this website for what's new in efforts to help sub-Saharan countries.

### Amnesty International
www.amnesty.org

Information about the current state of human rights throughout the world is available at this website.

### Reliefweb
www.reliefweb.int

This is the UN's Department of Humanitarian Affairs clearinghouse for international humanitarian emergencies. It has daily updates, including Reuters, VOA, and PANA.

### Target America
www.pbs.org/wgbh/pages/frontline/shows/target

Comprehensive website on terrorism which includes: a timeline of terrorist attacks, interviews with policymakers and newsmen, and an essay on the evolution of Islamic terrorism. It also includes related links.

# UNIT 1

# The World and the West, 1500–1900

## Unit Selections

1. **Aztecs: A New Perspective,** John M. D. Pohl
2. **The Mughal Dynasties,** Francis Robinson
3. **The Peopling of Canada,** Phillip Buckner
4. **The Real First World War and the Making of America,** Fred Anderson
5. **The Ottomans in Europe,** Geoffrey Woodward
6. **How American Slavery Led to the Birth of Liberia,** Sean Price
7. **Fighting the Afghans in the 19th Century,** Bruce Collins
8. **New Light on the 'Heart of Darkness',** Angus Mitchell

## Key Points to Consider

- How has Aztec civilization been clouded in mystery and misunderstanding? What does Pohl do to counterbalance this?

- What contributions did the Mughal dynasties offer to the peoples they conquered?

- How did Canada's two colonial experiences influence their "peopling"? What effect does this have on Canada today?

- What made the Seven Years' War a world war? What effect did it have on the American colonies? On the Native Americans?

- What was the extent of Ottoman westward expansion in the sixteenth century? How did the Western European nations respond to this expansion?

- What circumstances led to Liberia's founding? How have these circumstances affected its development?

- What lessons can be learned from British policies and actions toward Afghanistan in the nineteenth century?

- How did Joseph Conrad's book influence Western policies toward Africa?

## Student Website

www.mhhe.com/cls

## Internet References

**The Mughal Empire**
www.bbc.co.uk/religion/religions/islam/history/mughalempire_1.shtml
**The Ottoman Empire**
www.ottomanempire.com

Searching for trade opportunities, the small, seafaring nation of Portugal began the great European exploration of the fifteenth century. Portuguese navigators followed the western coast of Africa, eventually rounded the Cape of Good Hope, and sailed on to India and the spice islands of the Far East. They were the first Europeans to reach Japan, and they introduced the Japanese to both guns and Christianity.

The Japanese had not been very interested in the rest of the world and had gone so far as to suppress gun making in favor of honing the honored Samurai swords. It was a profound shock, therefore, when Matthew Perry of the United States arrived with his small flotilla and forced Japan to open it ports, under threat of naval gun power. However, following the forced opening of its ports, Japan undertook a large-scale industrialization that brought it power in the Far East and allowed it to avoid the humiliation visited upon China by Western nations.

Western nations, particularly Great Britain, followed the Portuguese and the Dutch to the Far East. At the end of the eighteenth century, an English delegation led by Lord George Macartney tried unsuccessfully to arrange a trade agreement with China. Meanwhile, the East India Company consolidated British power in India with Robert Clive's victory over the Indian and French force at the Battle of the Plassey during the Seven Years' War. Imperialism arrived through the dominance of a commercial enterprise.

The East India Company established trade in China and paid for the tea it bought with opium grown in India. Chinese efforts to halt this debilitating drug trade failed when the British government authorized the use of its warships to legalize the transactions. Five ports in Hong Kong fell under British influence, and other European nations moved in to join in the exploitation of China's weakness. In 1900, China's hatred of outsiders boiled over in the Boxer Rebellion. When the uprising was brutally suppressed by Western troops, China seemed on the verge of dissolution.

One example of successful resistance to European expansionism can be found in the vibrant military culture of the Ottoman Turks, whose army was the largest in Europe and whose navy ruled the shipping lanes of the eastern Mediterranean.

From 1354, the Ottoman Empire had advanced westward, overrunning Constantinople in the mid-fifteenth century and renaming it Istanbul. By 1520, the Ottomans were undisputed rulers of the Muslim world and were already casting their shadow over Western Europe.

Imperial cruelty and excess in Africa's Congo, fictionalized in Joseph Conrad's *Heart of Darkness,* along with press coverage of abuses in the region surrounding the Amazon, provoked public outrage and ultimately led to reform. Radical discussions from this period inspired human rights organizations such as Amnesty International and eventually led to the abolition of slavery.

European adventures in the Americas included both the Spanish military conquest of Mesoamerica and the much more incremental annexation of Canada. There, the conquest happened much more slowly and much less violently. So gradual was its takeover, as first a French colony and later a British one, that both cultures remain vibrant today. Although the majority of Canada is English-speaking, there is a thriving area of French language and culture in the province of Quebec.

# Aztecs: A New Perspective

JOHN M. D. POHL

As the warriors stand before the Great Temple of Tenochtitlán listening to speeches given by the emperor, they gaze out over the plaza looking for the faces of their proud families among the multitude who have come to witness their triumph. One mighty veteran gets a firmer grip on the hair of the prisoner kneeling at his feet and looks up at the towering pyramid to ponder the shrine of his patron god. It is the sworn duty of every Aztec soldier to carry on the legacy of Huitzilopochtli, Hummingbird of the South; to be ever vigilant, ever prepared to protect his family and his city from those who would destroy all that his ancestors had worked to accomplish.

The captive resigns himself to his fate; he knew the fortunes of war when he joined the army of his city-state in revolt against the empire. The priests approach and the warrior makes his presentation. Now is the time for the final conflict, the triumph, the conclusion of battle to be witnessed there in the central precinct by the Aztec people themselves. The captive will reenact the role of a cosmic enemy, living proof of Huitzilopochtli's omnipotence, of his power manifest in the abilities of the warriors, his spiritual descendants, to repay him for his blessings. The captive is pulled on to his back over the surface of a stone disk emblazoned with the image of the sun. He is held down by four priests, while a fifth drives a knife into his chest. The trauma of the blow kills him nearly instantaneously. Just as quickly the priest slits the arteries of the heart and lifts the bloody mass into the air, pronouncing it to be the 'precious eagle cactus fruit', a supreme offering to the solar god.

Every time I look upon the colossal monument known as the Aztec Calendar Stone, I try to imagine such rituals following Aztec military campaigns. Thousands of people participated— to reassure themselves that their investment in supplying food, making weapons and equipment, and committing the lives of their children to the armies would grant them the benefits of conquest that their emperors guaranteed.

Aztec civilisation has been clouded in mystery and misunderstanding for centuries. For many people, knowledge of the Aztecs is confined to vague recollections of the illustrated books of youth and their graphic depictions of grisly sacrifices. This may be more true in Britain, indeed in Europe, than in North America where we have been privileged to witness a remarkable rediscovery of the Aztec culture over the past two decades. Aztec 'sacrifice', for example, once perceived as a ruthless practice committed by a 'tribe' seemingly obsessed with bloodshed, is now seen as no more or less brutal than what many imperial civilisations have done to 'bring home the war' in the words of my colleague, the Harvard professor, David Carrasco.

Today we witness war on television to confirm for ourselves that what a government claims they are doing in the interests of national security is worth the cost in resources and human life. But ancient societies had no comparable means to convey the image of battle to the heartland of their culture. Roman triumphs were a means of doing just this, and were more important than battlefields for ambitious politicians, and we should not forget that those captives who were forced to march in their thousands to celebrate the glorious commander were condemned to horrifying deaths in the Colosseum. The Aztec rituals were no different.

In their songs and stories the Aztecs described four great ages of the past, each destroyed by some catastrophe wrought by vengeful gods. The fifth and present world only came into being through the self-sacrifice of a hero who was transformed into the Sun. But the Sun refused to move across the sky without a gift from humankind to equal his own. War was therefore waged to obtain the holy food that the Sun required, and thus to perpetuate life on Earth. The Aztecs used no term like 'human sacrifice' for their rituals. For them it was next-laualli, the sacred debt payment to the gods. Thus warfare, sacrifice and the promotion of agricultural fertility were inextricably linked in their religious ideology. Meanwhile for the Aztec soldiers, participation in these rituals was a means of displaying their prowess, gaining rewards from the emperor's own hand, and announcing their promotion in society. In addition, the executions served as a grim reminder for foreign dignitaries, lest they should ever consider making war against the empire themselves.

The very name 'Aztec' is debated by scholars today. The word is not really indigenous, though it does have a cultural basis. It was first proposed by a European, the explorer-naturalist Alexander von Humboldt (1769–1859), and later popularized by William H. Prescott in his remarkable 1843 publication The History of the Conquest of Mexico. 'Aztec' is an eponym derived from Aztlan, or 'Place of the White Heron', a legendary homeland of seven desert tribes called Chichimecs who miraculously emerged from caves located at the heart of a sacred mountain far to the north of the Valley of Mexico. The Chichimecs enjoyed a peaceful existence, hunting and fishing, until they were divinely inspired to fulfil a destiny of conquest by their gods. They journeyed until one day they witnessed a tree being ripped asunder by a bolt of lightning. The seventh and last tribe, known as the Mexica, took the event as a sign that they were to divide and follow their own destiny. They continued to wander for many more years, sometimes hunting and sometimes settling down to farm, but never remaining in any one place for long. When Tula, the capital of a powerful Toltec state that had dominated central Mexico for four hundred years, collapsed, the Mexica decided to move south to Lake Texcoco.

Impoverished and without allies, the Mexica were subjected to attacks by local Toltec warlords who forced them to retreat to an island where they witnessed a miraculous vision of prophecy: an eagle standing on a cactus growing from solid rock. It was the sign for Tenochtitlán, their final destination. Having little to offer other than their reputation as warriors, the Mexica hired themselves out as mercenaries to rival Toltec factions. Eventually they were able to affect the balance of power in the region to such a degree that they were granted royal marriages. Now the most powerful of the seven original Aztec tribes, by the early fifteenth century the Mexica incorporated their former enemies and together they built an empire. Eventually they were to give their name to the nation of Mexico, while their city of Tenochtitlán became what we know as Mexico City. The term Aztec is applied to the archaeological culture that dominated the Basin of Mexico in the fifteenth and early sixteenth century, but the people themselves were ethnically highly diverse.

Tenochtitlán was officially said to have been founded in 1325 but it was over a century before the city rose to its height as an imperial capital. Between 1372 and 1428, the Mexica emperors—called huey tlatoque or 'great speakers'—Acamapichtli (r. 1376–96), Huitzilihuitl (r. 1397–1417), and Chimalpopoca (r. 1417–27) served as the vassals of a despotic Tepanec lord named Tezozomoc of Azcapotzalco. They shared in the spoils of victory and succeeded in expanding their own domain south and east along Lake Texcoco. But when Tezozomoc died in 1427, his son Maxtla seized power and had Chimalpopoca assassinated. The Mexica quickly appointed Chimalpopoca's uncle, a war captain named Itzcóatl, as emperor. Itzcóatl allied himself to Nezhualcoyotl, deposed heir to the throne of Texcoco, the kingdom lying on the eastern shore of the lake. Together the two kings attacked Azcapotzalco. The siege lasted for over a hundred days and only concluded when Maxtla relinquished his throne and retreated into exile. Itzcóatl and Nezhualcoyotl then rewarded the Tepanec lords who had aided them, and the three cities of Tenochtitlán, Texcoco, and Tlacopan formed the new Aztec Empire of the Triple Alliance.

Itzcóatl died in 1440 and was succeeded by his nephew Motecuhzoma Ilhuicamina. Motecuhzoma I (r. 1440–69), as he was later known, charted the course for Aztec expansionism for the remainder of the fifteenth century and was succeeded by his son Axayacatl in 1469. Axayacatl had proven himself a capable military commander as a prince, now he sought to capitalise on the conquests of his father by entirely surrounding the kingdom of Tlaxcala to the east and expanding imperial control over the Mixtecs and Zapotecs of Oaxaca to the south. But by 1481, Axayacatl had died. He was followed by Tizoc, who ruled briefly but ineffectually. In 1486, the throne passed to Tizoc's younger brother, Ahuitzotl (r. 1486–1502), who proved himself an outstanding military commander. Ahuitzotl reorganised the army and soon regained much of the territory lost under the previous administration. He then initiated a programme of long-distance campaigning on an unprecedented scale. The empire reached its apogee under Ahuitzotl, dominating possibly as many as 25 million people throughout the Mexican highlands. Ahuitzotl was succeeded by the doomed Motecuhzoma II (r. 1502–20) who suffered the catastrophic Spanish invasion under Hernan Cortés.

The land mass of Tenochtitlán, the Aztec capital founded on a small island off the western shore of Lake Texcoco, was artificially expanded until eventually it covered more than five square miles. The city was divided into four districts. Each district was composed of neighbourhood wards of landowning families called calpulli, or 'house groups'. Most of the calpulli were inhabited by farmers who cultivated bountiful crops of corn, beans, and squash using an ingenious system of raised fields called chinampas, while others were occupied by craftspeople. Six major canals ran through the metropolis, with many smaller ones criss-crossing the entire city, making it possible to travel virtually anywhere by boat. Boats were also the principal means of transportation to the island. Scholars estimate that between 200,000 and 250,000 people lived in Tenochtitlán in 1500, more than four times the population of London at that time.

There were three great causeways that ran from the mainland into the city. These were spanned with drawbridges that, when taken up, sealed the city off entirely. Fresh water was transported by a system of aqueducts, of which the main construction ran from a spring on a mountain called Chapultepec to the west. The four districts each had temples dedicated to the principal gods, though these were overshadowed by the Great Temple, a man-made mountain constructed within the central precinct and topped by dual shrines dedicated to the Toltec storm god Tlaloc and the Chichimec war god Huitzilopochtli. The surrounding precinct itself was a city within a city of over 1,200 square metres of temples, public buildings, palaces, and plazas enclosed by a defensive bastion called the coatepantli or serpent wall, so named after the scores of carved stone snake heads that ornamented its exterior.

In November 1519, the band of 250 Spanish adventurers stood above Lake Texcoco and gazed upon Tenochtitlán. The Spaniards were dumbfounded and many wondered if what they were looking at was an illusion. The more worldly among them, veterans of Italian wars, compared the city to Venice but were no less astonished to find such a metropolis on the other side of the world. At the invitation of the Emperor Motecuhzoma, Hernan Cortés led his men across the great Tlalpan causeway into Tenochtitlán. He later described what he saw in letters to the Holy Roman Emperor Charles V. Cortés marvelled at the broad boulevards and canals, the temples dedicated to countless gods, as well as the magnificent residences of the lords and priests who resided with the emperor and attended his court. The Spaniard described the central market where thousands of people sold everything from gold, silver, gems, shells and feathers, to unhewn stone, adobe bricks, and timber. Each street was devoted to a special commodity, from clay pottery to dyed textiles, while a special court of judges enforced strict rules of transaction. All manner of foods were bartered: dogs, rabbits, deer, turkeys, quail and every sort of vegetable and fruit.

What happened once Cortés had entered the city is a long-familiar tale, retold from vivid reports of the Europeans themselves: though the Spaniards were initially welcomed, they seized emperor Motecuhzoma, held him hostage and forced him to swear allegiance to the king of Spain. In June 1520 Motecuhzoma was killed while trying to placate his subjects. Cortés was forced to retreat, but came back to beseige Tenochtitlán, which fell after three months in August 1521.

Some of the most dramatic recent changes to our perception of the Aztecs have come with a critical reappraisal of the histories of the Conquest itself. Spanish accounts traditionally portrayed the defeat of the Aztec empire as a brilliant military achievement, with Cortés' troops, outnumbered but better armed with guns and cavalry, defeating hordes of superstitious savages. The reality now appears far more complex. During the first year-and-a-half of the conflict, the Spaniards rarely numbered over 300 and frequently they campaigned with fewer than 150. Their steel weapons may have had an impact initially, but they soon ran out of gunpowder and by 1520 had eaten their remaining horses. So what accounted for their incredible achievement? They owed their success not so much to superior arms, training, and leadership as to Aztec political factionalism and disease.

With his publication in 1993 of Montezuma, Cortés, and the Fall of Old Mexico, Hugh Thomas exploded the myths of the Conquest, demonstrating that in nearly all their battles, the Spaniards were fighting with Indian allied armies that numbered in the tens of thousands. Initially these were drawn from disaffected states to the east and west of the Basin of Mexico, especially Tlaxcala, but by 1521 even the Acolhua of Texcoco, cofounders of the empire together with the Mexica, had appointed a new government that clearly saw an opportunity in the defeat of their former allies. The extent to which the Spaniards were conscious of strategy in coalition-building or whether they were actually being manipulated by Indians themselves is unknown. But on August 13th, 1521, when Cortés defeated Tenochtitlán, he was at the head of an allied Indian army estimated by some historians at between 150,000 and 200,000 men. Yet even this victory was only achieved after what is considered to be the longest continuous battle ever waged in the annals of military history.

By now, successive epidemics of smallpox and typhus—diseases unknown in Mexico prior to the arrival of the Europeans—were raging. Neither the Europeans nor the Indians appreciated that disease could be caused by contagious viruses. In fact successive epidemics would take away first 25, 50, and eventually 75 per cent of the population of an entire city-state within a year. By the summer of 1521, smallpox in particular had created a situation that allowed Cortés to assume the role of a kind of 'kingmaker,' appointing new governments among his allies, as the leaders of the old regimes loyal to the Mexica succumbed to sickness.

The Pre-Columbian city was totally destroyed during the siege of 1521 and the Spanish colonialists founded their own capital, Mexico City, on the ruins. After this, knowledge of Tenochtitlán's central religious precinct remained largely conjectural. The traditional belief that the Great Temple might lie beneath Mexico City's contemporary zocalo or city centre seemed to be confirmed in 1790, with the discovery of the monolithic sculptures known as the Calendar Stone and the statue of Coatlique, the legendary mother of Huitzilopochtli. Writings, drawings, and maps from the early colonial period appeared to indicate that the base of the Great Temple had been approximately 300 ft square, with four or five stepped levels rising as high as 180 ft. There were descriptions of dual staircases on the west side, stopping before two shrines at the summit. Only recently, however, has systematic archaeological excavation provided a more certain idea of what the Spanish invaders actually witnessed.

On February 21st, 1978, Mexico City electrical workers were excavating a trench, six feet below street level to the northeast of the cathedral, when they encountered a monolithic carved stone block. Archaeologists were called to the scene to salvage what turned out to be a stone disk carved with a relief in human form, eleven feet in diameter. The image was identified as a goddess known as Coyolxauhqui, 'She Who is Adorned with Bells'. According to a legend recorded by the Spanish friar and ethnographer Bernardino de Sahagún (1499–1590), there once lived an old woman named Coatlicue or Lady Serpent Skirt, together with her daughter, Coyolxauhqui, and her 400 sons at Coatepec, meaning Snake Mountain. One day as Coatlicue was attending to her chores she gathered up a mysterious ball of feathers and placed them in the sash of her belt. Miraculously, she found herself with child. But when her daughter Coyoxauhqui saw what had happened she was enraged and shrieked: 'My brothers, she has dishonoured us! Who is the cause of what is in her womb? We must kill this wicked one who is with child!'

Coatlicue was frightened but Huitzilopochtli, who was in her womb, called to her saying: 'Have no fear mother, for I know what to do.' The 400 sons went forth. Each wielded his weapon and Coyolxauqui led them. At last they scaled the heights of Coatepec. At this point there are many variations to the story but it appears that when Coyolxauhqui and her brothers reached the summit of Coatepec they immediately killed Coatlique. Then Huitzilopochtli was born in full array with his shield and spear thrower. At once he pierced Coyolxauhqui with a spear and then he struck off her head. Her body twisted and turned as it fell to the ground below the Snake Mountain. Then Huitzilopochtli took on the 400 brothers in equal measure and slew each of them.

Examination of the Coyolxauhqui stone led the National Institute's director of excavations, Eduardo Matos Moctezuma, to conclude that the monument had never been seen by the Spaniards, much less smashed and reburied like so many other Aztec carvings. Remembering that Coyoxauhqui's body was said to have come to rest at the foot of the mountain, the archaeologists began to surmise that Coatepec, or rather its incarnation as the Great Temple, might lie very nearby. It was not long before they discovered parts of a grand staircase and then the massive stone serpent heads, literally signifying the Snake Mountain Coatepec, surrounding the base of the pyramid itself. The Great Temple had been found by decoding a thousand-year-old legend.

Since 1980 the Mexican National Institute of Anthropology and history has carried out almost continuous excavations, uncovering at least six separate building phases of the Great Temple, as well as numerous smaller temples and palaces from the surrounding precinct. Excavations carried out by Leonardo Lopéz Luján and his associates have uncovered no fewer than 120 caches of priceless objects buried as offerings from vassal states within the matrix of the Great Temple. Further excavations, even tunnelling under the streets of Mexico City, to the north of the site have revealed an astounding new structure called the House of the Eagles (named for the stone and ceramic statuary portraying the heraldic raptor), which has yielded even greater treasures. Perhaps the most dramatic finds are frightening life-size images of Mictlantecuhtli, god of the underworld. Lopéz and his associates, examining images of Mictlantecuhtli found in pictographic books called codices, noted that they are depicted being drenched in offerings of blood. New techniques to identify microscopic traces of organic material were applied to the spot where the statues were found, that revealed extremely high concentrations of albumin and other substances pertaining to blood on the floors surrounding pedestals on which the statues once stood, a testament to the veracity of the ancient Aztec books.

One of the most remarkable discoveries was a stone box that had been hermetically sealed with a layer of plaster. Inside lay the remains of an entire wardrobe, headdress, and mask for a priest of the Temple of Tlaloc, the ancient Toltec god of rain and fertility whose shrine stood next to that of Huitzilopochtli at the summit of the pyramid. Despite the lavish depictions of Aztec ritual clothing in the codices, none was known to have survived the fires of Spanish evangelistic fervour. For the first time we have a glimpse of the perishable artefacts which played such a major role in Aztec rituals, pomp and ceremony.

During the course of excavations within the matrix-fill of the Great Temple, archaeologists have found the remains of objects very much like those well-known from earlier collections, together with hordes of other exotic materials. Investigators were initially puzzled by the discovery of hordes of shells, jade beads, greenstone masks, jaguar and crocodile bones, exquisitely painted vessels, textile fragments and quantities of other exotic materials. The clue lay in the Codex Mendoza, an pictographic book of Aztec civilisation compiled under Spanish supervision in 1541 and preserved in Oxford University's Bodleian Library. Here, the manuscript inventories the entire tribute of the empire for one year. Hieroglyphic place-signs name cities and provinces conquered throughout the fifteenth century. Pictographs for staple foods such as maize, beans, and squash appear, but the great majority of the pictographs represent precisely the same kinds of exotic goods found in the excavations.

Many ancient societies buried precious materials, including works of art. Economists argue that such practices served as levelling mechanisms when the supply of anything rare or labour intensive exceeded demand. The Aztecs compared war to a market place and it appears that there was more to this than just metaphor.

In societies like the Mixtecs and Zapotecs of southern Mexico, with whom the Aztecs fought nearly continuously for seventy-five years, the production and consumption of luxury goods in precious metals, gems, shell, feathers, and cotton was restricted to the elite. Commoners were even forbidden to wear jewellery. Royal women were the principal craft producers and the kings sought to marry many wives, not only to forge alliances but so that they could enrich themselves by exchanging the women's artistic creations through dowry, and other gift-giving networks. A king might marry as many as twenty times, so each palace could produce luxury goods to be measured by the ton. By 1200 CE, royal palaces throughout the central and southern highlands of Mexico began to engage in fiercely competitive reciprocity systems to enhance their positions within alliance networks. The greater the ability of a royal house to acquire exotic materials and to craft them into exquisite jewels, textiles, and featherwork, the better marriages it could negotiate. The better marriages it could negotiate, the higher the rank a royal house could achieve within a confederacy and, in turn, the better access it would have to materials, merchants, and craftspeople. In short, royal marriages promoted syndicates.

Historians are beginning to recognise that the Aztec strategy of military conquest was not only to secure supplies of food. It also sought to subvert the luxury economies of foreign states, forcing them to produce goods for the Empire's own system of gift exchange: rewards for military valour that made the soldiers of the imperial armies dependent upon the emperor himself for promotion in Aztec society. The outlandish uniforms seen on the battlefield must also have served as graphic proof of the kind of crushing tribute demands the Aztec empire could inflict. No less than 50,000 woven cloaks a month were sent by the conquered provinces to Tenochtitlán. For the kingdoms of southern Mexico, the prospect of being forced to subvert their artistic skills to the production of military uniforms to be redistributed to an ever more glory-hungry army of Aztec lords and commoners alike must have been a frightening proposition.

A great many Aztec artefacts were taken back to Europe by the Spanish; finely wrought jewels of gold, human skulls studded with turquoise mosaic, heraldic shields ornamented with the feathers of rare tropical birds, and dazzling codices all mesmerized the court of Habsburg Spain. Later these became highly prized by the nobility of Europe, in some cases passing between princes as ambassadorial presents. Others were seized as war booty and fell into the hands of collectors who valued them but were often at a loss to understand what they were or who had created them. It was only when a new generation of scholars and adventurers began to explore the ruins of Mexico and Central America in the nineteenth century that their meaning began to be appreciated. In November of this year, a major exhibition at the Royal Academy in London will be the first time that these have been brought together with the stunning finds of the past twenty-five years from the Great Temple site.

# The Mughal Dynasties

**Francis Robinson looks for the distinctively tolerant and worldly features of Mughal rule in India and that of the related Islamic dynasties of Iran and Central Asia.**

FRANCIS ROBINSON

Some ten years ago I was invited to contribute to a series of books covering rulers of the major societies of the world. My area was to be the Muslim world. There were far too many Muslim rulers, however, to fit into a single volume, so they were divided very roughly into two—the rulers of the western Muslim world and those of the eastern Muslim world.

Using a degree of selectivity, it proved possible to bring together some of the rulers of the eastern Muslim world up to about 1900 as a fairly coherent group. They were: the dynasties of the Delhi Sultanate, 1206–1526, which created the framework in which the subcontinent came, by the twenty-first century, to support one-third of the world's Muslims; the Il-Khanids, 1256–1340, the descendants of Chinghiz (Genghis) Khan through Hulagu (r.1256–65), who began to lay the basis of modern Iran; the Timurids, 1370–1506, the descendants of the last mighty Mongol conqueror, Timur [Tamerlane], who fashioned a brilliant Persianate civilisation in Iran, Central Asia and Afghanistan; the Mughals, 1526–40, 1555–1858, who ruled the greatest and richest of the Muslim 'gunpowder empires'; the Safavids, 1501–1773, who made Iran into a mainly Shia society, at the same time achieving new heights of artistic excellence; and the Qajars, 1796–1925, who valiantly strove to build up central power in Iran as they were increasingly hemmed in by pressure from Russian and British expansion.

Over several centuries these regimes had much in common. More often than not they were the work of elites of Iranian and Turkic descent, and in South Asia on occasion of Afghan descent. Iranians tended to provide the administrative skills and Turks the military muscle, although of course in South Asia the indigenous population played a major role. For the rulers themselves, Chinghiz Khan and his Mongol descendants were a powerful presence and legacy. For the Delhi Sultans the Mongols were a constant presence, harassing their northwestern border. The Il Khans were, of course, Mongols themselves in the process of being persianized. Timur (r.1370–1405) married a descendant of Chinghiz Khan. In consequence he and his descendants adopted the title Kuragan, meaning son-in-law. Babur (r. 1526–30), who founded the Mughal empire (Mughal

is the Persian for Mongol) was descended on his father's side from Timur and on his mother's from Chinghiz Khan. He and his descendants were profoundly aware of their Mongol inheritance. Abul Fazl's official history of the reign of his grandson Akbar (r.1556–1605) takes the family's ancestry back to the mythical Mongol goddess, Alanqoa. The Mughals themselves supported a genre of painting which placed them in the company of Timur or Chinghiz Khan and displayed the symbols of sovereignty and authority being handed down. The Mughal ruler, Shah Jahan (1627–58) emphasized the sense of inherited entitlement to rule nicely when, on a ruby given to his father, Jahangir (r.1605–27), by the Safavid ruler, Shah Abbas (r.1588–1629), he had enscribed the names of Timur and his successors, Shah Rukh (r.1409–47) and Ulugh Beg (r.1447–49), that of Shah Abbas, and those of Akbar, Jahangir and himself. This ruby was then placed in the centre of the breast of the peacock which formed the famed peacock throne. A century later this throne was part of the loot which the great conqueror, Nadir Shah (r.1736–47), carried back to Iran.

In this region of widely shared dynastic tradition, Persian was the language of government and the courtly arts. There was a shared high culture in which, for example, the poetry of Hafiz and Saadi, Rumi and Jami were enjoyed from Shiraz and Samarqand to Bengal and the Deccan. Alongside this there was a shared religious culture in which Arabic, the language of the Koran and the Traditions relating to the Prophet Muhammad, was the language of the *ulama,* the religious specialists. Men travelled freely across the region in search of patronage. Thus the Mughals in the sixteenth century, after being defeated in India by the Afghans, sought the support of the Safavid Shah Tahmasp (r. 1524–76) as they strove to reconquer their empire. But generally, the movement in search of patronage was in the other direction, from Iran and Central Asia to the rich courts of India. Thus, these regions of India, Iran and Central Asia had, in terms of government at least, much in common, a fact which was concealed by the onset of Western imperialism in the nineteenth and twentieth centuries, but which may in various ways be rediscovered today, as the tectonic plates of geopolitics shift once more and the links of Iran, the Indian subcontinent, Central Asia, and perhaps China, are fashioned afresh.

There are some facts about these dynasties which may come as a surprise to those who take an Orientalist view of the Islamic world. First, their rulers tended to be driven by considerations of power rather than faith. Thus, the early Il Khans spread their favours among Christians, Buddhists, Jews and Muslims. When Ghazan (r.1295–1304) converted to Islam, although the historian Rashid al-Din wrote of him becoming 'enlightened through the light of the religion of Muhammad streaming into his radiant inner being', there is little doubt that this was a ploy, for by indicating his identification with the faith of most Iranians, he strengthened his campaign for the Il Khanid throne. In a similar way, Shah Ismail (r.1501–24), the founder of the Safavid empire, aiming to build up the authority of his dynasty declared Shi'ism to be the religion of Iran. In the Safavid Sufi order, which Ismail headed, he was regarded as the incarnation of the hidden Shia twelfth Imam; by making Iran Shia he was arrogating this source of authority to his kingship. In a not dissimilar way, Nadir Shah responded to the way in which his authority was threatened by the religious aura, which still attached to his Safavid predecessors, by trying to launch a new form of Islam. He proclaimed a Jafari faith, following the sixth Shia Imam, Jafar al-Sadiq, which appeared to have the advantage of attracting both Shias and Sunnis.

For the Muslim rulers of India there was always the issue that they were ruling a vast non-Muslim population. All the Delhi sultans assumed titles which suggested that their purpose was the protection and advancement of Islam. But, when it came to the point, these Muslim rulers were dependent on Hindu bankers, clerks, craftsmen and labourers. At one point, it seems, in the second half of the fourteenth century in urban areas where Muslim authority was strong, Hindus were required to pay the *jizya* or discriminatory tax on non-Muslims. But for much of the Sultanate they seem to have been given the status of *dhimmis,* that is protected peoples of the book. Indeed, Jain sources speak well of the fiercesome Muhammad bin Tughluq (r.1325–51). The fact was that the logic of power meant that there had to be a gulf between the Islamic rhetoric of the official titles and the realities of ruling a large population of non-Muslims.

For most of the period of the great Mughals (1526–40, 1555–1707) rulers continued the inclusive policies towards non-Muslims of the Delhi Sultanate. They were particularly aware that their rule rested on an alliance between them and the warrior nobles of India, most of whom were Hindus. Thus, the emperors made a point of contracting marriages with the daughters of Rajput princes. Early in his reign Akbar abolished the Muslim right to make slaves of prisoners captured in war, repealed a tax levied on Hindu pilgrims and later abolished the *jizya*. He himself debated religious issues with *ulama* and with scholars of other faiths—Hindus, Jains, Parsis and Christians. He came to see the *ulama* as a danger to his empire of many faiths, reducing the support his state gave to them and making grants instead to the priests and scholars of other faiths. A Muslim ruler, he made it clear that people of all faiths in his empire should be treated equally.

Awrangzeb (r.1658–1707), the last of the Great Mughals went in a totally different direction. A devout man, he completed a transition, begun by his father, Shah Jahan, away from Akbar's inclusive approach to one in which he increasingly operated as the ruler of a Muslim state, following the holy law, governing for the benefit of Muslims and with the aim of converting infidels. Regulators of public morals were appointed for towns and cities; lands were restored to the *ulama;* a codification of legal judgments, the Fatawa-i Alamgiri was commissioned. Hindus suffered: temples recently built or repaired were demolished; Hindu pilgrims were taxed; Hindus paid twice the internal customs duties paid by Muslims; provincial governors were instructed to replace Hindu governors with Muslims; and the *jizya* was restored. Such policies helped to undermine the unity of the imperial system, which was already feeling the strain of considerable economic growth. So unusual were they in the context of Muslim rule in India that they are to this day regarded as an aberration.

A second surprising fact is that alcohol, and to a lesser extent drugs such as opium, were widely enjoyed by these Muslim rulers. Alcohol was part of the Il Khan way of life, which was certainly not sacrificed once they converted to Islam. Oljaitu (r.1304–16), for instance, died at aged thirty-six from digestive problems brought on by excessive drinking. In 1405, Timur, who was launched on a great expedition to China, died after drinking himself senseless over a three-day period. One of the reasons why Shah Ismail I (r.1501–24) of Safavid Iran lost the battle of Chaldiran to the Ottomans in 1514 was because his troops had spent the night before the battle carousing. Alcohol was the downfall of the four Safavid rulers who followed Shah Abbas. In the case of the fourth, Shah Sultan Husain (r.1694–1722) his sister, the forceful Princess Marlam Begum, herself a considerable drinker, turned this initially pious man into a drunkard so that the harem could keep him under its control.

Alcohol played a prominent part in the lives of a good number of the Muslim rulers of India. The chronicler, Afif, has a revealing story to tell of Firuz Shah Tughluq (r.1351–88), who liked to drink wines of different colours—yellow, red and white. One day, after prayer, he was enjoying a drink when a senior courtier called and he just had time to push his drinks tray under his bed. But he failed to push it far enough and the courtier was rendered speechless by what he saw. In his memoirs, Babur (r.1526–30), the founder of the Mughal empire, is disarmingly honest about his love of drinking parties and of the stupid things said and done under the influence of alcohol. In 1527, however, on the eve of the key battle for the future of India, he made a formal vow to give up drink. 'The thought of giving up drinking had long been on my mind,' he wrote, 'and my heart had continually been clouded by committing this illegal act.' He had all his gold and silver goblets smashed, the pieces distributed to the poor, and all the wine in his camp destroyed. His soldiers were forced to follow suit. Within a year or so Babur had regretted his action:

I am distraught to have given up wine

I do not know what to do and I am perplexed.

Everybody regrets drinking and then takes the oath;

But I have taken the oath and now regret it.

He was soon back to his old ways. Indeed, so prominent was alcohol in the lives of these rulers that it is much more a matter of note when, in a fit of piety, they make a point of forbidding it, as Shah Tahmasp (r.1524–76) of Iran did in 1530, and as the Great Mughal Awrangzeb did from early on in his reign.

The third surprising area was the role of women, who were invariably engaged in the ruling projects of their menfolk, as well as being great patrons, building mosques, madrasas and mausolea. At times they were major political players.

Among the best known was Sultan Raziya, who ruled the Delhi Sultanate from 1236 to 1240, and was, apart from the Mamluk Shajar al-Durr (r.1249–50), the only woman formally to rule in the pre-modern Muslim world. Her father, Iltutmish (r.1210–36) intended her to succeed him, so well had she managed affairs while he was away campaigning. After a stirring beginning in which she asserted her right to rule with popular support, she fell foul of the factional politics of her court.

Gawhar Shad, the wife of the Timurid ruler Shah Rukh (r.1409–47), dominated politics throughout his reign, losing control only at the end when she failed to place her favourite grandson on the throne. Her greatest legacy, for which she is remembered to this day, is the marvellous mosque with two assembly rooms that she built for the shrine of the 8th Shia Imam, Riza, at Mashhad, Iran. Another notable political player was Malik Jahan, mother of Nasir al-Din Shah of Iran (r.1848–96). For much of the early years of his reign she competed with the Shah's prime minister for influence over Nasir, at the same time keeping in touch with the British. She forced her son to have one prime minister, the able Amir Kabir, assassinated.

The vengeance of women was to be avoided. The Il Khan Abu Said (r.1316–35) developed a passion for Baghdad Khatun, the daughter of his leading general, Amir Choban. When Choban refused him his daughter, Abu Said had Choban and his sons killed and took Baghdad Khatun as his wife. She quickly gained an ascendancy over him and then had him poisoned, first, it was said, for the murder of her relatives, and second because he was in the process of transferring his affections to her niece. Another act of vengeance, for which the opportunity was long awaited, was that of the wife of the Mughal emperor Muhammad Shah (r.1719–48). Her son, Ahmad Shah (r.1748–54) had been blinded by the father of Shah Alam (r.1759–1806), in whose harem she lived. In 1788, she paid a large sum to an Afghan adventurer and his men to take control of the Red Fort in Delhi. The Afghan blinded Shah Alam and his sons, tearing out the emperor's eyes with his bare hands. It was, however, a limited revenge for the Afghan humiliated the old woman as well.

Court women played for high stakes, and died accordingly. Izzat Malik was the wife of Shaikh Hasan the Little, one of the last members of the Il Khan family. When in 1343 she thought that her husband had discovered an intrigue she had been conducting with one of his enemies, she took advantage of a time when he was very drunk and killed him by crushing his testicles. For her pains she was cut to pieces, some of her body being eaten and the rest fed to pigs.

It is with the Mughal rulers of India that we get the strongest sense of women as political players, although this could be because we tend to know more about them than about the women of other dynasties. Babur's memoirs are full of his respect for the women of his family and make clear how, when he was a teenager fighting to recover his patrimony in Central Asia, capturing and losing Samarqand twice, he relied on the political advice of both his mother and his grandmother. In a rather different way, the early years of Akbar's reign figure an episode revealing a woman as a political opportunist. When Akbar was a young emperor in his mid-teens, his former wet nurse, Maham Anaga, helped to bring down his able guardian, Bairam Khan, and came effectively to manage the government through her influence over the chief minister. She only lost control because her son, Adham Khan, became too full of himself and failed to show Akbar due respect. This led to a classic scene painted in the *Akbarnama*, in which Akbar has Khan thrown over the balcony of the harem so that his brains were dashed out on the terrace below.

Arguably, the political career of NurJahan was the most remarkable of those of Mughal women. The daughter of Jahangir's chief minister, Itimad Dawlah, the emperor fell in love with her in 1611, when he was forty-two and she thirty-four. A great beauty, highly intelligent, and a strong personality she quickly came to dominate the harem and her husband. Jahangir makes clear in his memoirs how much he depended on her support, caring for him when ill and lessening 'by degrees' his consumption of alcohol. As time went on he gave her a high profile in affairs of state: her name went alongside his on imperial edicts and he had coins struck with the inscription 'By order of King Jahangir, gold has a hundred splendours added to it by receiving the impression of Nur Jahan, Queen Begum'. Nur Jahan remained a major political force until Jahangir's death, after which she was defeated in the succession struggle. She retired to Lahore where she busied herself completing her husband's magnificent mausoleum and her own more humble one.

Major struggles for the succession were a feature of the reigns of the Great Mughals. As there was no primogeniture, the succession was open to the ablest and wiliest prince. The struggle was bitter; death tended to be the lot of the losers. The bitterest struggle was that to succeed Shah Jahan. It was started in 1657 when the Mughal made himself ill by taking an astringent aphrodisiac 'for already being an old man of sixty-one', Manucci records, 'he wanted to enjoy himself like a youth . . .' The line-up of four competing sons was as follows: Dara Shikoh, aged forty-two, the emperor's designated heir with a major interest in religions other than Islam; Awrangzeb, aged thirty-nine, energetic, devout and profoundly opposed to Dara's religious eclecticism; Shah Shuja, aged forty-one, a lover of pleasure; Murad Baksh, aged thirty-three, an able soldier of poor judgment. Two princesses were involved: Jahanara, head of the widowed Shah Jahan's household and supporter of Dara, and Rawshanara, plain and clever, and supporter of Awrangzeb. Dara was also assisted by his two sons. When the struggle was over, Awrangzeb was the victor and all the princes dead. Shah Jahan was confined to Agra Fort with Jahanara. Rawshanara had led the demand, after Dara was captured, that he be killed. Awrangzeb avenged himself on his father whom he said 'never loved him' by sending him Dara's head in a meat dish.

These dynasties were all concerned to create environments in which to display their power. The feature of Timur's buildings in his capital of Samarqand was their sheer size. When he thought that the gateway to his new Friday mosque was too low, he had it knocked down and personally supervised its rebuilding to a height of 41m (134ft). Shah Jahan, after finding the forts of Agra and Lahore unsatisfactory for royal ceremonial, built a new city for the purpose, Shahjahanabad, with this royal palace, the Red Fort, at the centre. So, too, Shah Abbas created Safavid Isfahan, with a magnificent piazza at its heart, as the focus of royal display.

Art, of course, was harnessed to dynastic purpose. The Timurids produced finely illustrated copies of Sharaf al-Din Yazdi's Zafarnama, *Book of Victory,* which recorded the triumphs of Timur. The Mughal emperors Akbar and Shah Jahan patronized illustrated histories of their reigns of which the latter's *Padshahnama* is the finest example. But nowhere was art used more strikingly than in Qajar Iran, where Fath All Shah (1797–1834) had large numbers of imposing portraits painted to promote his power and authority, and his image reproduced on articles of all kinds from pen boxes to mirror backs.

Art also offers a window on the growing impact of Europe. From the late sixteenth century Europeans appear in art and from the early seventeenth century aspects of European technique, such as perspective and light and shade, also appear. These are harbingers of the nineteenth and twentieth century

transmutations of these dynastic worlds symbolized by the overthrow of the last Mughal by the British in 1858 and that of the last Qajar by a Colonel of the Cossack Brigade in 1925. The following lines written in exile by the last Mughal, Bahadur Shah II, express the pathos of fallen greatness:

I am the light of no one's eye

The balm of no one's heart

I am no use to anyone

A handful of dust, that's all.

# For Further Reading

Francis Robinson, *The Mughal Emperors and the Islamic Dynasties of India, Iran and Central Asia, 1206–1925* (London, 2007); Babur, *The Baburnama,* trans., ed., annot., Wheeler M. Thackston, (New York, 1996); Jahangir, *Tuzuk-i Jahangiri or Memoirs of Jahangir,* trans., Alexander Rogers, ed. Henry Beveridge, 3rd ed., (New Delhi, 1978);Thomas W. Lentz and Glenn D. Lowry, *Timur and the Princely Vision: Persian Art and Culture in the Fifteenth Century* (Washington D.C., 1999); Milo Beach and Ebba Koch, *King of the World: the Padshahnama* (London, 1997); Layla S. Diba with Maryam Ekhtiar, *Royal Persian Paintings: the Qajar Epoch 1785–1925* (New York, 1998); Peter Jackson, *The Delhi Sultanate: A Political and Military History* (CUP, 1998); John R. Richards, *The Mughal Empire: New Cambridge History of India 1.5* (CUP, 1993); Roger Savory, *Iran under the Safavids* (CUP, 1980).

**FRANCIS ROBINSON** is Professor of History of South Asia at Royal Holloway, University of London. His new book *The Mughal Emperors and the Islamic Dynasties of India, Iran and Central Asia, 1206–1925* is published by Thames and Hudson.

# The Peopling of Canada

Phillip Buckner

Canada's experience of European imperialism has been both longer and more diverse than any of the major European colonies of settlement in the Americas. Indeed, parallels with those colonies are misleading for Canada alone was the creation not only of two imperial powers but of two distinct periods of European colonisation.

During the first period from the sixteenth to the eighteenth centuries all of the European colonies of settlement grew painfully slowly but none more painfully and slowly than the French colonies in Canada. Neither Acadia nor New France possessed the potential for plantation economies and the only exports that they produced of value to the mother country were fish and furs. The fisheries were of considerable economic importance, but did not require permanent settlements for their exploitation. The fur trade drew France into the interior of North America, but it could not sustain a large population base.

The French crown placed responsibility for colonisation in the hands of a succession of chartered companies until 1663 when it made a concerted effort to increase the population of New France. The costs were high and after 1672 the French monarchy returned primary responsibility for transporting colonists to French merchants. The flow of emigrants dwindled to a trickle. When Acadia was surrendered to the British in 1713, its population was about 1,000. At the time of its surrender in 1763 New France numbered around 75,000.

No more than a few hundred French settlers paid their own way across the Atlantic and there was a substantial preponderance of single, particularly single male, migrants. Peter Moogk estimates that about 10,250 migrants made their home in Canada between 1608 and 1760: 3,300 soldiers, 1,800 Acadians, 1,500 French women, 1,200 indentured workers, 900 slaves, 600 British subjects (most taken captive during the wars with the British), 500 male clergy, 250 self-financed migrants, and 200 deported prisoners. If these figures are correct, New France was even more of a military settlement than previously thought since soldiers formed a third of the total number of colonists. Since at least some of the soldiers and workers did not come from France, the origins of the population were also considerably more diverse than is traditionally assumed. The role of the French women, who had the highest retention rate of any group of migrants to the colony, was undoubtedly critical in the transmission of French culture, as was the role of the church, since all residents had to be Catholic.

Initially the chartered companies lacked incentive to colonise and the fur trade hindered agricultural development by employing large numbers of men in the interior of the colony. Yet after the first half of the seventeenth century the fur traders were aware that without a substantial base along the St Lawrence their furs and their scalps would end up decorating an Iroquois longhouse. The failure to create a larger colony had more to do with the imbalance of the sexes. Women of marital age continued to be outnumbered by men by more than two to one during the mid-seventeenth century and without a wife a male could not establish a viable farm. After 1700 the sexes came into balance but without substantial immigration New France grew slowly through natural increase.

Since half-a-million French Protestants left France between 1660 and 1710 the decision to exclude Protestants may have denied to the colony a valuable source of immigrants. Yet it is far from certain that a large number of French Protestants would have emigrated if allowed to do so. In any event the Catholic population of France was large enough to have supplied New France with all the settlers it required. Why then did they not go? One explanation emphasises the demands of the French army, which was many times larger than that of Britain's, and it is plausible that employment opportunities in the army reduced the number of potential emigrants.

But a large pool of itinerant landless labourers and unemployed artisans still existed in France and a peasant class suffering from high levels of feudal exactions and taxation. Some historians have therefore suggested that it was the land tenure system in France which discouraged emigration. In England the peasantry had lost their title to the land and had become tenants or wage labourers. In France, on the other hand, the peasants not only retained their titles but clung to the land tenaciously. But this hypothesis fails to explain why so many of those who did migrate subsequently abandoned New France. Something of the order of 27,000 French men and women emigrated but close to 70 per cent returned to France.

Historians have, in fact, been beguiled by the obvious comparisons with New England, which was created in one rush by a large number of families who came not to trade but to farm and who had the resources to establish viable communities. New France did not begin with this initial advantage and so could not offset the locational disadvantages of its climate, harsh environment and limited resources. Moreover, New France was almost continuously at war, with the Iroquois in the seventeenth century and the Thirteen Colonies in the eighteenth. It is hardly surprising that such a large proportion of the French immigrants were drawn from the military. New France began life as a fur trading post but ended it as a military outpost with a small colony attached to the base.

In the years immediately following the conquest the former French colonies received only a handful of British emigrants. Between 1763 and 1775, 125,000 emigrants from the British Isles sailed for British America, but virtually all of them went to the Thirteen Colonies. Indeed, the Thirteen Colonies, not the British Isles, was responsible for most of settlers who came to Canada prior to 1815. Americans came in three waves. The first consisted of some 7–8,000 New Englanders who occupied the lands forcibly vacated by the Acadians in Nova Scotia, and a few hundred Americans who went to Quebec. The second and largest wave were Loyalists, compelled to leave the newly established United States after 1783. Around 60,000 came to build new homes in the remnants of the first British Empire in North America. In the 1790s a third wave of American immigrants (erroneously described as Late Loyalists) came in search of land. The war of 1812–14 put an end to further migration from the United States but there was precious little about British North America that was British in 1815. By far the largest colony was Lower Canada with a population of about 335,000, of whom nearly 90 per cent were descendants of the original French emigrants. Outside of the urban areas, the French-Canadians had no need to learn English and they continued to live under their own civil law and to follow traditional inheritance practices. With virtually no migration from France for half a century French-Canadians had developed a strong sense of ethnic solidarity. In the remaining colonies the population was approaching 200,000, a substantial majority of them descendants of American migrants; most of their trade and their cultural ties were with the United States.

All this would change because of a second wave of colonisation from the British Isles after 1815. Over the next half century substantially more a million British emigrants poured into British North America. Many did not stay but moved on to the United States. Nonetheless, the population of Canada at the time of Confederation in 1867 was around 3½ million, nearly seven times what it had been in 1815. The migration to Canada was remarkably homogeneous compared with the much larger migration to the United States in this period. Except for a small influx of Germans, almost all of the immigrants came from the British Isles.

The sheer scale of the migration, which peaked in the quarter century from 1830 to 1854, meant that every province except Quebec had a majority composed of the British-born and their children by 1867. Even in Quebec the British minority had grown to nearly 25 per cent of the population.

The vast majority of the migrants paid their own way across the Atlantic. Since none came as indentured servants and slavery never took root, British North America was developed almost entirely by free labour. Male migrants slightly outnumbered women, but the majority came as part of a family migration, even though some members of the family often had to precede others. Most migrants, even those from urban areas, sought to acquire land of their own and most ended up in rural areas occupying family farms.

The frontier experience of these immigrants was remarkably short-lived. Since the majority came after 1830 and settlement was virtually complete by the 1860s, eastern British North America was transformed from a wilderness into a series of comparatively densely populated communities within a single generation. Nor did nineteenth-century British immigrants face a prolonged conflict with native peoples. They were not a kinder, gentler people than earlier migrants, but they settled in areas where, because of the ravages of European diseases and the prolonged conflicts of an earlier period, the native peoples were too few in number to offer effective resistance to the spread of settlement.

The British immigrants also overwhelmed the earlier American migrants. Lower Canada continued to have a substantial French-Canadian majority, but even the French-Canadians were compelled to make substantial changes in their society in order to survive within the second British Empire and within a Canada in which the British immigrants and their descendants formed a numerical majority.

Although migrants came from all parts of the British Isles, the Englist Canada that came into being in the first half of the nineteenth century was more Irish and more Scottish than the mother country. The Irish formed close to 60 per cent of the emigrants. Most of what has been written about the Irish in Canada has suffered from erroneous comparison with the Irish in the United States and an obsession with the Irish Famine. In fact, the mass movement of Irish to Canada peaked earlier than to the United States and the vast majority of Canada's Irish arrived before the onset of the Great Famine in 1845. The famine years did see an enormous increase in immigrants, but most of them continued on to the United States. In the later 1850s Irish migration to Canada dropped precipitously, at a time when Irish migration to the United States was dramatically increasing. Not only did Irish migration to Canada largely precede the famine but the majority of those who settled in Canada were Protestants, not Catholics.

Early nineteenth-century transatlantic Irish migrants were rarely destitute. More typically they came from comfortable farming classes who feared a future loss of status. They migrated as part of a family movement and were destined not to become indigent labourers but to acquire land and become agricultural pioneers. In the later years the income and skill level of the migrants dropped but the vast majority of those without resources were attracted to the United States. In many of the urban centres, in the lumber and railway construction camps, there were clusters of Irish labourers, but they were not the norm. Even the Catholic Irish were not so dramatically over-represented among the labouring classes as is usually assumed. Moreover, the Irish were significantly represented among the educated elite of the colonies; many of the judges, customs officers and surveyors were graduates of Trinity College, Dublin, and every colony had its Irish-born merchants, lawyers and doctors. In large parts of New Brunswick and the Canadas the Irish presence was so large that they did not so much overwhelm the existing settlers as absorb them.

The Scots were also disproportionately represented among the migrants, forming about 15 per cent of the total. Small numbers of Highlanders had begun to trickle into British North America before 1815. A people in transition from a clan-based society dependent upon subsistence agriculture, they moved across the Atlantic as part of communal groups under traditional clan leadership to protest against the economic transformation of the Highlands. But Highlanders composed a diminishing proportion of the migrants after 1815, because as economic conditions in the Highlands deteriorated, fewer and fewer could afford the costs of a passage. The majority of Scottish migrants came from the highly commercialised economy of the central Lowlands. By the early nineteenth century Lowland Scots were already a highly mobile people. Like the Irish, most moved as families and settled on the land as farmers, although there was a significant proportion of artisans among the migrants.

Not surprisingly, in view of the superior Scottish system of higher education and the over-supply of professionals in Scotland, Scottish university graduates played an important role in developing Canada's system of higher education and were strongly represented in the fields of law and medicine. Moreover, Scottish commercial links with British North America were strong. Scottish involvement in the fur trade increased the numbers of Scottish merchants in Quebec in the late eighteenth century but the real growth came with the expansion of the colonial timber and grain trades in the nineteenth. Scottish firms dominated the import and export trade of the colonies and provided the leadership in organising the Canadian banking system.

Less is known about the pattern of migration from England and Wales. Welsh migrants were comparatively few and probably came from groups suffering from the same kind of dislocation as the Scottish Highlanders. English migrants outnumbered Scottish, forming some 20–25 per cent of the total. They also migrated as families, though rarely as part of a community. Many were moderately successful farmers or skilled artisans and, particularly in the aftermath of the Napoleonic wars, the English influx included a substantial proportion of recently demobilised army officers. As with many of the Scottish and Irish migrants, this was probably not the first move for many of the English and in British North America many would move again to achieve eventual economic security for themselves and their families.

The migrants would take with them, and for a long time would preserve, the ethnic and regional distinctions that had divided them in the Old World. But nineteenth-century Britain was less fragmented than in the past. The prolonged wars with France had contributed to this process of unification and to the growth of a sense of British nationalism. There remained a good deal of popular unrest throughout the British Isles after 1815 but the rapid growth of the British economy in the middle decades of the nineteenth century, the opportunities offered by an expanding empire, and Catholic Emancipation in 1829 and the Great Reform Bill of 1832 channelled the discontent along constitutional lines and consolidated this new sense of British nationalism.

British immigrants carried these attitudes with them to the colonies. They were the children of the second British Empire, an empire infinitely larger and more impressive than the first. The heirs of the Loyalists already had a tradition of loyalty to crown and empire. The arrival of the British immigrants reinforced this tradition; indeed, they appropriated it. No group was more pronounced in their loyalty than the Protestant Irish who expressed their commitment to both Protestantism and the British constitutional monarchy through the Orange Order. In Canada the Orange Order expanded far beyond its ethnic roots and by the end of the nineteenth century about one-third of all English-speaking adult Canadian males belonged to it. Many Irish Catholics did not, of course, share the enthusiasm of the other British immigrants for the imperial connection, but those most disaffected made their way to the United States. While Fenianism had its supporters in Canada, it possessed nothing like the popular appeal it had either in Ireland or in the United States and was opposed by many leading Canadian Irish Catholics.

By the time of Confederation these immigrants had transformed the landscape. In 1815, except in Lower Canada, British North America had consisted of a series of thinly populated colonies. Most settlers were engaged in subsistence agriculture, although the fisheries were important and the timber trade had begun to develop. There were few urban centres and limited contact between the tiny provincial capitals and the outports scattered around the colonies. Except for small numbers of Americans and a trickle of Scots, there were few immigrants after the 1790s and population growth occurred largely through natural increase. In the half century after 1815 the population soared. All of the good arable land—and much of the not so good—was occupied and the land cleared of trees. Villages sprung up across the countryside and were linked by roads and by the 1850s in the more densely populated regions by canals and railroads. The newcomers were used to a competitive market economy and they quickly turned to the production of timber and wheat, the two great staple industries of early nineteenth-century Canada. They were encouraged to do so by the rapidly expanding British market in which colonial wheat and timber had a comparative advantage because of the system of protective duties imposed during the Napoleonic wars. Of course, subsistence agriculture persisted in remoter or less well endowed areas, but it usually had to be combined with some kind of wage labour in order to purchase manufactured goods, most of them now imported from Britain.

The commercial system was based on a chain of credit that stretched back to the mother country. Britain had a larger volume of trade with the United States than with Canada but there was not the same degree of dependency in the United States on the British market, which continued to absorb the bulk of British North America's exports even after the protective duties were removed. Most of British North America's imports also came from Britain, as did the capital that financed the railways of the 1850s and 1860s. British North America was not settled by small self-sufficient farmers gradually inching along the frontier. It was settled in one great influx by British immigrants who were quickly integrated into the nineteenth-century imperial economy.

The benefits of that integration were not universally shared. There was upward mobility in British North America. The earlier settlers benefited from later expansion and the inflation in land prices, but those who came out to the colonies with even small amounts of capital possessed an enormous advantage over those who did not. The latter group might eventually acquire land but it was more likely less desirable land suitable only for subsistence agriculture. By the 1860s many rural communities contained a class of backland farmers who were compelled to supplement their incomes by off-farm labour. In those industries requiring greater capital investment, such as the fisheries and the timber trade, most of the profits inevitably remained in the hands of British merchants and their colonial partners. In the urban centres disparities of wealth were even more pronounced. Social mobility was for those with capital or at least connections. Indeed, the real beneficiaries of economic growth were the colonial merchants, lawyers and administrators who acted as intermediaries for British merchants and investors. Inevitably they were largely drawn from among the British immigrants and quite naturally they were the most enthusiastic supporters of the imperial connection.

The colonies not only imported British manufactured goods and capital but also British engineers and technology, British troops to defend them during boundary disputes with the United States, British lawyers and judges to shape and to run the legal system, doctors from British medical schools to establish standards for the medical profession, British university graduates to teach in their colleges, British textbooks to use in their schools, and British architectural designs for their public buildings, their churches and even their homes. Particularly in the period after 1830, when most of the immigrants arrived, Britain was in the words of George Kitson Clark 'an expanding society,' spreading its influence across the globe, but few countries experienced the force of this pressure as Canada did. British North Americans were not immune to influences from the United States, but the distance between Britain and her North American colonies shrank during the middle decades of the nineteenth century. The passage across the Atlantic became easier and quicker. Colonial newspapers carried regular reports of events in Britain and they were seldom more than a few days out of date after the laying of the Atlantic cable.

The British North American elites frequently crossed the Atlantic to lobby British politicians, to arrange for loans from British bankers, to strengthen commercial alliances with British merchants, to visit friends and relatives they had left behind, or simply as tourists. A number of prominent British North Americans retired in Britain and members of the colonial elites eagerly sought titles and honours from the imperial government. Loyalty to the empire did not, of course, mean subservience, for British North Americans considered local self-government as part of their birthright and all of the colonies received the institution of an Assembly.

In Upper Canada and Lower Canada disputes between the Assemblies and the imperial Government led to rebellions in 1837. These rebellions reflected the growing anxiety felt by groups who did not want to see British North America more closely integrated into the second British Empire. French Canadians were legitimately fearful of the growth of a substantial British community in their midst and the rebellion of 1837 in Lower Canada was born of those fears. In Upper Canada the rebellion was a much smaller affair supported primarily by descendants of the pre1815 American migrants. In Lower Canada the rebellion was crushed by the combined might of imperial forces and the British minority; in Upper Canada the rebellion was so weakly supported that no imperial troops were required. In the aftermath of the rebellions the British Government soon realised that to retain the loyalty of its subjects, including the ever larger British-born population, it would have to give them control over their own internal affairs. The solution was the adoption of the principle of responsible government, a principle gradually extended to all of the colonies of settlement. The British Government would continue to play a part in the running of the colonies, but British North Americans now had the power to shape their own future as part of the larger empire to which they quite happily belonged.

Even most French Canadians came to accommodate themselves to the imperial connection. In 1846 one French-Canadian politician predicted that:

> *We will never forget our allegiance till*
> *the last cannon which is shot on this*
> *continent in defence of Great Britain is*
> *fired by the hand of a French Canadian.*

Not all French Canadians shared this enthusiasm but as the economy of Quebec became increasingly commercialised and the French Canadian bourgeoisie benefited from the prosperity generated by the imperial connection, the elite certainly did.

In 1867 British North Americans decided to unite into a single political unit, but they did not do so in order to create an independent state. Indeed, the majority of the immigrants of the post-Napoleonic period and their offspring felt themselves to be part of a common British culture. To them Confederation was seen as the best way of preserving the imperial connection. More British immigrants went to the United States than to British North America in the nineteenth century but there they became, in Charlotte Erickson's words, 'invisible immigrants,' forced to adapt to a society and a political culture that had been shaped by the descendants of those who had emigrated during the first period of European colonisation. In Canada, however, British immigrants came in such large numbers during the nineteenth century that they were able to overwhelm the existing settlers and lay the foundation for an enduring imperial connection.

# The *Real* First World War and the Making of America

**It has taken us two and a half centuries to realize just how important this conflict was.**

FRED ANDERSON

Two hundred and fifty years ago this winter, European courts and diplomats were moving ever closer to war. It would prove larger, more brutal, and costlier than anyone anticipated, and it would have an outcome more decisive than any war in the previous three centuries.

Historians usually call it the Seven Years' War. Modern Americans, recalling a few disconnected episodes—Braddock's defeat, the Fort William Henry "massacre," the Battle of Quebec—know it as the French and Indian War. Neither name communicates the conflict's immensity and importance. Winston Churchill came closer in *The History of the English-Speaking Peoples* when he called it "a world war—the first in history," noting that unlike the previous Anglo-French wars, this time "the prize would be something more than a rearrangement of frontiers and a redistribution of fortresses and sugar islands."

That prize was the eastern half of North America, and the war in which Britain won it raised, with seismic force, a mountain range at the midpoint of the last half-millennium in American history. On the far side of that range lay a world where native peoples controlled the continent. On the other side we find a different world, in which Indian power waned as the United States grew into the largest republic and the most powerful empire on earth. In that sense it may not be too much to give the conflict yet another name: the War That Made America.

Seeing what North America looked like on the far side of the Seven Years' War illuminates the changes the war wrought and its lingering influences. The traditional narrative of American history treats the "colonial period" as a tale of maturation that begins with the founding of Virginia and Massachusetts and culminates in the Revolution. It implies that the demographic momentum of the British colonies and the emergence of a new "American character" made independence and the expansion of Anglo-American settlement across the continent inevitable. Events like the destruction of New France,

while interesting, were hardly central to a history driven by population expansion, economic growth, and the flowering of democracy. Indians, regrettably, were fated to vanish beneath the Anglo-American tide.

But if we regard the Seven Years' War as an event central to American history, a very different understanding emerges—one that turns the familiar story upside down. Seen this way, the "colonial period" had two phases. During the first, which lasted the whole of the sixteenth century, Indian nations controlled everything from the Atlantic to the Pacific, north of the Rio Grande, setting the terms of interaction between Europeans and Indians and determining every significant outcome. The second phase began when the Spanish, French, Dutch, and English established settlements in North America around the beginning of the seventeenth century, inaugurating a 150-year period of colonization and conflict by changing the conditions of American life in two critical ways. First, permanent colonies spread disease in their immediate vicinities; second, they radically increased the volume of trade goods that flowed into Indian communities. The results of this transformation were many, powerful, and enduring.

Epidemic diseases—smallpox, diphtheria, measles, plague—dealt a series of deadly blows to native populations. Ironically, the Indians nearest the European settlements, and who sustained the earliest and worst losses, also had the closest access to trade goods and weapons that gave them unprecedented advantages over more distant groups. As warriors raided for captives to prop up their dwindling populations and pelts to exchange for European weapons, wars among native peoples became ever more deadly. The Five Nations of the Iroquois, in what is now upstate New York, grew powerful in the mid-seventeenth century by trading with the Dutch at Fort Orange (Albany) and seizing captives from Canada to the Ohio Valley to the Carolinas. Iroquois power, of course, had its limits. Tribes driven west and north by their attacks forged alliances with the French, who supplied them with arms, and encouraged them to strike back.

The Iroquois were already under pressure when England seized New Netherland from the Dutch in 1664. This deprived the tribes of an essential ally when they could least afford it. Iroquois fortunes spiraled downward until the beginning of the eighteenth century, when the battered Five Nations finally adopted a position of neutrality toward the French and British empires.

The Iroquois soon found that this neutrality gave them a new form of power. They could play Britain and France off against each other in the wars that the contending empires fought during the first half of the eighteenth century. By the 1730s a half-dozen Indian groups—Cherokees, Creeks, Choctaws, Abenakis, and various Algonquians, as well as the Iroquois—were engaging in balance-of-power politics that made any maneuverings of the French, the British—and the Spanish too—indecisive. While it lasted, this balance permitted Indian and European groups to develop along parallel paths. When it ended, however, the whole edifice of native power came crashing down.

The Seven Years' War brought about that shift and, in doing so, opened a third American epoch, which lasted from the mid-eighteenth century to the beginning of the twentieth. The shift was not immediately perceptible, for from beginning to end the war reflected the importance of Indian power. The fortunes of war in North America ebbed and flowed according to when the Indian allies of the Europeans decided to engage or withdraw. When, in 1758, the French-allied Indians on the Ohio chose to make a separate peace, Anglo-American forces could at last seize the Forks of the Ohio, the site of modern Pittsburgh and the strategic key to the transappalachian West, bringing peace to the Virginia-Pennsylvania frontier. The following year the Iroquois League shifted from neutrality to alliance with the British, permitting the Anglo-Americans to take Fort Niagara and with it crucial control of the Great Lakes. In 1760 Iroquois diplomats preceding Gen. Jeffery Amherst's invading army persuaded the last Indian allies of New France to make peace, facilitating the bloodless surrender of French forces at Montreal.

Recognizing the central role of Indians in the war certainly should not deny the importance of French and British operations in America or diminish the critical part played by the large-scale mobilization of the colonists. Those too were decisive and were part of the worldwide extension of the fighting. Britain's war leader, William Pitt, knew that the British army was too small to confront the forces of Europe on their home ground. He therefore used the navy and army together to attack France's most vulnerable colonies, while subsidizing Prussia and smaller German states to do most of the fighting in Europe. Similarly, from late 1757 Pitt promised to reimburse North America's colonial governments for raising troops to help attack Canada and the French West Indies, treating the colonies not as subordinates but as allies. This policy precipitated a surge of patriotism among the colonists. Between 1758 and 1760 the number of Anglo-Americans voluntarily participating in the war effort grew to equal the population of all New France.

Britain's colonists continued to enlist in numbers that suggest they had come to believe they were full partners in the creation of a new British empire that would be the greatest since Rome. Their extraordinary exertions made for a decisive victory, but one that came at a fearful cost. And that in turn had an impact that extended far beyond the Peace of Paris, which put an end to the hostilities in 1763.

Paradoxically, the war had seemed to damage the vanquished less than it did the victor. Despite the loss of its North American possessions and the destruction of its navy, France recovered with remarkable speed. Because the British chose to return the profitable West Indian sugar islands to France and to retain Canada, always a sinkhole for public funds, French economic growth resumed at pre-war rates. Because France funded its re-armament program by borrowing, there was no taxpayers' revolt. The navy rebuilt its ravaged fleet using state-of-the-art designs. The army, re-equipped with the most advanced artillery of the day, underwent reforms in recruitment, training, discipline, and administration. These measures were intended to turn the tables on Britain in the next war, which was precisely what happened when France intervened in the American struggle for independence. (The expense of that revenge tempered its sweetness somewhat, but it was only in 1789 that King Louis and his ministers, facing a revolution of their own, learned how severe the reckoning would be.)

For Britain and its American colonies the war had complex, equivocal legacies. Pitt's prodigal expenditures and the expansion of the empire to take in half of North America created immense problems of public finance and territorial control. The virtual doubling of the national debt between 1756 and 1763 produced demands for retrenchment even as administrators tried to impose economy, coherence, and efficiency on a haphazard imperial administration. Their goal was both to control the 300,000 or so Canadians and Indians whom the war had ushered into the empire and to make the North American colonies cooperate with one another, take direction from London, and pay the costs of imperial defense.

The war's most pernicious effect, however, was to persuade the Crown that Britain was unbeatable. The extraordinary battlefield triumphs of the previous years made this inference seem reasonable, and the perilous conviction that Britannia had grown too mighty to fail contributed to the highhanded tone imperial officials now used to address the colonists and thus helped sow the seeds of revolution.

Britain's American colonists had come to believe they were members of a transatlantic community bound together by common allegiance, interests, laws, and rights. Imperial administrators found this absurd. Even before the war they had been proposing reforms that would have made it clear the colonists were anything *but* legal and constitutional equals of subjects who lived in Britain. The outbreak of the fighting had suspended those reforms, and then Pitt's policies had encouraged the colonists to see the empire as a voluntary union of British patriots on both sides of the ocean.

**The war was a momentous American turning point.**

So when the empire's administrators moved to reassert the pre-war hierarchy, the colonists reacted first with shock, then with fury. What happened, they wanted to know, to the patriotic partnership that had won the war? Why are we suddenly being treated as if we were the conquered, instead of fellow conquerors?

During the 12 years between the Peace of Paris in 1763 and the battles of Lexington and Concord the colonists clarified their beliefs, using language echoing the broad, inclusive spirit of equality that had rallied them during the late war. In time those ideas became the basis of all our politics, but between 1763 and 1775 they were not yet founding principles. Rather, what took place in the postwar years was a long, increasingly acrimonious debate about the character of the empire, a wrangle over who belonged to it and on what terms and about

# The Seven Years' Movie

## A spectacular and painstaking PBS series brings the war to the screen

It's a good thing for Ben Loeterman and Eric Stange that they didn't have a passionate interest in the Thirty Years' War. Loeterman and Stange are the co-writers and two of the six producers for the forthcoming PBS broadcast *The War That Made America,* and it took them as long to make it as it took the French, British, colonists, and Indians to fight the real thing. "From pre-production to final cut," says Loeterman, "the planning was as elaborate as that of an actual military campaign. There were times when I felt we were fighting a war."

If so, the first enemy the filmmakers faced was ignorance. It's doubtful that many educated Americans could guess what war the production depicts on the basis of the title. "The French and Indian War," says the historian Fred Anderson, whose short history of the conflict, also titled *The War That Made America,* has just been published by Viking Books, "is the least known and least understood war in our country's history. North Americans don't even agree on the correct title for it; most Canadian historians call it the War of Conquest. Even those who know something about it usually know it through James Fenimore Cooper's **The Last of the Mohicans** or **the 1992 movie** with Daniel Day-Lewis. In that movie you don't know who's fighting who or why. All you know is that the French wear blue, the English wear red, and the Indians wear paint."

The four-hour production, one of the most elaborate dramatized documentaries of this type ever made, serves as a primer for history-minded viewers, one that will place the war in its proper international context. "The Seven Years' War was part of the first genuine world war," explains Anderson. "At the time, the struggle between the French and the British in North America seemed like a sideshow in a war that stretched from Europe to India." No one could know at the time that the "sideshow" would decide the fate of the North American continent and its Indian natives, who collectively constituted the third major player in the struggle.

Anderson says, "A painstaking effort has been made to show the war from the point of view of the natives, who were often forced to play both ends against the middle, knowing in their hearts that ultimately they would probably lose no matter who won." Numerous Iroquois and Canadian Mohawks were cast, contributing their own ideas on the characterization of their ancestors. In fact, the film was narrated by the Canadian Mohawk actor Graham Greene, best known for his performance in **Dances With Wolves.**

The Indians weren't the only ones caught up in circumstances they couldn't control. Colonials such as George Washington, an ambitious but insecure twenty-one-year-old army courier, were also caught in the clash of empires. Played by Larry Nehring, a classically trained actor and the artistic director for the Cleveland Shakespeare Festival, Washington was frustrated by his inability to rise to a position of prominence in the British army. He was a key figure in the war's first skirmish in 1754 and led the retreat in the Battle of Monongahela in 1755, in which his commander, the British general Edward Braddock, was killed. It's possible that had Washington been promoted to the level he believed his talents merited he might have viewed the later conflict between the colonies and the mother country much differently.

Unlike many historically based feature films (such as the first two versions of *The Last of the Mohicans, 1932* and *1936,* which were shot in California, and the *1992* version, which was shot in the Mid-Atlantic states), *The War That Made America* was almost entirely shot on the location of the actual events, in Pennsylvania and upstate New York all the way to the Canadian border. At least one American and one Canadian historian were on set at all times; there was even a military choreographer to supervise the marching and battle scenes. The film's dialogue and voice-over narration were derived from existing documents, letters, and journals, with the actors sometimes speaking their thoughts directly into the camera, a device that personalizes the characters in a manner uncommon to most documentaries.

*The War That Made America* is the result of the joint efforts of WQED Multimedia Pittsburgh and the French and Indian War 250 Inc., a partnership of the region's historic sites, foundations, and educational institutions. This unusual combination of historians, American Indian groups, and historical associations resulted in a film whose size and scope probably would have caused every major Hollywood studio to balk.

Another reason Hollywood would have refrained from making a film on the French and Indian War is the average American's lack of knowledge about the struggle that set America on the course for manifest destiny. Anderson sees that as a potential plus: "I don't think many viewers will approach the program with preconceived notions. I think they'll be fascinated to discover the rich background to a war that has all too often been relegated to a paragraph in most textbooks."

—Allen Barra

how it should function. The dispute became so bitter precisely because the colonists believed they were British patriots who had proved their loyalty by taking part in a vast struggle for an empire they loved.

The irony here is intense and bears examining. The most complete victory in a European conflict since the Hundred Years War quickly became a terrible thing for the victor, whereas the defeated powers soon recovered purpose and momentum. Even a decisive victory can carry great dangers for the winner. Britain emerged from the war as the most powerful nation of its day, only to find that the rest of Europe feared it enough to join ranks against it; it confidently undertook to reassert itself in America only to unite its colonists in opposition to imperial authority. Finally, when Britain used its military might to compel the fractious colonists to submit, it turned resistance into insurrection—and revolution.

And what of the Indians? for them, the war's effects were transforming, and tragic. By eliminating the French Empire from North America and dividing the continent down its center between Britain and Spain, the Peace of Paris made it impossible for the Iroquois and other native groups to preserve their autonomy by playing empires off against one another. The former Indian allies of New France came to understand the tenuousness of their position soon after the war, when the British high command began to treat them as if they, not the French, had been conquered. They reacted with violence to Britain's abrupt changes in the terms of trade and suspension of diplomatic gift giving, launching an insurrection to teach the British a lesson in the proper relationship of ally to ally. By driving British troops from their interior forts and sending raids that once again embroiled the frontier in a huge refugee crisis, the Indians forced the British to rescind the offending policies. Yet by 1764, when various groups began to make peace, native leaders understood that their ability to carry on a war had become limited indeed. Without a competing empire to arm and supply them, they simply could not keep fighting once they ran out of gunpowder.

## The war's effects were tragic for the Indians.

Meanwhile, the bloodshed and captive-taking of the war and the postwar insurrection deranged relations between Indians and Anglo-American colonists. Even in Pennsylvania, a colony

# The Clash of Empires

## The most ambitious exhibit ever on the war has just opened

When a young George Washington surveyed the confluence of the Allegheny and Monongahela Rivers, forming the Ohio, in 1753, he observed that the land there was "extreamly well situated for a Fort; as it has the absolute Command of both Rivers." After the English finally wrested control from the French in 1758, they christened the surrounding area "Pittsbourgh."

The 250th anniversary of this struggle is being commemorated by events and exhibits throughout the country, (www.frenchandindianwar250.org). But the center of the fighting then, and the commemoration now, can be found in the place where Washington made his assessment. The celebration includes a voluminous exhibition at the Senator John Heinz Pittsburgh Regional History Center (www.pghhistory.org). "Clash of Empires: The British, French & Indian War" will be on view there through April 15, 2006, when it will travel to the Smithsonian Institution in Washington, D.C. With nearly 300 artifacts painstakingly culled from more than 100 lenders in 12 countries, it is the largest exhibit ever on the conflict.

Even though the French and Indian War doesn't have the blockbuster appeal of many other conflicts, the story, as Andy Masich, president and CEO of the center, points out, is gripping. "It's the story of a young, red-haired George Washington who fired the first shot that set the world ablaze," he says, referring to the volley Washington exchanged with the ensign Joseph Coulon de Villiers, Sieur de Jumonville outside what is now Uniontown in May 1754. Washington, allied with the Seneca warrior Tanaghrisson, surrounded the French and defeated them handily in just 15 minutes. Then he watched in horror as Tanaghrisson split the wounded Jumonville's skull with an ax. The French retaliated for this brutal act two months later, surrounding Washington's forces at Fort Necessity. Washington signed a surrender document in French—a language he could not read—that was, in essence, a confession to the assassination of Jumonville.

That document will be on display as part of "Clash of Empires." "It makes the hair on the back of my neck stand up," says Masich. "To hold it, to see his signature, to see the rain spatters. To see the words that are the smoking gun that triggered a global war."

Other artifacts include remains of the wagons Benjamin Franklin secured for Gen. Edward Braddock, who suffered one of the worst defeats in British history on the Monongahela; a lead plate the French used to mark their territory; and ornate swords from both sides. These objects are complemented with paintings, dioramas, videos, and lifelike sculptures of period characters.

For many Americans, history begins in 1776, but as this exhibit shows, the Revolution was born of the French and Indian War. After the fighting had drained Britain's coffers, Parliament passed the Stamp Act, the first of the unacceptable taxes that spurred the colonists to rebellion. They would be led by Washington, who reported to the Continental Congress in his French and Indian War uniform.

—Elizabeth Hoover

that had never known an Indian war before 1755, indiscriminate hatred of Indians became something like a majority sentiment by 1764. When most native groups sided with the British in the Revolution, the animosity only grew. By 1783 Americans were willing to allow neither Indians nor the ex-Loyalists with whom they had cooperated any place in the new Republic, except on terms dictated by the victor.

In the traditional narrative mentioned earlier, the fate of native peoples is a melancholy historical inevitability; Indians are acted upon far more than they are actors. To include the Seven Years' War in the story of the founding of the United States, however, makes it easier to understand Indians as neither a doomed remnant nor as noble savages, but as human beings who behaved with a canniness and a fallibility equal to those of Europeans and acted with just as much courage, brutality, and calculated self-interest as the colonists. In seeking security and hoping to profit from the competition between empires, they did things that led to a world-altering war, which in turn produced the revolutionary changes that moved them from the center of the American story to its margins. No irony could be more complete, no outcome more tragic.

Finally, treating the Revolution as an unintended consequence of the Anglo-American quest for empire offers a way to understand the persistence of imperialism in American history.

We like to read the rhetoric of the Revolution in such a way as to convince ourselves that the United States has always been a fundamentally *anti*-imperial nation. What the story of the Seven Years' War encourages us to do is to imagine that empire has been as central to our national self-definition and behavior over time as liberty itself has been—that empire and liberty indeed can be seen as complementary elements, related in as intimate and necessary a way as the two faces of a single coin.

Changing our thinking about the founding period of the United States by including the Seven Years' War can enable us to see the significance not only of America's great wars of liberation—the Revolutionary War, the Civil War, and World War II—but of the War of 1812, the Mexican War, the Spanish-American War, and all of the country's other wars for empire as well. Those conflicts are not exceptions to some imagined antimilitarist rule of American historical development; they too have made us who we are. To understand this may help us avoid the dangerous fantasy that the United States differs so substantially from other historical empires that it is somehow immune to the fate they have all, ultimately, shared.

**FRED ANDERSON'S** most recent book is *The War That Made America,* which accompanies the PBS series and was just published by Viking.

# The Ottomans in Europe

GEOFFREY WOODWARD

## Introduction

> '*Now shalt thou feel the force of Turkish arms*
> *Which lately made all Europe quake for fear.*'

Christopher Marlowe's observation in Tamburlaine (1587) held true for most of the sixteenth century. The Ottoman army was the largest in Europe, its navy ruled the shipping lanes of the eastern Mediterranean, and its capital Istanbul was five times the size of Paris. Its resources seemed limitless, and its capacity to sweep aside opposition in the name of Islam gave the Turkish Empire an awesome presence. Indeed between 1520 and 1565 its momentum seemed unstoppable. Well might Christians in western Europe 'quake for fear'. This article sets out to trace some of the ways in which Europeans were affected by the Turkish Empire in the course of the sixteenth century. First, it considers the impact on the Balkans and the consequences for the Holy Roman Empire. Second, it looks at how Spain, Portugal and Venice were affected by the maritime expansion. Third, consideration is given to the argument that important military changes occurred in Europe as a result of Ottoman expansion. Finally, the strength of its Empire is evaluated and the question posed: did it really present a serious threat to Europe?

## Ottoman Western Expansion

Since 1354 the Ottoman Turks had been advancing westwards, overrunning Constantinople (and renaming it Istanbul) in 1453, gaining control of the Black Sea and the main routes to the Balkans and driving on to the eastern Adriatic. Owing to the exploits of successive Sultans, the Ottomans were, by 1520, the undisputed leaders of the Muslim world. For the rest of the century they cast their shadow over western Europe.

Suleiman 'the Magnificent' (1520–66) seized Belgrade in 1521 and, upon capturing Rhodes, evicted the Knights of St John and removed the last remaining obstacle to his domination of the eastern Mediterranean. The effect upon Europe was dramatic. The Holy Roman Emperor, Charles V, absent in Spain and Italy for most of the 1520s, delegated the administration and defence of his Austrian lands to his brother Ferdinand. It proved a timely move as Suleiman thrust aside the Hungarian armies at Mohacs, killed King Louis II of Hungary and, three years later, moved to the gates of Vienna. Though severe weather conditions led the Ottomans to withdraw after a two-month siege, Ferdinand and

his court had been forced to flee and he never forgot how close he had been to losing his capital. In 1532 Charles himself stood in the way of the largest army ever seen in Europe and repelled its assault on Guns, 60 miles south of Vienna. This, however, was to be a temporary respite and Suleiman's only military setback. In 1541 Ferdinand was forced out of Buda and six years later at Adrianople agreed to pay the sultan an annual tribute of 30,000 ducats in return for holding a small strip of western Hungary. Another abortive attempt to expel the Ottomans from Transylvania in 1550 confirmed that the Balkan frontier would remain 80 miles from Vienna and the Austrian Habsburgs would be treated as a tributary power.

In the second half of the century, the Habsburg emperors strengthened their frontier defences in anticipation of further Ottoman attacks and, apart from desultory fighting between 1552 and 1568, Austria was spared. In the wake of Suleiman's death in 1566, Selim the Sot (1566–74) and his successor, Murad III (1574–95), called a halt to the landward advances and, for much of this period, the Turks concentrated on defence rather than expansion. Like other European states, they were feeling the strain of administering their massive empire, a fact reflected by the state debts recorded every year after 1592. Indeed, peace would have probably lasted longer if Emperor Rudolf had not refused to continue paying his tribute. When Murad retaliated, war began again.

The Long War (1593–1606) started badly for the Ottomans with revolts occurring in their own vassal states. Dnieper Cossacks pillaged their supply lines and, worst of all, Persia invaded Anatolia in 1599. Moreover, at Mezokeresztes (1596), Hungarian troops demonstrated superior firepower and inflicted upon the Turks their first military setback for over a century. Hungarian and Transylvanian towns were won and lost in a series of sieges until all sides agreed upon a treaty in 1686 at Zsitva-Torok. The Habsburgs were confirmed in their possession of western Hungary, their tribute was annulled and Transylvania granted its independence. The Austrian-Turkish frontier had not moved since 1529 and it was now apparent that the western limit of the Ottoman Empire had been reached.

### (i) Turkish Rule in the Balkans

The impact of Turkish rule upon all sectors of Balkan society was profound. Most of its aristocracy were killed though a minority was absorbed into the ruling class when, in keeping with Ottoman practice, the sultan took over their lands. In contrast, the peasantry, who worked the land, paid most of the taxes and were liable for military service, were treated much better than before. They were protected by the new landlords and had their feudal services abolished. Apart from the frontier regions, most of the Balkans were spared that cultural and religious destruction usually associated with armies of occupation. Christians, though encouraged to convert to Islam, were allowed religious toleration and mixed marriages, and the comparative freedom and contentment enjoyed by its people is one of the most important explanations why the Balkans remained under Ottoman rule for over 400 years.

## (ii) The Impact on the Holy Roman Empire

Largely for reasons of geography, Charles V suffered more than most west European rulers. As 'the Most Catholic' King of Spain (1516–56) and Holy Roman Emperor (1519–58), he took his obligations seriously. The Ottomans were intent on a holy war against Christianity and the western Empire looked to him to counter them, but his political commitments consistently distracted him and forced him to confine his efforts to stemming the Turkish advance in north Africa. In this respect, he was spectacularly unsuccessful, losing at Tunis (1534), Algiers (1541), and Tripoli, Bougie and Penon de Velez in the 1550s. To add to his problems, German princes skillfully exploited the Ottoman threat by forcing him to make political and religious concessions. Charles himself later admitted that the Turkish threat had forced him to put aside religious issues. Indeed, at times of greatest peril—in 1527, 1532 and 1541—Charles compromised religion to attend to the Turks, and significantly his only triumph against the Lutherans in 1547 was secured in the knowledge that Suleiman was engaged in wars against Persia. The Turks also received considerable help from France. It was Francis I who first encouraged them to attack the Habsburgs and allowed them free access to the ports of Marseilles and Toulon to reduce the Emperor's power. Indeed, it can safely be said that the Ottoman Empire's western expansion owed a great deal to the political and religious disunity of Europe.

# Spain, Portugal and Venice
## (i) Spain

The effects of Ottoman expansion were felt as far west as Spain in the early sixteenth century. To reduce the possibility that Granadan Moriscos would receive help from Muslims in north Africa, King Ferdinand seized five coastal settlements, including Tripoli and Algiers, and secured Spain's sea routes between Sicily, Sardinia and Tunisia. However, the creation of a powerful Turkish fleet enabled it to conquer Egypt and renewed the threat to Spain's possessions. And the situation became critical when Barbarossa defected to the Ottoman fleet: Tunis and Algiers were lost and several north African settlements seized in the 1550s. Not only were Spanish communications with Milan, Naples and Sicily endangered but the mainland towns

of Malaga, Cadiz and Gibraltar also suffered raids from corsair pirates. It was just as well that the main Ottoman army was preoccupied with Persia.

Philip II of Spain responded to the Muslim threat in 1560 when his troops occupied the island of Djerba preparatory to an attack on Tripoli, but the expedition ended in disaster: 27 galleys were lost and 10,000 men were taken prisoner to Istanbul. The recovery of Penon in 1564 renewed Spanish spirits but celebrations were curtailed with the news that Malta was being besieged by 40,000 troops and 180 Ottoman warships. The subsequent relief of the island in September 1565 by the viceroy of Naples saved Sicily as well as Malta and marked the limit of Ottoman expansion in the western Mediterranean but, in spite of Suleiman's death the following year, its maritime power remained formidable. In 1570 Tunis, recovered by Spain in 1535, was again captured by the Turks and the Venetian island of Cyprus was attacked.

A Christian fleet, which was mainly Venetian but commanded by a Spaniard, Don John, met the Ottomans at Lepanto in the Gulf of Corinth. The ensuing battle (October 1571) saw two of the largest navies ever assembled and resulted in victory for the Christians. Though they lost 10 of their 208 galleys and 15,000 men, this was nothing compared with the losses sustained by the Turks. One hundred seventeen out of 270 Ottoman ships were captured, 113 sunk and 30,000 men killed. It was their worst defeat since 1402 and dispelled the myth of invincibility. Most historians have viewed Lepanto as a crucial battle, that ended the long conflict between Muslims and Christians. Thomas Arnold has recently argued that: 'After Lepanto, the Ottoman navy never recovered its earlier near-mastery of the Mediterranean'. The extant evidence in the Turkish archives, however, does not bear out this judgement, at least not in the short term. The sultan's reaction to defeat was to rebuild his fleet and double his resolve to control north Africa and the sea routes via Malta and Sicily. Just six months after Lepanto, the Turks had built 200 new galleys and captured Cyprus—a reminder that their potential to inflict a serious blow was still formidable. In 1574 a massive Turkish fleet seized Tunis and put the Spanish garrison in La Goletta to flight. Yet just when it seemed that the Ottomans were resuming the initiative, Selim died, and with him passed the last competent sultan for over a hundred years. Western Europe had been saved by a hair's breadth.

The expansion of the Ottoman Empire had two further direct effects upon Spanish affairs. For 20 years after Philip II's accession (in 1556), the problem had drawn resources away from the Netherlands and northern Europe and enabled the Dutch Revolt to gather momentum. Second, there was widespread belief in the 1560s that the Spanish Moriscos were in secret contact with the Muslims and the Ottoman court in Istanbul. Though some 4,000 Turkish and Berber troops fought alongside the Granadan Moriscos in their rebellion of 1598–70, letters from local Turkish rulers in 1574 suggest that the sultan was indeed contemplating a coordinated attack on Spanish lands. Philip II and the Inquisition continued to investigate reports of collusion. Though nothing was proved, it served to perpetuate the myth of the 'Turkish menace.'

## (ii) Portugal

Portuguese interests were affected both positively and negatively. Portuguese merchants in their search for gold had developed an alternative route to the Far East and Spice Islands that avoided the Turkish controlled east Mediterranean. This gave Portugal in the late fifteenth and early sixteenth centuries 'premier league' status. But its territorial and commercial expansion came at a price. Its long sea routes needed defending from the Turks, who had also reached the Red Sea by 1500 and the Indian Ocean by the mid-sixteenth century, and they were equally keen to secure the lucrative pepper trade with the Far East. Portugal, however, was more than up to this challenge. Its efficiently designed and well defended barracks saw off Turkish galleys which were less manoeuvrable in ocean waters, but the struggle for dominance of the spice trade was not won quickly or cheaply. Moreover Portugal had limited resources. As competition with Spain increased, it could ill-afford a struggle with the Ottomans for mastery of the Indian Ocean. It was precisely this threat of overstretch which made Portugal so vulnerable in the late sixteenth and early seventeenth centuries, due not so much to any Turkish incursion—this had long since passed—but to English, Dutch and French colonials, merchants and privateers.

## (iii) Venice

The Turkish threat to Mediterranean trade in general and to Iberian possessions in particular receded in the last quarter of the sixteenth century, but its impact was none the less considerable. A principal beneficiary for much of this period was the city-state of Venice. Since 1479 it had paid a tribute to gain access to the Middle East overland routes to Aleppo and Alexandria, and under Ottoman sufferance it remained the major maritime power in the eastern Mediterranean, handling most Ottoman trade with the west and successfully competing with Portugal for control of the pepper trade. Of course, Ottoman wars in the Red Sea, Persian Gulf and Mediterranean had disrupted trade but for most of the sixteenth century Venice itself avoided armed conflict. Indeed, by strengthening its fortresses and doubling the size of its fleet, it enjoyed rising profits from trade at least until the 1570s. However, the loss of Cyprus in 1571, rich in grain and wine, and Venice's failure to recover it, proved a turning-point in its history. In 1573 it gave up its claims to Cyprus and Dalmatia, returned lands in Albania and agreed to pay a large indemnity to normalise its trade arrangements with the sultan. The 1570s also brought new trading competitors when first French and then English merchants received Turkish 'capitulations' or privileges to compete with Venetian traders. By 1600, French merchants had displaced Venetians in the Levant, Dutch traders had won control of the east African trade and the English East India Company was ready to exploit the weakening condition of Spain, Portugal, Venice, and the Ottoman Empire.

## The Turks and the 'Military Revolution'

Historians have long recognised the significance of the wars with the Turks as an important, if not vital, element in the development of the 'military revolution' of western states. Victory for the cross over the crescent carried more than ideological and religious superiority. It proved, at least as far as west Europeans were concerned, that their military and naval tactics, equipment and application were also second to none.

There were some important differences between European and Turkish military developments. One lay in the line of fortifications built by several Christian towns in the 1520s which were modelled on the trace Italienne: these were earthen ramparts, low-walled bastions, and strategically located cannons which could repel the main Turkish assaults whether human or artillery. Although some fortresses fell to the Turks—Szigeth in Hungary (1566), Nicosia in Cyprus (1570)—they were the exceptions to the rule, and Vienna, Guns, Corfu and Malta all successfully withstood lengthy sieges.

A second important difference was that European armies placed more emphasis on drill and discipline, on practising defensive infantry formations of squares of pikes and arquebusiers, and of combining infantry, artillery and cavalry, confident that they could repel a Turkish cavalry and infantry attack. Treatises on military tactics encouraged generals to believe the way forward was to innovate. In one writer's opinion, a well-trained pike and arquebus detachment could withstand a Turkish cavalry assault, and another author claimed that a disciplined infantry would enable 'a few men to defeat the great multitudes of the Turks'. Although contemporaries could not prove it—there were no battles between Turks and Europeans in the sixteenth century—their confidence was not misplaced, as campaign after campaign confirmed in later centuries.

Third, the Turkish navy never developed the flexibility in ship design or strategy achieved by its European counterparts. As the Spanish and Portuguese adapted their ocean-going galleons to sail the Mediterranean and modified their galleys into three-masted carracks capable of both trading and fighting, so they were able to counter the Ottoman fleet and merchant shipping which was composed solely of galleys. Though the Turks almost always put more ships to sea, the Christians had a better fleet and superior cannon fire. After Lepanto, Turkish fleets warily avoided further engagements.

## Ottoman Decline?

To decide whether the Ottomans were in decline by the end of the sixteenth century, we must realise that ever since the seventh century the Turkish Empire had been expanding. As it did so, it became a military state geared for conquest and holy war. The sultan exercised, at least in theory, unlimited authority. The only conceivable challenge to his position came from his family, and such threats were negated by the traditional Ottoman practice of fratricide. By 1520, the Ottoman Empire was self-sufficient in food, minerals and land; the Islamic faith bound its people together and its army was second to none. Suleiman possessed the best field artillery, 87,000 devoted cavalry (known as sipahis) and 16,000 highly disciplined infantry (janissaries), whose sole objective was to wage war. Its western vassal states formed a buttress to defend the core principality of Anatolia, and so, of necessity, its frontier was in a permanent state of war. Since the fourteenth century, the Ottoman family had provided very able sultans. It was they who gave the Empire its dynamism. Under Suleiman, who fought 13 successful campaigns and some 40 battles, they had a leader capable of putting the fear of Allah into all Christians. Indeed, only his death in September 1566 prevented an estimated 300,000 troops from advancing upon the Austrian-Habsburg lands. The last naval engagement between Christians and Muslims may have been in 1573, but Spain's north African and Italian possessions remained vulnerable targets and Philip II considered it prudent to keep a fleet in excess of 100 ships in the Mediterranean for the rest of his reign.

The Ottoman Empire's strengths, nevertheless, hid long-term weaknesses. First, the sultans Selim, Murad and Mohammed, who followed Suleiman, began a line of ineffectual rulers whose authority was seriously undermined by a series of palace revolts. Second, by fixing Istanbul as the administrative capital, the Ottomans had unknowingly established limits to their western and eastern Empire. Some 99 days were needed to transport 100,000 troops from Istanbul to Hungary. This reduced the campaigning season to a few months at best, and made communications and supply lines difficult to sustain. Similarly, to reach Malta by sea entailed a journey in excess of a thousand miles, which raised questions as to the point of wanting to sail beyond it. Third, the Ottomans were beginning to fall behind western Europe in naval and military technology and tactics. In fact, it can be argued that only the lack of political and spiritual unity within Europe prevented western states

from exploiting Ottoman weaknesses. Already by the end of the sixteenth century Turkey's northern frontier of Azerbaijan and its central Asian trade were being challenged by the emerging state of Muscovy and its eastern frontier was threatened by the Safavids of Persia. For much of the century, the Ottomans had seen off challenges from these old rivals but victory eluded them in the Long War. It now seems clear that when both its western and eastern frontiers ceased to advance, the Ottoman state was vulnerable, and this was its condition at the end of the sixteenth century.

## Conclusion

The impact of the Ottoman Turks on sixteenth-century Europe was far-reaching. This explains why Charles V regarded them as a greater threat to Christendom than Luther; why Ferdinand II devoted the best part of his life to defending the Austrian heartlands; why Spain feared for its trade and dominions in the western Mediterranean and became paranoid over suspected links with Granadan Moriscos; why Portugal was prepared to neglect its transatlantic trade and colonies in order to defend its pepper monopoly with Asia; and why Venice saw its livelihood hang by a thread as Turkish fleets threatened to cut off its sea-borne trade. It also contributed to the 'military revolution' as European armies and navies learned how first to defend and then to defeat superior numbers and, in so doing, forged ahead of their eastern rivals. In this, as in so many other ways, the Turks played an important part in shaping European history.

# How American Slavery Led to the Birth of Liberia

**In 1820, a private American group established Liberia as a colony for freed U.S. slaves. But it was troubled from the start.**

SEAN PRICE

On January 25, 1851, Edward Blyden's ship dropped anchor just off the coast of Liberia. For the 19-year-old seminary student, it was the end of a weeks-long sea voyage and a kind of homecoming. To the very continent that Blyden's ancestors had left in chains, he was now returning as a free man. He could hardly contain his excitement as he wrote to a friend:

> You can easily imagine the delight with which I gazed upon the land of my forefathers—of those mysterious races of men. It is really a beautiful country. . . . The land is exceedingly prolific—teeming with everything necessary for the subsistence of man.

Along with beautiful scenery, Blyden was looking out over one of America's boldest social experiments. Liberia had been founded in 1820 as a colony for freed American slaves. A group called the American Colonization Society had purchased land on Africa's west coast to establish Liberia. Between 1820 and 1865, the society transported at least 12,000 people there. Shipping free blacks back to Africa seemed a sensible idea to the society's white founders and to some blacks, such as Edward Blyden. But the many controversies and problems that nagged at Liberia kept it from ever becoming the freed slaves' promised land.

## The Slavery Question

By the early 1800s, slavery had died out in the Northern U.S., but it thrived in the South thanks to the region's labor-hungry plantations. Over time some slaves were set free. Others bought their freedom.

This growing class of society—free blacks—troubled many slavery supporters, who often subscribed to views similar to Thomas Jefferson's. The third U.S. President and author of the Declaration of Independence believed slavery was a necessary evil that would one day die out. Yet he saw no place for free blacks in U.S. society when that day came. He once wrote that blacks were inferior and that, "when freed, [they are] to be removed beyond the reach of mixture."

One answer, for people who agreed with Jefferson, was to send African-Americans to Africa. If the thousands of free blacks already living in the U.S. could be successfully settled there, the thought went, then millions could later follow. Other whites, more sympathetic to the plight of blacks, thought sending them to Africa would allow them to live in freedom and without prejudice.

Against this backdrop, the American Colonization Society, a private group, was founded in 1816. It attracted luminaries including Daniel Webster, Henry Clay, and Francis Scott Key, as well as clergymen and philanthropists. It won support from slaveholders—such as Jefferson and the fifth U.S. President, James Monroe—and some antislavery activists.

## Why Leave America?

Some blacks were indeed eager to leave the U.S., but their main motivation was to flee racial hostility. Black abolitionist Martin R. Delany argued for emigration in 1852, saying:

> In the United States, among the whites, their color is made, by law and custom, the mark of distinction and superiority; while the color of the blacks is a badge of degradation.

Still, the idea of colonization angered many blacks and some white abolitionists, like William Lloyd Garrison. They saw it as a way to bolster slavery by getting rid of free blacks—among the few political allies of the slaves. They also believed sending blacks back to Africa made no more sense than shipping English-Americans back to England. As black abolitionist David Walker wrote in 1829:

America is more our country than it is the whites'. We have enriched it with our blood and tears . . . and they will drive us from our property and homes, which we have earned with our blood.

Nevertheless, the society pushed ahead with its plan. From local tribal chiefs, the group purchased a 36-mile-long strip of land next to present-day Sierra Leone for the equivalent of $300 in trade goods. (Some accounts say the purchase was made through intimidation and threats.) The colony's name was taken from the Latin phrase for "land of the free," and its capital, Monrovia, was named after President Monroe. Hundreds of well-wishers came to see off the ship *Elizabeth* on January 31, 1820, as it left New York with Liberia's first 86 black colonists and three white agents from the society.

## Quick fact: Liberia comes from the Latin phrase meaning "Land of the free."

# Disease and Dissent

Disease soon proved to be the colony's most dangerous foe. All three agents and 22 of the original colonists died of malaria, yellow fever, or other tropical illnesses. Between 1820 and 1843, disease killed about 22 percent of all new arrivals. Also, tensions quickly arose between the surviving colonists and their leaders. Liberia's early Governors—all white men—were picked by the society and ruled autocratically.

After several near rebellions, the society finally appointed Joseph J. Roberts, a free black from Virginia, as Governor in 1841. But the push for self-rule continued, and on July 26, 1847 Liberia proclaimed its independence, becoming the first black-run republic in modern Africa. Roberts was elected its President. Liberia's flag and constitution were modeled on those of the U.S.

## Quick fact 1847: Liberia became the first Independent black-run country in modern Africa.

Unfortunately, instability persisted. Ironically, Liberia's settlers—many of whom had once been in bondage—often discriminated against the native Africans, whom they considered uncivilized. The natives were excluded from voting and kept out of government. Even the country's Declaration of Independence asserted that "we the people of Liberia were originally inhabitants of the United States of North America." These practices frequently led to fighting between the settlers—known as "Americo-Liberians"—and the 16 ethnic African tribes that lived in the region.

During the 1800s, this turmoil discouraged prospective immigrants. By the 1890s, even Liberia's most fervent boosters could see that the experiment had largely failed.

Edward Blyden, who became a successful writer and speaker, mourned the promise for which his country had once stood. "We are keeping these lands, we say, for our brethren in America," he wrote. "But they are not willing to come. . . ."

The "Americo-Liberians" governed until 1980, when a bloody coup by native Africans helped trigger Liberia's current turmoil. But the seeds had been planted from its founding.

# Fighting the Afghans in the 19th Century

Bruce Collins

One of the abiding historical ideas of the nineteenth century is that of *Pax Britannica*. The 'long peace' from 1815 to 1914, with the one interruption of the Crimean War in the mid-1850s, encapsulates the essence of Britain's relationship with the major continental European powers. But, in fact, for people outside Europe the period witnessed an unremitting series of British military and naval interventions touching every part of the globe. For the most part, British generals and naval commanders ensured that these interventions were successful, or at least appeared victorious. The British experience in Afghanistan was an exception. Here, the first intervention of 1838–42 required considerable stage management to appear to have been even remotely successful, while the intervention in 1878–81 proved expensive even if ultimately it achieved its purpose. On both occasions military defeats were avenged, but the management of Afghan politics remained far more intractable.

In 1837, the Commander-in-Chief of the Bengal army, Sir Henry Fane, provided an official analysis arguing that the existing western and north-western frontier of British India was perfectly secure. Part of it, from the sea to Firuzpur on the Sutlej river, was 'covered' by the Thar or Great Indian Desert. At the other end stood the equally impenetrable Himalayas. The only exposed stretch was about 120 miles from Firuzpur to the Sutlej's upper reaches. Although scarcely a decade of the nineteenth century had passed without some frontier campaign affecting the borderlands of British India, good frontier garrisons, improving lines of communication to the main bases of British India and friendly relations with the Punjab, across the Sutlej, ensured that this border was secure. Yet, within a year, this impression had been shattered.

British intervention in Afghanistan stemmed from growing British concerns about Russian ambitions in central Asia. Throughout the eighteenth and early nineteenth centuries the Russians had rapidly expanded their central Asian empire. By the 1830s they had conquered Ural'sk and Turgay and parts of Akmolinsk. Before 1878, they had encroached as far south as Turkestan, acquiring Samarkand, Bukhara and Semirech'ye. The threat of Russian influence in central Asia and the effect this might bring to bear on Indian political opinion were of major concern to the British. Britain had effectively sealed India from any seaboard penetration by foreign rivals, but could the north-western boundary be vulnerable to actions that might encourage Indian princes to challenge British rule? Most policy-makers recognised that, whatever was being achieved through commercial and institutional development and through humanitarian, educational and religious 'improvement,' British rule ultimately depended on military force. Disaffection against British rule flourished below the surface sovereignty of the Raj. The government in India decided that any exertion of Russian political influence in Afghanistan posed an indirect threat to the integrity of the Anglo-Indian state.

From the late eighteenth century onwards, Indian rulers' compliance with British rule, and their reduction from rulers to subject aristocrats, had required coercion and usually war to effect. Yet, repeatedly, the British assumed that they could simply reshuffle Asiatic potentates. They approached Afghan affairs in a state of relative ignorance. Their first semi-official contact with its main eastern cities came only in the 1830s; earlier nineteenth-century diplomatic interest had focused on Persian relations with the country's western frontier area. In 1838, as it became clear that the incumbent emir of Afghanistan, Dost Mohammed, was toying with the notion of an alignment with Russia, the British decided that he should be replaced. They had in mind an ageing former Afghan emir Shah Shuja, who had spent some thirty years in exile in India. The Afghan empire had been forged from minor overlordships during the eighteenth century. The economy was poorly developed and involved relatively limited trading; Afghan leaders frequently depended on military raids on neighbouring lands, notably north-western India, to acquire ready cash through systematic plunder. By the early nineteenth-century an intense contest for power developed between two rival clans—the Suddozyes and the Barukzyes—of the Dourani tribe of the founding emir, Ahmed Shah. Dozens of off-spring of two antagonistic clan leaders provided numerous claimants to supreme power. Shah Shuja had already tried his hand by invading his country in 1834, but had been defeated in battle near Kandahar by Dost Mohammed. Nothing daunted, the Governor-General, Lord Auckland, felt that the regime in Kabul could be readily changed.

The British also mistakenly assumed that a local ally would assist in any military action that might result from their intervention. During the summer of 1838 it was expected that the Sikh ruler of the Punjab, Ranjit Singh, would provide the bulk of the force entering Afghanistan, but Ranjit refused to participate. Instead of having to furnish a contingent of 5,000 troops to supplement a Sikh army, the British found themselves having to commit 14,000 men from British India itself. Instead of crossing the Sutlej river and then passing through the Punjab and marching to Kabul from Peshawar via the Khyber Pass, the British were forced to take a wholly circuitous route to Kandahar.

Setting off in December 1838, the main British force from Firuzpur covered 1,000 miles in 135 days. There were no battles on the journey to Kandahar but the troops fought against harsh desert conditions, rugged mountain passes, food shortages, heat and deliberately contaminated water, under the constant threat of raids by mounted tribesmen. One officer described 'the heat, the dust, the desert wind, the myriads of flies and the stench of the dying and dead camels'. The camp 'smelled like a charnel-house' and no one could take three steps within the camp 'without seeing a dead or dying man or animal'.

Once they reached Kandahar the British force, together with Shuja's levies and perhaps 38,000 servants and camp followers, spent two months recouping while reinforcements were rallied. Shuja was installed as emir. The next stage was the 310-mile march from Kandahar to Kabul. On this route the only formal fighting of the eight-month campaign occurred at the fortified town of Ghazni. It lasted little over an hour. The British, who had brought no heavy guns on their march across the central valley of east Afghanistan, had to force their way into Ghazni by making a daring attack at dawn. They blew up one of the town's gates with 300 lbs of gunpowder and sent in an assault party of European light infantry. The party only just got the necessary support in time. As was so often the case in 'colonial' campaigning, the success of the operation depended on speed, daring, improvisation and high risk by a select minority among the forces available.

By the end of 1839 the British had secured their political objectives; Shah Shuja was installed and Dost Mohammed had fled. Most of the expeditionary forces had been withdrawn, but a significant British presence remained. However, the challenge of creating and maintaining a stable regime proved increasingly difficult. Autonomous tribal chiefs would not accept Shah Shuja's authority. The enthusiasm of British advisors for administrative and political reform led to changes in revenue-raising and in the privileges and powers given to local chiefs in Kabul, which provoked opposition. By May 1841, the British had deployed 16,000 troops within Afghanistan and on the immediate approach routes, with a further 9,000 on the route from Karachi to Quetta. Animosity intensified as local chiefs resented British raids upon individual valleys, involving the destruction of crops and attacks upon small forts. They also resented the widespread deployment of Hindu troops in a Muslim country, especially as eighteenth-century Afghans had been the arbiters of Hindostan's fate. A further contention was the sharp increase in the prices of vital commodities caused by the presence of a large foreign army and its demand for goods. Reforms in the organisation of the Afghan army drastically reduced the annual payments made to the Ghilzai tribes who controlled the Jalalabad-Kabul route. The Ghilzai responded by attacking a large caravan as it proceeded from Jalalabad up to Kabul in October 1841.

This attack occurred just as the British were planning a major withdrawal. During the autumn, Brigadier Sir Robert Sale, the commander of the frontal assault on Ghazni two years earlier, led a contingent from Kabul and pushed his way—often against opposition—to Jalalabad, to open up the direct line for that withdrawal. But in early November 1841, the British lost control of events in Kabul. A mob attacked and murdered the British resident, Sir Alexander Burnes. Tribal levies seized the commissariat fort. While the British hesitated in their response, numbers of tribal chiefs joined the rebellion. The ousted emir, Dost Mohammed's son Mohammed Akbar, arrived in the capital, assuming leadership of factions of the rebellion. The retiring British Envoy Sir William MacNaughten tried to negotiate a settlement with him, only to be murdered and dismembered on December 23rd. Against this increasingly turbulent background, Major-General William Elphinstone, the British commander, came to an agreement with eighteen prominent Afghan chiefs that they would guarantee a safe evacuation for the British garrison. On January 6th 1842, the British force of 4,500 soldiers, mostly Indian sepoys, and perhaps as many as 12,000 dependants, servants and camp followers, left Kabul. By this time Sale had established a defensive position at Jalalabad en route back into the Punjab.

The British retreat from Kabul to Jalalabad degenerated into one of the most appalling reverses in the history of British imperial intervention. Within days the perishing cold, food and supply losses and ambushes by tribesmen commanding higher ground over the narrow rocky mountain passes had taken their toll on the convoy. Frostbite and snow blindness rendered fighting men incapable of using their weapons. Hunger gnawed hard at the whole contingent. By the fifth day the number of soldiers capable of action amounted to perhaps only a tenth of the original force of 4,500 troops. This rapidly diminishing band of combatants were ruthlessly attacked by the Afghans at the pass at Jagdullak on January 12th; those that made it through the ambush made a miserable last stand at the Gundamuck Pass the following day. A few were taken prisoner, the remainder, including eighteen officers, were killed. Of the main force only one European survived the ordeal, escaping by the skin of his teeth. Surgeon William Brydon limped into Jalalabad on January 13th. Sale's garrison sounded the advance by bugle throughout that night in the hope that other survivors would make it in; not one did. It is not known exactly how many died; but the greater part of the garrison force and their followers perished. Some survived by deserting or by being taken prisoner. But the total lost probably exceeded 12,000.

In spite of the terrible human disaster, the British retained some major military assets. A force of 7,500 troops remained at Kandahar (a number far exceeding the number of soldiers lost in the Kabul withdrawal). A substantial reinforcement reached Peshawar in the Sikh kingdom in early February 1842. Sale's contingent held out at Jalalabad, surviving food shortages and Afghan attacks until the Peshawar relief force, having advanced up the Khyber Pass, reached the town on April 16th bringing to 15,000 the number of British troops there.

The defence of Jalalabad provided a heroic symbol of British resilience and resistance, a timely counter-point to the military ineptitude that had led to the destruction of the Kabul column. It also created the basis for a punitive expedition to be despatched to Afghanistan's capital. Forces from Jalalabad spread out into neighbouring valleys to punish local tribes. The British destroyed forts, burned villages, and cut deep rings around trees (which were so necessary to provide shade in the cruelly hot summers), in order that they would wither and die. The vigour of the British reaction was justified by a generalised demonisation of the Afghan population. As one officer, Thomas Seaton, later wrote, 'every crime, every sin of which human nature can be guilty . . . are as common and notorious as daylight, throughout Afghanistan'.

Strategically and politically, the British were committed to withdrawal from Afghanistan, but they now considered a variety of military measures to punish the Afghans. As the Duke of Wellington, a member of the Cabinet, wrote privately to the Governor General on March 30th, 1842: 'it is impossible to impress upon you too strongly the notion of the Importance of the Restoration of our Reputation in the East'.

British prestige was reasserted in various ways. The Kandahar garrison force marched across the country to Kabul and the large contingent at Jalalabad advanced westwards to meet it there. The two armies reached the capital on September 16th–17th, 1842. They negotiated the release of ninety-five British prisoners and then ceremoniously blew up the four great squares or bazaars at the capital's centre. The ritualistic destruction of prominent buildings became a recurrent practice of the British when they wished to assert their power, in the knowledge that they had little time to do so.

The Governor General, Lord Ellenborough, arranged massive ceremonial displays at Firuzpur to greet the forces on their return to British India in mid-December. Some 25,000 additional troops were assembled to form a welcoming line two-and-a-half miles long. Bands, banquets, balls and gun salutes all proclaimed victory and closure, not withdrawal and failure. The gates of Somnauth, symbolically important gate-portals to a major tomb long ago stolen from India by Afghan invaders, were now solemnly returned by the British and carried in procession across north-central India. Many British commentators criticised this empty triumphalism, but it formed a key element of Ellenborough's policy of rebuilding confidence in the Indian army.

Lastly, the British took advantage of political instability and tribal rivalry in the Sind to conquer and annex that area, to the south and southeast of Afghanistan, in early 1843. In deciding on the take-over in March 1843, Ellenborough noted, 'we must redeem the character we have lost in India'—both by acquisition and by the reformist energy to be applied to the new province's governance. The emirs of the Sind paid a heavy price for British reversals in Afghanistan.

Following the withdrawal in 1842, British relations with the restored Afghan emir, Dost Mohammed, proved broadly satisfactory. The entire north-west region was transformed in any case by the British acquisition of the Punjab in the 1840s. British forces were able to control the Punjab during the traumatic Indian Mutiny of 1857. There were no threats from Afghanistan then, but in the 1870s concern at Russian expansionism revived and dissatisfaction with a new emir in Kabul intensified. A number of long-running disputes and tensions came to a head in 1878, exacerbated by an assertive and politically unsubtle Governor General, Lord Lytton. A brief war ensued resulting in British diplomatic gains, the occupation of the Kuram valley, on the borderlands between Punjab and mountainous Afghanistan, and the installation of a permanent British representative in Kabul.

Yet, by apparently bowing to British pressure, the emir's regime succeeded only in enflaming tribal resentment. Dissident Afghan soldiers burned the British residency in September 1879, killing all its occupants including the British envoy, Sir Louis Cavagnari, By this time, enough British troops were available nearby for a prompt British reaction to be launched.

Within a little over a month of this attack, Major General Frederick Roberts (later Lord Roberts) marched into Kabul. The British plan was clearly laid out by Lord Lytton to Roberts. Lytton realised that immediate retribution was necessary in order to achieve results before British political attitudes softened towards Afghanistan. He wanted 'a prompt and impressive example' to be given to the Afghans. As the whole Afghan population had participated in 'a great national crime', Lytton stressed that 'any Afghan brought to death by the avenging arm of the British power, I shall regard as one scoundrel the less in a den of scoundrelism'. While British public opinion would require some judicial procedure, the viceroy felt it need be only 'of the roughest and readiest kind'. Roberts could inflict retribution, not justice, on reaching Kabul. During the next four weeks the British executed about 100 Afghans with little regard as to whether or not they had been directly involved in the assault on the residency. One senior officer noticed that 'we are thoroughly hated and not enough feared'. To sustain a large military presence during the winter Roberts sent out large parties of soldiers to seek food from the surrounding countryside. When they met resistance a predictable downward spiral of skirmishing, plundering foodstuff, and burning villages set in. Tribal levies attacked the British position outside Kabul in late December. By early 1880 the British had committed large numbers of troops from Peshawar to Kabul in order to secure a line of communication and base there for reinforcement and control.

The British found themselves in the midst of turbulent inter-tribal, inter-clan, and intra-family rivalries. In one regional contest for power around Kandahar, a British force of 2,600 troops met defeat at Maiwand in July 1880. In a humiliating rout, 43 percent of the British force was killed or wounded, an extraordinarily high level of casualties. This was a classic instance of a relatively small British force being exposed to superior enemy troop numbers and artillery fire. As so often, the British self-image of succeeding against overwhelming odds proved irresponsible. When their opponents were as well armed as the Afghans, then the British could not make significant headway against superior numbers. Instead, as at Maiwand, they marched into defeat.

But the British had sufficient manpower available to summon up a tremendous recuperative response. Roberts led 10,000 troops some 300 miles from Kabul to Kandahar and, immediately on arrival there, attacked the Afghan army outside Kandahar on September 1st, 1880. Roberts overcame the errors made at Maiwand. He had as many guns as his opponent and almost as many soldiers. He drove his enemy back by stages in a well fought flanking movement. His forces captured all the Afghan guns. This defeat broke the Afghan army apart. Regular troops within it returned to the northwest of the country and their original base at Herat. The tribesman returned to the widely scattered valleys. Although defeated in the field and dispersed, these dissident tribesmen were not necessarily crushed. Some military experts, including Roberts, argued that the longer term security for a pro-British regime required a British occupation of Kandahar. The Cabinet rejected that proposal and arguments for the break-up of Afghanistan. Following a number of major clashes between competing princes in 1881, a new regime was secured by the end of the year and the British were able to withdraw from the country. But at its height this intervention absorbed perhaps 48,000 troops, if those in the border towns of British India and along the lines of communication are included, and cost nearly 10,000 lives, the majority succumbing to disease.

An obvious question arises as to the extent to which the British adapted to the experience of mountain warfare. In 1841–42, the British had been hard hit by Afghan troops well positioned on hilly ridges. In 1878–79 Roberts had ensured the deployment of highly mobile troops to clamber up mountain ridges in order to outgun Afghan implacements. Also, the geographical route westwards from the Khyber pass and Jalalabad to Kabul, through which the British forces moved, and which was most open to mountain ambush, was fully guarded and controlled in 1879–81. Once in the main cities of Kabul and Kandahar, the British were reasonably secure, in that the Afghans had no heavy siege guns available to deploy against well fortified positions. The British made numerous efforts to control areas immediately around the main cities. Beyond those confined areas, the Afghan style of fighting created problems for the invaders. Protecting their own villages and valleys remained their priority. Yet the British could only penetrate those deep and divided valleys with difficulty and by dispersing their own forces. Roberts insisted that infantry battalions provide sixty mounted infantrymen each to help with mobility. But the capacity to move quickly and widely remained handicapped by problems of transport.

The Second Afghan war heightened notions of military commitment and of the existence of martial races both among the British (the Highlanders) and among the peoples of British India (the Sikhs and the Gurkhas). Roberts wanted to ensure that the relief force leaving Kabul for Kandahar in August 1880 would be highly committed as well as experienced. Recognising that soldiers who had been on active service for about two years might have become jaded, Roberts consulted his battalion commanders as to the battle readiness of their men. Only three reported that their troops might not bear the exertions of the campaign. To boost morale in what Roberts hoped would be a swift campaign, he promised soldiers that they would be allowed back to India immediately fighting ended. Those not up to forced marches were removed. Equipment was kept to a minimum. Roberts noted that the troops needed all their experience in loading and tending the baggage animals since Afghan drivers and support riders soon deserted the British in August 1880 on the march from Kabul to Kandahar.

Here then was a force whose individual strengths, weaknesses, and powers of endurance were well known to their commander and to each other. It possessed a great deal of experience and it travelled light. As usual in 'colonial' campaigning, the British deliberately mixed the units available, to ensure that the soldiers most likely to be fully committed to the cause would not all be concentrated together. Of a total of 9,713 troops (excluding officers), on the march to Kandahar, some 2,562 were British. Each of the three infantry brigades had four battalions of between 500–700 soldiers and each of those three infantry brigades contained one British and one Gurkha battalion. The other battalions in the army were virtually all Sikh or Punjabi. Thus both British and Gurkha forces were distributed in order to intensify competition between the different units and to give prominence within each brigade to the 'martial races'.

The main battle of September 1st was hard fought, essentially consisting of the British driving one flank of the Afghan force from its defensive positions and circling around the main Afghan point of defence to take the army's camp. The British, as usual, claimed to have inflicted heavy casualties, but the number of known Afghan dead (600), was not particularly high given the size of its army and the sheer weight of rifle and artillery rounds fired at them. At best the British killed one Afghan for every hundred shots fired and that assumed (wrongly) that none were killed by bayonets. The cavalry pursuit after the battle was not especially effective. It has been estimated that about a hundred Afghans were killed in a pursuit which took the cavalry around 15 miles from the field of battle itself. This suggests that there were relatively few wounded, since such soldiers would have lagged behind and been vulnerable in even a delayed cavalry chase. The battle did not therefore deliver a crushing military blow to the Afghans, but it brought about a powerful reversal which broke up the Afghan army and dispersed the tribal chiefs to their various homes.

In both campaigns, the leaders of British India treated Afghanistan as a pawn in a geographical contest to maintain Britain's position in India and her prestige as a world power. Both ultimately rested on the need for quick, highly visible victories and speedy subsequent withdrawal. Both ended by demonising the Afghans and by demonstrating that, in reacting to fierce Afghan resistance to their forced presence, retribution readily took precedence over justice.

And they left Afghanistan much as they found it. One hundred years ago the *The Daily Mail Year Book* described a populace of four millions desperately short of food and oppressed by 'rapacious' governors and nobles. British India subsidised the Emir whose power depended on the armed forces he controlled, while claimants—including some of those most deeply involved in the events of 1880–81—awaited opportunities for challenging for power from exile in India and Russia.

# For Further Reading

J.A. Norris, *The First Afghan War, 1838–1842* (Cambridge, 1967); Brian Robson, *The Road to Kabul, The Second Afghan War, 1878–1881* (London, 1986); M.E. Yapp, *Strategies of British India* (Oxford, 1980); Major-General Sir Thomas Seaton, *From Cadet to Colonel* (London, 1866); Field-Marshal Lord Roberts of Kandahar, *Forty-one Years in India,* 2 volumes (London, 1897); William Trousdale (ed) *War in Afghanistan 1879–1880: the Personal Diary of Major General Sir Charles Metcalfe MacGregor* (Detroit, 1985); Brian Robson (ed), *Roberts in India, The Military Papers of Field Marshal Lord Roberts, 1876–1893* (Stroud, 1993).

**BRUCE COLLINS** is a Professor at the University of Derby, and is writing a two-volume history of British military and naval power from 1775 to 1902.

# New Light on the 'Heart of Darkness'

**A century after the publication of Joseph Conrad's novel, Angus Mitchell reflects on the grim reality underlying the fiction, and the fight against slavery it inspired.**

ANGUS MITCHELL

In the spring of 1899, when *Heart of Darkness* was serialized in *Blackwood's Magazine,* its author, Joseph Conrad, could scarcely have predicted that he had penned one of the most provocative and controversial literary works of the next century. For a hundred years now this short novel has been a window through which Europeans have glimpsed the scramble for Africa by their empire-forging ancestors. Behind Marlow's river journey in search of Kurtz lie the great conflicts that seethed beneath the jingoism of Empire. The struggles between civilisation and savagery, nature and progress, cannibalism against culture, Christianity versus magic: all these opposites and others battle in the dense undergrowth of the narrative. *Heart of Darkness* was the first novel to attack concepts of Western progress and question dubious social Darwinist attitudes that were used to justify many brutal facets of Empire-building.

The debate over *Heart of Darkness* has grumbled on unabated ever since—to a point where it is now something of a cliche to mention it at all. The theme has attracted and sometimes obsessed the creative mind. Orson Welles adapted the story for radio. Film director Francis Ford Coppola made *Apocalypse Now* (1974), reinterpreting the weird nightmare to fit the psychedelic madness of American folly in Vietnam. Radical critics of Empire like Edward Said and the African writer Chinua Achebe have praised and lambasted the book respectively. A metaphyiscal dimension to *Heart of Darkness* makes it a hard book to pin down. The literary debate and the 'Conrad controversy' will doubtless continue for another century. Africa still lives in the shadow of horror and the significance of *Heart of Darkness* has matured with the vintage of the years.

But what worth has Conrad's imagining of *Heart of Darkness* for the historian? Was there an historical *Heart of Darkness*? Can it now be identified in history? Certainly in recent years there has been an effort to try and configure the fiction with fact. A number of African adventurers have been singled out as possible prototypes for 'the universal genius' Kurtz, whose great skill in collecting ivory at an up-river station eventually sends him over the edge: he turns from being the 'civilizer' into the savage.

The story begins on the banks of the Thames—the Imperial artery of commerce and civilization—but the main arena for the tale is another river altogether—the Congo. The historical framework of the narrative is set within and specifically alludes to the horror that lay beneath the surface of the Belgian King Leopold II's Congo Free State. Leopold is never mentioned by name in the novel, but he lurks in the shadows nonetheless.

*Heart of Darkness* appeared at a moment when horror began to take on a new graphic dimension in the European imagination and ideas on slavery demanded redefinition. During the 1890s rumours started to circulate widely that aspects of imperial policy were going terribly wrong. Conrad's ostensibly imaginative work gave these reports intellectual force. Following its publication new attitudes towards Africa emerged among radical humanitarian thinkers. Some started to wonder just where the flag of Imperial progress was leading.

The opening up of the tropical heart of Africa had been a rapid process. In 1800 Africa's interior south of the Sahara was unmapped terra incognita. At the Berlin conference in 1884–5 the colonial powers carved up Africa amongst themselves. Much of the territory by then had been traversed. The names of the epic adventurers responsible for opening up the interior: Sir James Bruce, John Hanning Speke, Sir Richard Burton, David Livingstone and Sir Henry Morton Stanley echo through classrooms even today. Their travel writings helped appropriate African territories in the Victorian imagination. Adventure stories sold newspapers. Adventurers, whether soldier-explorers, naval officers, missionaries or entrepreneurs, were the empire's own superstars.

But during the 1890s it became increasingly clear that the altruistic spirit that justified expansion for the European empire-builders was faltering. Atrocity stories began to percolate back through the ports. It was a horror more often sensed than witnessed. Clearly some aspects of the white man's administration had gone badly amiss. Imperial expansion had become a cover for ventures that increasingly subverted local life. There was much questionable military behaviour, and occasional military blunders. Some missionaries appeared to be tacit accomplices to the skullduggery, and the evangelising methods of muscular Christianity were also questioned. The leash constraining greed and exploitation was severed. The equation of commerce and

Christianity that had helped to abolish the slave trade had given way to a new horror: an unspeakable horror committed by Europeans in the name of civilisation.

In response, nineteenth century humanitarian endeavour was forced to reform. Traditions of thought condemning slavery and defending tribal lands and rights against foreign invasion—ideas rooted in the sermons of the church fathers Bartolome de las Casas and Antonio Vieira—found a new voice in Britain and elsewhere in Europe among emerging socialist and radical groups. Two societies had surfaced during the nineteenth century as self-appointed guardians of the rights of 'native people': The British and Foreign Anti-Slavery Society and The Aborigines' Protection Society. Both had to adapt to the new age of human rights abuse.

The Anti-Slavery Society was founded in the 1820s through the political drive of the 'Clapham Sect', Quaker beliefs and the work of a number of politicians including William Wilberforce and, later, Sir Thomas Fowell Buxton. Through a committee including a number of politicians, peers and bishops, it exerted enormous political pressure in both chambers at Westminster and in the corridors of the Foreign Office. In 1900 the future king, Edward VII, was the Society's patron. Its list of corresponding members included Joaquin Nabuco, the statesman and architect of abolition in Brazil.

Editions of its quarterly publication The Anti-Slavery Reporter at the turn of the century show that while its main centre of interest remained the 'native question' in Africa, its effectiveness was diminishing. There were sporadic and brief reports on slavery-related issues such as race relations in the United States, the system of Latin American slavery known as peonage, convict-leasing and Chinese labour. Coverage of countries such as Burma and Fiji showed that slavery was a global problem. Wherever slavery was discussed within the realms of the Empire, such as the desperate abuses against the aborigines of Western Australia, coverage was awkward. An obvious propagandist element clouded the views of the Anti-Slavery Society and is evident in stereotypical coverage of slave labour markets in Muslim lands such as Persia, Morocco, Zanzibar, Egypt or in Portuguese and German Africa.

The more effective outfit, after the abolition of the slave trade, was the Aborigines' Protection Society. Following the publication of a government Blue Book in 1837 drafted by William Gladstone, the A.P.S. was established in 1838 to stand up to 'the enormous wrongs inflicted on Aborigines by European colonization'. In its opening report it had targeted 'the restless spirit of adventure' and emigration arising from Europe's 'superabundant population' as two of the main reasons for escalating abuses. Again its committee attracted important politicians, churchmen and businessmen. By the late 1890s it had emerged as the most informed voice as a result of the active participation of members such as the radical Liberal politicians Sir Charles Dilke and James Bryce, the philosopher Herbert Spencer, and another rising Liberal, Augustine Birrell. Its asthmatic secretary, H.R. Fox Bourne, appointed in 1889, was prepared to stick his neck out on a number of issues; one of them was the Congo question.

In the aftermath of the Boer War attitudes to the Empire changed. A new humanitarian spirit was born, partly from popular objections to government policy in South Africa, including the use of concentration camps and the burning of Boer farms, partly through the inspiration of anti-imperialist campaigners like Emily Hobhouse. Humanitarian work was still seen as important to the advancement of political careers. Perhaps in an effort to divert attention away from the embarrassing excesses of British conduct in the Boer War, discussion catalysed around the Congo question. The search for a Heart of Darkness evident in fact inspired a series of Marlowesque river journeys by individuals intent on exposing the lie at the heart of the white man's civilisation. It also helped put the humanitarian movement on a new and more radical ideological footing.

In 1900 the African Society was founded in memory of the writer, ethnographer and traveller, Mary Kingsley, whose travels in West Africa in the 1890s had done much to increase public awareness of the rich cultural traditions of tribal life in the region. The new Society's honorary secretary, and the moving force behind its establishment, was the historian Alice Stopford Green, wife of J.R. Green, author of the popular History of the English People. The honorary treasurer was George Macmillan, proprietor of the publishing house. Among its committee members was the future Liberal prime minister, Herbert Asquith; Gladstone's disciple and biographer, John Morley; the anthropologist J.G. Frazer, author of The Golden Bough; and the governor of the Gold Coast, Matthew Nathan. The society's members were motivated above all to build up 'respect for native customs' and change public understanding on Africa and Africans.

In April 1903 a young, crusading journalist, E.D. Morel, began a weekly newspaper, The West African Mail. A founding principle of the paper was to supply 'reliable and impartial business intelligence' on West African issues and the inaugural issue ran a large picture of Winston Churchill—a recent convert to Liberalism from the Tories—accompanying a letter from him supporting Morel's venture. There were further good wishes from the two Liverpool shipping line owners Sir Alfred Jones and John Holt. Alice Stopford Green's name was also on the paper's masthead. But beside covering commercial news, Motel's deeper intention was to improve public awareness of atrocities in the Congo and expose the escalating stories of slavery emerging from the interior.

The Foreign Office decided to act when in March 1903 the House of Commons passed a resolution 'to abate the evils' in the Congo. They selected their most capable consul in Africa, Roger Casement, to carry out the investigation on their behalf. Casement had already spent almost twenty years in Africa, ten of them officially connected to the Foreign Office in a series of consular postings. But his consular position was a convenient cover for intelligence work. Early on in his consular career he had undertaken such work for both the War Office Intelligence Department and another department—whose activities have gone largely unrecorded—Commercial Intelligence, part of the Board of Trade. During the Boer War he had devised an unrealised 'special mission' to attack the Boer railway lines.

Casement's voyage into the interior in several ways mirrored Marlow's journey. The consul chartered a river boat and spent two months navigating and traversing territories he had travelled through in 1897, compiling evidence from victims and perpetrators of atrocities. On his return to London he met both Morel and Conrad. His report was published in

February 1904 in an abridged and edited form and represented the official government line. The national press grabbed at the story. There was an outcry across Britain. Casement himself handed the first cheque for 100 [pounds sterling] to Morel to set up the Congo Reform Association that over the next decade became the most radical humanitarian force in the Empire. It questioned fundamental principles of Imperial policy and ultimately forced Leopold II to surrender his personal control in the Congo.

Prominent journalists and radical-liberal newspapers and journals began to condemn the horrors that were happening in the name of imperialism across the globe. German atrocities against the Herreros in South West Africa (now Namibia); Japanese actions in Formosa (Taiwan); the hemp-kings of Yucatan and the slavery that had maintained Porfirio Diaz's long presidency in Mexico; reports about the US treatment of rebels in the Philippines—all built up a picture of global atrocities committed by the so-called civilisers.

The British journalist H.W. Nevinson made an investigation of slavery in Portuguese West Africa (Angola) published as *A Modern Slavery* (1906). Expensive libel suits by companies defending commercial practices in imperial enclaves attracted leading lawyers such as Rufus Isaacs and Sir Edward Carson. Public indignation was further excited by the contribution of other important literary heavyweights. Mark Twain wrote *King Leopold's Soliloquy*. Arthur Conan Doyle penned *The Crime of the Congo*. Thousands attended Congo Reform rallies across the country.

The publication of Red Rubber by E.D. Morel in 1906 made it clear that the worst atrocities had been committed to meet the spiralling demand for rubber as the burgeoning automobile and bicycle industries moved into top gear. 1906 was the year when Henry Ford started production of his Model T—the first mass-produced motor car. Demand for rubber now began to far outstrip the supply. As a result of both its insulating qualities for electrical wiring and circuitry and its use in the motor car industry, rubber became the defining commodity in imperial policymaking. In those crucial years between 1892 and 1914 when rubber was still tapped from tropical forests, before cultivated plantation rubber became the main supply source, desperate crimes were committed. The story of wild rubber is one of horror on an apocalyptic scale. Manipulation of the rubber market ignited a series of genocidal episodes across the twentieth century. It changed the face of the tropical regions of the world forever. Although in *Heart of Darkness* Conrad's character Kurtz's reputation had been built on his great renown in collecting ivory, it was the collection of wild rubber that led to the greatest tribal and environmental cataclysm of modern times. There were countless Kurtz-like white men imposing rubber tapping on indigenous populations across tropical Africa and the Amazon.

In 1909, in an effort to strengthen the front against abuse in Africa, the Anti-Slavery Society amalgamated with the Aborigines' Protection Society to produce the Anti-Slavery and Aborigines Protection Society. A former Baptist missionary who had spent many years in Africa, the Rev. John Harris, was elected as acting secretary. Within months of the merger the restructured society was involved in a new slavery scandal,

this time in the disputed frontier region of the north-west Amazon bordering Colombia, Brazil, Peru, and Ecuador. It was an episode that became known to history as 'the Putumayo Atrocities', and, once again it was Casement, by this time British Consul-General in Rio de Janeiro, who was recruited by the Liberal Foreign Secretary, Sir Edward Grey, to investigate the matter on an official level. Casement made two voyages to the Amazon in 1910 and 1911, again very much in the manner of Marlow; both journeys were cloaked in official secrecy. He uncovered a horror that paralleled and even exceeded the cruelty he had witnessed in the Congo. Again with press co-operation, the matter occupied newspaper columns around the world for many months.

The humanitarian work and achievement of both Morel and Casement was celebrated during 1911. By then both men were household names throughout the Empire. On May 29th, 1911, a public presentation was made to Morel in the Whitehall Rooms at the Hotel Metropole. Lord Cromer, the famous Imperial proconsul in Egypt, presided. There were dozens of letters from those unable to attend and rousing speeches from those who were present. The Bishop of Winchester said:

> Every candid and well-informed man knows now, and public men of all parties agree, that there had grown up on the Congo, and in its administration, one of those moral monsters which deface history and laugh in the face of the conscience of mankind. It might easily have gone on unknown: and even if dimly known behind the veils of distance and darkness, it might easily, even when known, have gone unattacked, except by some futile words of protest. That it did not do so was due, and due entirely, to Mr Morel. I am not ashamed to believe and say that for a great moral emergency the providence of God gave us the man.

The luncheon brought together a dozen bishops and as many peers and captains of industry. Andrew Carnegie, W.H. Lever, William Cadbury and John Holt were four of the better known industrialists who lent their names to the occasion. It became the defining humanitarian meeting of the age.

A few weeks later Casement received news of his knighthood, and in early August he embarked on a further trip up the Amazon to try and arrest the perpetrators of atrocities. Of Casement's three Marlowesque river journeys this remains the shadiest voyage of all. As he went up river Casement witnessed the end of the Amazon rubber boom and the collapse of the veneer of civilization built on the back of the rubber economy. Yellow fever had started to attack the three main communities at Belem do Para, Manaos and Iquitos. Rubber prices had slumped. Those who could afford to were leaving. On his return down-river Casement went to Washington and spent a few days with the British Ambassador, James Bryce, and also had a private meeting with US President William Howard Taft.

The publication of Casement's Amazon reports in a *Blue Book* in July 1912 brought the discussion in the newspapers to a height. Prime Minister Herbert Asquith was obliged to establish a Parliamentary Select Committee Enquiry and many of the corrupt practices supporting imperial commerce were exposed.

Rome issued a papal encyclical. Two years later legislation was passed by the Commons making British company directors responsible for their company activities abroad.

On the outbreak of war in 1914 many of those who had been united by humanitarian endeavour since the start of the century were divided in views and loyalty. Within hours of the outbreak of hostilities, Morel founded the Union of Democratic Control (UDC) along with James Ramsay MacDonald, Norman Angell and Charles Trevelyan. It became the most effective voice of dissent criticising the British government's entry into the First World War and attacked the official version of how the war had come about, accusing the Liberal government of deliberately spreading falsehoods. The loudest objections were raised against the practice of secret diplomacy and the control of foreign policy by a narrow clique of political insiders. Among those attracted to this movement was Bertrand Russell, and it says something for its influence that nine of its members became ministers in the first Labour cabinet of 1924.

Casement's career took a more revolutionary path. After his resignation from the Foreign Office in August 1913 he set about recruiting Irish Volunteers in response to the arming of the Ulster Volunteers by the Unionist leaders, Sir Edward Carson and F.E. Smith. When he left Ireland in July 1914, a month before the outbreak of the First World War, he had an army of over 12,000 volunteers at his disposal. A few days after he reached America the first shipment of guns for those volunteers was landed at Howth by Erskine Childers. The plan for this gun-running exploit had been hatched in the house of Alice Stopford Green in Grosvenor Road in London. In America, Casement raised further funds and planned open rebellion against the British Empire. In the autumn of 1914 he returned to Europe in an effort to get German support for the Irish independence movement. But the German high command prevaricated and a propaganda campaign began in the British press to blacken Casement's reputation in the public mind.

In April 1916, having failed to recruit Irish prisoners of war to join a pro-independence Irish Brigade, Casement returned to Ireland in a German U-boat, but British Naval Intelligence had intercepted a cypher detailing his plans for rebellion. His landing was expected and his capture at an Iron Age fort near Ardfert in County Kerry began the tragic chain of events of Easter week 1916. Many of those who had campaigned alongside Casement and Morel for Congo reform, such as Asquith, Sir Edward Grey, Winston Churchill, Herbert Samuel, and Sir Matthew Nathan, became the figures who now demanded Casement's execution for treason. Following a state trial Casement was the last of the sixteen Irish rebel leaders to be executed in the wake of the Rising.

In 1917 Morel was imprisoned under the Defence of the Realm Act for his continuing campaign against the war. Imprisonment seriously weakened his health and in November 1924 he died prematurely. The ethical policy that Casement and Morel had forced upon the Foreign Office and which galvanised radical liberal politics before 1914 has since then been conspicuously absent. In 1914 Britain and Belgium were allies in war and the whole matter of Congo reform hung in the air like an embarrassing smell. It was only during the 1980s that the Belgian state archive finally released important source material detailing the scale of the horror in the Congo. In Britain it was as recently as 1995 that the Open Government Initiative allowed proper independent historical examination of a number of aspects of the circumstances surrounding Casement's extraordinary career as an imperial intelligence operator-turned-humanitarian-turned-revolutionary.

At the end of *Heart of Darkness,* Marlow returns to Brussels in order to tell Kurtz's intended bride about his death. But instead of telling her the truth he lies and claims that it was her name that Kurtz had muttered with his dying breath. The humanitarian work that united many intellectual, political and religious figures before 1914 has remained a neglected region of history: a number of aspects of the story have been suppressed until today. Lies were told which survive as part of the historical record.

It is high time that this whole matter was better understood by historians. The ideals and action that gave rise to the anti-slavery movement and the efforts to protect indigenous peoples in the Congo, Amazon and elsewhere became the foundations upon which current humanitarian and human rights organisations, including Amnesty International and Survival International, were founded. Ideas of ethical foreign policy that are currently promoted as a motivating force behind New Labour's foreign policy can also be traced back to the radical discussions of this period.

The Congo reform movement and the Putumayo atrocities, that together provoked so much public anger between 1903 and 1914, were perceived as the last chapter in the long crusade against slavery, although that chapter is yet to be written up as history. Their significance has been deliberately obscured partly because of Morel's anti-war stance and his importance in the rise of the British Labour party, but more as a consequence of Casement's involvement with advanced revolutionary activities. What the story of this period reveals, however, is that Conrad's fictional narrative *Heart of Darkness* reflected both a truth and a horror at the core of Empire that some hoped would never be exposed by the facts.

## For Further Reading

Joseph Conrad, *Heart of Darkness,* edited by D.D.R.A Goonetilleke (Broadway Literary Texts, 1995); Frederick Karl and Laurence Davies, *The Collected Letters of Joseph Conrad (Cambridge University Press); Marvin Swartz, The Union of Democratic Control in British Politics During the First World War* (Clarendon Press, Oxford 1971); Wm Roger Louis. *'The Triumph of the Congo Reform Movement 1905–1908'* in Boston University Papers on Africa; Roger Anstey, *'The Congo Rubber Atrocities—A Case Study'* in African Historical Studies—Vol, IV, 1 (1971).

**ANGUS MITCHELL** edited *The Amazon Journal* of Roger Casement (Anaconda Editions, 1998).

# UNIT 2

# The Ferment of the West, 1500–1900

## Unit Selections

## Key Points to Consider

- What factors conspired to connect witchcraft to European women? What were the results?

- What influence did Martin Luther have on sixteenth century Europe? Why does this influence still resonate today?

- What impact did Queen Elizabeth I have on her times? What legacy did she leave?

- What reforms did Catherine the Great initiate to help the Russian people? How successful was she in achieving these reforms?

- How did Jean-Baptiste Colbert and Adam Smith each influence the history of economics? How were they different in their approaches to economic problems?

- In which ways did George Sand influence the lives of European women?

- Why was the French Revolution an important event in world history? What dangers did it unleash?

- What circumstances produced the Paris Commune of 1871? To what extent could it be considered a child of the French Revolution?

## Student Website

www.mhhe.com/cls

## Internet References

**The Adam Smith Institute**
  www.adamsmith.org
**Britannica.com: Mercantilism**
  www.britannica.com/eb/article?eu_53378
**Victorian Web**
  www.victorianweb.org
**The Witch Hunts Main Page**
  http://departments.kings.edu/womens_history/witch

The European voyages of exploration in the fifteenth and sixteenth centuries are representative of the spirit of adventure, curiosity, and greed that carried Western civilization to the ends of the earth. The unique character of Western civilization was shaped by many events, ideas, and people. Skillful manipulation of economic systems, the articulation of a secular worldview that was based on law, and the proclamation of democratic values had combined to create the West's legacy to the world.

Adam Smith, the first great economist, laid the foundations for the industrial revolution. He argued that if left alone (laissez-faire) the marketplace would be self-regulating. The invisible hand of market forces would regulate the economy. Manufacturers would produce all the goods that people wanted—and in the correct amounts. Without government interference, an oversupply would drop prices and provide a disincentive to suppliers. In times of scarcity, the reverse would occur, with demand driving prices up and inspiring suppliers to provide needed goods.

Smith's law of supply and demand has been modified by later conditions such as social welfare and the creation of large, multinational corporations, more powerful than governments. However, capitalism has not been overthrown by oppressed workers, as Karl Marx predicted. Instead, it has turned out to be a flexible economic system, more successful than either socialism or communism at present.

The free trade that Smith advocated has been modified as well. When Jean-Baptiste Colbert, finance minister for Louis XIV, used mercantilism to provide France a favorable balance of trade, other monarchs paid attention. Mercantilism called for the accumulation of bullion gold and silver as marks of a great nation. And, of course, mercantilism rested on the exploitation of colonies. When modern countries suppress free trade or try to protect their industries with tariffs, there are predictable protests at meetings of the World Trade Organization. Today, gold is no longer used as a form of money, and most of us receive our paychecks and pay our bills electronically, using electric current as our modern form of currency.

Catherine the Great of Russia, although a believer in absolute rule, also advocated "law-based" monarchy. A contemporary of Diderot, she was one of a group of leaders who came to be known as enlightened despots. Paradoxically, perhaps, she intentionally had no children, ensuring that her successors would be through the male line. Apparently, she considered herself unique.

In France, the nation's attempt to replace monarchy with democracy devolved into violence, offering a cautionary message to present-day democracies under threat that violence is a very imperfect tool for cultivating or maintaining democracy. And, this tendency, first observed in the French Revolution, was

repeated in the Paris Commune of 1871. Is violence an inevitable consequence of revolution?

One of the great ideological and political struggles at the end of the eighteenth century occurred in a peripheral frontier nation that would later become the United States. Victory over Britain unleashed a vigorous, capitalistic, argumentative people, determined to make democracy work. Benjamin Franklin, chief American representative at the Treaty of Paris negotiations that ended the War of American Independence, had hoped to avoid a break with Great Britain. Equally at home in London and Philadelphia, Franklin eventually came to see that America must shake off her shackles in order to fulfill her destiny as a great nation.

# The World, the Flesh and the Devil

**Robert W. Thurston looks at the politics of demonology and rethinks attitudes to witches and women between 1400 and 1700.**

ROBERT W. THURSTON

*All wickedness is but little to the wickedness of a woman . . . [She is] an evil of nature . . . [Women] are more credulous; and since the chief aim of the devil is to corrupt faith, therefore he rather attacks them . . . Women . . . are intellectually like children . . . [A woman] always deceives.*

As the Dominican monk Heinrich Kramer (c.1430-c.1505) sat down to write about witches in early 1486, he must have felt desperate. He had recently been sentenced to prison for theft, blocked by other clerics as he tried to convict women of witchcraft, and scorned and threatened by a bishop. Kramer (known as Institoris in some sources) needed to recoup the respect appropriate to a papal inquisitor, his position in 'Upper Germany', a swathe of present day Germany, France and Austria.

This was the inauspicious background to the creation of the *Malleus Maleficarum* ('Hammer of Witches'). First printed in 1486, the *Malleus* is often considered to be the pivotal work for the study of both the witch hunts, which lasted roughly from the 1420s to the 1690s, and the era's commentaries on women.

The book owes much of its fame to late nineteenth- and early twentieth-century scholars who were certain that superstition and fanaticism produced the hunts, while the Enlightenment's breakthrough to reason ended them. In 1878 the President of Cornell University, Andrew Dickson White, showed an early edition of the *Malleus* to 'his shuddering class', saying that it had 'caused more suffering than any other [work] written by human pen.' The narrator of Dan Brown's *The Da Vinci Code* (2004) echoes this claim:

> The Catholic Inquisition published the book that arguably could be called the most blood-soaked publication in human history. *Malleus maleficarum*—or *The Witches' Hammer*—indoctrinated the world to 'the dangers of free-thinking women' and instructed the clergy how to locate, torture, and destroy them. . . . During three hundred years of witch hunts, the Church burned at the stake an astounding five million women.

Not astounding but absurd—the old guesses of up to nine million victims have been revised downwards: recent estimates suggest 30-40,000 executions. Nor did 'the Inquisition' itself publish the *Malleus*. Germany, particularly along the Rhine, was the worst killing ground. France was a distant second, while England and even Scotland lagged far behind. Italy, Spain, and Portugal contributed relatively few victims to the pyres.

For all that estimates of the death toll have fallen recently, it still appears that females typically comprised about 75 percent of the victims. However, commentators on witchcraft between 1400 and 1700 divide sharply on three key points: whether or not women are intrinsically wicked; whether demons could perform real actions or simply create illusions; and whether witchcraft was truly practised. These divisions go far to explain why the witch-hunts were so erratic.

The reasons for the high proportion of female victims must be sought in more mundane factors than the demonologists advanced: the tasks that women performed, giving birth, suckling babies, preparing food, caring for children, and washing the dead, were just the ones that contemporaries suspected could provide opportunities and substances for evil acts.

The story of the *Malleus* and its author open the way to rethinking demonology in general. In the last decade studies of European demonology have focused more on widespread anxiety about heresy than on obsessions with women. When Kramer's work is seen in the context of the wider politico-religious struggles of the era, the *Malleus* appears less an assault on women than an attempt to use them—or stock images of them—to make points about correct belief.

Kramer had been arrested in 1482 for allegedly stealing silverware and money in the course of his inquisitorial duties. The Inquisition had arisen in the late twelfth century as the Church focused on combating heresy. Managed by the papacy and the Dominican and Franciscan Orders in its early phases, the Inquisition later developed various 'Holy Offices', for example in Portugal and Rome. Kramer, operating under the Pope and his own Dominican Order, was responsible in Upper Germany for investigating, arresting, and ordering the torture of suspected heretics, which by now included witches.

Before Kramer could actually be gaoled, the Archbishop of Craynensis (Albania) issued a call for a new Church council. Kramer seized this moment to write a strong defence of papal authority in opposition to conciliarism, the movement which argued that councils possessed higher authority than the Pope. Pope Sixtus IV, recognizing that Kramer's pen could be an important force on his side, dropped all charges against the monk and returned him to his inquisitorial post.

But Sixtus died in 1484, to be replaced by Innocent VIII. At this juncture Kramer, possibly supported by his inquisitorial partner Jakob Sprenger, complained to the new pontiff that ecclesiastical officials were hampering their efforts to combat heresy. Innocent responded by issuing the Bull *Summis desiderantes affectibus* ('Desiring with supreme ardour') in 1484, in which he enjoined all secular and Church authorities in Upper Germany to aid the two inquisitors.

Armed with this Bull, Kramer arrested some fifty women on the charge of witchcraft and put several on trial in Brixen, east of Innsbruck. He denied his prisoners legal counsel and had them tortured immediately, both gross violations of inquisitorial rules. His actions provoked strong opposition from officials appointed by the Bishop of Brixen, Georg Golser. These clerics finally agreed to try the women, but the case led to Kramer's downfall. When he questioned a defendant about her sexual practices and moral standing in her community, the judges found his query irrelevant and overruled him. The trial was quickly ended and the women released, as episcopal members of the court decided that Kramer had abused his position.

Golser wrote to a priest named Nikolaus criticizing Kramer for his 'completely childish' behaviour, a result of 'his advanced age' (he was about fifty-five). Kramer 'still wants perhaps to mix in women's affairs', the bishop continued, but 'I am not letting him do that, as formerly he erred almost completely in his trial'. Instead he advised him to return to his monastery in Innsbruck. But in the autumn of 1485, Golser informed Kramer that he had now become unwelcome in Innsbruck, warning him that a popular uprising against his witchcraft cases might develop. No such revolt occurred, but after a second threatening letter from Golser in early 1486, Kramer departed for Salzburg.

He then set to work on the *Malleus,* perhaps in the hope that a new book could salvage his standing. Hastily written by Kramer alone, and with glaring lapses in presentation of the argument and grammar, the text was printed late in the year. Sprenger's name became attached to the work in a later reprinting, which may have been a ploy by Kramer to give his book more scholarly weight.

While the *Malleus* offered little new on the theory of witchcraft, it did argue vehemently that witches existed, that women were particularly drawn to witchcraft and sex with demons, and that with demons' help, witches performed evil deeds. The book also presented sensational stories. For example, Kramer reported that in a certain city beset by plague, a dead 'woman was gradually eating the shroud in which she had been buried'. The pestilence would continue until she consumed the entire cloth. When the body was exhumed, half the shroud had been eaten. Aghast, an official cut the head from the corpse and threw it out of the grave; 'at once the plague ceased'.

After the *Malleus* appeared, Kramer continued his dubious or outright criminal behaviour. He implied that the book had direct papal approval by inserting Innocent VIII's Bull as the preface to an edition printed in 1487. But Innocent had merely written a standard directive reaffirming the authority of his inquisitors. The Bull repeats the conventional wisdom of the day on the sexual depravity of heretics, but not witches—it does not mention nocturnal flight and refers to the sabbat only indirectly. It did not single out women as Satan's whores.

Nevertheless, the *Malleus* has retained a leading role in studies of the witch persecutions because of its vitriolic condemnation of women. The most important reason for the Devil's appeal to females, Kramer argued, is that a woman is 'more carnal than a man, as is clear from her many carnal abominations'. The Dominican obsessively reiterated this point, concluding that 'all witchcraft comes from carnal lust, which is in women insatiable'. He did mention 'chaste and honest women', but the remark paled beside his overall misogyny. Clearly he feared women, as shown by the many references to impotence caused by witches and even to their removal of penises.

Kramer's career after 1486 demonstrates that by no means everyone agreed with him on witchcraft. He undermined his own cause by having a forgery endorsing his book inserted among letters from the theology faculty at the University of Cologne, which had offered only limited support for his ideas. Kramer then bribed a notary to label all the letters as true documents. The letters, along with the papal Bull of 1484, were bound with the *Malleus* in some reprintings, in an attempt to give it maximum authority. When this forgery became known, Kramer's reputation plummeted, and his ex-partner Sprenger opened prosecution against him for the forgery.

Kramer then moved on to the Mosel district, where he angered his superiors by approving a local community's effort to create counter-magic against dark forces by erecting a large crucifix. The Church could not openly approve such quasi-pagan measures.

Kramer's behaviour in Brixen had so discredited the concept of diabolical witchcraft that no further witch trials took place there. In 1490, the Dominican Order condemned him for excesses in his work. Although in 1491 the Nuremberg city council requested Kramer's assistance in witch trials and he obliged by writing a treatise denouncing laxity in the pursuit of witches, the city aldermen refused to publish it, perhaps because they had finally been informed about his past. He moved yet again, this time to Bohemia, where he died in about 1505.

While the *Malleus* represents an extreme strain in late fifteenth-century male attitudes toward women, it does not support the notion that misogyny was the pre-eminent factor behind the witch hunts. To begin with, the extent of the book's influence is far from clear. While some later works on witches drew heavily on the *Malleus,* its publication history was erratic. It appeared in two waves (sixteen editions were published between 1486 and 1520, and about the same number between 1574 and 1621), but none in the intervening fifty years, a crucial period in the rise of the witch trials. In 1526 the Spanish Inquisition denounced the *Malleus* as worthless. Nor were there further editions during another great round of hunts between 1620 and 1665.

The book's appeal is often explained in terms of its completeness in guiding witch-hunters, down to how to lead the witch into a courtroom (backwards). Yet, especially in view of the sensationalist qualities of the *Malleus,* it cannot be assumed that readers always accepted Kramer's arguments.

Sigismund, Count of Tyrol, had been so disturbed by Kramer's conduct at the Brixen trial in 1484 that he commissioned the jurist Ulrich Molitor to clarify the issues. Molitor's *De lamiis* [or *laniis*] *et phitonicis mulieribus* ('On Female Witches and Fortune-tellers', 1489) reached the traditional conclusion that while demons exist they can only create illusions, and cannot interact physically with humans. While Molitor agreed that women were more likely than men to enlist in Satan's service and should be tried for making a pact with him, he explained female attraction to demons by referring to specific circumstances such as poverty, hatred or other unspecified temptations, rather than to general female characteristics such as lust or defective character.

A stronger counter-attack against Kramer, Johann Weyer's *De praestigiis daemonum* ('On Demonic Illusions' or 'On Witchcraft'), appeared in numerous editions beginning in 1563. Weyer too maintained that Satan could only produce illusions; violent phenomena such as sudden illnesses or hailstorms had natural, not diabolic, causes. Evidence obtained under torture was worthless, and old women's voluntary confessions of witchcraft resulted from 'melancholy'.

Reading Kramer's work within the broad context of demonology makes it clear that the genre's primary goal was to defend the reality of demons and humans' physical interaction with them. This argument underscored the need for mainstream Christianity to engage in a sharper struggle against evil. The *Malleus* begins, 'Question the First. Whether the belief that there are such beings as witches is so essential a part of the Catholic faith that obstinately to maintain the opposite opinion manifestly savours of heresy'. No wonder Kramer argued for the existence of witches.

He sought a vivid means of supporting the notion that Satan could easily recruit some humans. Sex sells, and emphasizing purported female sexual transgressions was for Kramer a way of drawing on existing negative stereotypes to make demonic activity more plausible. Since women were traditionally considered the weaker sex and the Devil was definitely male, demonic copulation had to be overwhelmingly with females. Thus *incubi,* or demons who insert a sexual member into a human body, appear about nine times as often in demonological works as *succubi,* which are sexually receptive creatures.

In this and other respects, Kramer borrowed heavily from earlier works on witchcraft, especially Johann Nider's *Formicarius* ('The Ant Heap', 1435-37). The *Malleus* cites Nider at least fifty times. Though Nider had never been a witch-hunter, he was deeply concerned with heresy, particularly with the Hussite movement. A negotiator with the Hussites at the Council of Basel in 1433, he wavered between seeking their return to the fold and urging their destruction.

Nider noted that both sexes could be witches but argued that women's sexual 'weakness' often led them into the Devil's arms. Yet in contrast to Kramer, he was unwilling to break completely with the old doctrine that insisted Satan produced illusions, not acts, on Earth: two of the five books in *Formicarius* are concerned with 'false visions' and dreams.

Nider considered that demons posed a grave problem for true Christianity, because they allied with opponents of reform within the Church. He quoted St Paul in 1 Corinthians 11:19: 'For there must be also heresies among you, that they which are approved may be made manifest among you.' Heretics of all sorts were useful to the Church by demonstrating what *not* to believe and how not to act—and this included their reported copulation with demons. As this argument unfolds in *Formicarius* amid discussion of such topics as the importance of growing rye, it becomes clear that Nider's anxiety about wanton women is a small part of his larger concerns.

Although most witch-hunts occurred in German-speaking lands, the most developed demonology arose, surprisingly, in France during the mid- to late sixteenth century. Yet the many French treatises on demons by no means sparked large-scale witch persecutions. Indeed, trials in Francophone regions occurred mostly in eastern borderlands not then under the crown, especially Franche Comté and Lorraine. Normandy, long an integral part of the realm, did witness numerous cases, but there male witches far outnumbered females.

Lambert Daneau (1564), Jean Bodin (1580), Henri Boguet (1602), Martin Del Rio (1603 and 1611), and Pierre de Lancre (1612) were the leading French experts on witchcraft. Some of these men did think women were especially drawn to Satan. But, paralleling new work on Nider, historians such as Michael Bailey have seen these writers as preoccupied above all with political-cum-religious battles. Except for the Protestant Daneau, who fled to Geneva to write, the French authors were all zealous Catholics, writing in the wake of the Council of Trent (1545-63), which had adopted a host of new policies to strengthen the Church in the face of the Protestant challenge. They produced copious propaganda directed at the enemies of Tridentine reform: Catholic *politiques* (compromisers) as well as Protestants. How best to smear these opponents and solidify one's own ranks? Simple: by linking these enemies of the true faith to Satan.

The French demonologists directed particular fire at the Paris *parlement,* an appeals court whose jurisdiction covered a large part of the kingdom. The *parlement,* dominated for most of this period by religious moderates, was stubbornly sceptical toward the evidence for witchcraft accepted in lower tribunals. Unlike them, the Paris court used torture half-heartedly at best; of 185 appellants the court had tortured, only one confessed. The tribunal did not use physical duress in any witchcraft case after 1593. In 1624, the *parlement* required an automatic appeal to it from lower courts for all witch trials; by the 1640s the Parisian magistrates rejected witchcraft accusations altogether and even ordered that lower-court judges who tortured prisoners accused of the crime be punished themselves. The witch-hunters charged that these developments suggested the *parlement* had succumbed to diabolical influence.

Like Kramer, the French demonologists insisted that demons were real, flew about the earth and had intercourse with humans. Again like Kramer, they identified females as the likely candidates for diabolical connections. Yet they did not exhibit misogyny anything like Kramer's; most were rather even-handed about the sex of witches. In maligning all women, the *Malleus* occupied a special, perhaps unique, niche within demonology.

Since the existence of witches would confirm the earthly activities of demons, the concern to find them was, at root, related to a fear of atheism. More than a few observers argued that, if there were no witches, then the Devil might not be real either, which could mean that even God might be an unnecessary concept. Giordano da Bergamo may have been the first to say publicly that a belief in witchcraft was essential to true Christian faith. He wrote in 1470, well ahead of Kramer, and possibly he provided a stimulus for the Dominican's arguments.

The dread of atheism and its connection to discussions of witches appeared especially strongly in England. Clergyman Joseph Glanvill fulminated in 1668 against those who thought witches not real but merely 'creatures of melancholy and superstition'. To him, this was a notion fostered by 'ignorance and design'. And even though Meric Casaubon's *Of Credulity and Incredulity,* published in the same year, was sceptical regarding evidence of witchcraft, the author still believed in witches, or said he did, because to doubt was a step toward atheism. The Platonist Henry More evinced a similar concern. But as the belief that God intervened continually in the daily round of the natural world gave way in the late seventeenth century to the idea that he was the divine watchmaker, it became less important to believe that evil forces daily stalked good Christians.

The politics of belief in witches must also be seen against the background of a literary and theological debate on women known as the *querelle des femmes,* which ran from the late Middle Ages into the eighteenth century. This centred at first on the *Roman de la Rose,* a rambling poem begun by Guillaume de Lorris and completed by Jean de Meun around 1278. The poem is an allegory of courtly and carnal love but also a guide to manners, clothing, and the conquest of friends and lovers. Along the way, several characters deliver scathing attacks on women. Jealous Husband offers the worst tirade; he complains that a married woman reveals 'her evil nature'. His own wife is an 'evil bitch'. Husband defies anyone who says, 'I am overconfident in my attacks on all women'. Husband is sure that, 'All women get themselves laid', for the wish of each one 'is always to do it'.

A century later, Christine de Pizan replied to the misogyny she saw in the *Rose,* in her poem *The God of Love's Letter* (1399) and particularly in *The Book of the City of Ladies* (1404-05). She sparked a debate that dominated literary Paris in 1400-02, from which some twenty related treatises, letters, and sermons survive. Prominent men arranged themselves on both sides; one of de Pizan's foremost supporters was Jean Gerson, provost of the University of Paris.

The new demonology followed closely upon the *Rose* debate and in key respects was closely intertwined with it. Thus Nider's *Formicarius* of 1435-37 and Martin Le Franc's *Le Champion des Dames* (1440-42) contributed to a new stereotype of the witch as female, sexually assertive, and eager to be in league with Satan. But neither book is essentially misogynistic. Le Franc's main character is Defender (of women), who refers to the 'valiant Christine'. Le Franc describes how evil persons greet the Devil as their leader, proceed to have sex with him or each other, and receive lethal powders from him. For all that,

Defender maintains that women are essentially good and easily wins the debate.

Gianfresco Pico's *Strix, sive de ludificatione daemonum* ('Strix or The Deceptions of Demons', 1523), features a character who until the last page is sceptical that demons recruit humans. And in *De venificis* (1564), translated in 1575 into English as *A Dialogue of Witches,* Lambert Daneau's Theophilus also succeeds only after much talk in convincing his friend Anthony of the reality of witchcraft. These works do not insist that women are generally vile.

Alfonso de Spina, writing in 1458-60, qualified the issue of gender and demons by indicating that only old women became Satan's lovers. In 1584, Reginald Scot's influential *Discoverie of Witchcraft* all but denied the existence of demons on earth. Scot attacked the *Malleus* on logical grounds and was almost completely unconcerned with what women might or might not do. Other important voices directly defended women; Signor Magnifico in Baldesar Castiglione's *The Book of the Courtier* (1528) praises women and forgoes any mention of witchcraft.

The thorough-going misogynistic sentiments of the *Malleus* were largely discarded. While James VI of Scotland insisted in *Daemonologie* (1597), that there were twenty female witches for every male, the only reason he cited for the disproportion was women's greater frailty. After assuming the English throne in 1603, he refused to promote hunts and even stopped them on occasion.

Even as the witch-hunts intensified, powerful arguments continued to refute the idea that females were naturally evil. In the doleful story of the witch persecutions, misogyny by no means triumphed completely. Europeans could choose among competing views of the nature of women and their purported attraction to Satan. Political and religious questions often hovered just behind those debates.

# For Further Reading

Richard Golden, (ed)., *Encyclopedia of Witchcraft: The Western Tradition* (ABC-CLIO, 2006); Michael Bailey, *Battling Demons: Witchcraft, Heresy, and Reform in the Late Middle Ages* (Pennsylvania State University Press, 2003); Stuart Clark, *Thinking with Demons: the Idea of Witchcraft in Early Modern Europe* (Oxford University Press, 1997); Dylan Elliot, *Fallen Bodies: Pollution, Sexuality, and Demonology in the Middle Ages* (University of Pennsylvania Press, 1999); Jonathan L. Pearl, *The Crime of Crimes: Demonology and Politics in France, 1560-1620* (Wilfrid Laurier University Press, 1999); Eric Wilson, 'Institoris at Innsbruck: Heinrich Institoris, the Summis Desiderantes and the Brixen Witch-Trial of 1485', in Bob Scribner and Trevor Johnson, eds. *Popular Religion in Germany and Central Europe, 1400-1800* (St Martin's Press, 1996).

**ROBERT W. THURSTON** is Phillip R. Shriver Professor of History at Miami University, Oxford, Ohio. His new book *The Witch Hunts* is published by Pearson early next year.

# The Luther Legacy

Derek Wilson

Over the centuries Luther (1483–1546) has been variously identified as an advocate of absolute monarchy, democracy, individual freedom, intellectual repression, nationalism, internationalism, spirituality and secularism. The fact that so many later 'movers and shakers' have claimed the monk of Wittenberg as a progenitor of their own convictions is testimony to the stature of the man. Indeed, it would be difficult to identify any other individual who, without wielding political power or leading armies, more decisively changed the course of history. Even our supposedly post-Christian age cannot write him out of the record. Yet, we have to resist the temptation to recreate him in our own image. He was a religious figure; his battles were fought over theological issues that may seem to us obscure but whose implications touched every area of life, individual and corporate.

Jakob Burckhardt was essentially right in identifying the Reformation as an escape from discipline. For centuries the Church had held the monopoly of propaganda: its murals, stained glass, the polychromed paraphernalia of shrines and altars, the pastoral and educational activities of the clergy, all spoke of the awesome need for people to prepare for the world to come. That meant availing themselves of the prescribed means of grace entrusted to their spiritual superiors. The clergy held the keys to eternal bliss or torment. Any who did air doubts or proclaim a rival programme were heretics and were dealt with severely. The only spiritual authority emanated from Rome. Luther, however, insisted that there was another, higher, source of authority: the word of God written in the Bible. In his preaching and teaching—but above all in his public confrontations with spiritual and temporal leaders—he gave people permission to doubt everything the Catholic hierarchy taught; to judge it for themselves against the testimony of the Bible.

Any attempt to assess Luther's impact must begin with his redefining of the individual. His spiritual journey was an intensely personal one. In 1505 he forsook the legal career for which he had been destined and entered the Augustinian monastery at Erfurt, in order to save his own immortal soul. He was following the path of self-denial and holiness as prescribed by the Church for centuries. For at least eight years he gave it his best shot. He failed to find the consolation he sought because, as well as a sensitive conscience, he was blessed with a sharp, logical mind. He could see the flaw in the system of penitence that the Church preached: if contrition and abnegation were practised in the interests of self-preservation then they were selfish, hence sinful. His was not the first earnest soul to find itself on the treadmill of sin, confession, absolution, doubt, confession. It was a terrifying, never-ending predicament. Ever-present was the 'doom' image of Christ separating the sheep and the goats and consigning the latter to the torments of hell. Famously, Luther discovered in Paul's Epistle to the Romans (Romans 1.17) the sword to sever the Gordian knot: 'the righteousness (justice) of God is revealed from faith to faith . . . the just man will live by faith'. Like countless Christians before and since, he experienced an ecstasy of release.

He might have left it there and, as a good monk, preached justification by faith alone as a truth that could somehow be made to fit with the Church's traditional penitential system. But it could not. The maze of scholastic theology seemed to prevent access to the great central truth which he had discovered. His relentless logic persuaded him to suggest, in the 95 Theses by which he publicly challenged the Church in 1517, that the practice of selling indulgences—by which the buyers could secure remission from the penalties of sin in the next world—was a matter for urgent theological debate. When the papal regime refused to grant this debate, the real problem began. Luther defied the Pope, the Inquisition and the corps of Catholic theologians. Called before the Imperial Diet by the Emperor Charles V at Worms in April 1521, Luther refused to recant insisting, 'my conscience is captive to the word of God . . . Unless I am convinced by Scripture and reason [my emphasis], I will not recant'.

It is scarcely possible to exaggerate what those words implied. Luther was not just challenging the accumulated teaching of the Church; he was saying that any man or woman possessed of the open Bible could be his or her own theologian. If God had provided the Bible as a lamp to the believer's path, then as many people as possible should be encouraged to read it. So he translated it into German, and had his translation printed (New Testament, 1522, Old Testament, 1534). Within a few years hundreds of untrained lay people were writing devotional and polemical books and pamphlets. Gone was the assumption that people only needed those skills that enabled them to perform their God-given calling in a hierarchical society. Learning was now something to be valued for its own sake. In 1524, Luther wrote to the municipal authorities throughout Germany urging them to establish elementary schools for all children, including girls. The response was not dramatic but by 1580 half the parishes in Electoral Saxony had schools for boys and 10 per cent had made similar provision for girls. As the American historian Steven Ozment has suggested, 'It is not too much to call the early Protestant movement the first Western enlightenment'.

Luther replaced the authority of the Church with that of the Bible. But it was always the Bible and reason. With the plain text in his hand everyone could work out his own salvation and no longer needed the ministrations of an intermediary priesthood. This had far-reaching consequences. If truth is the exclusive preserve of a priestly caste, any system built on this foundation will be autocratic. But, if truth is to be found in a book which anyone can read, then authority can be challenged with divine sanction. The way lies open for the development of alternative polities, even democracy. To be sure, Luther himself drew back from the more revolutionary implications of the open Bible. He did not personally initiate debates on such issues as how to establish a godly commonwealth, whether tyrants might be deposed or the balancing of crown and parliament. But his courageous stand against the Pope and the Holy Roman Emperor, the political embodiments of traditional authority, fired the imagination and stiffened the resolve of more radical spirits throughout western Christendom.

Yet Luther never set out to challenge the establishment. That marks him out from most other religious reformers of his day. Wycliffe, Savonarola, Hus and other rebels and charismatic preachers usually had begun from a starting point of popular grievances—oppression, corruption, extortion. Many clothed their message in gaudy apocalyptic language, claiming they had been sent to cleanse the world in preparation for the Second Coming. Not so Luther. He wanted to restore the Church to its New Testament purity. In that desire he was at one with a large swathe of public opinion, including humanist scholars, kings and even the Emperor. There was a clamour for a general council of the Church to initiate reform. It was only when successive popes refused to concede anything which might weaken the power of Rome, that Luther concluded that the papacy must be the Antichrist, subverting the Christian community from within.

In terms of secular politics, an anachronistic but perhaps appropriate label for him is 'right-wing reactionary'. The political theory he found in the New Testament was that God ordained kings to maintain order and that all subjects (including clergy) were to render due obedience to them. It followed that secular rulers were charged with the reformation of the churches in their domains. He therefore advocated such measures as the ending of ecclesiastical jurisdiction in matters matrimonial and the restoration of ex-monastic property to lay ownership.

Luther had an abhorrence of anarchy. He shared the fear of rebellion and chaos that lay close to the surface of medieval life, but for him public disorder was a particularly sensitive issue because politico-religious upheaval in Germany gave his enemies a stick to beat him with. This explains why he reacted so violently to the Peasants' War of 1524–25, a widespread popular rising against secular princes by ordinary people some of whom drew socially radical conclusions from Luther's teaching. By doing so Luther forfeited the support of most of the populace. His notorious invocation of the German nobility to 'smite, slay and stab' any rebel, just as 'one might kill a mad dog' gave rise

to the accusation that he was in the pocket of the princes, a taunt that was in large measure justified. Having already enlisted the aid of the German warlords to protect him from the Church and the Emperor, Luther could not prevent his movement becoming hijacked by these men of power, who banded together in 1530 to form the Schmalkaldic League. Over and again Luther warned them not to wage war against the Emperor. If they did, they would have 'no good conscience before God, no legal ground before the Empire, and no honour before the world. This would be dreadful and terrifying.' (1528) But few people were listening. The new Protestant establishment had taken what it wanted from Luther and his politically non-confrontational agenda seemed to them hopelessly out of touch.

This raises the question of whether Luther should be seen as an apostle of absolutism. Some later autocrats certainly claimed him as a founding father. It is no coincidence that memorial statues of the reformer were erected in Worms and Wittenberg during the nineteenth century, a time of German empire-building; nor that Hitler, scrabbling around for anything that would justify his manifesto, claimed Luther as a fellow-traveller in Mein Kampf. But what would the man who had set his face against militarism in the service of the Protestant state have had to say to pickelhaubed soldiers who, in 1914, marched to the front singing his own hymn, Ein feste Burg?. This same 'apostle of absolutism' was also lauded by the German philosopher Johann Fichte in 1793 as the 'patron saint of freedom' who 'broke humanity's chain' and whose shade raised his hand in benediction over Frenchmen overthrowing the ancien regime.

Luther was certainly a German patriot. A basic element in his opposition to Rome was his loathing of 'effete Italians'. He shared the resentment of many of his countrymen at benefices and senior clerical appointments held by absentee shepherds who cared not a whit for their flocks and who creamed off Church revenues to finance a luxurious transalpine lifestyle. When Pope Julius II (1503–13) initiated an indulgence to pay for the building of his new basilica of St Peter's in Rome (1506), it was always going to be unpopular in the German states and his successor Leo X (1513–21) waited four years after Julius's death in 1513 before dispatching his agents thither. When Luther expressed his opposition to the project in the 95 Theses, he was echoing a complaint heard in every bierhaus and marketplace:

> Why does not the pope, whose wealth is today greater than the wealth of the richest Crassus, build this one basilica of St Peter with his own money rather than with the money of poor believers?

This resentment expressed itself in official protest at the highest level. At the very Diet of Worms where Luther was examined and condemned by the Emperor, the German estates also presented a catalogue of 102 'oppressive burdens and abuses imposed upon . . . the German Empire by the Holy See of Rome'. But a fissure had already appeared two years earlier in 1519 when the Austrian-born Holy Roman Emperor Maximilian I had been succeeded by the Spanish-born Charles V, giving Germany's political leaders another foreign entity against which to define themselves.

In the early sixteenth century the 'Holy Roman Empire of the German Nation', which was described in 1667 as 'a body that conforms to no rule and resembles a monster', was a hotchpotch of electoral, princely and ecclesiastical states and free cities that possessed only the vaguest of yearnings for a cultural identity. But the Reformation set its scholars, artists and historians on a quest for what marked the heirs of Charlemagne as a people distinct from others. Luther himself made one massive contribution to this. Between 1520 and 1546 he was personally responsible for a third of all the vernacular publications that emerged from German print-shops. He wrote in a vigorous vernacular which could be, by turns vulgar and poetic. His greatest achievement was the German Bible (published in 1534), which did more than anything else to merge regional identities. Scarcely less influential were the catechisms Luther wrote for his 'dear German people', which gave them shared versions of the Creed and the Lord's Prayer.

If 1517 and 1521 are important dates in the life of Luther, 1525 is just as significant. In the midst of the Peasants' War and at a time when he was engaged in a theological contest with Erasmus, Luther astonished all his friends and distressed some of them: he got married. When asked why he was taking this step at the age of almost forty-three, he explained that since he had been advising monks and nuns who had left the cloister to espouse matrimony he should set an example. It may have been nearer the truth that the lady made the running. Katharina von Bora was a strong-willed and determined woman, a Catholic nun seventeen years his junior whom Luther helped escape from a convent. The event divided Luther's mature life into two equal halves: it was twenty years since he had entered the cloister and he had just over twenty years left to enjoy family life. But he did not retire into humdrum domesticity. His new status was as much a demonstration of biblical truth as his opposition to indulgences had been. It declared that virginity and celibacy were not superior vocations. It exalted the nuclear family as the essential building block of society. It emphasized the importance of the home for the nurturing of children in the Christian way and for the exercise of hospitality. It involved him in that little world of intimate relationships with its joys and griefs where lay people actually spent their lives. In short, the Luther family which grew up in the old Augustinian convent at Wittenberg became the model Protestant paternalistic menage, a microcosm of the Church, where the head of the household was its bishop, gathering his children and servants around him for daily prayers and leading them to the church building for worship on Sundays. Over the years scores of university students lodged with the Luthers and it is thanks to some of them that we have the celebrated Table Talk, a collection of obiter dicta on all manner of subjects with which the great man regaled his guests at meal times.

Since the end of the Holy Roman Empire in 1806, Germany has endured successive identity crises that have impacted disastrously on the rest of Europe. The old north-south divide was resolved by Bismarck's Prussification of the new empire but resulted in a nationalist euphoria which the Iron Chancellor was powerless to control. So too the disasters of 1914–18 and 1939–45, which we can now see as a single conflict at the end of which Germany was once more divided, this time between east and west. The achievement of nationhood has cost Germany and her neighbours dearly. It is inevitable that partisans of a greater reich have wanted to enlist to their cause one of the greatest and most patriotic of Germans. At the turn of the twentieth century Lutheran leaders had to choose whether or not to support expansionist policies. Those who did so, such as the members of the German-Christian party, unhesitatingly used their founder's name to persuade the electorate that the triumph of the master race was written into the marrow of the German people and that Luther had set the nation on its inevitable course by his defiance of foreign interference. Thus the Luther-to-Hitler myth was born. But the reformer was never a nationalist in the modern sense of the word. He was, above all, a pastor. Many of his convictions were expressed in books and pamphlets written to help people who consulted him about their problems. Thus, for example, when a mercenary soldier came to him with a troubled conscience the result was another pamphlet (1526): *Whether Soldiers, Too, Can Be Saved.* Although he lived to a good age, Luther worked himself to death. It is characteristic of the man that he hastened his end by travelling through atrocious weather to sort out a dispute between a landlord and his neighbours.

Luther, then, touched life at every level—the individual, the family, the church, the state—and he did so not as a dry-as-dust philosopher but as a flesh-and-blood, fallible human being, agonising about the important issues which faced all his contemporaries.

He was a theologian who lived his theology. He put the Bible at the centre of everything and, as well as applying it to every problem of prince and peasant, he tried to live it himself. Indeed, no one more than Martin Luther resembles the flawed hero of which the sacred text affords so many examples. If we do not, now, find him simpatico it is probably because we cannot share his biblical world view.

This article first appeared in *History Today,* May 2007, pp. 34–39. Copyright © 2007 by History Today, Ltd. Reprinted by permission.

# Elizabeth I
## *Gender, Power & Politics*

SUSAN DORAN

Judging from the results of last year's BBC television poll of Great Britons, Elizabeth I is the best known and most admired English monarch, at least among those members of the public who decided to vote. Given her high profile in films and biographies, the Queen's relative success in the poll is perhaps unsurprising, especially as her life was so full of incident and drama. The evidence suggests, however, that it was specifically Elizabeth's ability as a woman to exercise power successfully in a man's world that earned her the votes and commanded the respect of today's viewers; she scored highest on her bravery and leadership qualities, while the comments of her supporters, as reported on the BBC website, emphasised her difficulties as a female ruler and her role as 'the ultimate British feminist icon'.

Recent academic opinion is usually less kind to Elizabeth. Christopher Haigh has described her as a bully and a show-off, while Susan Brigden seems to share the Elizabethan Council's irritation with their Queen's indecision, prevarications and sometimes faulty judgement. Nonetheless, whatever their views about the character of the Queen, many historians today share the preoccupation with Elizabeth's gender; they tend to stress the problems she faced as a female ruler in the patriarchal sixteenth century and the ways she attempted to circumvent them. I would suggest, however, that these difficulties have been overstated and that Elizabeth's methods of negotiating her gender have been partially misunderstood.

Of course, there is no question that early-modern society was deeply patriarchal in its structure and attitudes. Male primogeniture governed most property arrangements as well as the laws of succession to the crown. In theory, at least, women were not expected to assert any independent authority but were deemed subservient to male relatives whether fathers, brothers or husbands. The Scottish Calvinist preacher John Knox (c.1513–72) famously railed against female monarchy as an abomination in his *The First Blast of the Trumpet against the Monstrous Regiment of Women,* a work written in 1558 to contest Catholic Mary I's right to be queen. Yet, despite patriarchal attitudes, female rule was no great novelty in the sixteenth century; not only had women inherited the thrones of Castile, Scotland and England before Elizabeth's accession, but more importantly they had also been selected to act as regents in Spain, Scotland,

the Netherlands and France during the absences of their monarchs. Furthermore, Knox's views were extreme and reiterated by only a handful of other Protestants.

In fact, at the time of Elizabeth's accession, barely a murmur was heard querying the legitimacy of female rule. Catholics at home and abroad presumably did not think to use Knoxian-style arguments to challenge Elizabeth's right to the throne, because their claimant, Mary, Queen of Scots, was also a woman. In general, the prevailing sentiment within England in mid-November 1558 was not concern at the accession of another queen of England, but rather relief that Mary Tudor's reign—marked by harvest failure, epidemics and military humiliation—was now over, and that Elizabeth's succession was smooth and for all practical purposes undisputed without military intervention from France, Scotland or Spain. Protestants were obviously delighted by the new regime: Thomas Becon, who in 1553 had bemoaned the accession of a female ruler as God's punishment towards a 'people unworthy to have lawful, natural and meet governors', now accepted with joy Elizabeth as:

> . . . a most worthy patroness of all true religion and of learning, a most noble defender of all godly-disposed people [and] a noble conqueror of antichrist.

With Elizabeth on the throne, Knox himself hurriedly backtracked, even though he never actually recanted his earlier opinions. Other Protestant theologians, though, explicitly endorsed Elizabeth's right to rule and openly rejected Knox's arguments. In a letter to William Cecil in 1559, John Calvin (1509–64) reasoned that female rule was acceptable in countries where it had been established by law or custom and, furthermore, asserted that in exceptional circumstances God deliberately chose to channel His authority through women rulers, witness the Judge Deborah and prophetess Huldah in the Hebrew Bible. Possibly because Knox's views were not widely held, only two English writers felt impelled during the first years of Elizabeth's reign to write tracts refuting his *First Blast,* and only the work of one of them—John Aylmer's *Harborowe for faithfull and true subjectes*—was published (in 1559). In England, it seems, the monarchy was excluded from patriarchal assumptions and a female monarch was given rights by God which permitted her to rule over men.

Elizabeth justified her right to rule on the non-gendered grounds of the laws of inheritance, her father's will and the 1544 Act of Succession. At the same time, like her grandfather, Henry VII, and half-sister, Mary, she emphasised the role of God in preserving her from danger and placing her on the throne; during the Coronation procession of January 1559 she not only allowed herself to be identified with Deborah, the instrument of Divine Providence, but also compared herself to Daniel, who had been saved from the lion's den. Throughout the reign, Elizabeth claimed the same prerogatives as her male predecessors, adopted the same visual imagery and mottos on her coinage, and participated in traditional royal rituals, adapting them where necessary to suit a female monarch. Thus, on Maundy Thursday she washed the feet of poor women (instead of men) as part of the Easter ceremonies; on the feast of St George her ladies-in-waiting joined her in the Great Procession with the Knights of the Garter; and she sometimes chose to wear a magnificent gown rather than the customary martial attire. In the 1570s after the papal bull of excommunication, she decided to use the ancient form of royal magic and touch for the King's Evil (to cure the disease of scrofula) in order to emphasise her God-given sovereignty.

Despite the general acceptance of a woman's right to rule, there was at the outset of the reign some uncertainty about the extent to which Elizabeth would exercise power. Aylmer had assumed that the government would be in her name and on her behalf but executed by her Council and Parliament. Her first principal secretary, William Cecil, had initially presumed that the queen would leave the cut and thrust of decisionmaking to her most important councillors, particularly over areas of policy which fell within the male preserve of diplomacy and international affairs. But Elizabeth immediately made it absolutely clear that she intended to rule in deed as well as in name. She put her stamp on the membership of the Council by appointing several of her relatives and loyal friends, as well as associates of Cecil. Although she agreed to a change in title from Supreme Head to Supreme Governor of the Church of England, she made sure that the new settlement of religion reflected her own religious preferences as much (or more) than those of Protestant theologians or trusted ministers. Those royal injunctions of 1559 which ordered wafers to be used for communion, insisted on clerical dress, and safeguarded church music in cathedrals, were the product of her own desires, and indeed were anathema to most of her advisers. Similarly, royal proclamations of 1560 and 1561 designed to prevent further outbursts of iconoclasm, particularly those which threatened funeral monuments, were the work of her hand.

As time went on, Elizabeth continued to exercise power and to take the final decisions on policy. It was the Queen who prevented influential councillors and members of parliament from passing legislation in the 1560s and 1570s which would have excluded Mary, Queen of Scots, from the throne. Without Elizabeth's protection after 1569, moreover, Mary might well have knelt at the scaffold years before her execution in 1587.

As far as foreign policy is concerned, Elizabeth usually put her weight behind those more cautious councillors who wanted to avoid outright war with Spain during the 1570s and early 1580s and who preferred to follow a policy of giving underhanded aid to Protestants abroad while outwardly posing as a mediator in the struggle between Philip II of Spain and his rebellious subjects in the Netherlands. In consequence, despite considerable pressure from Walsingham, Leicester and other zealous Protestants, Elizabeth's government did not send troops to fight against Spain until late 1585.

In religious matters it was largely owing to Elizabeth that the English Church remained only 'halfly' reformed, and that moderate liturgical changes proposed by her bishops and backed by Archbishop Matthew Parker failed to pass through convocation in 1563 and Parliament in 1566. Had a more radical and less assertive monarch been sitting on the throne, a very different Church of England would have emerged in the second half of the sixteenth century.

Baffled by the Queen's failure to see the wisdom of their advice, Elizabeth's advisers often expressed their frustration in the gendered, sometimes misogynistic language of their day. Thus, they would criticise the Queen's feminine irresolution, female fickleness and womanly compassion towards papists and traitors. Nonetheless, their concern was more about what they saw as the Queen's mistaken policies and refusal to listen to good sense than about the inappropriateness of a woman taking decisions. Until at least the mid-1580s their frustration was a measure of Elizabeth's independence and their failure to persuade or browbeat her into following their own particular line of policy.

Elizabeth's independence was made more palatable to her councillors by the style of her leadership. But whether or not the qualities she exhibited in managing her male advisers can be labelled 'feminine' is a moot point, and writers today should really stop making simplistic assertions that Elizabeth capitalised on her 'feminine characteristics' to secure obedience and achieve her goals in statecraft. Like her father, Elizabeth displayed a mixture of radiating charm and unpredictable rages; like him, too, she demanded to be the centre of attention and enjoyed the flattery of courtiers (even if she had the intelligence to see through it). Unlike Henry VIII, though, she was immensely loyal to those she trusted, and men soon realised that they could present her with unwelcome advice without risking their necks. Her frequent refusal to be pro-active or pinned down to a particular line of action may have infuriated them, yet this flexibility and apparent indecisiveness always left open the possibility that she might rethink her position and change her mind. Consequently, until the later 1590s, when Elizabeth's skills of political management were waning, there was no need for anyone in the Council or at court to feel permanently excluded from power or entirely cut off from influencing the Queen, unless he unwisely overstepped the mark by questioning her authority.

Historians and literary critics have also suggested that Elizabeth dealt with the problems of her gender by adopting strategies that turned her into the iconic Virgin Queen: first by deciding to remain unwed and second by fashioning herself into the Virgin Mary for propaganda purposes. Each of these propositions present problems of interpretation. As far as Elizabeth's marriage is concerned, it has become almost a cliché that the Queen was determined to stay single so that she could rule as well as reign. Elizabeth, it is said, had learned this maxim from the sad experiences of Mary, who had allowed political power to slip into the hands of her husband, Philip of Spain, thereby dragging England into the disastrous Habsburg wars against France which resulted in the loss of Calais. Yet there is little evidence that Elizabeth rejected the idea of marriage as a deliberate act of will. On the contrary, far from being totally committed to the single life, Elizabeth on two occasions signalled that she wanted to marry a particular suitor. In 1560 she gave every appearance of being in love with Lord Robert Dudley; in 1579 she demonstrated a strong inclination to wed the French duke, Francis of Anjou. In both instances, however, the fierce opposition to her choice of husband, expressed in Council, at court and in the country at large, led Elizabeth to conclude that she would lose the support of influential subjects and create grave political difficulties if she went ahead with the match. In the case of Dudley, Cecil and other royal servants warned her that marriage to him would seriously damage her reputation and might even imperil her seat on the throne. They were probably right; the widespread rumours that Elizabeth had been involved in an adulterous relationship with her favourite and had conspired with him to murder his wife could only be allayed if she distanced herself from him. As for Anjou, most English Protestants abhorred his religion, disliked his French blood, and believed that Elizabeth's marriage to him would bring the wrath of God down on England. Once again, Elizabeth demonstrated political sense in ultimately rejecting his suit.

Despite the hostility targeted at Dudley and Anjou, Elizabeth was under intense pressure from her councillors and Parliament to end uncertainties about the succession by marrying and giving birth to an heir. Cecil, who had spearheaded the campaign against the Dudley match, found what he thought was a far better marital candidate in the Archduke Charles of Austria, a younger son of the Holy Roman Emperor Ferdinand. The Archduke, argued Cecil, was suitable in terms of his age, lineage and reputation, and would bring England an advantageous diplomatic alliance with the Habsburgs. In his enthusiasm for the match, Cecil persuaded himself that Charles's religion (he was a Catholic) would not prove a barrier to it. Elizabeth, though, was less keen on the Archduke. With Dudley out of the running she preferred to remain single, and besides she had heard unfounded rumours that Charles was deformed. Nonetheless, she found it impossible to withstand the pressure from all sides to marry; after all, the public image she had cultivated was that of a queen devoted to the interests of her subjects, even to the point of self-sacrifice. She therefore could hardly seem to be putting her personal preferences above the dynastic needs of her country. Consequently, in 1564 Elizabeth agreed to open discussions with the Austrians and soon afterwards she authorised envoys and councillors to negotiate a matrimonial treaty. From the start, however, Elizabeth insisted that the marriage had to be on her terms, terms which denied the Archduke any political power in England and compelled him to accompany her to Protestant church services and to forgo a public mass. It should not be thought that Elizabeth stipulated these conditions in order to sabotage the negotiations; Cecil and other supporters of the match also required them as safeguards for

England's political interests. Although the Austrians eventually agreed to the articles which excluded Charles from any role in government, the Archduke demanded access to the mass, if only a private one to be held in his own apartment. On this issue the negotiations broke down, for Elizabeth refused to permit any compromise over religion. No doubt she was heartily relieved to have found a get-out clause, but her decision was supported by a number of her councillors as well as her divines and London preachers. Thus, in the end it was the religious question and not gender concerns that caused the collapse of the Archduke Charles, matrimonial suit.

The image of Elizabeth as the Virgin Queen was not evident early in the reign, when Elizabeth's hold on power was arguably the least secure, nor was it she herself who first devised the image. The language and iconography of perpetual and powerful virginity first made their appearance during the Anjou matrimonial negotiations of 1578–81 as part of the weaponry employed against the match by its opponents. Thereafter, the figure of Elizabeth as the Virgin Queen gained currency as a courtly fashion with an intent both to flatter, and also in many cases (including that of Edmund Spenser's *Faerie Queene*) to criticise the Queen. Courtiers and poets were the main creators of the image, though certainly Elizabeth helped to promote it in her entertainments at court (such as the 'Four Foster Children of Desire') and in the miniatures she commissioned, where she was portrayed as the goddess Diana or Cynthia. Whenever Elizabeth was depicted or addressed as the Virgin Queen, it is very rare indeed to see any unambiguous allusions to the Virgin Mary. Far more common are the direct iconographic or poetic references to the classical goddesses Diana, Cynthia and Astraea or to Petrarch's chaste maidens, Laura and Tuccia. For all these reasons, there seems to be no case for claiming that Elizabeth appropriated the cult of the Virgin Mary as a strategy to secure acceptance as a female ruler.

Why did representations of Elizabeth as a Virgin Queen become so pervasive in poetry and portraiture during the 1590s? One strong possibility is that this mode of representation was thought a safe and effective way of depicting an elderly woman as a credible military and political leader of a country at war. Elizabeth's impenetrable physical body was a natural metaphor for the impregnable body politic withstanding invasion from a foreign king. At the same time, symbolic associations with the moon-goddesses, Diana, Phoebe and Cynthia, signified both England's sea-power and the Queen's immutability and continuing potency, despite her advancing age.

Arguably, Elizabeth experienced her greatest difficulties with her gender during the last fifteen years of her life, just when the image of her as the all-powerful Virgin Queen was taking hold. Until then, the gendered outbursts of courtiers and councillors had barely affected the tone of political life, as outward deference and respect continued to be shown to the Queen. During the 1570s, moreover, Elizabeth and her courtiers had engaged in chivalric and Renaissance courtly love conventions, made popular through Petrarch's poetry, and had absorbed Castiglione's *Il Cortegiano* (published in English in 1561 and Latin in 1571) as a working model for their behaviour at court. In consequence, Elizabeth's favourites had attended devotedly upon her and courted her with their love-poetry, elegies of praise, fine dancing and skill at the tilt. Christopher Hatton was one of the most successful of the exponents of the courtier's craft, earning his reward in lucrative grants of land and promotion to high office.

During the 1590s, however, disillusionment with Elizabeth's reign appears to have become entrenched, while misogynistic complaints about female rule became more outspoken. Robert Devereux, 2nd Earl of Essex (1566–1601), and other young male courtiers balked at playing the role of ardent and adoring suitors to an ageing and imperious queen. Military men held the monarch's gender responsible for a lack of energy and boldness in the prosecution of the war against Spain. Essex spoke for many of them when he complained in 1597 to a French envoy:

> They laboured under two things at this Court, delay and inconstancy, which proceeded chiefly from the sex of the queen.

At the same time, the presence of an adult male king, James VI of Scotland, waiting to inherit the throne made many of Elizabeth's courtiers impatient to see the end of female rule. John Harington, for example, mused that:

> . . . whensoever God shall call [Queen Elizabeth], I perceive we are not like to be governed by a lady shut up in a chamber from all her subjects and most of her servants, and seen seld but on holidays . . . but by a man of spirit and learning, of able body, of understanding mind.

With a male monarch on the throne, thought Harington, the privy chamber would again be staffed by men, and male courtiers would no longer be denied opportunities for intimacy and advancement.

Undoubtedly, Elizabeth's authority was affected by this new attitude at court. Once out of England, her military commanders flagrantly disobeyed royal instructions. During the Rouen campaign of 1591, for example, Essex conferred no fewer than twenty-four knighthoods in defiance of the Queen's express instructions. More seriously, during the Cadiz campaign of 1596 he planned to seize a base in Spain in total contradiction of Elizabeth's orders, and was only thwarted in his design by his co-commander, Lord Admiral Howard. Part of the problem was that Elizabeth was at a disadvantage in not being able to go in person to the battlefield. As an unmarried queen, moreover, she could not even call on her husband to act as a figurehead in her place, as had her sister Mary at St Quentin. But age was another factor. In the 1590s Elizabeth was old enough to be the grandmother of the new generation of courtiers, many of whom found her out of touch with their culture and aspirations. Their declining respect for their queen was demonstrated in the many sexual scandals that disrupted the court in the 1590s. Not only were a significant number of male courtiers prepared to flout Elizabeth's authority by embarking on illicit sexual relationships with maids of honour, but also every elopement and pregnancy that occurred was a stark reminder of 'her own physical and political sterility'. Nonetheless, despite her age, Elizabeth could on occasions impress observers with her majesty and intelligence: in 1596 her impromptu speech in Latin reprimanding a Polish ambassador who had offended her, so delighted English listeners that it was published; in 1601 her 'Golden Speech' which silenced complaining members of parliament was similarly printed and distributed to the wider populace.

All in all, Elizabeth's gender had less impact on political life than is generally assumed. The key political issues of the day were those that had dominated earlier reigns: religion, the succession and international affairs. While Elizabeth had her own style of leadership, she worked within the same institutional structures and adopted the same royal conventions as earlier monarchs. Even Elizabeth's image was not so very different from that of her male predecessors and contemporary kings; like them she emphasised her regality, religion and role as carer of her people. The part that Elizabeth's conservatism and reliance on tradition played in making female rule acceptable to male subjects should not be forgotten; she provoked no fears that the social and gender hierarchy would be subverted by female monarchy. In this sense, Elizabeth was no feminist icon. Her reign did however demonstrate that a woman could be an exceptionally successful ruler even in dangerous times. In this sense, she was!

# For Further Reading

Paul E.J. Hammer, "Sex and the Virgin Queen: Aristocratic Concupiscence and Court of Elizabeth I." *Sixteenth Century Journal 31* (2000); Susan Doran, *Monarchy and Matrimony: The Courtships of Elizabeth I* (Routledge, 1996); Susan Doran, "Virginity, Divinity and Power: The Portraits of Elizabeth I" in *The Myth of Elizabeth I* edited by Susan Doran and Thomas Freeman (Palgrave, Macmillan, 2003); Carole Levin, *The Heart and Stomach of a King: Elizabeth I and the Politics of Sex and Power* (University of Pennsylvania Press, 1994) and A.N. McLaren, *Political Culture in the Reign of Elizabeth I* (Cambridge University Press, 1999).

**SUSAN DORAN** is a lecturer in Early-Modern History at Christ Church Oxford. She is the editor of the catalogue *Elizabeth I: The Exhibition at the National Maritime Museum* (Chatto & Windus, 2003).

# The Return of Catherine the Great

Tony Lentin

After seventy years of neglect and dismissal in the Soviet period as a foreign adventuress, hypocrite and poseur, indifferent to the needs of 'the people' and marginal to the pre-occupation of Marxists with 'class struggle' and revolution, Catherine the Great (1762–96) is suddenly sweeping into favour in Russia as a focus of unprecedented interest both at the popular and the scholarly level. New lines of enquiry or the re-investigation of older ones have been set in motion. Revisionism, rehabilitation and research proliferate.

The process of rehabilitation began under the impact of glasnost, in the late 1980s and early 1990s with the publication of more positive assessments of Catherine by Alexander Kamensky and Oleg Omel'chenko. (See John Alexander, 'Comparing Two Greats: Peter I and Catherine' in *A Window on Russia*. Papers from the Vth International Conference of the Study Group on Eighteenth-Century Russia, edited by Maria di Salvo and Lindsey Hughes, La Fenice, 1996, pp. 43–50, and Kamensky's article, in Russian, 'The significance of the reforms of Catherine II in Russian history', ibid., pp. 56–65.) The wave of scholarly interest that followed culminated in August 1996 in an international conference in St Petersburg to mark the bicentenary of Catherine's death. Held under the auspices of the Academy of Sciences and a host of associated organisations, the conference was supplemented by an exhibition of paintings and artefacts at the Hermitage devoted to the Age of Catherine the Great. (See abstracts of conference papers in Mezhdunarodnaia konferentsiia. Ekaterina Velikaia: Epokha Rossiiskai Istorii, St Petersburg, 1996. Conferences have also been held in Germany: at Zerbst, Potsdam and Eutin.)

While it is true that Catherine never lost her German accent, Lydia Kisliagina puts her 'foreignness' into perspective by pointing out that she spent only the first fourteen of her sixty-seven years in Germany: the remaining fifty-three she lived in Russia, thirty-four of these as empress. In his opening address to the St Petersburg conference, Alexander Kamensky discussed Catherine's extraordinary political skills, her adroit management of power and people, her psychological penetration and ability to spot talent and draw it out and to inspire lasting confidence and loyalty. He reminds us that she provided three and a half decades of political stability and ministerial continuity with little significant opposition to her rule despite the constant and obvious claims of her son, Paul. This in itself was an extraordinary achievement, especially after nearly forty years of palace revolutions in the period preceding her accession.

Catherine directed her formidable tactical skills to particular ends. 'Russia is a European power' she declared in her equivalent of a political manifesto, the *Nakaz* or *Instruction of 1766*. Intended as a guideline for the drafting of a new code of law by a representative assembly duly summoned by Catherine in 1767, the *Nakaz* was banned in France as subversive. Catherine's emphatic assertion about Russia and Europe was full of political, cultural and social implications about the norms of thought, conduct and legality which she hoped to see established in Russia and about her own claims to be considered an exponent of 'enlightened absolutism'. (See O. A. Omel'chenko, "'Enlightened absolutism' in Russia", Coexistence, 32, 1995, pp. 31–38.)

Catherine is once more being taken seriously as an intellectual, engagee and writer (an inveterate 'scribbler', as she called herself and a ruler addicted to 'legislomania'). Committed to the values of the philosophes, she believed fervently in the power of enlightened ideas and legislation and energetically strove to put theory into practice by influencing and forming a 'public opinion' in Russia sympathetic to her objectives. She wrote moral tales for her grandchildren, school syllabuses and mildly satirical periodicals and comedies for her subjects in the lasting basic conviction that common sense, reason and moral conduct could lead to social progress and nurture a responsive and responsible 'civil' society in Russia. Education and enlightenment would create 'true sons of the fatherland' and even 'a new species of humankind'. In 1769 she founded the Smol'ny Institute, Russia's first girls' school, for the daughters of the nobility and bourgeoisie. In modelling the Institute on the latest pedagogical theories she showed a concern for the education of women as active (though not equal) contributors in the process of civilising society.

An international essay competition on the question of serfdom was intended to show that the empress held strong abolitionist views and to stimulate thinking in the same direction: the prize essay, recommending abolition, was chosen by Catherine in 1765. By her own very public example of inoculation against smallpox (in contrast to the royal families of France, Spain and Austria who refused to undergo it on religious grounds), she sought both to save lives and to demonstrate the real benefits of the Enlightenment faith in scientific empiricism and humanitarian zeal. Hospitals and the Foundlings' Home (1764) which she established also saved young lives which, in turn, she intended to turn into useful lives. (See Janet Hartley, 'Philanthropy in the Reign of Catherine the Great: Aims and Realities' in *Russia in the Age of the Enlightenment. Essays for Isabel de Madariaga,* edited by Roger Bartlett and Janet M. Hartley, Macmillan, 1990, pp. 167–202.)

Just as she also sponsored scientific expeditions to investigate Russia's natural resources and thereby benefit state and society, so the Russian Academy, which Catherine founded in 1783, was intended to make her subjects more conscious of the beauties of their language by systematising its rules and compiling a Dictionary of the Russian Language in order to place Russian on a par with Western and classical languages. Catherine herself contributed both to a burgeoning Russian literature and to the historical studies which she sought to encourage. Her enthusiastic approach towards her adoptive tongue may be contrasted with Frederick the Great's dismissive attitude towards the German language and letters.

Just as Russian scholars are at last able to acknowledge Western research on Catherine, so emerging studies in Russia are bound to make their impact on historical thinking on Catherine in the West. At present the leading monographs remain the work of Western scholars. The classic example is Isabel de Madariaga's monumental *Russia in the Age of Catherine the Great* (Yale University Press, 1981), reoffered in a popular abbreviated form as *Catherine the Great. A Short History* (Yale, 1990) and still more compendiously as an essay, 'Catherine the Great', in *Enlightened Absolutism. Reform and Reformers in Later Eighteenth-Century Europe,* edited by H. M. Scott (Macmillan, 1990, pp. 289–311). John T. Alexander tells a good story with verve and telling quotation in his *Catherine the Great. Life and Legend* (Oxford University Press, 1989), but has annoyed feminists by his detailed discussion of Catherine's life with her favourites.

Soviet historians have tended previously to emphasise Russia's spectacular territorial expansion in the period without considering Catherine's own crucial role in the formulation and direction of a dynamic foreign policy. In 1990 H. M. Scott examined Catherine's striking success in increasing Russian influence and prestige abroad, her remarkable flair for turning situations to advantage and her ever 'escalating ambitions' for influence not only at the expense of Turkey and Poland, but in the world generally. She brought Russian influence into the heart of Europe by acquiring the status of mediator in the War of the Bavarian Succession, holding the balance between Austria and Prussia; and to the Atlantic world through her promotion of the League of Armed Neutrality. (See H. M. Scott, 'Russia as a European Great Power', in *Russia in the Age of the Enlightenment,* pp. 7–39.)

Herself a bookworm, bibliophile and writer, Catherine believed passionately in the power of the printed word. She encouraged book production and the translation of foreign works into Russian as an obvious vehicle for spreading enlightenment. She decentralised publishing, hitherto a state monopoly, from state control by her decree of 1783 authorising the establishment of free presses in Russia, and by encouraging satirical journalism in the spirit of Steele and Addison. It is well known that by the time of the French Revolution she felt obliged to clamp down on several Russian writers and publishers of whom she had hitherto approved and to re-impose tight censorship. (See W. Gareth Jones, 'Novikov and the French Revolution', in *Literature, Lives, and Legality in Catherine's Russia,* edited by A. G. Cross and G. S. Smith, Astra Press, Nottingham, 1994, pp. 121–26.)

What is significant in current Russian historiography is that it does not play down her initial sustained efforts in this vein or dismiss them as insincere. Catherine personally brought her subjects into touch with the ideas and authors of the Enlightenment. No sooner did Marmontel publish his portrait of an enlightened ruler in *Belisaire* (1766) than Catherine had it translated and herself took part in the work of translation. After Voltaire's death in 1778, when flattering him could no longer be an issue, she asked to be sent a hundred sets of the latest edition of 'my master's works, so that I can have them distributed everywhere. I want them to serve as models; I want them to be studied, learned by heart; I want them to provide food for thought'.

Historians have always been uneasy about Catherine's fondness for the public image, the theatricality of her court and what Joseph II called the 'Catherinisation of the Princess of Zerbst'. There is no doubt that in the cultivation of her own legend she was obsessively concerned both with contemporary applause and with her future reputation. (See David Griffiths, 'To Live Forever: Catherine II, Voltaire and the Pursuit of Immortality' in *Russia and the World of the Eighteenth Century.* Proceedings of the Third International Conference organised by the Study Group on Eighteenth-Century Russia, edited by R. P. Bartlett, A. G. Cross, K. Rasmussen, Slavica Publishers, Ohio, 1988, pp. 446–68.) Yet as we see from Peter Burke's *The Fabrication of Louis XIV* (Yale, 1992), the cultivation of an image of gloire and grandeur through the arts and in ceremony could play the central part in enhancing the credibility and effectiveness of absolute monarchy. (For an outline of Catherine's use of the arts, see Allen McConnell,

'Catherine the Great and the Fine Arts' in *Imperial Russia 1700–1917. State, Society, Opposition. Essays in Honor of Marc Raeff,* edited by Ezra Mendelsohn and Marshall Shatz, Northern Illinois Press, 1988, pp. 37–57.)

Catherine's flair for the grand occasion should be seen as a counterpart to her detailed instructions on protocol to her ambassadors abroad: it transmitted her own prestige and Russia's, it spread the message of Russia's enlightenment and power. If she laid it on with a trowel, this probably also reflected her consciousness of a lack of lawful claim to the throne and the unprepossessing circumstances of her accession. (On the murder of her husband, Peter III. Oleg Ivanov has published some important articles in *Moskovsky Zhurnal,* Nos. 9, 11–12, 1995 1–3, 1996.)

This murky background had not merely to be lived down but transcended and magicked away by the grandeur of her chosen figurative persona as 'Minerva Triumphant' and 'All-wise Mother of the Fatherland', suggesting the advent of wisdom and enlightenment in the person of the spiritual descendant of Peter the Great. Catherine's victory celebrations over Turkey were breathtaking demonstrations of state power, while Oleg Nesterov reminds us of the ambitious symbolism of naming her grandsons after Alexander the Great and Constantine the Great.

Yet Catherine could successfully combine imperial grandeur and its neo-classical expression in architecture and the arts with a cluster of more intimate attitudes associated with Roman humanitas and Enlightenment humanite and a personal informality that set strangers at their ease. Natal'ia Vulich explains how the buildings which Catherine commissioned from Charles Cameron were intended to combine symbols of stoic greatness with ideas of epicurean friendship. The recent conference in St Petersburg began and ended in Catherine's private Hermitage Theatre at the Winter Palace, designed for her by Quarenghi and combining classical splendour with informality and agreement. The conference closed with a performance of items from a grandiose Russian 'historical drama' set to music by eighteenth-century Italian and Russian composers to a libretto written by Catherine herself in 'imitation of Shakespeare'. It was first performed in the self-same theatre in 1790.

On the vexed problem of serfdom, which, whatever her original hopes clearly expressed in the *Nakaz,* nevertheless reached its apogee in her reign, Alexander Kamensky took a swipe at the cliches of Marxist historiography and insisted on Catherine's absolute sincerity in wishing to mitigate serfdom, but pointed out that at the time of her accession the nobility had only just consolidated a near total monopoly in serf-ownership and did not take lightly to attempts to infringe their newly won privileges. Catherine attacked serfdom at her peril. She could try persuasion, but ultimately her powers were limited and she always recognised the need to take public opinion with her.

The Pugachov rebellion of 1773–4 made her particularly sensitive to the risk of any fresh shocks to the social or political order, and she came to accept the inevitability of gradualness. (See Roger Bartlett, 'The Question of Serfdom: Catherine II and the Russian Debate and the View from the Baltic Periphery' in *Russia in the Age of the Enlightenment,* pp. 142–66, and 'Defences of Serfdom in Eighteenth-Century Russia' in *A Window on Russia,* pp. 67–74.)

What went wrong? Despite her unflagging energy and conscientiousness, Catherine became increasingly aware from experience of the enormity of what she had taken on with such initial confidence. Russian historians still suggest answers in terms of the unfavourable reactions of her advisers to some of the proposals in the *Nakaz*; of the lack of a 'third estate' which she hoped to nurture; of the upheaval of the Pugachov rebellion and of the French Revolution, which made her perceive dangers in some of the ideas which she had formerly encouraged. Nevertheless, both Kamensky and Omel'chenko emphasise the extent and depth of her overall achievements across the reign and her fidelity to her original aims. She used the information gleaned from the Legislative Commission as the groundwork for the reorganisation and regularisation of provincial and municipal government on a solid basis, so that, as Omel'chenko claims, "the law reforms of 'enlightened absolutism' were basically realised in 1774–87".

Throughout her reign Catherine remained an avowed believer in absolute rule as a historical and political necessity in Russia, even if, as Omel'chenko argues, she was at the same time "the greatest theoretician and practician of 'law-based' monarchy" in eighteenth-century Europe, who laid down guidelines for the exercise of power and in 1787 even contemplated introducing some form of 'fundamental law'. At all times she remained true to her *Nakaz,* where she declared that "the ruler of Russia is absolute: for no power, other than that concentrated in his person, can operate with the effectiveness required by such a vast state . . . Any other form of government would be . . . fatal to Russia".

Catherine tempered her exercise of power with fact and affability. "Be gentle, humane, accessible, sympathetic and liberal", she urged in a set of maxims intended for herself and copy of Fenelon's Telemaque, adding, however, "and never let this kindness undermine your authority". Her own touch remained sensitive and sure. All her proposed measures were most carefully prepared, going through many drafts at her hands, were referred by her to special advisory commissions and tested out on her advisers.

The classic victim of her reaction against her earlier optimism was Alexander Radishchev, exiled to Siberia after the publication in 1790 of his *Journey from St Petersburg to Moscow,* which hit out at absolutism and by implication at her own government. Even before that she revealed occasional hints of depression and doubts about the durability of her achievements. In a note of 1787 she minuted: "will not my labours, care and warm concern for the good of the Empire be in vain, for I do see that I cannot make my frame of mind hereditary".

Mikhail Safonov, however, dismisses the persistent rumour that Catherine intended to exclude Paul from the succession in favour of her grandson, Alexander. On the contrary, according to Safonov, she wished to establish the succession on the firm basis of primogeniture in the male line (the principle enacted by Paul himself). If this is so, it is a paradox, that this legendary woman sought to prevent any other of her sex from following her own example.

ANTONY LENTIN is Reader in History at the Open University. His latest book is an edition and translation of *Peter the Great: His Law on the Imperial Succession,* 1722. The Official Commentary. (Headstart History, Oxford, 1996).

# From Mercantilism to the 'Wealth of Nations'

**The Age of Discovery gave rise to an era of international trade and to arguments over economic strategies that still influence the policies of commerce.**

MICHAEL MARSHALL

We live in an era when continual economic growth is almost considered a birthright, at least in the developed world. It has become the benchmark of the health of a society, guaranteeing an ever-expanding prosperity. The current president of the United States even finds that his extensive misbehavior is overlooked by a majority of Americans because he happens to be presiding over an extended period of economic growth and optimism.

If annual growth drops below about 2 percent, planners and politicians start to get nervous, while a recession (negative growth) is considered a serious crisis. Where will it all end? Can such growth continue—with periodic setbacks, of course—indefinitely? We do not know and usually do not care to ask.

One thing is clear, however. It was not always so. For most of human history it has not been so. In western Europe in the period 1500–1750, output increased by a mere 65 percent, by one estimate, or an average of 0.26 percent a year, even though the population grew about 60 percent. For most of this period, 80 percent or more of the population worked the land. Studies of wage rates in England and France suggest that the working poor had to spend a full four-fifths of their income on food alone.

So this was not an economically dynamic society. There was relatively little disposable income, that being enjoyed by the prosperous elite of landed aristocracy and, increasingly in this period, merchants. Consequently, there was no prospect of creating a mass domestic market for new products. Most wealth was still tied up in the relatively static commodity of land, and agriculture was the major measure of a country's wealth.

Yet in the period from the voyages of discovery in the late fifteenth and early sixteenth centuries [see "Columbus and the Age of Exploration," THE WORLD & I, November 1998, p. 16] up till the Industrial Revolution there occurred what has been called a "commercial revolution."

The story of that revolution, which I will tell here, weaves together a number of significant themes. The upshot of the Age of Discovery was the emergence of a network of global trade.

The consequences of that trade, and the measures taken by increasingly centralized European governments [see "The Ascent of the Nation-State," THE WORLD & I, March 1999, p. 18] to control and direct it, produced the system later labeled, most notably by Adam Smith, mercantilism. This was the practice of imperial rivalry between European powers over global trade, and it gave impetus to the disagreements between Britain and its American colonists that led to the American Revolution. Critical consideration of these issues gave birth to Smith's theoretical study of economics, which culminated in the publication of his masterwork *The Wealth of Nations*.

## Protecting Bullion Reserves

Smith wrote: "The discovery of America and that of a passage to the East Indies are the two greatest and most important events recorded in the history of mankind." No doubt he exaggerated, but nothing was more important in the unfolding of this story. The Spanish conquistadores went to the New World in search of El Dorado. They found little gold but plenty of silver at Potosi in Peru and in northern Mexico. This silver became the lubricant of the machinery of an emerging global economy.

It flowed into Spain, from where much of it went to the rest of Europe, especially Holland, to pay the debts the Hapsburg rulers had incurred through the religious and dynastic struggles in their German possessions and in the Spanish Netherlands. Some of it then flowed to the Baltic to pay for the timber, rope, and other shipbuilding materials that the region supplied, especially to Holland and Britain. The bulk of it, though, went to Asia to satisfy the growing European demand for spices, silk, Indian calico, and later, Chinese tea.

Without the silver that demand could not have been satisfied: Europe had nothing that Asia wanted to import in exchange. That situation would not change until after the Industrial Revolution, when clothing from the Lancashire cotton industry in the north of England found a market in Asia. Even then problems

# The Commercial Revolution

Voyages of discovery in the fifteenth and sixteenth centuries resulted in a growing network of international trade. Silver from the New World became the lubricant for the machinery of an emerging global economy.

Fearing the success of their rivals, European governments imposed trade restrictions to protect their national interests.

Viewing commerce as an arena of conflicting national interests at times thrust competing European powers into war.

Advocates of free trade criticized mercantilist policies, suggesting peace could arise from mutually beneficial terms of trade.

Clashes over trade were significant factors in the antagonisms that led to the American Declaration of Independence.

The growth of economic relations between America and Britain after the Revolutionary War suggests that the free traders were right.

Underlying this thinking was the assumption that markets and the amount of trade were relatively fixed, and that gaining a larger share of the pie necessarily meant depriving another country of part of its share. Trade was thus conceived as an arena of national competition and even conflict, a form of war by other means.

# Colbert and French Mercantilism

Advocates of free trade in the late eighteenth and the nineteenth centuries strongly criticized this aspect of mercantilist policy. They proposed that peace was one of the benefits of free trade, since it tied trading partners in mutually beneficial exchanges that could only be lost through war. Neither side was totally right. Circumstances always affect cases, and the mercantilist policymakers were pragmatists who reacted to the situation before them.

## Advocates of free trade proposed that peace was one of its benefits.

The most systematic practitioner of mercantilist policies was undoubtedly Jean-Baptiste Colbert, finance minister for France's Louis XIV in the later seventeenth century. Colbert used the considerable power of the Sun King's state to increase its wealth through the promotion of French trade and manufactures. He certainly banned the export of bullion, but his policy was aimed at replacing bullion as the means of payment for necessary imports with the earnings from the export of French manufactures.

To that end he developed selected industries by state subsidies and bringing in skilled foreign artisans. He particularly encouraged high-value products such as quality furniture, glass, and tapestries, and the quality of French workmanship in these areas became legendary throughout Europe. He used tariff barriers to protect industries that faced serious foreign competition. Wanting to develop the French cloth industry in the face of the well-established British cloth trade, he doubled the duty on imports.

Thus emerged the classic mercantilist pattern that, because it came about in a piecemeal, pragmatic manner, has only existed in its complete form in the writings of historians. The export of domestic raw materials was largely discouraged, so that domestic manufacturers could enjoy their use. The export of sheep and raw wool from Britain, for example, was heavily regulated for the benefit of the domestic textile industry. The export of manufactures was encouraged as the means to a favorable balance of trade and the bullion inflows that came with it.

The import of foreign manufactures was restricted since this adversely affected the balance of trade. Raw material imports were looked on favorably to the degree that they could be used in or support domestic manufactures, although a large agricultural country like France, under Colbert, aimed at as much self-sufficiency as possible.

Colbert realized that encouraging French industry had little point if its products could not then be exported. That meant commercial shipping and a navy to protect it. Colbert had before him the example of the Dutch. They were the dominant

remained. The economic reason for the shameful opium trade in the early and mid-nineteenth century, when opium grown in India was exported illegally to China, was to earn exchange to pay for tea without having to export silver.

Silver was not without problems. So much of it flowed into Europe in the sixteenth century that it caused serious price inflation. The Spanish economy, in particular, was considerably disrupted, a significant factor in Spain's gradual decline. During the seventeenth century, from a peak around 1600, the supply of silver began to decrease. The demand for goods from Asia, however, did not. The result was a net outflow of silver bullion from Europe, a shrinkage of the money supply, and as a result, economic recession.

No economic theory existed at the time, and no contemporary thought argued that governments should not regulate such matters affecting national wealth in the national interest. So they did. The ad hoc system of tariffs and other measures influencing trade and manufactures that came to be known as mercantilism began to emerge.

The context in which this happened was one of increasingly centralized emerging nation-states that were spending a greater portion of the total national income than in the past, especially in the frequent times of war. They exercised closer control over more aspects of life in pursuit of national policy than in the past, especially through the taxation needed to fund wars. Trade with the New World nurtured the idea that commerce could be a source of national wealth and strength just as much as agriculture and should be developed to that end.

Spain, Britain, and France all banned the export of gold or silver bullion, but this proved to be like trying to stop water from running downhill. The belief was that bullion represented the national wealth or treasure, and that trade should be conducted so as to amass a surplus of it. A country would then have a reserve to cushion itself from the economic effects of adverse fluctuations in the supply of gold and, especially, silver.

economic power in Europe in the early and mid-sixteenth century through their skills in trade and shipping.

The Dutch dominated North Sea fishing, annoying the British by taking huge catches of herring from Britain's east coast, developing a factory-style industry for salting the catch, and then exporting it throughout Europe. They dominated the carrying trade from the Baltic to western Europe, were major carriers of imports to Europe from the Americas and from the East, and grew rich through their control of the lucrative reexport of those imports throughout Europe from their initial port of entry in Amsterdam.

To support these efforts the Dutch dredged and improved their rather shallow harbors and developed specialized forms of shipping, both for fishing and for moving bulk materials. They also developed financial instruments to ease the flow of trade and extend the use of credit. Most notably, they established the Bank of Amsterdam, a public bank that offered a source of capital very different from the government funding of chartered companies that had marked the enterprise of discovery and trade in the sixteenth century.

Colbert built up a merchant marine to rival that of the Dutch and ensure that French trade was carried in French ships. Under his direction the merchant fleet grew from a mere 60 ships of 300 tons or more to over 700 ships of that size. He provided for the protection of French maritime commerce by building up the French navy from 20 ships to 250 by the time of his death in 1683.

He always viewed commerce as an instrument of national policy, and merchants had little say in his decisions. This was unlike the situation in England, where various merchant groups formed influential lobbies on the Crown's commercial policies. The prizes of commerce remained for him a zero-sum game: France's gain must be someone else's loss. He created a successful glass industry in Paris by inviting Venetian glassblowers to teach their skills. He later boasted that the successful royal mirror factory that resulted was depriving Venice of one million livres a year.

## Commerce and Conflict

Colbert's attitude was much derided by the later free-trade economists, most notably Smith. The Scottish philosopher David Hume, a contemporary and good friend of Smith's, wrote on the subject: "I shall therefore venture to acknowledge that, not only as a man, but as a British subject, I pray for the flourishing commerce of Germany, Spain, Italy and even France itself."

It was an irony, too, and one that later critics did not fail to point out, that a considerable contribution was made to the growth of French transatlantic exports by industries that did not receive Colbert's nurturing support. Iron and coal, hardware, and the cheaper cloths produced by the textile industry in Normandy all developed through their own enterprise.

Nevertheless, Colbert's legacy was a foundation for rapid and successful French commercial development in the eighteenth century. Between 1715 and 1771 the total value of French foreign trade grew eightfold until it almost matched British trade. The value of French exports multiplied more than four times between 1716 and 1789. Colbert must have been doing something right.

Nor were the policymakers of the time completely wrong in their view of commerce as conflict to gain the largest share of a fixed prize. It is certainly true that bilateral trade is mutually beneficial. If a country wants to export its goods, its potential trading partners must have the means to pay for those goods. So it is in the exporter's interest that partners have their own successful export markets, perhaps in the original country's own home market, to generate the revenue needed to buy its exports.

This is not true of the carrying and reexport trade, however. The Dutch had grown rich on this trade, and the British and French set out to take it away from them. Both ended up fighting trade wars with the Dutch over the issue. In the second half of the seventeenth century, Britain passed a series of Navigation Acts, which required that goods shipped in and out of British ports, and to and from British colonies, had to be carried in British ships.

This struck at the heart of the Dutch trade, hence the tensions that led to war. At issue was who would distribute the new colonial imports throughout the rest of Europe. The Dutch gradually lost out to the French and British. Between the 1660s and 1700 British exports grew by 50 percent. Half of that increase came from the reexport of colonial imports, mostly to Europe.

As a result, the eighteenth century was the Anglo-French century in terms of commerce. I have already mentioned the spectacular growth in French trade. The value of British trade grew threefold between 1702 and 1772, and British shipping grew at a similar rate, reaching over one million tons by 1788. This phenomenal growth represented a tremendous amount of new wealth, most of it associated with colonial trade, especially that of the New World.

The bulk of British trade in 1700 was still with Europe, but by 1776 two-thirds of its overseas trade was outside Europe. Between 1700 and 1763 the value of British exports to America and the West Indies multiplied fivefold, while the value of imports from those areas grew fourfold. Anglo-French rivalry resulted in a number of wars throughout the century. It is small wonder, given the importance of colonial trade, that parts of those wars were fought in North America and in India, over strategic control of its sources.

## 'Badges of Slavery'

The Atlantic trade not only was the most substantial but it also formed an interlocking network. From the plantations of the southern colonies of America, the Caribbean, and the Brazilian coast, tropical staples—tobacco, cotton, sugar, coffee, cocoa, rice—flowed to Europe. European manufactures flowed back west, supplying the plantation economies with necessities they did not produce themselves. European cities, especially those on the Atlantic, grew and prospered on this trade. From Cadiz and Lisbon in the south, through Bordeaux and Nantes in France, to Bristol, Liverpool, Glasgow, and the burgeoning entrepôt of London in England, they all became part of the Atlantic economy.

A city like Liverpool benefited from importing, refining, and reexporting sugar and tobacco. It also benefited from a new and

**Figure 1** Slaves on the deck of the bark *Wildfire,* brought into Key West, Florida, on April 30, 1860. Carrying 510 slaves, the ship violated the 1809 slave trade law that prohibited slave importation. This engraving was made from a daguerreotype for *Harper's Weekly,* June 2, 1860. Blacks were rarely allowed on deck except for occasional "exercise."

Note: Library of Congress.

increasingly significant part of the Atlantic economy—slavery. Plantation agriculture is labor intensive, and the plantations of the Americas looked to West Africa to supply that need. Ships from Liverpool or Bristol, or Lisbon for that matter, would sail to West Africa and trade cheap manufactured items to local chiefs in return for live bodies.

These were then shipped across the Atlantic—the Middle Passage—to the Caribbean or the American South, where those still alive after the horrors of the voyage were sold. The ships then returned home laden with cotton, tobacco, or sugar. In the case of Portuguese ships, they would sail to Brazil and return with Brazilian produce.

European manufactures were also exported to the settler societies of the Americas. The half million Spanish settlers in Mexico and Peru paid for these with silver. As the supply of silver slackened and Latin American society became increasingly self-sufficient, this trade became less important.

The North American trade continued to burgeon. European manufactures were paid for by the products of the region. The question arose as to what those products were to be, and who should determine that: the colonists or the government in London? At this point, questions of mercantilist policy become questions about the future of the American colonies, in other words questions about independence. Adam Smith addressed both sets of questions in *The Wealth of Nations.*

He described the regulations by which London sought to control the American economy as "impertinent badges of slavery." They were intended to ensure that the American economy would complement the British economy, but that, of course, also meant subordinating the one to the other. The American colonies were viewed as a supplier of those staples mentioned above and a protected market for British manufactures.

The colonies were by no means expected to develop industries that might compete with those in Britain. In 1699, Britain sought to ban the woolen industry in America and prevent any intercolony trade in woolen goods. In 1750 a similar ban was applied to steelmaking and the manufacture of finished products from iron.

The role of the New England colonies was to reduce British reliance on the Baltic region for naval materials and certain types of shipbuilding timber. Thus, these strategically sensitive materials—essential for building the ships of the Royal Navy that protected British commerce—would be under British political control. These products were allowed into Britain duty-free, as was pig iron, in that case to reduce British reliance on Swedish and Russian sources. But the pig iron was not to be any further refined in the colonies, lest it compete with the British iron industry.

Being true Englishmen jealous of their liberties, the colonists chafed under these restrictions. Political conflict inevitably resulted, and many commentators in Britain considered that the costs of that conflict outweighed any economic benefit from trying to restrict the natural economic development of the colonies. Matters came to a head in 1776, the year in which both the Declaration of Independence and *The Wealth of Nations* were published.

## New Economic Directions

Smith had definite views on the American economy and on the system of tariffs and trade regulations that had helped produce the conflict. Unlike the views advocated by other contributors to the debate, however, his arose from the context of an extensive theoretical consideration of how wealth is created. It is only a slight exaggeration to say that he invented economic theory.

He can certainly be considered the originator of classical economics. It was his ideas that were first developed and interpreted by David Ricardo and then by John Stuart Mill in *Principles of Political Economy.* At the end of the nineteenth century they were revived and revised as "neoclassical" economics by Alfred Marshall. Even the economic ideas of Karl Marx and, in this century, John Maynard Keynes, started from the principles first enunciated by Smith, although they then moved in very different directions.

His book discusses systematically the basic economic questions: a theory of price or value; wages, profits, and rents; the role of labor; how wealth is distributed among owners of the different factors of production; the role of capital, money, and the banking system; and taxation and the national debt. He famously introduced the concept of the division of labor, explaining how it increases productivity and also is limited by the extent of the market.

He held a dynamic view of the economy. National wealth resulted from the flow of income over time rather than from the size of the stock of capital held. His theory anticipated the actuality of burgeoning economic growth produced by the Industrial Revolution. It differed significantly from the assumptions that lay behind mercantilist policies.

Smith and his good friend Hume refuted the argument that trade should be managed in such a way as to maintain a positive balance so as to earn bullion. Hume pointed out that if bullion flowed out of a country its prices would fall, which would render its exports more competitive, thus increasing the flow of export earnings into the country until balance was restored. In other words, Hume and Smith thought of the economy as a dynamic self-regulating system. In Smith's most famous phrase, it was as if an "invisible hand" harmonized individual economic actions pursued out of self-interest into an overall balance that served the public good. It worked best without government interference.

Economic historian Peter Mathias sums up Smith's arguments on this topic admirably, saying that

> a system of freely operating market prices, under naturally competitive conditions, would ensure the lowest effective prices to the consumer and produce the most efficient allocation of resources between the different branches of economic activity. The ultimate test of efficiency and welfare thus became a freely moving price level not distorted by legislative interference.

On the basis of this argument, Smith launched into a critique of tariffs, subsidies, and monopolies, all the tools of the commercial policy of the era that he dubbed mercantilism. "Consumption," he argued, "is the sole end and purpose of all production," yet under the mercantilist system the consumers' interest was sacrificed to that of producers, who sought special favors from the government for their particular industries.

With such views he could not help but be critical of contemporary British policy toward the American colonies. He thought that Britain could rightly impose its own taxation system on the colonies but only in the context of colonist representation at Westminster. (He was, incidentally, a friend of Benjamin Franklin's, and the two discussed these issues when Franklin was in London.) He thought, too, that Britain could extend its customs laws to America provided that *all* internal barriers to trade were abolished.

Smith thus conceived of the British Empire as a vast and free internal market for each and all of its component regions. He even envisaged that the seat of the empire should not remain fixed in London but should move "to that part of the Empire which contributed most to the general defense and support of the whole."

## The Discussion Continues

Economic relations between Britain and America after the Revolutionary War suggested that the free-trade arguments promoted by Smith and his fellow critics of the system of colonial regulation were right. After 1782, British exports to the United States began to grow more rapidly than those to any other region. By 1836 about a quarter of Britain's total exports went there, while the United States provided 80 percent of Lancashire's cotton.

Such evidence boosted free-trade ideas, which became increasingly influential in the nineteenth century, especially in Britain—whose manufacturers, of course, stood to gain the most by them. But the argument that Smith first articulated against mercantilist policy is still going on today. Countries still remain very sensitive about their balance of trade. In the United States, a Republican presidential candidate, Pat Buchanan, argues for greater protection for American industry, in the face of widespread free-trade thinking in both parties.

Back in the 1970s, the Carter administration bailed out Lee Iacocca's Chrysler Corporation because it was thought that the damage to the economy as a whole and the social cost of the resulting unemployment were worse than paying the cost of a bailout. Right now the United States is entering into a tariff war with western Europe over Caribbean bananas. The Europeans want to reserve 25 percent of their banana market for producers in their former colonies. Without that guaranteed market those producers probably could not survive. The United States is arguing for unrestricted free trade in bananas, which would benefit the mighty Dole Corporation. Whoever is right in the argument, its roots lie in the system of Atlantic trade and colonies that developed in the seventeenth and eighteenth centuries.

The "commercial revolution" of the eighteenth century generated a huge increase in trade and wealth. This all happened under a system of mercantilist policy. Whether that policy nurtured the development or, as Smith argued, it took place despite the policy is a question that can probably never be resolved.

What can be said is that the commercial revolution was an important prelude to the Industrial Revolution. Some of the capital generated from trade found its way into the new manufacturing industries. Perhaps more important was the development of extensive new global markets, for it is questionable whether in the absence of those markets European domestic demand could have grown enough to sustain the rapid growth of the new industries. As it was, those industries found an already established international network of markets through which their new products could flow.

MICHAEL MARSHALL is executive editor of *The World & I*.

From *The World & I*, May 1999, pp. 18–31. Copyright © 1999 by World & I Online. Reprinted by permission.

# A Woman Writ Large in Our History and Hearts

**The free-spirited author George Sand scandalized 19th-century Paris when she defied convention and pioneered an independent path for women.**

Robert Wernick

It can be plausibly argued that one of the critical steps toward the emancipation of women and the expansion of their world was taken one afternoon in November 1830, at the lovely chateau of Nohant in the center of France. Today, thousands of pilgrims visit that literary shrine each year, arriving from the world over to pay their respects to the famous writer who spent half her life there, George Sand.

The visitors find everything so peaceful here, the 18th-century architecture so airy and comfortable and elegant, the dining table set so properly with its place cards for M. Flaubert and M. Turgenev and Prince Jerome Napoleon. The walls are so stately with their family portraits and pale-blue paper, the views so lovely of the rich fields and woodlands of the old province of Berry, that it is hard to associate this gracious place, recently subject to a loving restoration, with a revolutionary event. George Sand's stand for freedom, taken in these spacious rooms, could be said to have had greater consequences than that year's uprising in Paris, which had overthrown the last of the Bourbon kings.

George Sand was not yet George Sand in 1830. She was the baroness Aurore Dudevant (née Dupin), 26 years old, a handsome, hot-blooded, thoroughly unhappy woman living with her husband and two little children on the estate she had inherited from her grandmother. She was rummaging through her husband's desk that day, looking for some paper she had misplaced, when she came across a bulky envelope with her name on it and written below it the words "Only To Be Opened After My Death." Since it was addressed to her, she saw no reason not to open it. The missive turned out to be full of violent abuse, all the resentments and disapprovals that had been simmering for the eight years of a marriage between two people who had nothing in common.

It was perhaps the pretext she had been looking for; in any event, something snapped inside her at that moment. She summoned her husband and told him that she was tired of living with a drunken oaf who fell asleep when she talked about books

or played the piano, and that she was moving to Paris to make a living there by writing books. She would live her own life in her own way. She needed his consent to do it, for though the property and most of the money was her own, the law decreed that a married woman was incapable of handling her own business affairs and that all the checks had to be signed by the husband. This particular husband was a great hunter and a heavy drinker, but he was no match for her in character. She bullied him into accepting her terms and giving her a small allowance when she went off to Paris. He could have had no idea that he was helping to inaugurate a new era in human history.

Within a few weeks, the baroness had packed her bags and kissed her children goodbye. (She and Casimir would manage to share custody of the children for a while; eventually, they would live with her.) She took the diligence for Paris, where she attracted immediate attention by wearing masculine attire, featuring trousers, top hat and cravat, a sight calculated to turn heads anywhere. Almost immediately, she began selling articles and short stories to newspapers and became an active member of a hitherto all-male circle of talkative, turbulent students and artists. She was living in rooms overlooking the Seine with a curly-haired young man named Jules Sandeau; they had met at a party the previous year and Sandeau had told her that he was a writer.

They agreed to collaborate and in short order had written two novels that were snapped up by a publisher. Sand did not want her given name on the title page, for the public would not take such a book seriously, and so they concocted a joint asexual pseudonym, J. Sand. When she realized that she was doing most of the work, she decided to strike out on her own.

She produced a remarkable novel called *Indiana*, about a beautiful young bride married to a dull brute. Her heroine is wooed by a cynical cad for whom she is willing to sacrifice all, but he prefers instead to make a safe and conveniently profitable marriage. In the end, she discovers her true love and disregards opprobrium in order to run off with him. Indiana, wrote

Sand, represented "Choice at odds with Necessity; she is Love blindly butting its head against all the obstacles set in its path by civilization."

A friend suggested that she might lure all the J. Sand fans into buying the book by changing a single letter, which no one would be likely to notice. So the author's name became G. Sand, and the *G,* she decided, would stand for George. It was the name by which she was to be known forevermore. *Indiana* was an instant success. She wrote another novel, and then another.

That was to be only the beginning of her aspirations.

The pants she wore were primarily a matter of practical convenience: you could not work in newspaper offices and run around with all the bright young writers and artists or even sit in the orchestra at theaters (ladies were supposed to sit in expensive boxes) if you were hobbled by ballooning skirts. They were also, like the cigars she smoked, an unmistakable signal of revolt: they announced her intention to turn law and society and traditional modes of thought upside down and put an end to the age-old tyranny of men over women.

She was going to live like a man, make money like a man, have love affairs the way every famous man from Saint Augustine to Lord Byron had done, and do it all without giving up any of what the world regarded as traditional feminine attributes: she would be a good cook and housekeeper, managing half a dozen servants and a sizable estate. She would be a good mother, and she would be flighty and flirty, letting emotion run her life when the right lover came along.

She was only trying to be completely honest and completely independent: "I ask the support of no one, neither to kill someone for me, gather a bouquet, correct a proof, nor to go with me to the theater. I go there on my own, as a man, by choice; and when I want flowers, I go on foot, by myself, to the Alps." After all the millennia of female servitude, she would be Spartacus showing the way to freedom.

She was not quite as radical as she sounded to the horrified conservatives of her day. She did not propose to do away with marriage; she only wanted the wife to have equal rights with the husband. She wanted marriage to stop being a business arrangement between families and become a loving union between two human beings.

Since she was a child of the Romantic Age, she had high standards for love. She maintained that life should be ruled by emotion and instinct, by the heart rather than the brain. In practice, however, she was not quite that simpleminded.

She would follow her heart anywhere, but the love she dreamed of had to involve the complete "embrace of twin souls." Such accords and embraces were as hard to come by in the 19th century as they are in the 20th, and it is no wonder that her love life was marked by a series of disillusionments. So was her political life, where her hatred of oppression and poverty led her to join revolutionary causes with boundless enthusiasm, only to find that when her heroes came to power, after years of shouting for the people, they soon began to think only of Me Me Me.

Underneath the swirling tides of her romantic impulses was a bedrock of common sense. Where other Romantics like Lord Byron and Alfred de Musset would turn from unattainable ideals to cynical debauchery and early death, she had the capacity for looking over her ideals coolly and, finding them wanting, going on to something else. But she never lost her faith that the future was brighter than the past and that the future did indeed mean freedom. "My profession," she said, "is to be free."

A proposal to live by this code was amazing enough coming from a somnolent backwater in the hidebound society of early 19th-century France. Still more amazing was that she got away with it. By the time she died in 1876 at the age of 72, mourned by adoring grandchildren and local villagers, she was universally recognized as one of the giant figures of the era. Though little of her vast output is still read today, she counts as one of the notable writers of France.

She understood, cannily, that literature was one of the few domains where women had the slightest chance of getting ahead in the world. There was no hope in the church or the state or commerce, but there was a long if subdued tradition of women in the arts. A handful of successful women novelists had received grudging recognition: Fanny Burney, Madame de Staël, Jane Austen. They had all operated on the sidelines.

Aurore Dupin was going to get into the thick of the professional literary world. She knew she could write well and she had plenty to write about. Few novelists have had so much family and youthful background to draw upon.

On her mother's side, she came from the back alleys of Paris, where her grandfather had peddled birds. On her father's, she was related to the last three Bourbon kings of France, through her great-great-grandfather Frederick Augustus, elector of Saxony and king of Poland. By his favorite mistress, Countess Aurora von Koenigsmark, the most beautiful woman of her time, Augustus produced the most famous of his 360 or so illegitimate children, the Maréchal de Saxe.

De Saxe was one of the most successful of French generals—there is a great broad avenue named for him in the heart of Paris. He in turn had numerous offspring, including one Aurore de Saxe. She married a rich tax collector named Dupin de Francueil and became one of those handsome free-thinking, art-loving aristocratic ladies who set the tone of French life in the 18th century. She was a friend of Voltaire and Rousseau; she used to tell her granddaughter that, in the days before the revolution, living well was an art: everyone went on enjoying good food, savoring intellectual conversation, delighting in good music every day of their lives. (As her granddaughter observed, it was a great life if you were assured of a steady income of 500,000 francs a year.)

Aurore de Saxe had one son, Maurice, who served in the military, fighting for the revolution and for Napoleon. After the battle of Marengo he met up with the beautiful Sophie Delaborde, who had made what living she could in cabarets, dancing and meeting army officers. He married her a month before the birth of their daughter, and despite the efforts of his mother to annul the marriage, the little girl was born with an honest name, Aurore Dupin.

By the time she married the baron Casimir Dudevant at the age of 18 in 1822, Aurore Dupin had lived in a Paris garret, in her grandmother's chateau, in a palace in Madrid (when her father was aide-de-camp to General Murat, who had just gobbled up Spain for his brother-in-law Napoleon Bonaparte). She

ANNUAL EDITIONS

had, from afar, witnessed a battle and seen Napoleon review his troops. She had experienced the tragedy of her father's death: he had been killed when his wild Spanish stallion threw him against a tree near Nohant on his way home one night. She had fed pigs with the neighboring peasant children and had spent three years in a school for young ladies of good family run by English nuns in Paris.

The convent was the very place inhabited by her grandmother during the Reign of Terror. Then it was a jail, and Madame de Saxe was locked up there. (One day, or so one story goes, her 15-year-old son had come to whisper to her how he and his tutor had crept in the dead of night to the apartment from which they had been expelled, and had detached the seals that the police had put on the doors. They searched out and burned compromising documents that would have sent her to the guillotine and resealed the doors without waking up a soul.)

Aurore Dupin knew how to gallop astride a horse (to the outrage of respectable neighbors who expected her to ride side-saddle like a lady). She knew how to sew, draw and play the piano. She could speak fluent English and had a command of Latin. And she could tell stories that would hold her mother and her aunt spellbound.

She also had inherited a remarkably robust constitution from the kings and tavern-keepers who were her ancestors. She could walk for miles in a day and delighted in hiking the Alps. In her later years, she swam in the Indre River at what was then the very advanced age of 70.

She had a truly extraordinary capacity for work. Whatever was going on at any time in the breakneck pace of her complex life—whether it was Chopin or Liszt playing piano in the living room, or revolutionists being shot down on their barricades outside her window in a Paris street, or Jules Sandeau climbing a ladder to her bedroom while her husband snored down the hall, or 18 people coming to dinner—she was never far from her writing desk. She herself might be traversing the countryside collecting plants and flowers or nursing sick neighbors. She might discourse into the small hours with artists, actresses, revolutionary agitators. Or she might design and sew the costumes for her son's marionette theater, or stay up all night talking and drinking and running her fingers through some young poet's hair. No matter: she unfailingly turned out her 20 or more pages a day. Even so, the royalties were hardly ever sufficient to pay for her lavish hospitality, her boundless generosity to friends, lovers, neighbors, political causes.

The work did not exhaust her energy. "Unceasingly I see her hovering anxiously over me," wrote Chopin of the ghastly winter they spent in Majorca, where it rained all the time, where he spat blood and people avoided them like lepers, "nursing me all by herself, for God preserve us from the doctors of that country, making my bed, cleaning my room, depriving herself of everything for me, watching over the children as well . . . add to this, that she continues to write." In fact, she finished a novel in Majorca.

Balzac would write after a visit to Nohant: "She lives almost exactly as I do. She goes to bed at six in the morning and gets up at midday, whereas I go to bed at six in the evening and get up at midnight. But naturally I fitted in with her arrangements,

and during three days we talked from five in the evening after dinner, until five in the morning." By keeping such hours, the burly Balzac wore himself out and died before he was 52. Little (barely five feet) George Sand took it all in her stride. She was working on yet another novel (she wrote about 70 in all) when she died in 1876 at the age of 72.

She had written, in addition, many short stories, 24 plays, ten volumes of autobiography, essays, book reviews, political pamphlets and an estimated 40,000 letters, of which 22,000 have been printed. Her complete works now number 160 volumes, and they do not include hundreds of newspaper and magazine articles, or the thousands of lost letters, some of which were burned by their recipients to keep them from the eyes of their children.

She wrote about everything that came to hand: love, adventure, foreign lands and secret societies, Roman prelates and rapacious pirates, corrupt noblemen and hardworking peasants, absolutely anything that she fancied.

In her day she was one of the half dozen most widely read novelists of the Western world. She was extravagantly admired by people as different as Dostoyevsky, Walt Whitman and Elizabeth Barrett Browning (who wrote two sonnets dedicated to "Thou large-brained woman and large-hearted man, Self-called George Sand!" She was extravagantly denounced as well: by the Vatican, which repeatedly put her on the index of books no good Catholic was allowed to read, and by Charles Baudelaire, who called her a "latrine," a "great fool" and a "stupid creature."

Her reputation as a writer has not stood up very well, and though feminist scholars have revived interest in her works, it is unlikely that she will ever regain the worldwide popularity she acquired in her lifetime. Librarians and booksellers report few requests for her books. She is too long-winded and preachy, her optimism too syrupy, for modern tastes. Witness this passage from *Indiana*, wherein the heroine decries the wrongs visited upon her: "The law of this country has made you my master. You can bind my body, tie my hands, govern my actions. You are the strongest, and society adds to your power—but with my will, sir, you can do nothing. God alone can restrain it and curb it. Seek then a law, a dungeon, an instrument of torture, by which you can hold it—as if you wished to grasp the air, and seize nothing." But there are many unexpected pleasures to be derived from dipping at random into that immense mass of work, for she had a keen eye and a warm heart and a lively forthright style.

She may seem old-fashioned today, a writer of "charming improbable romances for initiated persons of the optimistic class," as Henry James called her, but in her time she was hailed, or reviled, as an innovator, bringing something radically new into literature. She was one of the first novelists, male or female, to treat marriage not as the goal and fulfillment of a maiden's desire, but as a fact of life, which in most cases meant a commercial contract leading to a life of submission and servitude.

She was a trailblazer, too, in dealing with a class of people that had largely been neglected by playwrights and novelists and historians alike: the working poor.

George Sand was among the first serious writers to attempt an account of their lives. She knew perfectly well that, even

58

in a fairly prosperous region like Berry, the rural poor were condemned to a hard, squalid, stifling life. She didn't dare to show all the squalor, for fear of alienating her bourgeois readers, whom she wanted to make aware of the fundamental decency and dignity of these people. So her picture of the life of poverty is apt to seem sentimental to the modern reader.

She never had the gift for creating unforgettable characters like her contemporaries Balzac and Dickens—at least in her novels, for in real life she did create one character that seems sure to live on indefinitely. That character is, of course, George Sand, a fascinating and complex mixture of passion and reason, wildness and domesticity, frankness and hypocrisy.

In the summer of 1833 she wrote her friend and confidant the critic Sainte-Beuve: "I have fallen in love, and this time very seriously, with Alfred de Musset. . . . You may, perhaps, think that a woman should conceal her feelings: but I beg you to realize that I am in a quite exceptional situation, and am compelled, from now on, to live my private life in the full light of day."

These are words that would come naturally from the lips of any Princess of Wales or Hollywood starlet today. In 1833 they were—for a woman—quite revolutionary indeed.

She was not, like so many of today's celebrities, just putting on a show for the public. She was always following her heart, or her good sense when she realized her heart had led her astray. One way or the other, it made good copy everywhere.

The whole world was watching as she departed with Alfred de Musset, the delicate dandified poet six years her junior, for Italy, land of dreams and desire, from the moment they got aboard a paddle steamer in Marseilles on December 20, 1833. Coldly summarized, the couple's voyage looks as if it had been scripted a hundred and fifty years later by Woody Allen. The Mediterranean was rough, and George strode the deck blowing smoke at the elements. Alfred, who was sick as a dog, wrote a furious little quatrain to protest the reversal of traditional gender roles.

He got his revenge when they arrived in Venice at the hotel Danieli and George contracted a bad case of dysentery that knocked her out for days. Alfred went out night after night to drink and gamble, and pick up girls along the canals. A handsome young doctor named Pietro Pagello came to bleed George regularly.

Back in the hotel after she was healed, Alfred collapsed with what different biographers describe as typhoid, or perhaps brain fever. He saw George and Pietro Pagello drinking tea out of the same cup. In his fever he saw much more, and threw a violent jealous fit.

Alfred gallantly went back to Paris alone. George stayed on happily in Venice till summer, then took Pagello back to Paris with her and introduced him to her friends as a famous archaeologist. (As usual, the romance did not work out.) Alfred eventually threw himself back into George's arms. There were passionate midnight meetings, the inevitable Sturm und Drang, and finally they broke up for good.

George, who had written two novels, a novelette and two essays about Venice during her stay there, eventually wrote a book about the whole experience. So did Musset. So did Alfred's

brother, and the actress who succeeded George in Alfred's affections. Doctor Pagello lived on in Venice till the age of 91, a local celebrity because of his liaison with the famous, or infamous, George Sand.

Within a month of her finally writing off Musset, she was passionately in love with a married man, a well-known lawyer named Michel de Bourges. Unlike most of her other lovers, he was quite a bit older than she was, and ugly and bald. But he had a golden tongue. He helped win the case against Baron Dudevant for separation (there was no such thing as divorce in France at that time).

But in 1837, less than two years into the affair, she broke things off. She had learned that, among other transgressions, her beloved had already taken another mistress.

Shortly afterward, she sat down to write a letter to herself coolly analyzing the impossibility of remaining attached to a man who wanted only her devotion and submission, who was not going to leave his wife or his comfortable way of life for her. That was the end of Michel de Bourges, and in 1838 she was willing and ready to take on Frédéric Chopin.

Chopin was a delicate, tubercular, morbidly punctilious, morbidly jealous genius, "frail as a snow-drop," said an American visitor, Margaret Fuller. To him George Sand would play alternately lover, muse, worshipful mother and devoted nurse for eight years. They were the years during which he wrote most of his best piano compositions and she some of her best novels, including the one that has been the most popular down to the present day, *La Mare au diable* (The Devil's Pool). It is a simple tale of love in the Berry countryside, of love triumphant over social convention, which she wrote in four days.

They were also years of squabbles with her daughter, Solange, now an adolescent with a roving eye. When it roved to Chopin and he responded, a tangle of jealousies and resentments ensued, also involving her son, Maurice, and Augustine, a poor cousin whom Sand had adopted. Augustine fell in love with Maurice, to the intense annoyance of Solange. She managed to turn Maurice against Augustine, Chopin against Maurice, George against Chopin. Solange married a brute of a sculptor who once attacked Maurice and George with a hammer. Everyone blamed everyone else, and the affair with Chopin, which might have gone on till his death a couple of years later, petered out unpleasantly.

Political turmoil followed domestic. Revolution erupted in 1848, spurred on by a wide variety of malcontents, from conservative republicans to socialists of various stripes. Sand, sympathetic to the plight of the people, poured out revolutionary rhetoric in countless pamphlets and open letters. A brief republic soon gave way, in a series of stages, to a Bonapartist dictatorship, headed by the nephew of Napoleon I, Louis-Napoleon Bonaparte. Republican and socialist hopes alike were dashed.

But as Sand grew older, she was losing her taste for adventure. She spent more and more time in Nohant, and it was a quieter time than any she had ever known. She had the longest lasting of all her love affairs, 15 years with a young painter named Alexandre Manceau, a devoted companion to whom she was very attached. She even left her estate for a time, moving with Manceau to a Paris suburb until 1865, when he died of tuberculosis.

She settled into an active old age at Nohant, playing with her grandchildren, writing and producing elaborate marionette shows with her son, entertaining guests by the dozen and writing novels steadily. She was an international celebrity by now; people came to see her from Russia, from America, everywhere. And although young people continued to adore her as a standard-bearer of revolt and liberation, her views of the world had calmed down considerably: she had in due course grown to detest radicalism; now she was all for moderation.

She never gave up her capacity to "live life as it is, without being ungrateful, fully aware that joy is neither enduring nor assured." Her last great affection, a purely platonic one this time, was for Flaubert. He admired her wholeheartedly, though he could never understand her taste for playing rowdy practical jokes when he wanted to talk about literature.

And when he wrote to her from the Swiss mountains where he had been sent to calm his nerves, "I am not a *man of nature,* I would trade all the glaciers in the world for the Vatican Library," she snapped back that he himself was a part of nature and he had better get used to it.

Nature was with her to the end. Almost the last words she uttered, when she was dying in agony of an intestinal cancer, were *"laissezverdure,"*—"let greenery"—perhaps because she was thinking for the last time of the great cedar trees at Nohant, planted at the birth of her two children almost half a century before.

If she had a time machine and were to come back to Nohant today, she might find much to displease her in modern life, but Nohant itself would undoubtedly have its consolations. Her house is much the way she left it, and so are the rolling grainfields and woodlands around it. The sturdy farmhouses of her neighbors look much the same; the farmers are little changed, though they now use tractors instead of teams of oxen for their planting.

She would be saddened by the loss of so many traditions: the ox-cart ruts that are now paved roads, the people who have been taught by their television sets to speak French instead of the throaty Berrichon patois she loved.

But then she was a creator of tradition, too, and she would take a generous delight in watching the women drive up on their visits to what is now a national monument, women who may keep house the way she did but also have careers such as she made for herself, as doctors, lawyers, cabinet ministers, professors of gender studies and presidents of international conglomerates. She would recognize them all as her grandchildren. "One day," she had predicted, "the world will understand me, and if this day never comes, no matter, I will have opened the way for other women.

The cedar trees still stand on the grounds of her estate.

Frequent contributor **ROBERT WERNICK** has written recently on sound bites and on the nativist political party of the mid-1800s, the Know-Nothings.

# A Disquieting Sense of Deja Vu

HOWARD G. BROWN

Extremist violence threatened liberal democracy, posing grave challenges for a political class riven by systemic corruption and bitter partisanship. Leaders resorted to whatever tactics could help them retain power, regardless of the consequences to the political system. Citizens quickly grew disillusioned by democratic politics, and voter participation declined at each election. The government, fearing that mere policing could not preserve the republic from threats to its security, turned to the army. A prolonged regional insurgency, fueled by a heavy-handed military occupation, grew ever more vicious and bloody. Foreign elements eager to see the regime fail took the opportunity to foster an all-out civil war. At the same time, the government and the media turned the possibility of violence against ordinary people into a pervasive climate of fear. To counter the threat to individual and collective security, the government resorted to a range of exceptional measures that infringed civil liberties and violated the Constitution. In the process, the steadily expanding power of the state was used to consolidate major changes in the social and political order.

While that account may sound familiar today, those events actually occurred more than 200 years ago, during one of the most neglected periods in modern French history—the years of France's first constitutional republic, from 1795 to 1804. What people know about the French Revolution is generally limited to the years 1789 to 1794—the fall of the Bastille; "liberty, equality, fraternity"; a short-lived constitutional monarchy; the trial and execution of Louis XVI; foreign war against the monarchies of Europe; civil war in the Vendée; and, above all, the Terror of 1793–94, when thousands of supposed counterrevolutionaries were sent to the guillotine. Even better known is the figure of Napoleon Bonaparte, the military genius who came to power in 1799, steadily concentrated authority in his person, and emerged as emperor in 1804.

Because it falls between the thrill of revolutionary idealism and the glory of Napoleonic conquest, France's failed effort to establish liberal democracy in the late 1790s has been generally ignored, even by historians. Yet it is the decade between Robespierre's bloody reign of virtue and Napoleon's bloodier reign of military prowess that reveals the true difficulties inherent in trying to preserve the principles of liberal democracy and the rule of law in a republic threatened by extreme violence. It is the nature of France's first constitutional republic—its struggle to reconcile liberty with security and to defend a liberal democratic constitution while at the same time violating it—that deserves our attention today.

It is especially instructive to note parallels between America's growing role since September 11 as the world's policeman and efforts made to establish a liberal democracy in France in the decade after the Terror. Such a comparison draws attention to the cover that the "state of exception" (as Carl Schmitt and Georgio Agamben have termed skirting the rule of law in times of emergency) can provide for consolidating a new political order. Such a comparison should also alert us to the possible hazards of shifting the sources of political legitimacy from popular participation and the rule of law to defense of the homeland and personal safety. The consequence could well be a form of "security state" more characteristic of an authoritarian regime based on national plebiscites than a representative democracy based on the rule of law.

France's fledgling republican government may have been better equipped to bring order to France in the late 1790s than the U.S. government is able to act as the antiterrorist policeman of the new world order. Nonetheless, the disparities are not as great as they may at first appear. France was a vast, populous, and diverse country in the 18th century. Even sensational news took at least four days to spread from Paris to the Pyrenees. France also consisted of highly distinctive regions, whether considered economically, linguistically, or culturally. Once revolutionaries had abolished noble lordships, dispossessed the Roman Catholic Church, and overthrown the monarchy, their attempt to impose the "one and indivisible republic" provoked a combination of foreign war, civil strife, and economic chaos not seen in Europe for 150 years. The trauma of the Terror in 1793–94 and the wave of revenge killings that followed in 1795 left the country in tatters and politicians with few means to stitch it together again.

Moderate republicans responded to the chaos that followed the Terror by adopting a liberal democratic constitution. This created the Directory, a five-man executive that ran France from 1795 to 1799. The new constitution was both a strategy to rally Frenchmen behind the new regime—and thereby consolidate revolutionary changes in the social order—and a goal in its own right: to embody key principles of the early revolution, such as liberty, equality, and representative democracy, in a secular republic. The Directory's legitimacy was to be based on annual elections and a strict adherence to the rule of law.

This included a code of police and judicial procedures that fully embodied the modern concept of due process. However, given the nature of the anti-republican opposition, which was rooted in popular religion and led by traditional rural elites, efforts to preserve the constitutional republic soon compromised the liberal democratic principles on which it was based.

The greatest compromises derived from the republic's handling of civil strife in western and southeastern France, a response akin to the United States' involvement in Afghanistan and Iraq today. Though mindful of both the excesses of the Terror and the need to establish its legitimacy as a constitutional regime, the Directory found it necessary to use the army to impose its authority. In the west, a peasant rebellion first ignited in the Vendée and, ruthlessly repressed in 1793–94, flared up again in the summer of 1795. The guerrilla insurgency spread so rapidly over the west that the government gave the region over to the army. Eight months of intensive operations, including hunting down the main guerrilla leaders, finally brought the region to heel. This was more subjugation than pacification, however, and sporadic violence continued to threaten local governance for years to come. A protracted "dirty war" of ambushes, kidnappings, reprisals, arbitrary detentions, and double-dealing divided the populace and discredited the regime.

In contrast to the west, the civil strife in southeastern France was largely urban. Rather than relying on the army alone, the Directory sought to overcome the region's intense factionalism and vendetta violence through an evenhanded application of the Constitution and due process. That largely failed. Local leaders and magistrates continued to persecute their political rivals, using urban militias and secret murder gangs to assist them. Army commanders and government commissioners came to rely on local strongmen for advice. By the summer of 1797, the region was almost entirely in the hands of men determined to subvert the government in Paris.

In addition to regional strife, France suffered from widespread banditry. Every day the government received a host of reports containing lurid details of intercepted couriers, gang-style robberies, stagecoach holdups, and assaults on those who bought land expropriated from the Church or emigrants. The scourge of banditry fell heaviest on property holders, merchants, and local officials—the social basis of the republican regime—but almost anybody who lived in an isolated farmhouse or ventured beyond town walls was a potential victim. At least that was how the government and newspapers made it seem.

Republican officials had come to share a general "banditry psychosis." Such thinking turned many isolated crimes into behavior explicable only as organized banditry. Newspapers, which exploded in the early 1790s, helped to spread news about the wave of lawlessness. Frenchmen suddenly became aware of events in distant parts of the country as never before. The increased flow of information to agents of law enforcement, which was often interpreted as evidence of organized crime, as well as unprecedented circulation of news about various crimes committed around the country, helped to generate a pervasive climate of fear.

Matters became most alarming when republicans explained virtually all resistance to authority, including insurgency in the west, factional violence in the south, and brutal robberies perpetrated elsewhere, as "royalist conspiracy" and "counterrevolution." By tarring its opponents, including bandits and even ordinary draft dodgers, as royalists and counterrevolutionaries no matter what their differences, the regime painted them all as manifest threats to the republic. The government also claimed that the plague of farmhouse break-ins and highway robberies was part of England's war against France. Although the English did lend sporadic support to the guerrillas in the west, as well as to various royalist conspirators, the regime's own aggressive policies clearly generated the vast bulk of violent opposition.

These various threats to the republic, fear of which was kept in the forefront of public consciousness, led to a number of repressive responses by the government. Many of these violated the principles on which the republic was ostensibly based. For example, the Directory gave local army commanders authority to declare numerous towns and cities under state of siege. This gave them even more police powers than proclaiming martial law. So effective was the state of siege that in 1797, lawmakers made it a permanent instrument of government, despite contravening the Constitution in the process. By late 1799, more than 200 municipalities, including many important towns and cities, had been declared under a state of siege and subjected to military rule.

The late 1790s also witnessed a growing use of military justice to try civilians. Initially, only counterrevolutionary rebels captured in armed gatherings were deprived of proper jury trials. In September 1797, military commissions were authorized to judge and execute emigrants who had fled the revolution, but then returned. Emigrants were the "unlawful combatants" of their day, deprived of their civil rights more for what the government feared they would do than what they actually had done. A few months later, regular military courts were authorized to judge and execute civilians charged with aggravated robbery. When these two laws lapsed in 1800, the government resorted to roving military commissions to judge accused rebels and bandits in the west and south. Recently discovered records show that regardless of important differences between them, each of these types of military justice produced hundreds of executions. Given its sheer frequency, the firing squad deserves a place alongside the guillotine as a symbol of the First Republic.

The regime employed other methods of protecting the republic while violating its Constitution. Republicans provoked a great deal of opposition through their handling of religion. Priests who refused to take an oath of loyalty to the republic were banished from the country. If they returned from exile or emerged from hiding, they were subject to death or deportation. The lucky ones, namely the aged and infirm, were merely interned indefinitely. Furthermore, when renewed warfare abroad brought a resurgence of violence at home, lawmakers passed the infamous "law of hostages" authorizing the arbitrary arrest and possible deportation of local nobles and relatives of rebels in areas of civil unrest.

All of these exceptional measures violated individual rights enshrined in the Constitution. Although such measures were justified as necessary to preserve the republic, they easily became the means of continuing to transform the social and political order at the expense of the Church and traditional elites. Such exceptional measures discredited the Directory's claim to liberal democracy and prepared the ground for a more authoritarian regime. Most people lost faith in the possibilities of democracy and instead craved security and stability. Bonaparte's coup d'état in 1799, which replaced the Directory with the three-man Consulate, appeared as merely another blow to election results and was greeted largely with indifference.

Rather than abandon exceptional measures altogether, the new Consular government first sought to regulate them. Just when lawmakers began objecting to Bonaparte's growing authoritarianism, a failed attempt to blow him up gave Bonaparte the popular support he needed to push through new security measures. These included creating a hybrid between military and civilian justice known as Special Tribunals, which operated without juries and without appeal. Though established only in certain areas and confined to a narrow set of rural crimes, Special Tribunals accounted for as many executions and sentences to hard labor as all other criminal courts combined. This form of regulated exceptionalism ensured that less than 15 years after the Declaration of the Rights of Man and Citizen, the French state was meting out more penal repression than had the absolutist monarchy of the 1780s. By 1802 the fledgling French republic had succumbed to the personal dictatorship of Napoleon Bonaparte.

The American republic is more robust and will not experience a similar fate anytime soon. That is no reason, however, to ignore the threat posed to liberal democracy by repeated recourse to exceptional measures in the name of homeland security. Holding prisoners in legal limbo for years, sending defendants before special military tribunals, conducting warrantless surveillance of phone calls—all actions undertaken without legislative or judicial oversight—are the sort of emergency measures that any democracy has reason to fear. Being oblivious to hypocrisy and history alike entails grave risks; it could well allow a permanent "state of exception" to be used to consolidate a more authoritarian world order at the expense of genuine liberal democracy.

**HOWARD G. BROWN** is a professor of history at the State University of New York at Binghamton and the author of *Ending the French Revolution: Violence, Justice, and Repression From the Terror to Napoleon* (University of Virginia Press, 2006).

# The Paris Commune

Robert Tombs explains why the Paris Commune of 1871, which ended with the most ferocious outbreak of civil violence in nineteenth century Europe, is still a subject of intense historical interest and controversy.

ROBERT TOMBS

Before daybreak on 18 March 1871, several thousand cold and miserable French troops trudged up the steep streets of Montmartre, the hill overlooking northern Paris, to capture by surprise hundreds of cannon parked on the summit by dissident units of the Paris National Guard, the citizen militia. Seizing these heavy weapons was to be the first step towards reimposing the national government's authority on the unruly capital. Since the beginning of the war with Germany the previous July, which had led to a four-month siege of the city, Parisians had become increasingly disaffected from their rulers. The end of the war had left Paris ungovernable, as most of the regular army was demobilised while the National Guard kept its guns. The newly elected National Assembly, which had a royalist majority, was far away in Bordeaux. The government it appointed, led by Adolphe Thiers, intended to assert its authority over Paris. The Montmartre expedition was the outcome.

It led to one of the most famous, and fateful, scenes in French history. Thousands of local National Guards, together with women and children, turned out to obstruct and argue with the outnumbered and visibly unenthusiastic soldiers. The streets became jammed with people, horses and cannon. A few shots were fired by both sides, but generally the soldiers ignored their officers' orders to force back the crowds. Some handed over their rifles and went off 'arm in arm, fraternising and singing' with the civilians. Two generals were grabbed by the crowd and later shot in a neighbouring back yard.

Across the city, people threw up barricades, as in 1848 and 1830. The government and the army high command, convinced that they had lost control, retreated with all available troops to Versailles, ten miles south-west of Paris, where the National Assembly arrived from Bordeaux on 20 March. The Central Committee of the Republican Federation of the Paris National Guard—an unofficial body set up in February to co-ordinate the activity of the militia battalions, hence their popular name of 'Fédérés'—established a provisional authority at the Hotel de Ville, the city hall.

A week later, elections in which over a quarter of a million voters took part chose a city council mainly composed of revolutionaries—veteran democrats from 1848, radical journalists, labour militants, patriotic National Guards—who assumed the title of Paris Commune. 'Commune', the French term for the basic unit of local government, signified grass-roots democracy, and also consciously recalled the first revolutionary Paris Commune of 1792; it did not imply communism. The red flag and the 1793 revolutionary calendar were adopted, according to which they were in Germinal Year 79. The proclamation of the Commune was a joyous popular ceremony, described by the writer Jules Vállés (a member of the Commune) as 'calm and beautiful as a blue river'. The cheering, singing and marching crowds believed that 'the Free City of Paris' would begin a new era as a 'democratic and social republic'. Every previous insurrection that had successfully gained control of Paris had gone on to rule France.

## The Origins of the Commune

The roots of the Commune lay in the Parisian 'revolutionary tradition', which had already overthrown conservative regimes in 1830 and 1848. Many Parisians aspired to an egalitarian 'democratic and social republic'. Republicanism had been revived by campaigns against Emperor Napoleon III in the late 1860s. It was radicalised by the effects of the disastrous Franco-Prussian War (July 1870–January 1871), which led to a rapid and unstoppable German invasion of France. The defeated emperor was overthrown in a republican revolution on 4 September 1870, but the moderate republican government that replaced him managed neither to defeat the Germans nor to negotiate with them. The invaders besieged Paris from September 1870 to January 1871. Parisians were armed and enrolled in a mass National Guard.

Starved into surrender, they angrily blamed the government for their defeat. Moreover, they were determined to preserve the Republic from a possible monarchist restoration. The events of Montmartre detonated this already explosive situation.

## The Commune: Aims, Membership, Activities

The new Commune represented the left wing of Parisian politics. About half were middle-class (journalists, lawyers, small

# Timecheck on the Paris Commune

**1870**

| | |
|---|---|
| (July) | France declares war on Prussia |
| (1 Sept) | France defeated at Sedan |
| (19 Sept) | Siege of Paris begun by Prussians |

**1871**

| | |
|---|---|
| (Jan) | Bombardment of Paris, followed by capitulation |
| (Feb) | National Assembly elections; Thiers forms government |
| (1 March) | German troops enter Paris |
| (18 March) | Rising of the Paris Commune; Thiers leaves for Versailles |
| (6 April) | Communards besieged by troops of National Assembly |
| (1 May) | Versailles troops begin bombardment of Paris |
| (21 May) | Versailles troops enter Paris and begin a week of bloody fighting and reprisals |
| (28 May) | Last Communard barricades captured |
| (31 August) | Thiers elected President of France |

businessmen, master craftsmen), and the other half white-collar workers or skilled manual workers, often labour leaders, from the main Paris trades (metal-working, jewellery, furniture, clothing etc). It is noteworthy that among this heterogeneous group there was not a single unskilled labourer. Unlike in earlier revolutions, they were not national politicians; few had more than a local reputation. The better known include the elderly neo-Jacobin journalist Charles Delescluze, the socialist bookbinder Eugéne Varlin, and the painter Gustave Courbet. The aims of the Commune leaders were above all to defend the Republic and to assert the autonomy of Paris as the republican capital. Their immediate acts were aimed at those they saw as the republic's enemies: the Catholic Church (which was disestablished), the regular army (which was abolished, at least for Paris), and the police and bureaucracy, which were to be democratised and turned over to ordinary citizens—a project which barely got off the ground. In the free and somewhat anarchic atmosphere, grass-roots initiatives were permitted or encouraged, for example in education and the arts.

The Commune's supporters, usually known as 'Communards' or 'Communeux', were broadly 'the people': the manual and white-collar wage-earners, self-employed craft workers and small business people who composed the majority of Parisians. They were comparable with participants in earlier revolutions in 1848, 1830 and even the 1790s. One described himself as follows:

'I am the son of a good patriot of 1792 . . . Journeyman cabinet-maker at 18 years old . . . working during the day, studying at night, history, travels, political and social economy, making propaganda and taking part in all republican movements . . . Arriving in Paris in 1854, two years later I set myself up as a furniture restorer . . . I employed 1 to 3 workers, paying them 50 centimes per day above the official rate and propandising them too . . . In politics I want the broadest possible sovereignty of the People [and] all the Reforms our defective social and political organisation demands.'

Women played a much-remarked role. They were prominent on 18 March, when the insurrection began. Later, led by activists such as Nathalie Le Mel, Louise Michel (subsequently a well-known anarchist) and the Russian Elisveta Tomanovskaya, they were public speakers, organisers of co-operatives and schools, military nurses and—so conservatives alleged—wielders of rifles and petrol-bombs. There is some debate as to how extensive and how new their activity really was; but it has recently been argued that the Commune marked a new stage in women's political assertiveness.

Given expectations of what revolutions were like, this one seemed remarkably calm, even somnolent, at first. Noted one visiting Englishman, 'The first thing that struck me on my arrival was the extreme tranquillity of the streets.' The city's tangible calm was partly because much of the administrative machinery ran as usual. It was also because many thousands of middle-class Parisians had left. Others continued to flee, especially men of military age determined to avoid fighting for the Commune or taking the risk of opposing it: some bribed sentries to let them shin down the city ramparts. Others kept off the streets. Consequently, the city centre and residential western quarters, wrote a British visitor, were like 'London on a wet Sunday'. It is harder to find contemporary impressions of the working-class districts where the Commune had most of its supporters. An English journalist, after stressing the emptiness of the city centre, described Montmartre as 'full of life, the shops open, and the streets thronged with women and children'—many of the men would have been on military duty. At the Place du Trône the usual Gingerbread Fair was held, with 'nearly as many booths as usual, and acrobats, conjurers, fat ladies and other monstrosities were not wanting'.

There were also more political entertainments. Acts of ceremonial destruction were staged to signal the defeat—at least symbolic—of the people's enemies, and these became more spectacular as the situation deteriorated and morale needed a boost. On 6 April, National Guards from the La Roquette district burnt the guillotine taken from its shed near the local prison. Several churches were systematically wrecked. An exhibition in May of human remains discovered in the crypt of Saint-Laurent church and said to be those of girls raped and murdered by the priests—one of several occurrences of anticlerical street-theatre—attracted crowds of sightseers. On 15 May Thiers's house was demolished by decree of the Commune as a reprisal for Versaillais bombardment of the city. On 16 May occurred the most spectacular demolition, which caused worldwide interest: that of the Vendome Column, in the centre of the city, which commemorated Napoleon I's victories.

Economic reforms were far less dramatic—principally encouraging workers' co-operatives, forbidding night work in bakeries, cancelling war-time rent arrears and returning small items free from the municipal pawnshops. These were seen by some at the time (and by many later commentators) as social experiments of great significance. But there was never any question of seizing private business or financial institutions, such as the Bank of France. Karl Marx criticised this as timidity, but few French socialists favoured state control of an economy still dominated by small businesses. The Commune's only clear ideological split, on 1 May, was over whether to hand emergency dictatorial powers to a five-man Committee of Public Safety (another reference to the 1790s). The majority, mainly neo-Jacobins and followers of the authoritarian revolutionary Auguste Blanqui, voted in favour, against a minority, mainly socialists, who opposed on grounds of democratic principle.

## Chaos or Festival?

The life of the Commune was dominated not by ideology or legislation, but by civil war. Skirmishes began on 1 April 1871. A Parisian march on Versailles on 3 April failed. The Versaillais regular army began siege operations on 11 April. For the rest of April and May, the Commune faced the huge task of organising, arming, equipping, feeding, paying and leading its part-time democratic citizen army in continuous fighting in the suburbs against ever-increasing numbers of Versaillais, who eventually totalled 130,000 men. Most contemporaries and historians have emphasised the disorganisation and indiscipline of the Fédérés, about 170,000 strong on paper; but, given the improvised and largely voluntary character of their effort, a balanced picture would give more credit to their two-month defence. They were aided by Paris's massive fortifications and the huge stock of weaponry built up during the German siege. Nevertheless, chances of survival were slim: they could not defeat the regular army in battle; they had no significant help from the rest of France (sympathetic uprisings in Marseilles, Lyons, Toulouse and other cities were quickly extinguished); and the German army was camped in their rear, ready to intervene if required. The Versaillais and the Germans contemplated imposing a blockade, but it was never seriously implemented. Food therefore remained available at only slightly higher prices, and Parisians were not again reduced, as under the German siege, to horsemeat and rats.

Life during the Commune has often been portrayed as either chaos or festival, which may be different ways of describing the same things. The first element was the absence of usual routines linked with work, due to the interruption of normal economic life and the subsistence of most working-class Parisians on National Guard pay and rations. Except for usually brief periods of duty, this left most men with free time for socialising, politics and (an accompaniment to both) drinking. The second element was the weakness or absence of conventional authority from above, as public order was largely in the hands of the National Guards themselves and their elected officers. This meant an overturning of the usual hierarchy: middle-class people could be ordered around by workers, which sometimes involved harassment by the officious, the bullying and the drunk. It also meant a much-criticised level of disorganisation, with much arguing and milling around. But it also meant an unprecedented level of freedom and equality. The third element was the decentralisation of initiative, which created a wonderful opportunity for political enthusiasts to make speeches, to run clubs, committees and newspapers, and to take practical action—whether starting co-operatives, opening schools or

wrecking churches. Fourth, ignorance of much that was happening inside and especially outside the city meant that both friends and enemies of the Commune had little notion of how long it would last and what the outcome of the conflict might be. For all these reasons, the period from March to May seemed outside normal time. The sentimental way of describing it after the event was as *'le temps des cerises'*—'cherry time'—the title of a song written by a member of the Commune, Jean-Baptiste Clément.

> **Life during the Commune has often been portrayed as either chaos or festival, which may be different ways of describing the same things.**

## Blood, Destruction and Myth

Cherry time came brutally to an end on 21 May, when the first Versaillais troops clambered over the shell-torn south-western ramparts. By the next morning, over 100,000 men had overrun the western districts of the city, capturing thousands of Fédérés almost without resistance. The troops were acclaimed as liberators by throngs of mainly middle-class residents, who showered them with money, food and wine. The atmosphere soon changed in what was to be known as 'La Semaine Sanglante' ('Bloody Week'), the most deadly and destructive few days in the history of Paris, the most ferocious outbreak of civil violence in Europe between the French Revolution of the 1790s and the Bolshevik revolution of 1917. In Richard Cobb's memorable phrase, it was like an appalling level-crossing accident at the end of a school outing to the seaside. The disaster would give the Commune a new legend and meaning. From being a rather timid, incompetent and verbose municipal revolution, it became an epic of popular heroism and sacrifice. A sympathetic critic put it bluntly: 'The Commune, which would have sunk amid ridicule, took on a tragic dignity.'

The Versaillais troops, in overwhelming number, used cannon fire to smash their way across the city from west to east. Several thousand Fédéré diehards built hundreds of street barricades. Some began to set fire to buildings, first to slow the Versaillais advance, later as a reaction to defeat. Symbolic monuments were gutted, badly damaged or narrowly rescued from the flames, including the Tuileries Palace, the City Hall, the Palace of Justice, the Finance Ministry, the Louvre and Notre Dame. Panicky rumours spread that the Communards were trying to destroy the whole city, and that women *firé-ráisérs—petroleuses*—were burning private houses. This—along with the pent-up fear and anger the Commune had inspired over the previous weeks—led to an increasingly savage reaction against Communard prisoners and suspects. Neighbours denounced each other to the troops; landlords denounced tenants, and shopkeepers customers.

The Versailles army slaughtered prisoners by the hundred. Often, being wounded, having a recently-fired gun, a right shoulder bruised by the kick of a rifle butt, gunpowder stains or any other suspicious characteristic meant summary execution: mass slaughter continued for some days in public parks, behind prison walls and most notoriously in the Pére Lachaise cemetery against the 'Fédérés' Wall'. Angry Fédérés shot several dozen hostages in retaliation, including the Archbishop of Paris. The last flickers of resistance, in the working-class eastern quarters, were stamped out on 28 May. Convoys of Fédéré prisoners were mobbed as they were marched off to Versailles. The number of Communards, or suspected Communards, killed in the street fighting, shot clown summarily, or executed after hasty court-martial will probably never be known for certain. At least 10,000 bodies are known to have been buried in Paris as a result, but most historians assume the total to have been much higher. Many conservatives applauded the carnage as the way to guarantee a generation of peace. This intensity of civil violence was unique in Europe between the French and Russian revolutions, and it left deep scars. To this day an annual commemoration is held by French socialists at the *Fédérés'* Wall.

---

**The Versailles army slaughtered prisoners by the hundred. Often being wounded, having a recently-fired gun, a right shoulder bruised by the kick of a rifle butt, gunpowder stains or any other suspicious characteristic meant summary execution: mass slaughter continued for some days.**

---

# The Significance of the Commune

The Commune has been variously interpreted, The first and most influential commentator was Karl Marx, busy in London as events unfolded sending advice to contacts in Paris and formulating reasons why the Commune was an event of historic significance. He and his followers hailed it as the dawn of the age of proletarian revolution and the pioneer of a new form of popular revolutionary government, the dictatorship of the proletariat. They praised the courage of its 'martyrs', and the song L'Internationale, written by Commune member Eugène Pottier, became their revolutionary anthem. In the years that followed, the lesson of the Commune was a bone of contention between socialists who implicitly or explicitly abandoned revolution in favour of electoral politics and trade unionism, and those who insisted that violent revolution was the only route to socialism. Marx and especially Lenin argued that the Commune's failure proved the need for less 'decency', more ruthlessness and more disciplined leadership in future: the Communards had 'stopped half way . . . led astray by dreams of . . . justice'; their

'excessive magnanimity' had prevented them from 'destroying' the class enemy through 'ruthless extermination', and so they themselves had been massacred. The Soviet Union claimed to have succeeded where the Communards had failed. As a symbolic gesture, Lenin's body was wrapped in a red Fédéré flag.

Recently, historians have broken away from the Marxist interpretation, stressing the specifically French, republican and Parisian nature of the Commune. It was, writes Jacques Rougerie, the end of an era, 'dusk not dawn'. Francois Furet concludes that 'in this Paris in flames, the French Revolution bade farewell to history'. However, some historians and sociologists, especially in America and Britain, have suggested that in other ways—as a specifically urban revolution, or in certain of its cultural aspects, or through the participation of women—the Commune can be seen as dawn as well as dusk. Debate will certainly continue.

L' Internationale

Arise, you wretched of the earth!
    Arise, you inmates of hunger's prison!
Reason is rumbling in Its crater,
    Its final eruption is on the way.
Let us wipe clean the slate of the past,
    Arise, enslaved multitude, arise,
The world will completely change:
    We are nothing, let us be everything!
This is the final conflict:
    Let us form up and, tomorrow,
The Internationale
    Will encompass the human race.

This poem was written by Parisian transport worker, and member of the Commune, Eugène Porttier. Translated into Russian, it became the Soviet national anthem until 1944. But was the Paris Commune a revolutionary beginning or end?

# Reference

David Barry, *Women and Political Insugency: France in the Mid-Nineteenth Century* (London, Macmillan, 1996).

Francois Furet, *Revolutionary France, 1770–1880* (Oxford, Blackwell, 1992).

Roger V. Gould, *Insurgent Identities: Class, Community and Protest in Paris from 1848 to the Commune* (Chicago, University of Chicago Press, 1995).

Karl Marx, *The Civil War in France* [London, 1871] (new edition, Peking: Foreign Languages Press, 1966).

Plessis, Alain, *The Rise and Fall of the Second Empire, 1852–1871* (Cambridge University Press, 1985).

Tombs, Robert, *The Paris Commune 1871* (London, Longman 1999).

---

**ROBERT TOMBS** is Reader in French History at Cambridge University and a Fellow of St John's College.

---

From *History Review*, September, 1999, pp. 36–41. Copyright © 1999 by History Today, Ltd. Reprinted by permission.

# UNIT 3

# The Industrial and Scientific Revolutions

## Unit Selections

## Key Points to Consider

- What were Isaac Newton's major contributions to the history of science? How does his work continue to influence our world today?

- Why has John Locke's work had such universal appeal? What is his greatest legacy?

- What factors made the Industrial Revolution possible? What positives and negatives did it create?

- What role did the slave trade play in Great Britain's rise to power in the modern world? What was its price?

- What changes took place in Japan during the Meiji Regime during the last half of the nineteenth century? What role did the nation's first railroad play in these new developments?

- What contributions did Engels make to Marx's work? Is "No Marx without Engels" a valid statement?

- What effect did Sputnik have on the United States? What legacy has it left to the world?

## Student Website
www.mhhe.com/cls

## Internet References

**Center for Mars Exploration**
    http://cmex-www.arc.nasa.gov
**Sir Isaac Newton**
    www-gap.dcs.st-and.ac.uk/history/Mathematicians/Newton.html
**Sputnik**
    www.history.nasa.gov/sputnik

The roots of these two revolutions lie in a dramatic shift away from authority and toward observation, away from concept and toward evidence. When Abu Ali al-Hasan, a scientist living in what is now Basra, Iraq, solved the riddle of light, roughly a millennium ago, he refuted both Ptolemy and Aristotle. With a simple appeal to experience—asking people to look at the sun—he established that the source of light is outside the eye.

Sir Isaac Newton continued this pragmatic tilt with his explanatory laws—each based originally in keen observation. Watching an apple fall from a tree led him to postulate the existence of gravity. His most extraordinary discovery was that the same laws that held under the apple tree applied throughout the universe. Humans had come to realize their ability to understand the cosmos. Armed with the confident expectation that the basic laws underlying natural processes could be deciphered, human ingenuity set to work solving human problems.

We should not think of the industrial and scientific revolutions the way we think of political revolutions, such as the French and American Revolutions. Both of those were relatively quick and definitely dramatic. What we call the industrial revolution was, instead, centuries in the making, reaching back to the Middle Ages for its fundamental concepts. Powerful intellectual and religious assumptions needed to be modified before individuals dared to probe nature's deepest mysteries.

The mechanization of labor began in England, where resources, need, and opportunity combined to spur invention. Having used up its forest resources, Britain turned to coal for fuel. As miners dug deeper for coal, water accumulated in the pits, hampering progress. Thomas Newcomen, in the early eighteenth century, designed a practical steam engine to pump and drain the water. From coal mining and steam power had come a source of portable energy that was more reliable than either wind or water power had been.

Ironically, Chinese scientists had developed the concepts of mechanization and mass production as early as the eleventh century. Unlike the British, however, the Chinese chose not to pursue their initial advantage. For reasons that remain unclear, the implications of this technology were never explored. Within a relatively short time, China fell behind in the race toward technological mastery. Japan, by contrast, imported industrial technology and used it to build a modern rail system that revolutionized and modernized the country. The decision of the Meiji government to modernize Japan on its own terms led to the introduction of the telegraph, telephone, and wireless radio.

It was the West, however, that fully exploited the possibilities of industrial technology. A good example of this is the laying of the transatlantic cable that connected nations on both sides of the Atlantic Ocean in 1866. This stunning achievement provided instant communication among Western nations and around the world, forever altering political and economic realities. Living in what is called an "information age," we can easily see how the flow of information determines success or failure in business, military, and social systems.

© Brand X Pictures/PunchStock

Equally revolutionary in the history of ideas were the theories of Charles Darwin and Sigmund Freud. As technology speeds up communications, and as we have access to greater and greater quantities of information, we remain puzzled about our own place in the cosmos. Darwin's claim that humans are descended from apes was deeply shocking to people who had come to think of themselves as a little lower than the angels. And Freud's contention that we are prisoners to our subconscious urges further eroded assumptions of human uniqueness and intellectuality. Our scientific and technological progress has been amazing. But, we have yet to match that progress in the development of our social systems. Are we more enlightened than our counterparts of 500 years ago? Have we surpassed them in morality? Although Sputnik and its many successors have opened the cosmos to our exploration, it seems that the "full human and humane heritage" of the scientific and industrial revolutions remains unexplored.

# In God's Place

**With his discovery of gravity, Newton taught that understanding the cosmos is not confined to the divine.**

ALAN LIGHTMAN

Giovanni di Paolo's 15th-century painting "The Creation of the World and the Expulsion from Paradise," which hangs in the Metropolitan Museum of Art in New York, offers an unexpected synthesis of Western art, religion and thought.

The picture has a split-level appearance. On the right is the title scene: a grove of fruit trees, the Garden of Eden and the frail, ashamed figures of Adam and Eve being shoved out by an angel. The left half is dominated by concentric spheres. At the middle is the earth, center of the universe, encircled by the planets and sun. An outermost sphere contains the stars, all straight out of Aristotle's "On the Heavens." Above this cosmic hierarchy floats a divine God, who gravely reaches down with an index finger to spin His heavenly spheres.

This painting presents a doubled portrait of the fierce boundary between human and divine. Aristotle made all terrestrial phenomena out of earth, air, water and fire. For the moon, the sun and the stars, however, he decided he needed to introduce a completely new kind of substance: the *divine* ether. Adam and Eve were banished from Eden for crossing a more local boundary and eating from the tree of knowledge, God's knowledge. As it turns out, the forbidding separations of substance and place in Aristotle's cosmology seem to resonate with the forbidden knowledge, transgression and guilt in Judeo-Christian theology. In both cases, and on both sides of di Paolo's painting, the proper domain of human existence and understanding is severely restricted.

Indeed, for centuries Western culture was ingrained with the notion that some areas of knowledge are inaccessible, or forbidden, to human possession. In this view, humankind is entitled to comprehend only what God deigns to reveal. Zeus chained Prometheus to a rock for giving fire, the secret of the gods and the wellspring of advanced civilization, to mortal man. St. Thomas Aquinas (1225–74) distinguished between scientific knowledge, discoverable by the human mind, and divine knowledge, "higher than man's knowledge." Divine knowledge could "not be sought by man through his reason, nevertheless, once . . . revealed by God [it] must be accepted by faith." When Dante

asks the divine Beatrice about the mysteries of the moon, she replies that "the opinion of mortals errs where the key of sense does not unlock." When Adam, in Milton's "Paradise Lost" (1667), questions the angel Raphael about celestial mechanics, Raphael offers some vague hints and then says that "the rest from Man or Angel the great Architect did wisely to conceal, and not divulge His secrets to be scann'd by them who ought rather admire."

The idea that there are limits to the rightful scope of human knowledge is, of course, partly a cultural belief. Surrounding it is an entire worldview, an understanding of how the cosmos is put together, spiritually and physically, and where we fit into the grand scheme. But the idea is also deeply psychological. It is an introspection, a state of mind that subtly imprisons individual thinkers as well as societies, and its effects and ramifications cannot possibly be weighed. No one can say how the history of civilization would have changed if God had never forbidden us to taste from that tree. However, a number of developments over the 16th and 17th centuries did succeed in introducing a new belief: that the entirety of the universe, at least its physical parts, was knowable and discoverable by human beings. This new belief, a belief in the unfettered entitlement to knowledge, was the most important intellectual development along the lengthy time line of the past millennium.

Perhaps the most glorious culmination of the new thinking was Isaac Newton's "Principia" (1687). This monumental treatise established fundamental ideas like inertia and force, articulated general laws of motion of bodies under general forces and proposed a specific law for the force of gravity. Newton's book was unprecedented in the history of science and played a pivotal role in the birth of modern science. But what was most important about Newton's work was not his particular law of gravity, great as it is, but the universality and unbounded application of that law. The same gravity that caused an apple to fall from a tree also caused the moon to orbit the earth, and these trajectories, and an infinity of others, could be mathematically calculated from equations that the English physicist and mathematician had discovered on his own. The heavenly bodies were, after all, physical things, like rocks—or inkwells tossed in frustration against a stone fireplace. The "Principia" dealt a mortal blow to Aristotle's strong division between earthly and cosmic phenomena.

Beneath Newton's idea of the universality of gravity, in turn, lay the implicit assumption that the physical universe was knowable by man. This was a new idea in the evolution of human self-awareness, a psychological turning point, a liberation, an empowerment. Without this idea we might never have had Newton. Nor would we have had the intellectual and scientific breakthroughs that followed: Lavoisier's discovery of oxygen and the beginnings of modern chemistry, Mendel's seminal work on genetics, Dalton's concept of the atom, Darwin and Wallace's theory of evolution and natural selection, Maxwell's formulation of the laws of electricity and magnetism, Einstein's relativity, Hubble's discovery of the expanding universe, Watson and Crick's unraveling of DNA and countless other scientific discoveries.

Even Newton's contemporaries realized that the great physicist had achieved something far deeper than his individual laws. Roger Cotes, in his introduction to the second edition of the "Principia," wrote that Newton had reached "discoveries of which the mind of man was thought incapable before. . . . The gates are now set open." Submersed in a scientific and technological culture as we are today—a culture that has been so totally shaped by telephones and microchips, daily reports on the genes of disease or the recession rate of galaxies—it is hard for us to conceive any limitations in knowledge. All things are our province. The universe is our oyster. We are mostly oblivious to the intellectual history that led us to this point. And we take for granted the active part being played by our own psyches.

What produced the new psychology found in Newton's "Principia"? Certainly, changes in religious thought played a role. Martin Luther's proclamations of 1517, which sparked the Protestant Reformation, helped diminish the authority of the church. Despite Luther's vicious anti-Semitism, his argument that every person should be able to read and interpret the Bible for herself, without lock-stepping with the priesthood, encouraged a certain freedom of mind. This religious freedom spread. For example, the subject matter of art turned from almost exclusively religious themes to landscapes, still lifes, interiors and other broad explorations of the secular and natural worlds. Compare Masaccio or Michelangelo with Rembrandt or Vermeer.

There were scientific discoveries as well. On Nov. 11, 1572, soon after sunset, the Danish astronomer Tycho Brahe sighted an intensely bright object in the constellation Cassiopeia that he realized had not been there before. Brahe was the first person to prove that such novae lay beyond the orbit of the moon, within the celestial realm. Brahe had discovered an exploding star, and his discovery exploded the centuries-old belief that the stars were eternal and constant. The divine perfection of the heavens was further questioned when the Italian physicist Galileo turned his new telescope to the moon in 1610 and found the surface "to be not smooth, even, and perfectly spherical, as the great crowd of philosophers have believed about this and other heavenly bodies, but, on the contrary, to be uneven, rough and crowded with depressions and bulges."

Also of enormous influence, in the decades just preceding Newton, were the scientific and philosophical ideas of René Descartes. Most of the great thinkers throughout history have debated the kind of knowledge that is knowable by the human mind, but philosophers before Descartes assumed that at least some certain knowledge already existed. Descartes, for the first time, began a philosophical system by doubting everything, even his own existence. After convincing himself of his own reality ("I think, therefore I am."), he entered a long meditation that eventually established the existence of God.

Descartes helped us to question. He also prefigured Newton's idea of universality of physical law by proposing a universal mechanism himself, namely his "vortices," which swirled here and there through space, like whirlpools in an ocean, directing the motions of planets and other heavenly bodies. Although Descartes's vortices lacked quantitative description and proved finally unworkable, they had the psychological import of explaining and unifying a vast range of terrestrial and cosmic phenomena under one rational system.

One way of looking at these developments is that they altered and clarified the distinction between what one could call a physical universe and a spiritual universe. Little by little, the sacred geography of Aristotle was replaced by a more amorphous and subtle map of the world. In this map, there exists a material universe, which includes all matter and energy: electrons and atoms, light and heat, brains and stars and galaxies. This vast cosmos is subject to the inquiries of science and to rational mathematical laws that we can discover with our minds.

---

**Science can push back the equations of modern cosmology to less than a nanosecond after the 'big bang,' but it cannot answer the question of why the universe came into being. Science can, in principle, explain all human behavior in terms of biochemical processes in the brain, but science can never determine what is ethical behavior.**

---

Coexisting with this physical universe is a spiritual one, not quantifiable, not located in space, not made of atoms and molecules but, to believers, pervasive nonetheless. Each universe poses an infinity of important questions. It is the physical universe, not the spiritual, that is the domain of science. Science has everything to say about the physical universe and nothing to say about its spiritual counterpart. Science can push back the equations of modern cosmology to less than a nanosecond after the "big bang," but science cannot answer the question of why the universe came into being in the first place or whether it has any purpose. Science can, in principle, explain all human behavior in terms of biochemical processes in the brain, but science can never determine what is ethical behavior.

These new perceptions did not happen quickly, neatly or with finality. Like all deep psychological seeds, the idea that some areas of knowledge are off-limits to human beings is not easily excised from our consciousness. The scientist in Mary Shelley's "Frankenstein" (1818), a novel significantly subtitled "The Modern Prometheus," laments, "Learn from me . . . how dangerous is the acquirement of knowledge, and how much happier that man is who believes his native town to be the world, than he who aspires to become greater than his nature will allow." Some of the horror at the first test of the atom bomb in New Mexico was surely that we had unleashed forces greater than our nature. Soon after the Second World War, J. Robert Oppenheimer, the head of the Manhattan Project, told an audience that "we thought of the legend of Prometheus, of that deep sense of guilt in man's new powers." The troubled public reaction to Dolly, the first adult mammal to be cloned, shows that our fear remains. The sheep's human manipulators were described by *The New York Times* as having "suddenly pried open one of the most forbidden—and tantalizing—doors of modern life."

Most likely, each new door opened will continue to disturb us and play upon our guilt. We are advanced and we are primitive at the same time. We are Newton's flight of mind and we are Prometheus chained to a rock, we are Watson and Crick and we are Adam and Eve. All of it, all of the centuries of liberation and imprisonment, creation and dread, live together in one house. And each new door opened will disturb us. Yet we will keep opening the doors; we cannot be stopped.

**ALAN LIGHTMAN,** the author of *Einstein's Dreams,* is Burchard Professor of Humanities and a senior lecturer in physics at M.I.T.

# John Locke: Icon of Liberty

**Mark Goldie traces the ways in which people across the political spectrum have used and abused the ideas of the philosopher who died 300 years ago this month.**

MARK GOLDIE

The english do not celebrate their philosophers. In Paris there is a rue Descartes. In Edinburgh there is a statue of David Hume. But in England there is no public fanfare for John Locke (1623–1704), the tercentenary of whose death falls on October 28th this year. You will find his portrait in the National Portrait Gallery, but demand is insufficient for a postcard to be on sale. Perhaps Locke would not have minded that accolades are conferred instead on his friend Isaac Newton. He modestly wrote in the preface to his *Essay Concerning Human Understanding* (1689) that he was but an 'under-labourer in clearing ground' for such 'master-builders' in the 'commonwealth of learning' as Newton and Boyle.

Nor would Locke have wished his life to be remembered. He was indifferent to biography and reticent, even secretive, about himself. When the philosopher Damaris Masham wrote her memoir of him, she could not report his year of birth, though they had lived together for fourteen years from 1690. Like another of his friends, Sir Christopher Wren, whose epitaph in St Paul's Cathedral invites us to 'look around', Locke's epitaph at High Laver in Essex invites us to 'learn from his writings' rather than engage in 'dubious eulogies'.

Yet Locke has not escaped canonisation, and it was for his writings that he became an icon. Today he is lauded in the United States far more than in his own country. There, because of his *Two Treatises of Government* (1689) in which he argued that, to be legitimate, a government required the consent of its people, he is hailed as 'the philosopher of freedom', the 'founder of liberalism'. The American political tradition is grounded in Year One, the Revolution, and it invokes Founding Fathers. The belief is in-grained that Locke was the inspiration behind Adams, Jefferson, and Washington. When the American newspapers of the 1760s denounced George III they quoted the *Two Treatises*. Governments, wrote Locke, may not 'levy taxes on the people' without 'the consent . . . of their representatives'. In 1773 the *Boston Gazette* hailed the American edition of the *Second Treatise* as providing 'a better view of the rights of men . . . than all the discourses on government . . . in our language'.

In contemporary America Locke or, rather, an imagined heritage 'Locke', is a mascot of right-wing think-tanks. The Locke Foundation and Locke Institute teach the virtues of free enterprise and the evils of big government. LibertyOnline offers the *Two Treatises* in its virtual library, where it is placed in a litany of great texts of freedom from Magna Carta to Ronald Reagan's 'evil empire' speech against the Soviet Union. The National Rifle Association cites paragraph 137 of the *Second Treatise* as an authority on the right to carry arms. The Arizona State Court Building, opened in 1991, has inscribed upon it words from paragraph 202: 'Where law ends, tyranny begins'.

Locke had once been a British icon too. British Whigs thought of their own regime as grounded in Year One, the Revolution of 1688. Only later did the British insist on telling themselves a myth of organic continuity. The Whigs made Locke a hero of 'Revolution Principles'. Locke encouraged this reading by a remark in the preface to the *Two Treatises*. He announced that his book would 'establish . . . King William . . . in the consent of the people'. An exile in Holland in the 1680s, where he had fled the regimes of Charles II and James II, Locke had sailed back to England in the wake of William of Orange's invasion, and published his *Two Treatises* in the autumn of 1689.

He did not become an icon immediately, however, and he was never an uncontested one. He was revered more for his philosophy than for his politics, and it was his *Thoughts on Education,* not the *Two Treatises,* that ran second to the *Essay Concerning Human Understanding* in numbers of reprints during the eighteenth century. As many historians have insisted, there was far more to political thought in the eighteenth century than Locke and the ideas of consent, the social contract and the right of revolution. The Tories castigated him as a fanatic 'Commonwealth-man', a fomenter of rebellion and anarchy, and a deistical underminer of Christianity. The first pictorial representation of 'Locke on government' appeared in 1710 in a Tory cartoon attacking the Whig pamphleteer Benjamin Hoadly, where Locke appears on the bookshelf behind Hoadly's desk. In one version, Oliver Cromwell stands over Hoadly's shoulder, with regicide's axe in hand; in another, it is the devil who stands there. Ironically, in the reign of Queen Anne Tory hatred of Locke served to make his name better known as

# Life and Works

Locke was born in Wrington, Somerset, in 1632, the son of a country attorney who fought on the Parliamentary side in the Civil War. He attended Westminster School and Christ Church, Oxford, and in 1667 he entered the household of the Earl of Shaftesbury, who became Lord Chancellor but who later led the Whig movement against Charles II. Locke fled to Holland in 1683, returning in the wake of the Glorious Revolution of 1688–89. He then began to publish his books, which had long been in gestation. In the 1690s he served on the Board of Trade and Plantations, advising on colonial and commercial policy. He was involved in the Great Recoinage and the end of press censorship. A polymath, he wrote on philosophy, politics, religion, education, economics, and medicine. He spent the last fourteen years of his life at Oates in Essex, in the household of Damaris Masham, a philosopher. He died in 1704.

Locke's chief philosophical work is the *Essay Concerning Human Understanding* (1689). It insisted that the purpose of philosophy was not to produce systems but to clarify thinking, and argued that all human knowledge derived from experience. *The Two Treatises of Government* (1689) attacked divine-right absolutism and advocated a right of revolution against tyranny. The task of government was to protect our natural rights and no government was legitimate unless grounded in the consent of the people. In *A Letter Concerning Toleration* (1689), he argued against coercion in religion. Churches were voluntary associations and the saving of souls was no business of the state. *Some Thoughts Concerning Education* (1693) was a handbook for parents in the nurturing and character formation of children.

The last of Locke's principal works was *The Reasonableness of Christianity* (1695), minimalist as to Christian doctrine, and reflecting his fear of clerical power and of religious 'enthusiasm' or fanaticism.

a theorist of politics. One of his critics was the Tory feminist Mary Astell, who attacked Whig philosophy because it deposed monarchical tyrants while leaving husbandly tyranny intact. 'If all men are born free, how is that all women are born slaves?'

Despite Tory assaults, Locke became an icon. The trend was set round 1730 by George II's consort, Caroline of Ansbach, who commissioned a bust of Locke for her hermitage at Richmond. He was one of five heroes installed there, with Boyle, Newton, and the latitudinarian clerics Clarke and Wollaston. *The Gentleman's Magazine* ran a poetry Competition which made the grotto famous, and yielded reams of egregious verse.

> Within on curious marble carv'd compleat,
> Majestic Boyle claims a superior seat,
> Newton and Locke, Clarke, Wollaston appear,
> Drest with the native robes they us'd to wear,
> Immortal bards, and as divine their name,
> Dear to their country and as dear to fame.

The *Magazine* published panegyrics to the wisdom of Caroline, the people's princess:

> When her majesty consecrated these dead heroes, she built herself a temple in the hearts of the people of England; who will, by this instance of her love to liberty and public virtue, think their interests as safe in the hands of the government as their own.

If Caroline brought Locke to Court, other adepts at political garden art placed Locke among the heroes of the Country opposition. About the same time, Lord Cobham transformed his estate at Stowe near Buckingham into a rural allegory of the fate of political liberty under the rule of perverted Whiggery. In his Elysian Fields he built a sturdy Temple of Ancient Virtue and a ruinous Temple of Modern Virtue. The ensemble culminated in the Temple of British Worthies. Here he placed busts of Elizabeth I, William III, John Hampden, Milton, and Locke. To these he added the Black Prince, a model for the current Prince of Wales, Frederick, who, it was hoped, would restore liberty when his father died. Lastly came King Alfred, whom Cobham called the 'founder of the English constitution'. The inscription under Locke is as follows:

> JOHN LOCKE, who, best of all philosophers, understood the powers of the human mind; the nature, end, and bounds of civil government; and, with equal courage and sagacity, refuted the slavish systems of usurped authority over the rights, the consciences, or the reason of mankind.

Stowe became a site for tourists, and remains so. Gilbert West's versified guidebook of 1732, *The Gardens of . . . Lord Viscount Cobham*, hailed each bust in turn, dwelling in Locke's case on religious toleration:

> Next Locke, who in defence of conscience rose,
> And strove religious rancour to compose:
> Justly opposing every human test,
> Since God alone can judge who serves him best.

Shortly afterwards, Voltaire published his *Letters on England*, which ignited Locke's European fame. In Georgian England, Locke became constantly vaunted. John Clarke's *Essay upon Study* (1731) recommended reading Locke's books every year, 'even the driest'. Samuel Richardson's novels *Pamela* and *Clarissa* treated the reader to meditations on Locke's *Thoughts on Education*. In Francis Coventry's children's book *The History of Pompey the Little* (1751), young Lady Sophister tells Dr Rhubarb that Locke is her favourite philosopher. It was said of William Warburton that he had Locke's works 'bound up in small detached pieces, for the convenience of carrying them with him'. Locke was lauded in poetry, for instance in Isaac Watt's *To John Locke* (1706) and in James Thomson's *Seasons* (1730).

The radical publisher Thomas Holles named a Dorset estate 'Locke Farm'. The merchant Sir Gerard Vanneck decorated his library at Heveningham Hall, Suffolk, with medallion portraits, Locke standing alongside Homer, Virgil, Shakespeare, Milton, Dryden, Pope, Prior, Voltaire, and Rousseau. In 1809 a subscription was launched to place a statue of Locke in St Paul's Cathedral. Richard Westmacott's model was open for inspection at his workshop and subscribers were to receive from Messrs Boulton—the firm that built Watt's steam engine—a bronze or silver medal. In 1835 a statue of Locke was placed by the Duke of Bedford in his Temple of Liberty at Woburn. The tympanum carried a relief of Liberty, bearing her spear and cap of liberty, attended by Peace and Plenty.

Locke became a plastercast saint of the blandest kind. In the 1730s, Samuel Strutt had remarked that in Locke 'a great many as implicitly believe, as Roman Catholics do transubstantiation'. A century later Henry Acton wrote that 'his life appears to have been one uninterrupted course of innocence, piety, and goodness', he was 'one of the noblest intellectual benefactors of his race'. To Locke, wrote Leigh Hunt in 1810, 'every Englishman owes love and reverence'.

Yet the story of Locke's reputation is more complex. Politically, he seems to have become domesticated and tamed during the first half of the eighteenth century. In a compilation of 1753 called *Of Civil Polity,* selections from Locke were combined with extracts from popular sermons. Locke was cast as a preacher of social duties and family values. Then, after 1760, he was seized upon by radical movements which, in the wake of panics provoked by the American and French Revolutions, provoked renewed Tory counterattacks against him.

During the last thirty years of the eighteenth century a struggle ensued for his soul. The engagement began with the use of Locke by pro-Americans in the Stamp Act crisis, and, in domestic politics, in debates over George III's alleged ambitions to revive royal power. Between 1778 and 1783 there were half-a-dozen tracts specifically addressing Locke's politics. In 1785, the philosophical writer William Paley (1743–1805) observed that, in recent years, in

> . . . the language of party, in the resolutions of popular meetings, in debate, in conversation, in the general strain of those fugitive and diurnal addresses to the public, which such occasions call forth, it was impossible not to observe the prevalency of those ideas of civil authority which are displayed in the works of Mr Locke. The credit of that great name, the courage and liberality of his principles, the skill and clearness with which his arguments are proposed, no less than the weight of the arguments themselves, have given a reputation and currency to his opinions.

In 1783 a Dublin tract complained that 'even shopkeepers might be heard quoting Locke'.

Locke had become the common currency of a new populist politics. He was cited by the Wilkites, the Societies for Constitutional Information, and the London Corresponding Society, in their campaigns for a wider franchise and regular elections. Locke became a hero of the Dissenters, who demanded an end to their civil disabilities. He was the cynosure of latitudinarian Anglicans who wished to ease their consciences of the doctrinal impositions of the Established Church. He was quoted by the friends of the American and Irish causes.

In the House of Commons in 1776, John Wilkes recited from the *Two Treatises* in demanding 'fair and equal representation'.

For the political reformer John Cartwright, Locke's remark that every man must consent upon coming of age was used to support his campaign for annual parliaments, on the ground that prolonged parliaments were a deprivation of each young man's right of formal entry into civil society. In 1795, the radical lawyer Thomas Erskine contrived to turn paragraphs 157–8 of the *Second Treatise* into an argument for universal manhood suffrage. It was a usage which persisted in the *Black Dwarf* and *Northern Star,* the newspapers of the Chartists in the 1840s.

By the late eighteenth century, Locke was doing service in a decisive shift in political ideas away from the traditional ideal of the tripartite constitution of King, Lords and Commons, towards the democratic conception of the sovereign people, and a theory of representation grounded in personhood rather than property. A critic of these movements, Baptist Noel Turner, complained that the old idea of the aristocracy as the 'intermediate power', the counterbalance between crown and people, was in danger of destruction by the craze for a 'democratical' reading of Locke. 'The majesty of the people' will reduce the king to 'a mere signing clerk'.

Locke underpinned the two most signal political testaments to appear from the leaders of Rational Dissent, Joseph Priestley's *Essay on the First Principles of Government* (1768) and Richard Price's *Observations on the Nature of Civil Liberty* (1776). Here a distinctively modern liberalism emerged, marked by an accent on free enquiry and the value of pluralism in modes of life and opinion. In 1787 Charles James Fox cited Locke in a Commons debate on the repeal of the religious Tests. Dissent and pro-American sentiment came together in a cartoon of 1768. Called 'An Attempt to Land a Bishop in America', it showed a ship carrying a bishop being attacked by colonists. One man shouts 'No Lords Spiritual or Temporal in New England'. Another carries a flag declaring 'Liberty and Freedom of Conscience'. And a third waves a book, inscribed 'Locke'.

In the 1780s and 1790s Locke's *Two Treatises* was abridged and anthologised in a series of popular tracts. Extracts appeared in Thomas Spence's brazenly populist *Pig's Meat* (the title a reference to Edmund Burke's sneer against 'the swinish multitude'). A handy forty-two page pamphlet, *The Spirit of John Locke,* extracted Locke on consent, constituent power, restraints on governmental tyranny and revolution. 'Men being all free, equal, and independent' was its opening line, from paragraph 95 of the *Second Treatise*. The jurist Sir William Jones translated Lockean precepts into vernacular simplicities in his *Dialogue between a Scholar and a Peasant.* His brother-in-law was prosecuted for sedition for distributing it.

That Locke became the instrument of libertarian politics will not surprise modern readers. That he became an instrument of what might be called, at least in shorthand, 'socialist' politics, will surprise some, especially in the American neo-con think tanks. By the close of the eighteenth century, at a time of rural poverty, economic dislocation, crisis in Poor Law provision, and steadily diminishing scope for commoners' rights of access to natural resources, manifestos multiplied on behalf of the rural poor against oppressive landlords. Locke's basing of property-right in labour and his stipulation of a natural right to the means of subsistence served such campaigners well. An intellectual tradition of 'Lockean socialism' ran from Thomas Spence's *Rights of Man* in 1775 through to Thomas Hodgskin's *Natural and Artificial Right of Property* in 1832. Spence imagined communitarian utopias. Hodgskin used the newly coined word 'capitalism' to define an economic system which he saw as contrary to Locke's principles. In 1796 the radical John Thelwall, with Locke in hand, denounced the 'territorial monopolist' and defended the right of common access to 'the means of being usefully industrious . . . the common right of all'. George Dyer, in his *Complaints of the Poor People of England* (1793), cited Locke for the principle that the gifts of nature remain in common till a man 'by his own industry' acquires a right over them. Providence had never decreed that

> . . . the squire may shoot a partridge or a pheasant, though the labourer shall not; or that Sir Robert may draw the fish out of the river, and that his poor tenant shall be imprisoned for the same action.

For conservatives, Locke had become a dangerous figure, an icon in need of smashing. In 1783 Baptist Noel Turner issued a *True Alarm . . . A Descant on the Present National Propensity*. The 'present national propensity' was the deployment of Locke on behalf of the 'many-headed majesty' of 'king-people'. Yet, even in Turner there was a note of apology for Locke, a desire to protect him from himself, for Locke's exaggerations were, he said, 'natural enough . . . at the first dawning of liberty'.

A breeze of criticism of Locke gathered into a storm. The sense that Locke's philosophy had been misappropriated increasingly turned into a conviction that it was erroneous. An intense debate on Locke in the years 1778–83 opened with the pugnacious Josiah Tucker's *The Notions of Mr. Locke and his Followers*. Tucker became obsessed with repudiating Locke. He turned his tract into a much longer *Treatise Concerning Civil Government* (1781). It was the most intelligent and sustained critique of Locke of the century. He again repeated himself in an essay of 1783, on 'The Evil Consequences Arising from the Propagation of Mr. Locke's Democratical Principles'.

These were not just books for scholars. The cartoonists noticed the bookish battle for Locke too. A radical print of 1783 showed a pile of books, by Locke and the republican Algernon Sidney and Catherine Macaulay, on the floor, parcelled up for sale. On the desk were books by Josiah Tucker and his colleague, Soame Jenyns. Seated at the desk, a government fox pens a manifesto in favour of kingly prerogative and war against America. Out of doors, a speaker addresses the crowd, 'Lord North . . . butchered your American brethren . . . The king is your servant—Each of you gentlemen ought to have voices in the House of Commons'. The poets joined the fray too. William Mason's *The Dean and the Squire* lampooned a conversation in a Bond Street coffeehouse between Dean Tucker and Squire Jenyns. Tucker opens:

> *Squire Jenyns, since with like intent*
> *We both have writ on government,*
> *And both stand stubborn as a rock*
> *Against the principles of Locke.*
> *Let us, like brother meeting brother,*
> *Compare our notes with one another.*

Jenyns, who was a facile and shallow polemicist compared with Tucker, breezily announced that he had refuted the Whigs' philosophy:

> *I controvert those five positions,*
> *Which Whigs pretend are the conditions*
> *Of civil rule and liberty;*
> *That men are equal born—and free—*
> *That kings derive their lawful sway*
> *All from the people's yea and nay—*
> *That compact is the only ground,*
> *On which a prince his rights can found—*
> *Lastly, I scout that idle notion,*
> *That government is put in motion,*
> *And stopt again, like clock or chime,*
> *Just as we want them to keep time.*

'Sblood! . . . controvert them all?', exclaimed the dean, impressed at Jenyns' brisk temerity.

The attack on Lockeanism signalled the revival of Toryism and the emergence of modern conservatism. The new conservatism was of diverse sorts. In Tucker, it took the form of a secular argument which viewed liberty and authority as the fragile products of political evolution, threatened by the naive dogma that by natural birthright men are 'free and equal' and subject to nothing but what they choose. Others appealed to divine providence and the sanctity of ordained hierarchies.

The French Revolution, and Edmund Burke's savage assault upon it, dealt a heavy blow to Locke's reputation. Burke himself was silent about Locke in his *Reflections on the Revolution in France* (1790), but others filled the gap. 'Mr Locke', blustered William Jones in 1798, is

> . . . the oracle of those who began and conducted the American Revolution, which led to the French Revolution; which will lead (unless God in his mercy interfere) to the total overthrow of religion and government in this kingdom, perhaps in the whole Christian world.

'With Mr Locke in his hand' that 'mischievous infidel Voltaire' had set about destroying Christianity. In 1798 there appeared the first edition of the *Two Treatises* to carry editorial footnotes. This was the work of an Irish Protestant bishop, Thomas Elrington, whose aim was to mitigate Locke's text by adding conservative readings in the notes. One footnote, on the right to overturn governments (paragraph 223), said that 'the answer Mr Locke gives is . . . partial and imperfect . . . as the events of the present time but too clearly prove'.

Whether Locke was an author of sedition became a matter of courtroom debate in the treason trial of the boot-maker and agitator Thomas Hardy in 1794. His defence counsel insisted that Hardy had said no more than what Locke had said, and hoped that Locke remained a sufficiently respectable symbol to save Hardy from the gallows. Hardy was indeed saved, but Locke fell victim to the Counter-Enlightenment. In 1815 his portrait was taken down from the hall of his old college in Oxford, Christ Church, from which he had been expelled by order of Charles II in 1684. The Dissenting journal *The Monthly Repository* lamented that this was 'Locke's second expulsion from Oxford'.

In the nineteenth and early twentieth centuries, Romantics, utilitarians, Marxians, Evangelicals, and high churchmen all had their different reasons for passing Locke by. In the second half of the twentieth century, interest in Locke's political ideas revived, especially after the collapse of Marxism and with the resurgence of several contested varieties of liberalism. Today, of the one hundred volumes in the series Cambridge Texts in the History of Political Thought, Locke's *Two Treatises* is the bestselling item.

# For Further Reading

John Locke, *Two Treatises of Government,* ed Peter Laslett (CUP, 1988) or ed. Mark Goldie (Everyman, 1993); *John Locke, Political Essays,* ed. Mark Goldie (CUP, 1997); John Locke, *Selected Correspondence,* ed. Mark Goldie (OUP, 2002); John Locke, *A Letter Concerning Toleration,* ed James Tully (Hackett, 1983); John Dunn, *Locke: A Very Short Introduction* (OUP, 2003).

**MARK GOLDIE** teaches history at Cambridge University. He is editor of *The Reception of Locke's Politics* (6 vols., London, 1999) and *John Locke: Selected Correspondence* (Oxford, 2002).

# The Workshop of a New Society

**The industrial revolution gave an utterly new shape to Britain's economy, its population, its cities and its society. But not quite as fast as is supposed.**

## 1670–1850

Britain's industrial revolution was more than that. In most senses, it was a revolution of society too. A mainland population of maybe 6m–7m in 1700 was put at 10.7m by the first official census in 1801, 20.9m in 1851 and 37.1m by 1901. A nation of countrymen went to town. Agriculture's share of male employment fell between 1700 and 1850 from about 60% to about 25%; industry's rose from under 20% to around 50%. And as industrialists built steam-powered factories near the markets, the one Briton in six living in town in 1700 became by 1850 one in two.

The industrial change, however, was neither as swift nor as complete as is often thought. Tradition describes a roaring take-off between 1770 and 1830, driven by a handful of technological innovations, such as textile machinery and James Watt's improved steam engines; and, hey presto, Britain is "the workshop of the world". In fact, the process had begun in the 17th century and was still incomplete in the 1830s, by when only a few industries—mining, metal-working, textiles, brewing—had taken to "factory" methods.

Technological change, important as it was, was not the be-all and end-all. Nor yet did it start with the machine-builders. They depended on earlier advances in iron technology that enabled that industry to produce, in quantity, better and cheaper iron goods such as components for the new machines or for structural use. And, from around 1670, other factors were at work.

One was the development of coal as a fuel, as the cost of wood rose. Next, the growth of thriving rural industries, supplementing farm incomes, which laid the basis for a skilled industrial workforce. Third, the increasing commercialisation of manufacturing, to meet rising demand for cheaper cloth and metal goods from the growing urban elites in Britain and mainland Europe, and from British colonies.

Britain was helped too by easy access to the sea, political stability and light regulation of trade, finance and industry. It also developed a highly specialised workforce, speeding up the development of new products and processes. Industrial output, according to one modern estimate, rose by 0.7% a year between 1700 and 1760, by 1.3% in the 1760s and 1770s, 2.0% in the 1780s and 1790s, and 2.8% between 1800 and 1830.

Work changed, and more than that, as manpower and water power gave way to steam and machines, and rural craftsmanship to urban factories manned by unskilled labour. For some, work vanished. Rural weavers put up a desperate fight for their jobs, marching, petitioning Parliament and burning mills and machinery such as Daniel Burton's textile factory in Middleton, Lancashire, in 1812, but all in vain.

The new factory workers who took their place were mostly unskilled, and earned less than the craftsmen had. Yet for the many men, women and children who flocked to the factory gate, the pay on offer was better than they had earned as farmhands or servants. And as one skill died, new ones were needed: those of tool- or machine-builders, or—almost a new class—foremen.

One aspect of factory life was universally hated by the workforce. Considerations of productivity and safety led employers to regulate all aspects of life in the factory: working hours, breaks and movement inside "the works." Many workers resisted what they saw as infringements of individual freedom, and some of the traditions of the small workshops survived for a while. Employers had to fight hard for the demise of "Saint Monday", when men went to the pub after work on Saturday and did not return until Tuesday morning, disrupting production in spite of (or by) their frantic efforts to catch up by the end of the week.

The clergy and the good-hearted middle classes worried much about their inferiors' morality, as men and women in the mass flocked into the new workplaces. Some industrialists tried to prevent workmen entering parts of the factory where women worked—without much success. In time, awkward-squad parts of the middle class began to worry about the employers' social morality too: Mrs. Gaskell's "North and South" offers an early illustration.

Outside "the works" too, conditions altered greatly. Overcrowding, in jerry-built housing in the much-polluted new towns, brought ill-health; at its worst, the devastating cholera epidemics of 1831–32, 1848 and 1854–55. Despite efforts by some employers, charities and eventually local authorities, improvement was slow before the end of the 19th century. Yet a new, mass urban society was born, and not all of its life was the misery depicted by writers from Dickens to D.H. Lawrence. Our deprived Victorian ancestors were quite good at enjoying themselves.

The most obvious beneficiaries of the industrial revolution were the new "barons" such as the Whitbreads in brewing, the Guests in iron or the Strutts in the cotton industry. But the landed classes too profited, from mineral royalties, rises in urban land values and their own investment in industrial concerns. The greatest gainers, though, were the working class, whose living standards rose from 1820 onward, after 70 years of stagnation. This rise accelerated between 1870 and 1900, when real wages, consumption and life expectancy all rose sharply.

Simultaneously, new forms of leisure emerged, which became synonymous with the British working class: football matches, social clubs, seaside resorts. By 1900, the ordinary Briton was better paid, fed, clothed, housed, educated, perhaps amused and certainly better represented in politics, than his forefathers could have dreamed of.

Not everyone was content. Lawrence was soon to pour out his ample bile on the machine world. In 1933, J. B. Priestley lamented that it was "as if the country had devoted a hundred years of its life to keeping gigantic sooty pigs. And the people who were choked by the reek of the sties did not get the bacon." Actually, they got quite a lot. Whether that was a fair share is a separate story.

# Slavery and the British

JAMES WALVIN

The enforced movement of more than eleven million Africans onto the Atlantic slave ships, and the scattering of over ten million survivors across the colonies of the Americas between the late sixteenth and early nineteenth centuries, transformed the face of the Americas. It also enhanced the material well-being both of European settlers and their homelands. The cost was paid, of course, by Africa: a haemorrhage of humanity from vast reaches of the continent, the exact consequences, even now, unknown. Though they were not its pioneers, by the mid-eighteenth century the British had come to dominate Atlantic slavery, a fact which in turn helped to shape much of Britain's status and power.

Historians have become increasingly interested in the concept of an Atlantic world: a world that embraced the maritime and littoral societies of Europe, Africa and the Americas, and one in which slavery played a crucial role. The Atlantic system developed a gravitational pull that drew to it many more societies than those formally committed to African slavery. Even the economies of Asia were ultimately linked to African slavery. European ships, bound for the slave coast of Africa, brimmed not simply with produce from their home towns, their hinterland and from Europe, but also with goods transhipped from Asia. Firearms from Birmingham, French wines, Indian textiles, cowrie shells from the Maldives, food from Ireland, all were packed into the holds of outbound ships, destined to be exchanged for Africans.

The bartering and trading systems on the coast fed a voracious demand for imported goods that stretched far deeper into the African interior than Europeans had seen or visited. In return, the traders who settled on the coast, and the transient captains, gradually filled the holds of their ships (suitably rearranged for human cargoes) with Africans.

European, American and Brazilian traders flitted nervously up and down the west African coast, always anxious to make a quick exchange and quit the dangers of the region for the welcoming currents that would speed their Atlantic crossing to the expectant markets of the Americas. We have details of some 26,000 voyages throughout the recorded history of the slave trade. Once described as a 'triangular trade,' it was in fact a trading system of great geographical complexity, with routes cutting from Brazil to Africa, from North America to Africa and back, between Europe and the Caribbean—and of direct routes from the slave colonies back to the European heartlands. Ships crisscrossed the north and south Atlantic Caribbean, ferrying Africans and goods needed by all slave societies, finally hauling the vast cargoes of slave-grown produce back to European markets, to sate the appetite of the Western world for tropical and semi-tropical staples. This trading complexity was compounded by commercial transactions with native peoples on the frontiers of European settlement and advancement across the Americas.

This vast network, lubricated by slavery, drew together hugely different peoples from all over the world. Africans in the Caribbean dressed in textiles produced in India, used tools made in Sheffield, and produced rum drunk by indigenous native peoples of the Americas. Tobacco cultivated by slaves in the Chesapeake was widely consumed, from Africa itself to the early penal colonies of Australia.

Though Africans were present in many of the early European settlements in the Americas, the drift towards African slavery was slow. Europeans tried a host of agricultural and social experiments in the Western Hemisphere before the mid- and late-sixteenth-century Brazilian development of sugar cane cultivation. Sugar had long been grown on plantations in the Mediterranean (it came later to the Atlantic islands), before being transplanted into the Americas in the late sixteenth century. But sugar plantations, even in their early form, were labour-intensive, and there was not enough labour available among local peoples, or migrating Europeans. Africa, though, could be made to yield people in abundance. From small-scale, haphazard origins (with Europeans tapping into local slave systems), the demand for labour in the New World spawned violent networks of slave-trading along the African coast and deep into the interior.

By the time the British forged their own early seventeenth-century settlements in the Caribbean and North America, black slavery had already taken root in Spanish, Portuguese and Dutch settlements. Informed by this earlier experience, and able to borrow the technologies of sugar cultivation, backed by Dutch money, and with domestic political support, the British found the commercial opportunities afforded by slavery irresistible. But they, too, tried other systems at first.

Sugar changed all. First in Barbados and the Leewards from the 1630s, then in late seventeenth-century Jamaica, British settlers converted ever more acreage into cane cultivation. In Barbados, sugar cultivation hastened the rise of larger plantations and the decline in the number of smallholdings—and, of course, a growing proportion of the population was black and enslaved. In 1650 there were perhaps 300 plantations on the island, by 1670, some 900. The black population in Barbados stood at about 20,000 in 1655 but less than thirty years later it had risen to over 46,000. In the same period, the white population had declined. The conversion of Barbados to a plantation society based on African slave labour was a pattern repeated across the Caribbean.

In the Chesapeake colonies of Virginia and Maryland, the drift to slavery followed local lines of tobacco cultivation (again on plantations), though they differed in size (and nature) from the sugar plantations of the West Indies. Later, in the early eighteenth century, rice cultivation (also on plantations) in the Carolinas was also driven forward by slavery. Though all depended on imported Africans, each region developed a distinctly different slave system. Plantations varied from crop to crop. Slave demography, social life and culture took different trajectories across the enslaved Americas. But one universal fact remained unflinching: the reduction of African humanity to the status and level (in law, economic and social usage) of property.

From the first, the slave's status clashed with a number of European legal and political practices and conventions. Europeans were turning their backs on bondage in their own continent at the very time they were creating and perfecting African slavery in the Atlantic economy. In turn, the expansion of slavery—British ships carried three million Africans between 1680 and 1807—spawned a confusion of justifications, many of which came to hinge on ideas of race; for what could be the justification for the relegation of humanity to the level of chattel, even when colonial (and imperial) law decreed it so? There consequently evolved a protracted social and political debate about colour and 'race' that entered the intellectual bloodstream of the Western world. By the time the slave systems reached their mature form in the English-speaking colonies in the mid-eighteenth century, to be black was to be enslaved: a piece of chattel. The obvious contradictions in such practices and beliefs were there for all to see. Nonetheless, the political (and legal) tensions generated by the property-status of slaves remained. Ultimately, this ideological core of the slave system was fatally fissured by the seismic impact of the French Revolution of 1789 and the *Declaration of the Rights of Man and the Citizen* passed by the Constituent Assembly in France the same year. And in Britain the assertion of equality encapsulated in the abolitionists' motto 'Am I not a Man and a Brother?', adopted in 1787, would ultimately prove corrosive of slavery.

But slavery and the Atlantic slave trade still continued. Even after 1789, the intellectual or political attachment to black freedom was often overridden by economic considerations. For much of its history, slavery had had its critics. But its basic commercial value served to marginalise whatever criticisms were raised by churchmen, philosophers and even political economists. For a long time the material well-being, visible on both sides of the Atlantic, that slavery brought to so many hushed all protest.

The benefits of slave labour could be seen, initially, in the colonies themselves. Africans and their local-born offspring converted swathes of the settled Americas to profitable agriculture.

Though often little more than toe-holds on the American land mass and Caribbean islands, plantations became the means of bringing a luxuriant wilderness into commercial cultivation. Slaves re-ordered the confusions of the natural habitat into fields and fruitful land-holdings, the whole linked by man-made trails and pathways, to local river or coastal docks. Each plantation colony developed its own, often small-scale, urban centres. Towns, cities and ports were both centres of local political power and entrepôts forming a crossroads with the wider world, where goods (and peoples) flowed in from Europe and Africa, and whence produce and profits were dispatched back, across the Atlantic, to Europe.

From the sixteenth to the early nineteenth century, European conflicts were also played out in the Americas, as each emergent colonial power sought to gain advantage over its rival. In the islands, Europeans built massive fortifications to keep other marauding Europeans at bay, and to prevent their own settlements from being destroyed or usurped. The magnificent fortifications that survive along the Caribbean island chain testify to the military threat experienced by each colonising nation, and to the vast expense invested in securing their strongholds. In time, however, the greatest threats came not from other Europeans, but from the enslaved armies toiling reluctantly for their colonial masters. The slave colonies, and the planters in their rural retreats, were permanently embattled against an encircling slave population they vitally needed but never trusted.

Colonial slave societies were held in place not simply by naval and local armed defences, but by ad hoc federations of militia and armed whites (and by the late eighteenth century even by black troops) marshalled to over-awe and stifle any outburst which might erupt from the slave quarters. Throughout the British slave colonies, violence and resistance among the slaves was endemic (as they were wherever slavery existed). But so too was savage and remorseless repression. Slaves resisted their bondage in a variety of ways. From enslavement in Africa, to life in the squalor of the slave ships, through to the more settled but often brutal life on the plantations, slaves found ways to resist. Most spectacularly in the form of open revolt or rebellion, resistance more commonly took the form of mundane acts of non-compliance: feigning stupidity, failing to do what was required, sabotaging owners' plans and instructions, or simply by presenting the sullen reluctance that whites reported across the slave colonies. There were great dangers here for the slaves: resist too much, too far, and retribution would result in all too predictable a fashion. This was true for healthy young men in the fields (generally the most 'troublesome' group) and for their mothers and sisters working as domestics in white households. How far to go—the boundary between the tolerable and the dangerous—was always an early lesson young slaves had to learn from their elders. Throughout, physical assault, a simple cuff or beating, was an ever-present reality.

Not surprisingly, slaves ran away in all slave societies, though physical circumstances often determined what was possible. Barbados for example—much the same size as the Isle of Wight—offered few obvious escape routes once the island had been fully conquered and put into sugar cultivation. But in other colonies where geography allowed, slaves formed 'maroon' societies: communities of runaways, living beyond the pale of plantation life. Maroons were deeply disliked by planters and military alike. Seen as an obvious goal for potential runaways, they were viewed as a threat in many senses. Yet efforts to destroy them generally failed in the teeth of fierce resistance and the physical difficulties of the local environment (mountains or jungle, ideal country for what were, effectively, guerrilla bands.) Where the British could not bring maroons to heel, they were ultimately forced to [work] with them, conceding their independence, most importantly in return for the handing back of further would-be runaways.

Newspapers throughout the slave colonies were filled with advertisements for slave runaways. Most common was the slave runaway heading for a loved-one. While many were clearly on the run from their plantation or owner most were simply seeking family and friends: a lover or spouse, a child or parent. Runaways might more easily escape notice in urban communities. Curiously, at times, slave owners seemed not to mind when slaves ran away (when food was short, for example, or when the demands of the agricultural year were slack), on condition that they returned—eventually. Always, of course, slaves had to prove their right to roam. Unless they had an obvious task to do, slaves on the move were inevitably suspect, and runaways generally moved furtively, needing the help of other slaves for food or shelter. There were, however, many other slaves with a legitimate reason to be on the move—to and from their own markets, between plantations and the nearest river or port, transporting exports and imports, goods and beasts, along the lines of local (and even international) communication.

Open revolt bloodied the history of the slave colonies. The insurrection of the 1790s in the French colony of Haiti was the only example of slaves in the Americas succeeding in the complete destruction of the system that oppressed them, though not for want of trying elsewhere. African slaves (many with military experience in their African homelands) tended to be more resistant than those born in the New World, with numbers trying, but invariably failing, to escape their bondage by plots, revolt and physical defiance. Failure was measured out in bloody retribution by means of summary executions, dismemberments and exemplary tortures which colonial penal codes (to say nothing of plantocratic instinct) made possible. Nowhere was the 'bloody code' more bloody, and more widely used, than in the slave islands. And each failed slave revolt saw a tightening of plantocratic repression: a vicious cycle of resistance and repression which showed no prospect of change.

One element in the growing British disenchantment with slavery was with the brutality required simply to keep the slaves in their place. What might have gone unquestioned in 1700 had, by the 1820s, become unacceptable. By then there was a changing sensibility about slavery that was partly religious, partly secular but which, when placed in the context of growing economic doubts (was slavery really more efficient than free labour?) helped to undermine the metropolitan attachment to a system that had served Britain so well for two centuries. Moreover, as British missionaries began to win over increasing numbers of slaves to their chapels and churches, they reported back to their British congregations the full nature of slave experience and sufferings, to the growing concern of fellow British worshippers.

What kind of system was it that persecuted black Christians, their preachers and their places of worship? By the 1820s few doubted that the British slave system was doomed.

From the late eighteenth century, the adoption of Christianity transformed slave life in the islands. From the first, slaves had evolved distinctive cultures from one colony to another, which blended Africa with local European and colonial life. Belief systems and languages, folk customs (from cooking to health care and dress) and family patterns imported from the slaves' varied African communities, were transformed by the process of enslavement, transportation and settlement in the Americas. Africans in the slave quarters may have sought out their 'own people' (whose language and habits they understood) but they were also forced into the company of other Africans, local-born slaves and Europeans, with whom they had to live and work. The creole cultures that grew from such blendings imposed a distinct style and tone on each and every slave society.

Despite the ubiquitous repression and violence of slavery, slave-owners learned that they secured the best returns on their human capital not by unrelenting pressure, but by allowing free time: breaks at weekends, at high days and holidays. The calendar of the local agricultural year or the Christian Year provided slaves with a breathing space. In those breaks from drudgery, slaves evolved their own particular social activities, investing their breaks with ritual and ceremonies: dressing up in elaborate fashion (in sharp contrast to the everyday dress of the work place), enjoying particular customs with music, food, drink and elaborate carnival. Equally, the patterns of family and community life—notably birth, marriage and death—evolved their own distinctive patterns and rhythms. Outsiders were often amazed at the vigour and material bounty displayed by slaves in their social life. Where and how did they acquire such elaborate clothing and finery: jewellery and musical instruments, money for lavish food and drink? In fact, they bought such luxuries from the fruits of their own labours. Individual skills (such as music-making, nursing, sewing or craftsmanship) could generate earnings. Gardens and plots, tending animals, cultivating foodstuffs and so on, gave slaves the material wherewithal for barter and trade, for sale and purchase. Such efforts formed the basis of the slave markets which came to characterise the slave islands. All this took place after the normal working day: at evenings, weekends or in other free time. It meant that even in their rare moments of leisure slaves had to toil. Whatever advancement they made (and many clearly did make their lives more comfortable) came from their own sweat and application.

The greatest beneficiaries of slave efforts were of course their owners and their imperial backers. This brings us to the thorny issue of profit and loss. For more than fifty years, historians have squabbled about the economics of the British slave system. What role did slavery play in the transformation of Britain itself? More especially, what was its significance in enabling Britain to become an industrial power from the late eighteenth century onwards? Equally, were Britain's decisions to turn its back first on the slave trade (1807), and then on slavery itself (1834), economically inspired? At one level it is implausible to discount the importance of the Atlantic slave system, it was so massive, its ramifications so ubiquitous, its defenders so tenacious in their attachment to it. In the development of Liverpool, for instance, can we ignore the some 6,000 slave voyages that departed from that port? And can we adequately grasp the nature of Bristol's (or London's) earlier, seventeenth-century involvement in the slave trade and settlement of the slave colonies? Moreover, the accountancy of the system—the facts and figures so carefully researched and teased apart by historians in the past twenty-five years—do not always convey the full social impact of slavery on Britain itself. Whatever the level of profit (or loss) of particular voyages, of specific trading companies and plantations, here was a system that by the mid-eighteenth century had become part of the warp and weft of British life itself. To those at home, slavery was, in general, out of mind and out of sight. Yet its consequences, most obviously the fruits of slave labour (the sugar and rum, the tobacco, rice and coffee) served to transform the social life of Britain (and the West in general.) Africa was obliged to consume vast amounts of Western produce in return for bartered slaves. Plantation societies were kept alive by British imports, from the hats on the slaves' heads, to the hoes in their hands, from equipment in the fields, to the wines on the planters' tables. And a host of British ports, with their immediate economic hinterland, thrived on supplying the whole, filling the ships, plying African markets and the American plantations with vital goods and services: with their manpower (black and white), their finance, firepower and military defences. In the enslaved Atlantic, Britain may have ruled the waves. But even the victorious Royal Navy, hard at its massive task of protecting the British colonies and the sea-lanes from the predatory threats of other Europeans, kept its men at their unenviable tasks by lavish helpings of rum. And who made the rum?

The results of slave labours were inescapable, from the smoke-filled atmosphere (courtesy of Virginian tobacco) of London's myriad coffee houses, to the insatiable appetite of British common people for sugar to take with the tea. Yet the slaves were thousands of miles distant. What gave the slave system a local, British focus was that small band of blacks, living in London, mainly domestics, sometimes slaves, who flit in and out of view; in parish registers, fashionable portraits, as the subject of legal arguments, and often the victims of aggression by employer or owners. They serve as a reminder, however apparently removed from the centre of Atlantic slavery, of other Africans, measured in their millions, whose brutal enslavement and transportation was so fundamental a part of the rise to greatness of eighteenth-century Britain.

# For Further Reading

Robin Blackburn, *The Making of New World Slavery* (Verso, 1997); David Eltis, *The Rise of African Slavery in the Americas* (Cambridge University Press, 2000); *The Oxford History of the British Empire: The Eighteenth Century* P. J. Marshall, ed, (Oxford University Press, 1998); James Walvin, *Making the Black Atlantic* (Cassell, 2000).

---

**James Walvin** is Professor of History at the University of York.

# Samurai, Shoguns and the Age of Steam

RON CLOUGH

In 1853 Commodore Matthew C. Perry of the U.S. Navy arrived with a small fleet in Tokyo Bay and coerced the Japanese into bringing to an end a period of 250 years of self-imposed seclusion. This seclusion had not been total, and knowledge of developments in other parts of the world had been brought to Japan via Dutch and Chinese traders who had been granted licenses to trade at Nagasaki, Japan's only official gateway to the outside world, and also from a few Japanese castaway sailors lucky enough to have avoided execution on their return—the almost invariable fate reserved for those feared to have been contaminated by contact with foreign lands.

The government of the Tokugawa shoguns, the military caste who controlled the Emperor, was therefore well aware of the ominous advance of Western power towards the East, and of the defeat of China, from which much of its culture derived, by superior European technology in the Opium War of 1841. In this way, even before Perry's arrival, the Japanese knew of the existence of railways. The first confirmed mention of railways appeared in 1846 in the Fusetsu-sho (regular reports of activities outside Japan presented by the Dutch to the shogunate), which referred to a French plan to build a railway across the Isthmus of Panama, and they were mentioned fairly regularly after that.

In 1851 Nakahima Manjiro, a returned shipwrecked sailor fortunate enough to have escaped the usual execution, gave an account of a railway journey he had made in America in his Narratives of a Castaway:

> Usually when people go on trips they go by a fire burning vehicle known as a 'reirote' [railroad]. This device is shaped like a ship, water is boiled in a cauldron, and with the three of the hot water the device can run about 300 ri [1,200 kms] in a day. When you look outside the house-shaped object, it's as though you were a bird in flight, and there's no time to get a good look at things. They have iron laid along the vehicle's path.

On April 26th, 1860, the first samurai had cause to ride on a train. This was Muragaki Norimasa, who travelled by train between Panama and Colon while on a mission to exchange instruments of ratification of the Japan-U.S. Treaty of Friendship and Commerce. He was surprised that several people could ride together, his previous experience of passenger travel having presumably been limited to the palanquin:

> It's as though a flock of birds was perched on one branch in such a way that the birds are jostling one another.

An attendant on the same mission, Tamamushi Yasushige, made detailed technical notes of everything he saw: rolling stock, signals and track.

Once Japan had opened up there was an immediate influx of foreign officials and merchants who manoeuvred to further their interests with the shogunate, the stability of which became increasingly threatened by the shock of events. The government did not have the strength to resist the 'barbarians,' as many reactionary samurai wanted, and was therefore seen as vacillating and ineffective. The slogan 'expel the barbarians' gradually gave way, in the cold light of experience, to the more practical 'enrich the country and strengthen the military,' with the long-term aim of being able to stand up to the West after taking in its technology. This technology was seen as an important factor in bringing about a new era of 'civilisation and enlightenment.' The shogunate eventually collapsed after a brief civil war in 1867–68 in the face of opposition from the samurai of the western clans, who attached themselves to the cause of the Imperial family which had been cloistered in the old capital of Kyoto during the period of seclusion. A young British diplomat, Ernest Satow, had earlier predicted the likelihood of an Imperial victory over the shoguns and had advised his senior, Sir Harry Parkes, to favour the Imperial forces, whereas the French, also struggling to gain influence, had tended to side with the shogunate. Parkes' tireless lobbying of the new government paid off in the favouritism shown towards the British when it came to awarding contracts for technical advice. The first railways in Japan thus came to have a distinctly British flavour about them.

Notwithstanding the machinations of foreign diplomats, the first proposal for a railway had come from a samurai, Godai Tomoatsu of Satsuma, in 1865, for a line from Kyoto to Osaka, which was rejected. Given the upheavals of the period, it is not surprising that several proposed schemes came to nothing before work finally commenced. One application was accepted by the shogunate on January 17, 1868, for a railway from Edo (now Tokyo) to Yokohama from the American A.L.C. Portman, but this was thwarted when the shogunate collapsed. In commercial terms the demise of this project was fortunate for Japan, as Portman had been guaranteed a full concession to build the railway, whereas the new Meiji government, rejecting the policy of allowing concessions to non-Japanese, ensured that Japan avoided China's fate of having its railways in hock to foreign interests.

In principle the new government was in favour of a railway and accepted the logic that the first route should link Tokyo with other important towns along the populous southern seaboard such as Yokohama, Nagoya, Kyoto, Osaka, and Kobe. This route, the section of which connecting Tokyo and Kyoto was known as the Tokaido, or Eastern Sea Route, was a logical first choice, and it followed that the first sections to be built should be those linking the treaty ports of Yokohama and Kobe to Tokyo and Osaka respectively. Raising capital for such expensive projects as railway construction was not an easy matter, however, particularly as the government wanted to keep foreign investment to a minimum. In the long run the Japanese managed to fund much of the construction themselves, but recourse to foreign loans was occasionally made. Such was the case for the Tokaido line, for which the decision to start building was finally taken in December 1869.

Before this government-sponsored scheme, Thomas Glover, a British merchant living in Nagasaki, laid down a short line along the dockside of that city. A locomotive named the 'Iron Duku' was imported to provide the power. This name was presumably a Japanicised form of the 'Iron Duke' of the Great Western Railway in England, of which it seems to have been a replica.

The Tokaido line project was to be carried out under the auspices of the newly-created Ministry of Works (Kobusho). Horatio Nelson Lay, an Englishman who had run the Chinese Customs service, was approached to negotiate a 1 million [pounds sterling] loan in London, with customs revenues as security. The Japanese, with a sketchy knowledge of British history, may have assumed a connection—wrongly—between Lay and his famous naval near-namesake, and thus considered him trustworthy. They were wrong on this point also. An American business rival, peeved at losing the contract, informed the Japanese government that Lay was fleecing them by charging twelve-and-a-half percent interest on money which he had raised at nine-and-a-half percent in London. His services were dispensed with and responsibility for the loan was passed to the Oriental Bank.

Not surprisingly, there was opposition to the project from traditionalists, and those who feared a heavier tax burden, from traders such as innkeepers along the route, and from hauliers who might feel the pinch of competition, as well as from nationalists who felt the country was being 'sold out' to foreign interests.

Nevertheless in 1870 Edmund Morell, an Englishman who had worked on railways in New Zealand, a country with similar terrain to that of Japan, arrived to take charge of construction. He decided on a 3'6" gauge. The narrow gauge was chosen in the expectation that there would not be a high demand for capacity. This mistaken decision was to bedevil the Japanese railways for years, and remains a problem to this day.

Cultural differences between the British advisers and the Japanese were not easily overcome. The British engineers constantly complained of obstruction by the officials and the inefficient methods of the workmen. E.G. Holtham, who

supervised reconstruction of the Tokyo-Yokohama section in 1877, wrote:

> My native assistants were some of them of a very dreamy temperament, and considered the first thing necessary in all calculations involving inches was to reduce every dimension into decimals of a foot, to six places of decimals at least, and then resorted to books of logarithms to throw some light upon their subject. In this way about a week was required to ascertain how many bricks went to a given-size wall.

Another bone of contention was the insistence of the samurai on wearing their swords, a jealously-guarded status symbol, while being instructed in the use of the surveying instruments. The steel in the swords affected the readings, and it was only after much argument that they were persuaded to discard them temporarily. Also, they found it demeaning to engage in manual labour, whereas the British engineers had no qualms in rolling up their sleeves to help out. For their part, the Japanese complained of the arrogance and overbearing attitude of the British. Evidence of this is found in a phrase-book of the Japanese language published shortly after the opening of the railway, which presumed that the following expressions would be necessary for travel in that country:

> 'You must put on another carriage.' 'I insist on another carriage being put on.'
>
> 'I will complain to the Chief of the Railroad Department if you don't put one on.'

Morell died in November 1871 of either pneumonia or tuberculosis, with work on the section only half-completed. Despite their differences, Morell's work was greatly valued by the Japanese, and a statue of him can now be seen at Sakuragicho Station in Yokohama.

The line was opened to passenger traffic on a single track from Shinagawa, in the southern suburbs of Tokyo, to Yokohama in July 1872. Goods traffic followed on September 15th, 1873. The official opening ceremony at Shinbashi, nearer to Tokyo's centre, took place on October 12th, 1872, with the Emperor himself presiding and many foreign and local dignitaries in attendance. The Emperor took a return trip to Yokohama. Thomas Hart, the British engine driver, was taken to task because, in his anxiety not to be late into Yokohama, he actually arrived early and caused embarrassment among waiting officials who were not ready to receive the Emperor. As an example of nineteenth-century culture shock, it is said that many Japanese stepped out of their shoes when boarding the train as if they were entering a house, and were mortified when the train drew out and the shoes were left behind on the platform.

The railway was largely British-staffed, from engineers and foremen-platelayers to drivers and ticket-collectors. The firemen were Japanese from the outset, however. One European was both ignorant and patronising when he said of the employment of Japanese drivers:

> It would be all very well so long as the train was on a straight line, but I doubt if any Japs could be trusted to steer the engine round those curves!

The first Japanese, in fact, drove a train on the Tokyo-Yokohama section in April 1879.

In the peak years of employment of foreign labour in 1875–6, of foreign employees on the railways ninety-four were British, two American, two German and two Danish. The British were engaged not only as engineering advisers, but also as artisans such as stonemasons and blacksmiths. William Cargill, the Superintendent of Communications, received the highest regular salary: 2,000 [pounds sterling] a month, of any foreign worker in Japan in the Meiji era.

There were three classes of travel, referred to initially as upper, middle and lower, which were renamed first, second and third in 1897. Upper class passengers mainly comprised civil and military officials and foreigners. The middle class fare from Shinbashi to Yokohama was twice that of the lower, and the upper class three times. Despite the expense, the new form of transport proved popular with the paying public. Rates for carrying freight were very competitive. One estimate claims that freight costs between Tokyo and Yokohama were slashed to one-seventieth of the cost of previous methods of transport. In the first full year of freight operations 46,000 tons were carried by rail. By 1887 this had risen to 578,000 and by 1897 to 1,583,000.

In 1872 ten daily trains ran in each direction between Shinbashi and Yokohama, all scheduled to leave on the hour and to take forty-five minutes for the 29 km journey. Locomotive power was provided by ten tank engines made by the Vulcan foundry of Newton-le-Willows in England, which ran until 1930. One is now preserved in Tokyo's Transport Museum. Britain also provided all the passenger cars and goods wagons. These consisted of fifty-eight double-axle wooden passenger coaches divided into three classes, with eighteen seats for the upper, twenty-two for the middle and thirty for the lower class.

Opinions on the new railway were divided. The traveller Isabella Bird wrote in 1878:

> The Yokohama station is a handsome and suitable stone building with a spacious approach, ticket offices on our plan, roomy waiting rooms for different classes—uncarpeted, however, in consideration of Japanese clogs—and supplied with daily papers.

Henry Faulds wrote in 1874:

> The line, constructed by British engineers, is, on the testimony of a distinguished American railway constructor, 'as firm as a rock,' the gauge is somewhat narrower than the usual British gauge; the engines are of British build, somewhat too light, perhaps, but effective and extremely elegant in appearance, while the carriages, with the exception of those in third class, have the seats arranged lengthwise, like our tramway cars.

More professional critics were not so effusive. The engineer E. G. Holtham, writing in 1877, said the railway was 'a model of how things should not be, from the rotting wooden drains to the ambitious terminal stations.' R. H. Brunton, another British engineer, was more caustic still:

> The construction of this line ... was, perhaps not unnaturally, attended by a series of the most unfortunate mischances and mistakes—buildings were erected, pulled down, and re-erected in other places; numerous diversions were made; bridges were strengthened after completion; rails were twisted in every conceivable form and laid in such a way that it seemed impossible for a train to run over them ... the main cause of this somewhat deplorable condition of affairs was that the European staff engaged to direct operations ... supinely permitted interference of the native officials with their operations.

The Tokaido line was finally completed from Tokyo to Kobe in July 1889. British advisers and workers helped with construction at the western end throughout the 1870s, but it had always been envisaged that the employment of foreign labour would be a temporary expediency. After the peak year for foreign employment, 1876, the number of Britons working on the railways declined rapidly to just a handful by the early 1890s. One of these was Richard Trevithick, grandson of the man who designed the world's first steam locomotive. The younger Trevithick, in turn, designed the first steam locomotive to be built in Japan.

The opening of the Tokaido line made it possible to travel from Tokyo to Kobe in just over twenty hours. The speed, low cost and high capacity offered by the freight service was a major factor in the development of the industrial belt along the south coast of Japan, which today forms an almost continuous conurbation between Tokyo and Kobe.

Japan's railway network matured during the 1920s, by which time all major towns had been connected. After a speedy recovery from the chaos of the Second World War, Japan's railways were rapidly modernised and transformed into the highly efficient system much admired and studied by foreigners today. The student has become the teacher.

---

**RON CLOUGH** has lectured in Japanese at the University of Hertfordshire. He is the author of *Japanese Business Information: An Introduction.* (British Library, 1995).

# No Marx without Engels

TRISTRAM HUNT

It is a truth now universally acknowledged that capitalism's most insightful philosopher is Karl Marx. For over a decade, the one time ideological ogre 'responsible' for the killing fields of Cambodia and excesses of the Soviet Union has been lauded as the first thinker to chart the true nature of the free market. 'Marx's Stock Resurges on a 150-Year Tip' was how the *New York Times* marked the 150th anniversary of the publication of *The Communist Manifesfo*—a text which, more than any other, 'recognised the unstoppable wealth-creating power of capitalism, predicted it would conquer the world, and warned that this inevitable globalisation of national economies and cultures would have divisive and painful consequences.' In 2005, the French politician-cum-banker Jacques Attali went further, to pinpoint Marx as the first great theorist of globalisation. Today, in the midst of a once-a-century crisis of capitalism, *Das Kapital* has raced to the top of the German bestseller lists and even President Sarkozy has been caught leafing through its pages.

But as with so much of the Karl Marx myth, the role of his lifelong friend and ideological ally Friedrich Engels has been airbrushed from history. The coauthor of *The Communist Manifesto*, cofounder of Marxism and architect of much of modern socialism, is nowhere to be seen in this shower of admiration. Yet when it comes to the Marxian analysis of capitalism, any credible account must have Engels alongside Marx. For Marx only gained his unique appreciation of the functioning of capitalism thanks to Engels' first-hand experiences. Moreover, it was Engels who went on to edit the crucial passages of *Das Kapital* which dealt with the inherent instability of the capitalist model. If we are to look for the origins of one of the most salient criticisms of the market system, we should start with Engels.

Friedrich Engels was delivered straight into the furnace of the nineteenth century. The historic transformations he would make his life's work—in urbanisation, industrialisation, social class, and technology—were there at his infancy. Born in 1820, he grew up in the polluted, overcrowded manufacturing district of Barmen-Elberfeld (modern day Wuppertal, western Germany), known at the time as the 'German Manchester'. 'The purple waves of the narrow river flow sometimes swiftly, sometimes sluggishly between smoky factory buildings and yarn-strewn bleaching-yards,'was how Engels described his birthplace. 'Its bright red colour, however, is due not to some bloody battle . . . but simply and solely to the numerous dye-works using Turkey red.' From his earliest days, amid the acrid stench of workshops and bleaching yards, Engels was exposed to a witches' brew of industrialisation: the eye-watering pollution which blanketed his home town's mixture of intense poverty and ostentatious wealth.

Contributing to the town's prosperity was the firm of Caspar Engels und Söhne, a successful yarn business and bleachery. Established by Engels' great-grandfather Johann Caspar in the mid-18th century, by the 1830s it was a major Barmen business renowned as much for its philanthropy as profitability. Down the generations, the Engelses provided homes, gardens and even schools for family employees.

As a result, Engels spent his early years mixing easily with ribbon-makers, joiners and craftsmen, fostering in him a class-free ease which would later serve him well. But none of this could disguise the human cost of the cash-nexus that Caspar Engels und Söhne were engaged in: the factory workers, as a youthful Engels put it, 'in low rooms where people breathe in more coal fumes and dust than oxygen'; the 'totally demoralised people, with no fixed abode or definite employment, who crawl out of their refuges, haystacks, stables at dawn.'

Engels' career path was always meant to entail the family firm and, in 1837, he was withdrawn from school and dispatched to Bremen to be taught the mysteries of spinning and weaving as a clerk to linen exporter, Heinrich Leupold. Engels'work in Bremen mainly involved handling international correspondence: there were packages to Havana, letters to Baltimore, hams to the West Indies, beans from Haiti. In this free-trading, former Hanseatic city, he came to know the ins and outs of the export business, currency deals and import duties. But Engels, a romantic young man given to the poetry of Shelley, Heine and Goethe, found it numbing stuff and sought refuge in what became a lifetime's passion: bottled beer. 'We now have a complete stock of beer in the office; under the table, behind the stove, behind the cupboard, everywhere are beer bottles', he boasted to his sister Marie.

After a year's military service in Berlin and time spent among the radical circle of so-called 'Young Hegelians', who offered reinterpretations of the work of the Prussian philosopher, Engels was then sent to Manchester to complete his training. His employer, Ermen and Engels, had been established in 1837 when Engels' father sold his share of the family firm and invested it with the Ermen brothers. The guiding force behind the company, Dutch-born Peter Ermen, had come to Manchester in the mid-1820s and worked his way up from being a worker in a small factory to establishing a multinational cotton-thread business run with the help of his brothers Anthony and Gottfried. Investment by Engels senior allowed the company to open a new mill in Salford for the production of cotton thread. This district to the west of Manchester was renowned for its fine-count mercerised cotton and its weaving, and the mill—next to Weaste station, alongside the Manchester and Liverpool railway line—was ideally situated both for bringing raw cotton from the Mersey docks and drawing water from the nearby river Irwell for bleaching and dyeing. It was here that the privileged, intellectual Engels mucked in with a 400-strong Mancunian workforce, starting off among the cotton-spinning machines 'in the throstle-room'.

Working for the family firm while living within a community exploited by cotton capitalism quickly made the contradictions of Engels' position painfully apparent. As he put it in a heartfelt letter to Marx some years later, 'huckstering is too beastly . . . most beastly of all is the fact of being, not only a bourgeois, but actually a manufacturer, a bourgeois who actively takes sides against the proletariat. A few days in my old man's factory have sufficed to bring me face to face with this beastliness, which I had rather overlooked.' But even if he worked for the bourgeoisie, Engels didn't have to socialise with them. 'I forsook the company and the dinner-parties, the port-wine and champagne of the middle classes, and devoted my leisure-hours almost exclusively to the intercourse with plain working men.'

The result of such intercourse was Engels' astonishing book, *The Condition of the Working Class in England* (Leipzig, 1845). Here was a far richer, more detailed, more coruscating indictment of the brutalities of capitalism than his youthful Barmen critique. With almost vicarious pleasure, Engels listed the maiming and physical disfigurements that accompanied life on the factory floor: 'The knees are bent inward and backwards, the ankles deformed and thick, and the spinal column often bent forwards or to one side,' he wrote of the effects of the long hours spent in the cotton mill. In the mining industry, the labour of transporting coal and iron-stone was so punishing that children's puberty was unnaturally delayed.

Marx was entranced by the work ('what power, what incisiveness and what passion') and its remarkable accumulation of evidence. It was a source to which he turned again and again for concrete evidence of capitalism's inhumanity.

'As far as concerns the period from the beginning of large-scale industry in England down to the year 1845 I shall only touch upon this here and there, referring the reader for fuller details to Friedrich Engels' *The Condition of the Working Class,*' he wrote in an early note to Volume I of *Das Kapital.* 'The fullness of Engels' insight into the nature of the capitalist method of production has been shown by the factory reports, the reports on mines, etc, that have appeared since the publication of his book.'

But *The Condition* was more than just a catalogue of atrocities. With astonishing intellectual maturity, the 24-year-old Engels applied the (religious) notion of human alienation which he had absorbed from the Young Hegelians to the material realities he witnessed in Victorian Britain and thereby crafted the ideological outlines of scientific socialism. So much of what would later be regarded as mainstream Marxist thought—the nature of class division, the inherent instability of modern industrial capitalism, the creation by the bourgeois of their own gravediggers, the inevitability of socialist revolution—were all first embedded in Engels' brilliant polemic.

When Engels completed his Manchester tutorial in 1844, he did not expect to see Lancashire again so soon. But in 1850 he was back in Cottonopolis. After the failure of the 1848–49 continental revolutions, both Marx and Engels had sought refuge in England and, with no other obvious source of income, the Ermen and Engels heir reluctantly returned to the fold. His sister Marie smoothed his return with tact. 'The thought has come to us that you may perhaps wish to enter business seriously for the time being, in order to ensure yourself an income; you might drop it as soon as your party has a reasonable chance of success and resume your work for the party,' she wrote in an elegantly crafted letter sent with the blessing of her parents.

So while Marx busied himself at the British Museum writing *Das Kapital,* Engels was forced back into 'accursed commerce'. But he did so at a most propitious time as the mid-Victorian boom catapulted the Manchester cotton industry toward unprecedented prosperity. Ermen and Engels did especially well thanks to the invention of the sewing machine and, with it, increased demand for just their type of thread. With surging orders, the company moved offices to 7 Southgate (into a warehouse overlooking the courtyard of the Golden Lion public house) and purchased another mill—the Bencliffe Mill in Little Bolton, Eccles—in addition to their Victoria Mill at Salford.

It was a dull, tedious but certainly lucrative existence. In 1860, Engels' cut of the company profits stood at £978, taking his annual income to over £1,000 which is not far off £100,000 in today's money. Most of these riches cascaded south, from Manchester to London, to fund Marx's determinedly middle-class lifestyle. There were post office orders, postage stamps, £5 notes, a few pounds snaffled from the Ermen and Engels cash box, and then far more weighty sums when pay-day arrived. 'Dear Mr Engels', as

Jenny Marx was apt to address him, was regularly allocating over half his annual income to the Marx family—totalling between £3–4,000 over the 20-year period he was employed. Yet it was never enough. 'I assure that I would rather have had my thumb cut off than write this letter to you. It is truly soul-destroying to be dependent for half one's life,' begins a typical letter from Marx before pleading for an emergency loan.

But Ermen and Engels yielded more than just a living allowance. It also provided the essential data for Marx's analysis of capitalism: 'I have now reached a point in my work on economics where I need some practical advice from you, since I cannot find anything relevant in the theoretical writings,' Marx wrote to Engels in January 1858. 'It concerns the circulation of capital—its various forms in the various businesses; its effects on profit and prices. If you could give me some information on this, then it will be very welcome.' There followed a series of questions on machinery costs and depreciation rates, the allocation of capital within the firm and calculation of turnover in the company book-keeping. Over the next five years, the requests for information kept coming as Engels' years of grafting in the Manchester cotton trade helped to construct the empirical foundations of *Das Kapital*. 'Could you inform me of all the different types of workers employed, e.g. at your mill and in what proportion to each other?' Marx inquired in 1862. 'For in my book I need an example showing that, in mechanical workshops, the division of labour, as forming the basis of manufacture and as described by Adam Smith, does not exist . . . All that is needed is an example of some kind.' 'Since practice is better than all theory, I would ask you to describe to me very precisely (with examples) how you run your business,' began another round of queries.

Engels' contribution went beyond the statistical as he became Marx's sounding-board for his emerging economic philosophy. 'Let me say a word or two about what will, in the text, be a lengthy and complex affair, so that you may LET ME HAVE YOUR OPINION on it,' Marx began a letter of August 2nd, 1862. He then launched into an explanation of the difference between constant capital (machinery) and variable capital (labour) offering an early draft of the 'surplus value' theory of employee exploitation which was at the core of *Das Kapital*. Engels responded in kind, raising a number of methodological objections to the way in which Marx was calculating the value of a factory worker's labour and its relative compensation in labour-wage rates. But Marx rarely enjoyed too close a questioning and breezily replied that any such criticisms could not properly be treated 'prior to the 3rd book . . . if I wished to refute all such objections in advance, I should spoil the whole dialectical method of exposition.'

But after Marx's death in 1883, Engels was left in charge of editing Volume III and the problem still wasn't solved. However, what Engels did do was to change Marx's intent on a number of crucial passages with significant ideological repercussions. This was most obviously the case in the much debated Part III, 'The Law of the Tendency of the Rate of Profit to Fall', in which Marx had outlined how profits tend to decline under capitalism as labour-saving technology progressively reduces the scope for extracting surplus value from living labour. Marx connected this falling profitability to the vulnerability of capitalism itself. But whereas the original manuscript referred to the 'shaking' of capitalist production, Engels spoke far more definitively of the 'collapse' of capitalism. A small change, but one with far-reaching consequences for later Marxists who repeatedly looked for a systemic 'crisis' or 'breakdown' of capitalism to usher in the communist dawn. It is a theme that has recently resurfaced in commentary on the credit crisis.

Yet all such attributions of originality on Engels' behalf would have been anathema to the man himself. He always regarded Marx as the 'first fiddle', the genius who 'stood higher, saw further, and took a wider and quicker view than all the rest of us.' However, it is fair to say that Marx would not have been able to achieve half his intellectual legacy without the legwork of Engels. More than that, Engels had a deep feel for the true human costs of capitalism; despite his own exploitation of the Ermen and Engels proletariat, he offered a moral critique of political economy that Marx found hard to rival. And today it is his voice that resonates most powerfully in those countries at the sharp end of global capitalism—most notably the emerging markets of Brazil, Russia, India and China. For here all the horrors of breakneck industrialisation—capitalism transforming social relations, destroying old customs and habits, turning villages into cities, and workshops into factories—display the same savagery which Engels recounted in nineteenth-century Europe. With China now claiming the mantle of 'Workshop of the World', the pollution, ill health, political resistance and social unrest prevalent, for example, in the Special Economic Zones of Guangdong Province and Shanghai appear eerily reminiscent of Engels' accounts of Manchester and Glasgow. Compare and contrast, as the scholar Ching Kwan Lee has done, Engels' description of employment conditions in an 1840s' cotton mill—

*'In the cotton and flax spinning mills there are many rooms in which the air is filled with fluff and dust . . . The operative of course had no choice in the matter . . . The usual consequences of inhaling factory dust are the spitting of blood, heavy, noisy breathing, pains in the chest, coughing and sleeplessness . . . Accidents occur to operatives who work in rooms crammed full of machinery . . . The most common injury is the loss of a joint of the finger . . . In Manehesfer one sees not only numerous cripples, but also plenty of workers who have lost the whole or part of an arm, leg or foot.'*

—with the testimony of a Chinese migrant worker in Shenzhen in 2000:

*'There is no fixed work schedule. A 12-hour workday is minimum. With rush orders, we have to work continuously for 30 hours or more. Day and night . . . the longest shift we had worked non-stop lasted for 40 hours . . . It's very exhausting because we have to stand all the time, to straighten the denim cloth by pulling. Our legs are always hurting. There is no place to sit on the shopfloor. The machines do not stop during our lunch breaks. Three workers in a group just take turns eating, one at a time . . . The shopfloor is filled with thick dust. Our bodies become black working day and night indoors. When I get off from work and spit, it's all black.'*

FRIEDRICH ENGELS, a child of the Industrial Revolution, speaks now with remarkable authority and insight to our own global age of exploitation and immiseration. It is his impassioned criticisms of the market model in action which should echo down the decades. Engels is an essential part of our newly acknowledged truth.

# Sputnik + 50
## *Remembering the Dawn of the Space Age*

RON COWEN

> *Well, I say the fun has just begun*
> *We're on Sputnik Number One*
> *A' flying through outer space*
> *At a rockin' rollin' pace*
> *Oh! We're gonna get out kicks*
> *On a little ole thing called a Sputnik*
> > —Sputnik (Satellite Girl)

In the fall of 1957, pitcher Lew Burdette's fastball gave the Milwaukee Braves a surprise World Series win over the New York Yankees. In Little Rock, Ark., white mobs rioted after nine black students dared to attend Central High School. On television, *Leave It to Beaver* made its debut. But for many people across the globe, the most riveting show was playing out overhead.

Reaching an altitude as high as 940 kilometers, a shiny aluminum sphere was circling Earth 14 times a day. Scientists tracked its orbit, while ham radio operators tuned in to its alien "beep-beep"—a sound that radio and television stations around the globe rebroadcast to millions. Some feared that the beeps were a sinister code that would help the Russians drop a nuclear bomb. Others simply marveled at how a 184-pound hunk of metal could rocket into the sky and stay there.

The space age began on Oct. 4, 1957, when the Soviets launched Sputnik, the first artificial satellite to orbit Earth. "Soviet Fires Earth Satellite Into Space," blared the *New York Times* headline. "Myth has become reality: Earth's gravity conquered," read the banner of France's *Le Figaro*.

Fifty years later, satellites for science, surveillance, and communication have become commonplace. But if Sputnik was supposed to usher in an era of human colonies on the moon and astronauts rocketing off to other planets, that part of the story seems to have sputtered.

First stage If the U.S. public was caught off guard by Sputnik's launch, the country's scientists were not. Two years earlier, they and their Soviet counterparts had agreed to launch satellites carrying scientific instruments during the International Geophysical Year, beginning in July 1957, during which the sun would reach the peak of its 11-year activity cycle.

In the United States, the Army, Navy, and Air Force argued over which of them should build a rocket that could put a satellite into Earth orbit. The Soviets, meanwhile, forged ahead. During the summer of 1957, they even announced the two radio frequencies at which their satellite would broadcast—but not when it would launch.

To make sure of beating the Americans to the punch, the Russians shelved plans for a scientifically sophisticated satellite and went with a far simpler model, building the device in just a month without the help of blueprints.

On the evening of Oct. 4, *New York Times* reporter Walter Sullivan was at the Russian embassy in Washington, D.C., attending a reception for scientists, when he received an urgent telephone call from his Washington bureau chief. Tass, the Russian press agency, had just announced the launch of Sputnik—Russian for "traveling companion." Sullivan shared the news with the U.S. scientists at the gathering, who made an impromptu speech congratulating their Russian colleagues. The party then repaired to the embassy's rooftop so that everyone could try to catch a glimpse of the satellite.

In fact, Sputnik was visible, but just barely. It was a mere 23-inch-diameter sphere with four swept-back antennas that, up close, gave the satellite a sleek, sci-fi look. It had but a single watt of power to transmit its radio signals. The duration of the beeps indicated the temperature and pressure, and that the craft had not been punctured by a meteorite.

That night, 22-year-old engineering student Sergei Khrushchev was with his father, Nikita, in Kiev. The Soviet leader was meeting with Ukrainian officials when he got a phone call and returned to the room smiling. "He told me a great thing has happened" Sergei Khrushchev now recalls.

"We had entered a new age," Khrushchev says, but at first "we didn't understand all the significance." The next day's edition of *Pravda*, the official Russian newspaper, carried just a brief mention of the launch. "It was a shock to the West," he says. U.S. scientists and leaders thought that "the Soviet Union was far behind them. We didn't think we were far behind."

Sputnik "changed the dynamics on Earth of what our society [was] going to be like," says historian Roger Launius of the Smithsonian Institution's National Air and Space Museum in Washington, D.C. "The ability to fly in space has utterly transformed our lives. Sputnik marks the beginning."

Despite the Cold War, fear wasn't the first reaction of most Americans, Launius says. By coincidence, anthropologist Margaret Mead and a coworker were doing a survey about spaceflight just as Sputnik launched. What they found, says Launius, was "overwhelmingly a sense of excitement."

And there were some light-hearted responses. Jerry Englerth, who worked at Eastman Kodak and called his band Jerry Engler and the Four Ekkos, penned a rockabilly tune about Sputnik and went on tour with Buddy Holly. A bartender invented the Sputnik cocktail, a blend of vodka and grape juice—from sour grapes, of course. Sputnik burgers included Russian dressing and a satellite olive on a toothpick.

In rural Indiana, 7-year-old Steve Dick got a new puppy, which his family promptly named Sputnik. "I don't remember being scared at all . . . it was just an awesome thing that people watched as it went overhead," recalls Dick, now NASA's space historian in Washington, D.C.

But before long, fear took hold. "I think it was the result of a concerted effort on the part of several groups," says Launius. The Democrats, including presidential hopeful Lyndon Baines Johnson, realized that they could turn the Russian feat into a critique of President Dwight D. Eisenhower's administration. Many other groups—national-security personnel, aerospace-industry executives, space scientists who suddenly had access to the White House, and space-exploration enthusiasts who had been tagged "space cadets" and largely dismissed as kooks—saw a chance to push their views on a fascinated but anxious public, says Launius.

In response, Eisenhower tried to dismiss Sputnik, noting its lack of data-gathering equipment. Members of his administration called Sputnik "a silly bauble."

But there was also a growing rhetoric, like this verse by G. Mennen Williams, the Democratic governor of Michigan:

*O little Sputnik, flying high*
*With made-in-Moscow beep,*
*You tell the world it's a Commie sky*
*And Uncle Sam's asleep.*

Second surprise the anxiety and recriminations may have abated, but less than a month later, on Nov. 3—just in time to celebrate the 40th anniversary of the Bolshevik revolution—the Soviets launched Sputnik 2. Ten times as heavy as Sputnik 1, the satellite carried into orbit the first live cargo, a dog named Laika—which made a strictly one-way journey. The U.S. press promptly dubbed the dog Muttnik.

At Red Square in Moscow, throngs cheered chief Sputnik engineer Sergei Korolev as well as Nikita Khrushchev. "A birthday flexing of Red biceps," *Life* magazine called it.

The second Russian launch further agitated the Eisenhower administration. "The thing to remember is that anything put on a rocket [was] also only a shadow away from putting a nuclear weapon on top of an intercontinental ballistic missile," notes Air and Space cultural historian Margaret Weitekamp. "There were peaceful purposes [for the satellites], but they were also a demonstration to the world of the capability of the Russian [military presence in space.]"

On Dec. 6, the press was invited to Cape Canaveral, Fla., to witness the U.S. response to Sputnik. Newsreel cameras rolled as a modified Navy Vanguard rocket carrying a small satellite lifted off the launch pad. It rose just 4 feet before erupting in a fireball, sending the grapefruit-size satellite in its nose cone hurtling across the sands. The next day's headlines provided the postmortem: "Flopnik," "Dudnik" "Kaputnik."

Wernher von Braun, whose earlier plan to adapt an Army rocket had been ditched in favor of the Navy's project, was now brought back into the game. On Jan. 31, 1958—with no press in attendance—von Braun's Jupiter-C rocket successfully launched the first U.S. satellite, Explorer I. A Geiger counter on the satellite recorded the first evidence of what are now known as the Van Allen radiation belts, bands of energetic charged particles trapped by Earth's magnetic field.

In March, President Eisenhower founded NASA, the National Aeronautics and Space Administration, a civilian agency devoted to space exploration. Spurred by what would soon become a well-worn phrase—"Soviet children are playing chess while American children are playing checkers"—politicians poured money into math and science education. Educators revised the K–12 science curriculum and introduced the baby-boom generation to "new math." Every classroom, it seemed, got an overhead projector as its new, high-tech weapon against the Russians.

Nevertheless, "there were 5 to 6 years of almost unparalleled Soviet dominance" in space, notes Launius. The highlight may have come on April 12, 1961, when Yuri Gagarin became the first person to orbit Earth, circling once in a Vostok spacecraft.

Eisenhower always maintained that there was no space race, but he couldn't really afford to say otherwise, says Weitekamp. "Because if we were in a race, the Soviets [had] beaten the pants off the Americans. They had the first satellites, the first man in space, the first woman, the first time to have two capsules [in space together], the first rendezvous."

Jolted into action, Eisenhower's successor, John F. Kennedy, decided that the United States should embark on a major project that would eclipse Russian superiority. After consulting his advisors, including LBJ, Kennedy spoke before a joint session of Congress on May 25, 1961, and announced "the goal, before this decade is out, of landing a man on the moon and returning him safely to Earth."

Through 1972, NASA focused almost exclusively on that goal with the Apollo missions, which put 12 men on the lunar surface, beginning with Neil Armstrong's "one small step" on July 20, 1969. But after Apollo, just as the country was undergoing a cultural upheaval, NASA found itself without a clear-cut goal. "I kind of imagine all these military-buzz-cut engineers who pop their heads up and suddenly they're in an environment of stagflation, their budget shrinking instead of exploding, and it's a whole other ball game," says Weitekamp.

Says space-policy analyst John Logsdon of the George Washington (D.C.) University, "Kennedy decided to go to the moon to be there first. Period. And we got there first and then stopped."

Lasting lessons "What we've learned from Sputnik is that a shock can get you started . . . but you'd better have a good, sustainable science initiative to [keep] going," says Logsdon. "We haven't done a very good job of providing goals for ourselves in space." For the first decade after Sputnik, "we had this competition with the Soviet Union and then we chose what turned out to be a dead-end—space shuttle and space station."

The shuttle ended up being an unwieldy, costly, and ultimately dangerous way to take astronauts into space—especially after 3 decades of use. The space station has been roundly criticized by scientists for draining NASA's budget while having limited research value.

Plans for a human presence beyond Earth's orbit seemed to get a boost with President George W. Bush's 2004 announcement that NASA would return people to the moon and then go on to Mars. But those plans lack the financial support that Kennedy and LBJ garnered, notes Logsdon. They also appear to lack broad support from politicians and the public.

In many ways, the visions of space exploration that flowered soon after Sputnik, including complex space colonies, didn't materialize. Von Braun envisioned human flights to Mars, using a nuclear-powered rocket, by 1984.

But in other respects, Sputnik's legacy has endured. Among the remarkable accomplishments over the past 50 years, says Logsdon, is that "we've revolutionized our knowledge of the solar system and the universe, primarily through robotic missions." In addition, "satellites are now managing the world," he adds. With some 850 operational devices now circling Earth, satellites are at the core of worldwide communications, the Global Positioning System, and data gathering on topics as vital as global warming.

Today, it's taken for granted that "every local news station has access to [regional] satellite views" to forecast storms, notes space historian David DeVorkin of the National Air and Space Museum.

Most satellites are now launched by private industry. "There are more launches on a regular basis than people realize," says DeVorkin. "There's a booming business in launching satellites and a whole space industry."

The race among entrepreneurs into space exploration is heating up. As a follow-on to the $10 million Ansari X prize, awarded in 2004 to the first private company to fly a piloted craft twice into space within a 2-week period, the Internet company Google last month announced a new space competition: the $30 million Lunar X prize to the first company to land a robotic rover on the moon and beam pictures back to Earth.

Does the United States need another Sputnik to spur space exploration? Competition pushes progress, says Launius. "Mickey Mantle and Roger Maris were both great home run hitters, but neither of them did as well as when they competed with each other."

For DeVorkin, the new Sputnik—the crisis at hand begging for a U.S. response—is global warming. "U.S. space technology is extraordinarily good at understanding global systems and the Earth-sun connection," he says. A fleet of data-gathering satellites could be used by climate scientists needing to better understand and address global warming.

"It's a question of personal moral responsibility," says DeVorkin. "We don't deserve to go [further] into space" unless this problem is solved. A program devoted to the study of global warming would involve international collaboration more than competition. Scientists—and society—still have the chance to build on Sputnik's legacy, DeVorkin says, by using the technology developed during the space race to "galvanize and really focus on self-preservation" of the planet.

From *Science News*, October 6, 2007. Copyright © 2007 by Science Service Inc. Reprinted with permission.

# UNIT 4

# The Twentieth Century to 1950

## Unit Selections

## Key Points to Consider

- What were the main characteristics of twentieth-century warfare? What might the future variations be for this century?

- What were the positive and negative results of the Versailles Treaty? Does it rate "two cheers"?

- How did the Nehru/Gandhi dynasty manage to rule India for much of the twentieth century? What have been the effects of their efforts?

- What characteristics contributed to the Chinese xenophobic attitude toward the West? How do they continue to influence today's diplomacy?

- How extensive were the atrocities committed by Japanese armed forces in Nanking? What circumstances conspired to "cover up" these atrocities?

- What was new and revolutionary about the Nuremberg War Crimes Trials? What legacy did they leave to posterity?

- What circumstances led to the Cold War from 1945–1947? Who bears responsibility for it?

- Why was Truman's recognition of the new state of Israel a courageous act?

## Student Website
www.mhhe.com/cls

## Internet References

**First World War.Com**
www.firstworldwar.com
**U.S. Holocaust Memorial Museum**
www.ushmm.org
**World War 2 Timeline**
www.worldwar2.net

At the beginning of the twentieth century, the British Empire spread around the world. Britain's navy ruled the seas and Britain acted as the world's policeman. Britain's financial strength was equally unsurpassed, and the pound sterling was the money standard for world markets. Still, other nations—notably, Germany, Japan, and the United States—were rising in prestige and power.

At the same time, the prestige and power of the West was diminishing, as the twentieth century brought World War I, the Great Depression, World War II, and the Cold War. The first World War left 10 million dead and a heritage of cynicism caused by the barbarism of trench warfare. Great Britain emerged exhausted, the great debtor nation of the world; and the Soviet Russians began their long experiment with communism by executing Nicholas II, the last czar of Russia. Only after the fall of the Soviet Union in 1989 was it possible to identify and rebury the remains of the czar and his family. The rumor that Anastasia, the czar's daughter, had survived was finally laid to rest.

In the 1930s, the Great Depression undermined the financial strength of the West and raised questions about the stability of the capitalist economic system. Fascism fed on this economic misery, and Adolf Hitler began his demagogic career. The Nazis attempted to form a "perfect" society, in part by eliminating Jews, Gypsies, and other so-called undesirable people. Women in the Third Reich were assigned the role of producing children to replace fallen warriors.

Fighting in World War II began first in Asia, with the Japanese invasion of China in 1937. The Japanese conquest of Nanking was marked by its brutality, which included torture, rape, and murder. Although this event was long known, historians have written about it only recently. After a four-year-long struggle, the war in the Pacific came to an end when the United States dropped two atomic bombs on the Japanese cities of Hiroshima and Nagasaki. The Japanese surrendered.

As allied armies captured various portions of Germany in the European theater of war, they found death camps. Barbarism on this scale was deeply shocking and the horrors of the holocaust demanded a rethinking of human morality. When the rule of law was reasserted, German leaders, not the German people, were to be held accountable. The Nuremberg trials set a precedent for subsequent war crimes trials. After Japan's surrender, the Allied powers also conducted war crimes trials in Tokyo for the Japanese leaders of the Pacific portion of the war.

© Library of Congress, Prints and Photographs Division [LC-USZ62-7449].

The aftermath of Word War II and the Holocaust included the formation of the state of Israel. Support from the United States was crucial, and Israel continues to consider the U.S. a key ally today. Another legacy of the two great wars was a decades-long standoff between the two remaining superpowers—the Soviet Union and the United States. Now that the Cold War has ended, Is the world safer or more dangerous?

The first half of the twentieth century also witnessed struggles for national independence. In India, Gandhi and Nehru combined moral and political leadership to achieve their shared goal of home rule in India. Long independent, India today is divided by provincial and religious strife. The shared vision of Gandhi and Nehru might again have relevance as Hindus and Muslims clash over disputed areas in Kashmir.

And, in China, Mao Zedong communist-inspired revolution turned China into a world power. Today, China is an economic and nuclear giant. However, after a century of what it sees as national humiliations inflicted by foreign powers, China appears xenophobic to the West. Nationalism, which inspired the unsuccessful Boxer Rebellion a century ago, remains a potent force in contemporary Chinese politics. As the remaining superpower, the United States is often perceived by China as a threatening foreign power.

# From Boer War to Timor: Warfare in the Twentieth Century

Keith Suter

The century that is ending has been dominated by war. This article examines five features of warfare this century: guerrilla warfare, the increase in military power, the role of the mass media, scepticism about the effectiveness of war as an instrument of national policy, and the long search for peace.

## Guerrilla Warfare

The century ended much as it began, with guerrilla struggles in sprawling empires, imperial powers having difficulty beating small guerrilla forces fighting on a terrain the guerrillas knew well and with the support of the local population.

In the 1880s, Britain sought the unification of the whole of South Africa under the British flag. The stumbling block came from the two Boer republics: the South African Republic (Transvaal) and the Orange Free State, which wanted to retain their independence. The British deployed extra forces to their colonies. The South African Republic, wishing to seize the military initiative, issued an ultimatum to Britain on October 9 1899 calling for the removal of all imperial forces from the republic's borders within 48 hours with the alternative of formal war. Britain did not comply with the demands of the ultimatum and war began on October 11. The Boers invaded the British colonies and besieged the British garrisons at Ladysmith (Natal), Mafeking and Kimberley (Cape Colony). After further initial defeats, the British fought back and beat the Boers in conventional battles. In March 1900 the Boers began the second phase: a protracted guerrilla war. The British responded with a scorched earth policy and by placing women and children, both black and white, in concentration camps. The war dragged on until 1902, when the Boers surrendered and were given generous terms: the British were glad that the war was over. It had been a much bigger campaign than Britain had anticipated. (See *Reviews,* p.325–6.)

Three quarters of a century later, Indonesia was not so fortunate. Suharto's Indonesia invaded the Portuguese colony of East Timor in late 1975, expecting a quick victory. Indonesia is the fourth most populous country in the world (now at about 210 million) with one of the world's largest armies. The Portuguese colony had about a million people. About 200,000 people

perished in the war, thereby making the war, in per capita terms, one of the most violent this century. But Indonesia could not beat the East Timorese resistance. The 1997 Asian economic crisis was a severe blow for Indonesia and Suharto was driven from office in May 1998. His successor, Dr Habibie, set East Timor on the path to independence. The Indonesian Parliament voted in October 1999 for East Timor to be transferred to the United Nations as a transitional arrangement to its becoming independent.

Guerrilla warfare is the weapon of the weak against the strong. It is the war of the flea. An elephant can fight another elephant but it is powerless against the irritations of a flea. It is also an equal opportunity form of fighting: everyone can play a part (as British troops found out in the 1970s and 1980s in Northern Ireland against children throwing rocks and Molotov Cocktails). The weak may not be able to defeat the strong but they can drive them crazy (as the Israelis found out in the 1980s in the *Intifada,* when young alienated Palestinians rebelled against the Israeli occupation).

Excessive firepower is no guarantee of success in a guerrilla war. A century ago, the British were trying to beat the Pathans on the North West Frontier of India. Their modern machine guns were of little use in the mountainous terrain; their opponents' antiquated 'jezail' flintlocks did better because of their longer range and accuracy. The US's great power in Vietnam did not produce a victory 1965–75. Nor did it work for the Soviet Union in Afghanistan 1979–85. Now one wonders how it will work in Chechnya.

Guerrilla warfare is now the most common form of fighting. The modern trends in warfare are for groups to try to break away from an existing country to create their own country (as in the Balkans in the 1990s), or for a group to try to overthrow its government and so form its own government (as throughout Africa since World War II). Guerrilla warfare is the preferred technique in both cases.

This means that it is dangerous being a civilian. A key component of conventional warfare was the clear distinction between professional soldiers and the civilians—one protected the other and in return received a special status in society. Senior officers have a priority standing in orders of precedence at official government functions as a part of the reward for being willing to lay down their lives for protecting the rest of society.

However, the percentage of civilians being killed in warfare has increased. A tradition of war was that military personnel and buildings were to be the only targets. Nowadays, the targets could be anything—including office blocks and passenger aircraft. Civilian deaths may now be as high as 90 per cent of the total deaths in warfare. During the period of the Vietnam war, more US Ambassadors were killed worldwide than generals in Vietnam.

## The Increase in Military Power

The century may have begun and ended with guerrilla warfare but the largest casualties were created with conventional warfare, especially in the two world wars. One explanation for the dramatic increase in firepower is the mobilization of the scientific community to produce ever more destructive weapons.

A second explanation is the pendulum effect in defence and offence and the role of extra firepower as the key to breaking the deadlock. A century ago, with the machine gun, the initiative was with the defender, who could fire at oncoming troops. The defender was then, of course, at a disadvantage when he had to attack the other side.

The World War I trench warfare stalemate was broken by the English use of the tank. The Germans perfected the use of the tank to move quickly through defensive lines in the early years of World War II. Bomber aircraft became more important in World War II than in World War I, and the use of atomic weapons brought the war against Japan to an abrupt end in August 1945.

On a rate based on the number of potential deaths, nuclear missiles are cheaper than most other forms of killing. Their limitation arises, ironically, from their extensive capacity to kill. They are too destructive to use in the usual military campaigns. Nuclear weapons would destroy that which the attacker would like eventually to control.

Additionally, for the first time in history, a powerful country cannot defend its people from an attack. Nuclear missiles cannot be shot down. Even if the proposed Strategic Defense Initiative ('Star Wars') had gone ahead and it could have shot down some missiles, only about two per cent of Soviet missiles were needed to destroy the US's main cities. Meanwhile, all societies will remain vulnerable to guerrilla groups using nuclear explosive devices. For the nuclear weapon cannot be disinvented. That knowledge is here to stay.

In June 1917, General Sir Hubert Plumer captured Messines Ridge. His 'all-arms offensive' required the use of tanks, aircraft, artillery and mines. When 17 mines exploded on June 7 (with 957,000 pounds of explosive), they created what was then one of the greatest explosions in world history. However two failed to detonate. The 18th mine exploded in 1955, without killing anyone. The other is still down there waiting to go off.

This is an example of how the wars of the twentieth century will reach into the twenty-first and possibly even twenty-second centuries. Peace has returned to Cambodia but Cambodians are still dying or getting their arms or legs blown off at a rate of 200 to 300 per month by some 4 million land mines left behind

on the killing fields. Since Cambodia has a population of about 8 million, this means that there is still one mine for every two Cambodians. Cambodia's civil war may have been the first war in history where more people were killed by mines than by any other armaments. Cambodia has the world's highest rate of amputees. If Western Europe had a similar rate, it would have 6,275,000 land mine injuries a year—almost the population of Switzerland. Cambodian amputees have a limited future. There is no social welfare programme to look after them, they are a burden on their families, buildings are not wheel-chair accessible. The prevailing religious fatalism means that people hurt by mines are often regarded as being 'punished' for sins committed in an earlier life, and so there may be little sympathy for the victims.

The situation in Afghanistan is also grim. It has 10 million mines. Using current mine-clearing techniques, it will take 4,300 years to render only 20 per cent of Afghan territory safe.

There are at least 100 million mines deployed around the world in 62 countries. About 800 people a month die because of mines. Land mines are permanent sentries. They remain at war for up to about 75 or 100 years—until they rust away, explode or are de-mined. From 1945 to 1977, 15 million mines placed in World War II were cleared from Poland, yet 4,000 people were killed there by mines and 9,000 injured over the same period. In Egypt, Libya, Tunisia, the Netherlands and the Russian Federation, mines dating back to the Second World War still endanger civilians. One of the main rail lines into London had to be closed in October when an unexploded German bomb was uncovered near the tracks.

Indeed, the mines laid in recent civil wars, such as in Cambodia or Afghanistan, by one generation could, in theory, cause injury among the mine-layers' grandchildren—or even great grandchildren—in the next century.

## The Role of the Mass Media

The mass media represent a battle front. British journalists (such as the young Winston Churchill) received assistance from British officers in the Boer War anxious to keep British public opinion sympathetic to the war effort. In World War I, journalists received officer status, with the media conscripted as part of the war effort. Censorship was also important in World War II. Maintaining morale remains a vital task. This applies to both the defence personnel and their next of kin and friends at home. They want to be reassured that the war is worthwhile.

Advances in science have affected the mass media. In the 1960s signals were bounced off the one broadcasting satellite Telstar—and it was necessary to wait for Telstar to get in the right position for the day for the signal to be bounced off it. Much of the Vietnam War television footage had an even longer wait: it was flown in by air. Vietnam was the first televised war—but it was not 'live' television.

Now a string of satellites can bounce the signal off each other and take it around the world. The 1991 Gulf War was the first 'live' televised war. A US officer who was with the advancing forces and who had been given by the Saudi Government a cellular telephone (another example of the information technology revolution) told me that he used to ring his wife in the US (who was watching the war on CNN) to find out what was going on because she had a better overall view of the war than someone in the midst of it.

It is a matter of speculation of what television would have done to the conduct of World War I trench warfare, if the audiences at home had seen the appalling nature of that war.

There is now an even greater attempt by governments to influence the mass media. It was what the mass media had done to the coverage of the Vietnam War, that made the British Government determined to control the media coverage of the 1982 Falklands War. The Government limited the number of journalists in the UK naval force, and it censored the material broadcast (including banning the broadcasting of gory material on the destruction of *HMS Sheffield*).

The US learnt from the UK's handling of the Falklands War when it came to planning the Gulf War coverage and later that on Kosovo. Attacks and subsequent press conferences were timed to fit in with 'live' broadcasts back to the US for prime time television.

The truth often does come out eventually. Over a year after the Gulf War ended, for example, the media reported that Allied ground forces in the Gulf War outnumbered the Iraqis by more than three-to-one at the start of the hostilities and the Bush Administration had vastly overestimated the Iraqi military's fighting strength. There was also the Pentagon's admission that its so-called 'smart' bombs and Tomahawk cruise missiles were not nearly as successful at hitting their intended targets as previously stated. The ground-launched Patriot missile, used against Iraqi Scud missiles, also turned out to be less effective than advertised.

Finally, people now know they are poor. In all previous eras, people were poor but they did not know it. They lived in small villages, with the rich people in their castle or country house. Life was settled, and few poor people could journey out of the village.

On a recent trip to Bangkok, for example, I was struck by the way in which so many people live in huts over or near rivers and canals, where they lack adequate roads, clean water and sanitation—and yet they all have small colour television sets. Now people in Third World villages can see how well Texans live (because of *Dallas*) and how good life is in Australia (because of *Sylvania Waters*). Texans and Australians may not take these programmes too seriously but there is a tendency for other people to believe what they see on television.

Third World governments are therefore under pressure to satisfy immediate consumer demands rather than creating appropriate infrastructure for the long-term development needs of their countries. Marginalized young people can see that they are missing out on the good things of life and so are attracted to alternative leaders who promise them a better life. In Algeria, Egypt and Turkey, for example, extremist Islamic groups attract such people. In earlier years, they would have joined communist groups but communism is now discredited. Instead, they now follow extremist Islamic leaders and use guerrilla tactics. As the rich become richer and the poor become more numerous, so there will be increased scope for violence.

# Is War Worthwhile?

Benjamin Franklin said two centuries ago that there was never a good war or a bad peace. He would feel vindicated by some of this century's warfare. For example, the Gulf War began in August 1990 with Iraq's invasion of Kuwait. The person who lost it—President Saddam Hussein—remains in power. All the leaders who beat him have long since lost power, notably George Bush, Margaret Thatcher and John Major.

First, it is no longer clear just when a war ends. As far as Saddam Hussein is concerned, the Gulf War is not over. He had a setback in 1991 but he is still battling on. Much the same could be said about Argentina and the Falkland Islands: Argentina lost the 1982 round but remains determined to get the islands. The conflict—or conflicts—in former Yugoslavia of the early 1990s are still not settled despite all the peace negotiations.

Second, it is no longer clear just who 'wins' a war. Germany and Japan lost World War II but their economies are stronger now than many of the countries which won it. With the introduction of the Euro based so much on German financial power and the UK pound not even included in the Euro scheme, the UK could be eclipsed by the country it beat in two world wars.

The US won the Cold War but has found little joy in doing so. The Cold War damaged the economies of both the US and USSR. The US fought the Cold War to contain Soviet expansionism. The US is now troubled that Moscow is too weak to govern the country and so is lending money to Moscow, but this helps Russia to fund the war in Chechnya.

# The Long Search for Peace

In August 1898, the Russian government issued a circular, 'The Tsar's Rescript', calling for a conference to discuss the 'maintenance of general peace and possible reductions of excessive armaments which weighed upon all nations'. The Tsar had been advised by his ministers that he could not afford both guns and butter: military expansion and social reform. Therefore he hoped to avoid a further round of military expenditure by negotiating an overall reduction in international military expenditure. (See *Contemporary Review Vol. 274, No.1 600, p. 242.*) This also fitted with the mood of the times: the twentieth century was going to be an even greater era for Europe and so war was being seen as a barbaric relic of a less modern era.

In May 1899 representatives of the world's major governments met in The Hague. They failed to agree on any system for ending war as an instrument of national policy, though much progress was made in regulating how warfare was to be fought (The Hague Conventions). The second round, in 1907, also failed to end the reliance upon war as an instrument of national policy. The third round could not be held because World War I was underway.

A century later, disarmament is still on the international agenda and with only partial successes. Treaties cover some nuclear weapons, biological and chemical warfare and land mines. Much of the world has been designated nuclear-weapon free. But the Tsar would see that the world in 1999 is still confronted with the challenges he saw in 1899.

A culture of peace is needed to replace the culture of war. This would mean unlearning the culture of violence that has pervaded human existence in thousands of ways. It would mean questioning the institutions, priorities and practices that undergird the culture of violence.

I have proposed a holistic approach—the triangle of peace—based on disarmament, conflict resolution and the search for economic and social justice.

One side of the triangle is the removal of existing weapon systems: disarmament and arms control, which is what was sought at The Hague in 1899. But governments are not going to disarm in a security vacuum and so there have to be alternative ways of settling disputes: hence the second side of the triangle—conflict resolution. Such techniques include diplomacy (with one government talking directly with another government), arbitration (where governments have their disputes settled by recourse to international law and international courts), and mediation (where a third party tries to find a way of settling a dispute through negotiation).

The third side of the triangle is economic and social justice. If you want peace, you have to work for justice. It is necessary, then, to look for the underlying causes of violence. This work requires attention to such matters as the protection of the environment and respect for human rights.

The world can find money for war but not for peace. If it does not develop a culture of peace, then an article written on warfare in 2099 will not be much different from this one.

---

KEITH SUTER is the author of *The Triangle of Peace* (Perth, Western Australia: Trinity Peace Research Institute, 1990).

# Two Cheers for Versailles

MARK MAZOWER

The Versailles Treaty settlement was, from the moment of its birth, unloved as few creations of international diplomacy have been before or since. Hitler and Churchill were united in its condemnation; so were commentators from the American anti-Soviet diplomat and historian George Kennan to the British Marxist E.H. Carr. One is hard put to find a school textbook with anything good to say about the achievements of the Paris peacemakers. Yet curiously we still live in the world they shaped: were the foundations laid more carefully by them than we like to think? The argument that the defects of Versailles led to the outbreak of another world war is commonplace; yet one might as easily argue that its virtues underpinned the peace after 1945.

Some suggest that Versailles was based on principles inconsistently applied. The charge is obviously true. The right of national self-determination was granted at Germany's expense, and the Anschluss with Austria, which Social Democrats in Vienna wanted in 1918, was prevented by the Great Powers and only achieved after the Nazis broke the League of Nations system and marched in twenty years later. But international affairs are not a matter of logic alone, and the principle of consistency must be matched against considerations of power politics or geography. National self-determination could never have been applied across the board; the basic issue is whether a better principle existed for the re-ordering of Europe.

More serious an accusation is that the peace settlement was not so much inconsistent as ineffective: it was based upon an inaccurate appraisal of the European balance of power and deprived of the means of its own defence by American withdrawal and British indifference. At Paris the Great Powers ignored the fact that the almost simultaneous collapse of Germany and Russia had produced an anomalous situation in eastern Europe. The French, who of all the Great Powers felt most immediately threatened, thought the only safeguard of their own security—if the League was not to be equipped with an army of its own—was alliance with grateful clients like the Baltic states, Poland, Czechoslovakia, Romania and Yugoslavia. But it should have been obvious that the newly independent states formed there would be unable alone to ensure stability in the region once these two Great Powers reasserted themselves. The Treaty of Brest Litovsk of early 1918 had shown what intentions the Germans of the Kaiserreich harboured in that area; after 1939, Hitler's New Order pushed the principle of German (and Russian) hegemony one brutal stage further. But this is less an argument against the Versailles settlement itself than against the refusal of the Great Powers who sponsored it to back it up with armed force before 1939.

Thirdly, it is often felt that the whole approach to Germany after the Treaty was flawed. The enemy was humiliated but not crushed, burdened by reparations yet unopposed when it rearmed and marched into the Rhineland. It is true that the contrast is striking with the policies pursued towards Germany after the Second World War when long-term economic assistance was provided and by governments not the markets, and when the Bundeswehr was quickly incorporated within west European defence arrangements. But the economic problem after 1919 was not so much reparations as the shaky structure of international lending and, in particular, the shock of the world depression. The Allies were helped to learn from the mistakes of the inter-war era by the Cold War, which divided Germany, and made Europe's German problem a question of reunification rather than of territorial expansion and revanche in the East.

Finally, there is the accusation common to conservatives and Communists alike that the Versailles peace settlement was overly ideological. For some, it was an extension of nineteenth-century liberal moralising, a combination of British utilitarianism and American idealism—a basically philosophical approach to the world which lacked realism or understanding of the political passions which animated people in Europe.

Alternatively, it was—behind the veil of noble sentiments—an anti-Communist crusade whose liberalism masked a fundamentally reactionary and deeply conservative goal: the containment, if not the crushing, of Bolshevism. Outflanked gradually by other more determined and forceful anti-Communist movements of the right, European liberals lost their enthusiasm for defending the Versailles order and sat back to watch fascism take over the task of saving Europe from red revolution.

One question, however, confronts the critics of Versailles: what were the alternatives? It was not, after all, as if the Powers had willed this new liberal order of independent, democratic nation-states into existence. They had certainly not been fighting the Great War to this end. On the contrary, as late as 1918 most Entente diplomats still favoured the preservation of the old empires in central Europe in the interests of continental stability. Of course, after 1919 the conflicts and tensions produced by the new states of the region made many people nostalgic for what the Austrian writer Stefan Zweig, looking back to the Habsburg era, called 'the world of yesterday'. Fragmentation since the war seemed to have harmed the region both politically and economically, especially once the world depression forced countries into an impoverished self-sufficiency.

Yet it was a rare blend of nostalgia and realpolitik which lay behind much of the antipathy to Versailles. The makers of America's new role in Europe after 1945, for example, who had grown up looking closely at these problems, held Versailles responsible for the instability of interwar Europe. Adolf Berle, Roosevelt's assistant secretary of state between 1938 and 1944, believed that French generals had been responsible for breaking up the Austro-Hungarian Empire and wanted some kind of reconstitution of that entity to ward off the Russians. Hitler, he advised the president on the eve of Munich, was perhaps 'the only instrument capable of re-establishing a race and economic unit which can survive and leave Europe in balance.'

George Kennan, a younger man but more influential than Berle in defining the Cold War policy of containment, took a very similar view in the late 1930s. In his despatches from Prague he wrote:

It is generally agreed that the breakup of the limited degree of unity which the Habsburg Empire represented was unfortunate for all concerned. Other forces are now at work which are struggling to create a new form of unity . . . To these forces Czechoslovakia has been tragically slow in adjusting herself . . . The adjustment—and this is the main thing—has now come.

It did not take long for someone as astute as Kennan to realise that the Nazi New Order was not going to stabilise central Europe in the way the Habsburgs had done. But the reason for this, in his mind, was not the apparently obvious one that Hitler's whole upbringing had turned him into a German nationalist critic of the Austro-Hungarian monarchy. It was, rather, what Kennan conceived as the excessively democratic character of Hitler's Germany and the limited involvement of Germany's aristocracy in the Third Reich. More aristocratic government was Kennan's answer to Europe's problems. It is hard to imagine a more far-fetched or unrealistic approach—the Habsburgs were marginalised between the wars even by Hungary's reactionary regent Admiral Horthy, and the most successful Habsburg aristocrat of that era was the bizarre and premature proponent of European union, Count Coudenhove-Kalergi. Perhaps only an American conservative intellectual like Kennan could have taken the prospect of a Habsburg restoration seriously. European conservatives, closer to the ground, had fewer illusions. 'The Vienna to Versailles period has run its course,' wrote the historian Lewis Namier in February 1940.

Whatever the weaknesses of the system created in 1919, a return to previous forms is impossible. They have been broken, and broken for good.

It was not aristocrats that had kept the old empires together but dynastic loyalty, and this had vanished.

If dynasticism no longer offered an alternative principle to the Versailles order, then what of the rival ideologies of right and left? This was where root-and-branch critics of Versailles had to bite the bullet. Most anti-Communists between the wars had no difficulty in swallowing the idea of an authoritarian revision of the Versailles settlement. What made them hesitate was a quite different proposition; the reality of life under the Nazi New Order. The difference between a right tolerable to most conservatives and an extreme and ideological fascism was that, for instance, between King Alexander's royal dictatorship in Yugoslavia, and Ante Pavelic's genocidal Ustase state in Croatia, or between King Carol's Romania and that of the Iron Guard, with its bloody pogroms, in the winter of 1940–41. Above all, the New Order was based on the idea of German racial superiority, and few anti-Communists could stomach this once they saw what it meant in terms of practical politics.

If one agreed with Namier that 'no system can possibly be maintained on the European Continent east of the Rhine which has not the support either of Germany or of Russia,' then the only ideological alternative to Nazism was Communism, or more precisely the extension of Russian rule westwards into Europe. Just as Versailles's critics on the right had seen Germany's move east after 1933 as confirmation of their own prejudices, so critics on the left similarly interpreted the course of events after 1943 as a happy necessity. Historians like E.H. Carr saw this as realism replacing the idealism of Versailles. It was apparently not felt to be realistic to point out that all the historical evidence pointed to the unpopularity of Communism among the majority of the populations who now had to endure it. In only one country in central Europe, Hungary, had a Bolshevik regime held power for any length of time before 1945, and that still brief experience—the Bela Kun regime of 1919—had only confirmed how unpropitious the soil was for such experiments. Today we are unlikely to see Communism as an attractive alternative to the principles embodied in the Versailles order: yesterday's 'realism' looks riddled with its own form of wishful thinking.

One of the reasons Bela Kun fell from power in 1919 was that he had not understood the strength of Hungarian nationalist feeling. So long as it had appeared to Hungarians that Bolshevik Russia might help them get back their traditional lands, they were prepared to tolerate Kun. But once it appeared that the Allies would not let this happen, Kun lost any popularity he had once enjoyed and he was easily defeated. The power of nationalism was the chief force to emerge from the First World War in Europe, and was the main political factor facing the architects of a new postwar settlement. From our perspective at the century's end, it hardly looks as though fascism and Communism were able to handle European nationalism better than the peacemakers at Versailles. Hitler's New Order proceeded by ignoring all nationalisms except the German, and lost Europe in consequence. Communism believed that eventually nationalist antipathies would vanish, subsumed within an internationalist struggle: but time ran out for the Communists before this happened. If we want to find guidance in the past for how to tackle the problems of nationalism that remain in Europe, we cannot do better than return to the diplomats who gathered in Paris eighty years ago.

In the Bukovina (a former province of the Habsburg empire), Paris seemed very far away in the spring of 1919. But events were occurring there which help us chart the trajectory of anti-semitic violence from the unorganised pogroms of the nineteenth century to the more systematic population engineering of the twentieth. A manifesto was posted up in the village of Kamenestie, written in Romanian:

> Order to all the Jews in the village. Those Jews who are still in the village are asked to go to the city or somewhere else. You can leave in good condition [sic] and without fear in ten days. It will be made unbearable for those who stay beyond the limit.

Throughout the little villages of the Bukovina, pogroms were taking place in late 1918. 'Following the example of the neighbouring villages,' runs an account from Petroutz,

> The peasants decided to drive the Jews out of this place. On the night of November 17th, they attacked the Jewish families Hermann, Feller and Schubert, broke doors and windows and took away everything they found. A scroll of the Law was torn to pieces by the marauders. After the robbery they burned everything that remained. All three families fled to Suczawa.

The Jews were the chief targets of ethnic violence in the Bukovina, as they were elsewhere in eastern Europe, in Galicia for instance, or in Lithuania. But the war of nationalities could not be reduced to antisemitism: Poles were fighting with Ukrainians, Germans and Lithuanians. Across much of Europe there fell a double shadow: ethnic as well as class war. Bolshevism was contained by a combination of land reform, reformist social democracy and the military defeat of the Red Army in the Russo-Polish war. But the nationalist enmities and suspicions which exploded into violence as the First World War ended, and which generated casualties on such a scale that some historians have compared them with the violence which erupted under Nazi rule after 1941, these proved harder to tackle.

Ethnic civil war emphasised in the most unmistakable way that the peacemakers in Paris were not sketching their maps on a tabula rasa. On the contrary, they were as much responding to circumstances as shaping them. East European critics of Great Power arrogance often forget today how far the Versailles settlement was brought into being, not by the Powers, but by local nationalist elites and their supporters. New nations were pressing their claims on paper, in the streets and by force of arms, as the war approached an end. Serb, Croat and Slovene delegates issued the Corfu Declaration in July 1917 and declared the new tripartite Yugoslav nation 'a worthy member of the new Community of Nations.'

The Provisional People's Government of the Polish Republic proclaimed 'the authority of Polish democracy' in its November 1918 manifesto. The Czech National Committee seized power in Prague as early as October 28th of the same year in the name of the infant Czechoslovak state. Much of the subsequent fighting from the Baltic to the Balkans was designed to conquer as much territory as possible for the new states, to see off rival claimants and to settle scores with Jews, Germans, Muslims and other hated, despised or feared peoples. Between 1920 and 1923, the Treaty of Sevres was signed, scrapped and replaced by the Treaty of Lausanne as the struggle between Greece and Turkey shifted first one way then the other, culminating eventually in the forced population exchange of some two million people.

It is to the credit of the Versailles peacemakers that they confronted the problem of ethnic violence head on. They were aware of the chief defect of the Wilsonian principle of national self-determination—namely that if it was interpreted territorially and not merely as a grant of cultural autonomy, then on its own it ruled out either an equitable or a geographically coherent settlement of the problems of central and eastern Europe. No one, after all, was proposing to give the Kashubians, the Polesians, the Pomaks, or any of the other small ethnic groups of the region a state of their own. They, and several other larger peoples like the Jews, the Ukrainians and the Macedonians, would remain under the rule of others. In other words, the creation—or better, the recognition—of nation-states at Versailles was accompanied by its inescapable shadow, the problem of minorities.

Fearful in particular that Poland's appetite for territory might destabilise the whole area, the Powers obliged the reluctant Poles to sign a treaty granting the country's very sizeable minority population certain rights. The Polish treaty formed the basis for a series of similar treaties imposed in 1919 and 1920 upon most of the states of central and eastern Europe. The result was that for the first time an international organisation—the League of Nations—assumed the right to intervene in a member state's internal affairs on behalf of minority populations.

This right, however, was very limited and scarcely used at all by the League. Most countries feared doing away with the idea that a state was sovereign within its own borders, and even the Great Powers who had sponsored the Minority Rights Treaties trod warily. They had resisted calls to universalise the regime of minority rights on the grounds that 'the League cannot assume to guarantee good government in this matter throughout the world'. By 1929 they were very reluctant to act at all against member states accused of rights violations. British foreign secretary Austen Chamberlain warned that,

> We have not reached such a degree of solidarity in international affairs that any of us welcome even the most friendly intervention in what we consider to be our domestic affairs.

This attitude discouraged the most dynamic lobbyists for Europe's minorities, the Germans and the Jews. Until 1933, they worked together in the European Congress of Nationalities to try to give the Minorities Treaties teeth. Thereafter their paths diverged. But Hitler's rise to power can be seen in the context of the failure of the League to protect Europe's minorities. Where the League's rather timid use of international law had failed, the Nazis used force; their 'solution' involved forced population transfer, resettlement and ultimately genocide. And after 1944 many of these instruments were turned on the Germans themselves as they were driven out of Poland and the former Habsburg lands.

Yet we should not write off the peacemakers of Versailles too quickly. Despite the horrors of the 1940s, which virtually eliminated both the Jews and the Germans from much of eastern

Europe, many minorities remained across the region. However, instead of building on the League's tentative efforts to construct an international regime of minority rights, the architects of the post-war order enshrined in the United Nations deliberately retreated from the problem and tried to dress up its reluctance to deal with it with meaningless persiflage about 'human rights'. As a result, when issues of minority rights came to the fore after the collapse of Communism in eastern Europe in the decade after 1989, most obviously in the context of the disintegration of Yugoslavia, the international community possessed no coherent strategy for tackling the problem.

The consequences have been all too visible in Bosnia and Kosovo. The United Nations was less equipped to tackle the fundamental problem of minority rights than its predecessor, the League, had been. It delivered food and tried to keep the peace without a clear doctrine of what kind of peace it should keep. The contrast between the self-confident and articulate liberal universalism of the 1920s and the post-modern evasions of the 1990s was all too conspicuous. In Kosovo, too, the contrast with the Versailles generation does not flatter our own times. NATO intervention in Kosovo could, as articulated somewhat optimistically by Tony Blair, be interpreted as marking a new doctrine of foreign affairs, according to which state sovereignty may be overridden to prevent massive violations of minority rights. Yet, NATO's attacks on the Serbs, in the absence of any UN mandate, do not indicate any great confidence in international law and institutions. The United States, which has been leading the charge, is, after all, opposed to the creation of an International Criminal Court. If inter-war Europe suffered because international guarantees were never acted upon, we may suffer in the 1990s through military action taken without any reference to international law at all, the late twentieth-century equivalent of gunboat diplomacy handled by a post-Holocaust generation of politicians.

The very least, then, that we can say for Versailles is that it recognised and articulated the major problems for European stability at that time. What was more, there was no palatable alternative to the nation-state then, or since. Where the peace was found wanting between the wars was in the will to uphold it. Today NATO is turning itself into the kind of force which the peacemakers of 1919 lacked. But do its political masters have a clear grasp of what kind of Europe they wish to defend? They could do worse than cast their eyes back to the work of their predecessors eighty years ago.

# For Further Reading

I. Claude, *National Minorities: An International Problem* (Harvard, 1955). James Headlam Morley, *A Memoir of the Paris Peace Conference, 1919.* (London, 1972). J. Harper, *American Visions of Europe* (Cambridge, 1996). C. Fink, '*Defender of Minorities': Germany in the League of Nations 1926–1933.* (Central European History, 5:4, 1972). R. Brubaker, Nationalism Refrained: *Nationhood and the National Question in the New Europe* (Cambridge, 1996). E. Kulischer, *Europe on the Move: War and Population Changes, 1917–1947.* (New York, 1948).

**MARK MAZOWER** is a Visiting Professor of History at Princeton University. He is the author of *Dark Continent: Europe's Twentieth Century (1998).*

# One Family's Tryst with Destiny

**As India celebrates six decades of independence on this year, Jad Adams examines how, in the world's largest democracy, one family has come to take centre stage in politics, as if by divine right.**

JAD ADAMS

For forty of the sixty years since independence, a member of the Nehru-Gandhi dynasty has ruled as prime minister in India. The family came to personify the struggles and triumphs of the entire nation—an identification they did everything to promote. The story of how the family intertwined its fate with that of the nation starts with its fiercely ambitious founder, Motilal Nehru (1861–1931), who rose from poverty to become a leading lawyer and member of the Indian National Congress, and set out to make his son, Jawaharlal Nehru (1889–1964) the greatest man in the world.

By the time Jawaharlal was born, his father's wealth was legendary and his home at Allahabad, Anand Bhavan (Abode of Joy), a by-word for luxury. The child grew up with tennis courts, a swimming pool, lawns with sparkling fountains, rich furnishings and a retinue of liveried servants. It was the first house in Allahabad to have electricity and water laid on; it soon had flush toilets and hot and cold running water. The Nehru family were Brahmins, the highest caste of Indian society, traditionally destined as priests or scholars. Every birthday Jawaharlal was weighed in public in a huge balance against grain and other goods that were then distributed to the poor—an early example of the relationship between his physical being and that of the people of India, a theme that was developed throughout his life.

Jawaharlal was sent to England for his education at Harrow, Trinity College, Cambridge and the Inner Temple. Spending so many of his formative years away from his country he became, he later wrote, 'a queer mixture of East and West, out of place everywhere, at home nowhere.' Back in India he served in the High Court at Allahabad; and became involved in the independence movement, a cause in which he met Mohandas Gandhi in 1916. When some peasants came to his house looking for Gandhi, hoping to share their tales of oppression with him, Jawaharlal, at a loose end, went home with them and this experience was his first revelation of living India. As he described it:

> They looked on us with loving and hopeful eyes, as if we were the bearers of good tidings, the guides who would lead us to the promised land. Looking at them and their

misery and overflowing gratitude, I was filled with shame and sorrow, shame at my own easy-going and comfortable life and our petty politics of the city which ignored this vast multitude of semi-naked sons and daughters of India, sorrow at the degradation and overwhelming poverty of India.

As he travelled around India, his sister Krishna, and sometimes his wife Kamala, would accompany him. 'Slowly,' Krishna recalled, 'he grasped the psychology of the masses and began to feel a thrill at being able to influence vast crowds.' His act of taking family members on these rigorous trips was (consciously or not) building the Nehru legend that the family in some mystical way had a unique relationship with India.

A former moderate in nationalist politics, Motilal Nehru was voted president of the Indian National Congress in the wake of the Amritsar massacre in 1919, and again at the key session in Calcutta in 1920 when he dramatically backed Gandhi's call for withdrawal from British-run courts, elections, legislatures, schools and colleges, and for the boycott of official functions and foreign goods. The reason for Motilal's about-turn was not policy, but family: he knew Jawaharlal would go with Gandhi; Motilal voted to be on the same side as his son when the battle started.

Out went the Western kitchen, crystal, china and wine cellar in Allahabad, along with the horses and carriages; the staff was drastically reduced and the Western clothes sacrificed on a giant bonfire. The stories of the Nehrus' wealth were often wildly exaggerated, as were the tales of how low they now abased themselves (they still lived very comfortably by Indian standards) so that the mythic element of the renunciation could shine through. This destiny was not thrust upon the Nehrus; they fashioned it themselves.

In 1928 Motilal Nehru presented a draft constitution for a future India under dominion status within the British Empire. Embracing universal adult franchise and equal rights for women, the Nehru report was the basis of the constitution India would adopt twenty years later—an example of the way Nehru skills helped define the nation. When Gandhi put his name forward for the presidency of the 1929 Congress at Lahore, Jawaharlal was embarrassed and tried to refuse the honour, but Motilal was overjoyed and hymned the occasion with a Persian adage, 'What the father is unable to accomplish, the son achieves.' Indira, Jawaharlal's twelve-year-old daughter, was present to see power pass from father to son.

Motilal renamed his house Swaraj Bhavan (Abode of Freedom), and donated it to the nation in April 1930, a year before his death. It attracted crowds of devotees anxious to catch a glimpse of the family. 'The verandas of the house were full of these visitors of ours,' wrote Jawaharlal, 'Each door and window had a collection of prying eyes.' Among pictures of the gods and Indian heroes, the bazaars sold pictures of Jawaharlal and his wife Kamala with the inscription *'adarsha jori'* ('the ideal couple')—rather ironically, considering their less than ideal married life.

## On one occasion Indira Gandhi was obliged to tell a visitor, 'I'm sorry but my grandfather, father and mummy are all in prison.'

The family, and Jahawarlal especially, spent long spells in jail for their anti-British activities. On a famous occasion Indira was obliged to tell a visitor to the house, 'I'm sorry but my grandfather, father and mummy are all in prison.' Jawaharlal wrote regularly to Indira during his absences—and in 1929 published the correspondence as *Letters From a Father to His Daughter.* His lengthy account of Indian history from the Indus Valley civilization through British rule and the independence struggle, *The Discovery of India,* written while he was in prison for the last time, even included events from his own life, such as the death of his wife Kamala. The family's activities, their relationships, and literally their worldview, were being made public property. Jawaharlal was writing them into history.

The 1935 Government of India Act gave self-government to the Indian provinces. During the first elections in 1936–37, Jawaharlal went on a national campaign on behalf of Congress, travelling 50,000 miles by plane, train, car, bicycle, cart, steamer, paddle boat, canoe, horse, elephant, camel and on foot. One time the crowd waiting to see him was so packed that when he arrived he had to walk on their shoulders to get to the front to address them. He is said to have addressed ten million people and been seen by many more.

When Indira Nehru married a nationalist activist, Feroze Gandhi, in 1942, the Labour MP Stafford Cripps, an old family friend, was a guest at the wedding. A cabinet minister in Churchill's coalition government, he was in India to broker a deal to end independence agitation—a deal Congress turned down. Indira's cousin Nayantara said, 'It was quite usual in our family for a very personal, private event to be somehow involved with matters that were happening in the world and in the country. So we took it for granted that the Cripps Mission

should be somehow mixed up with Indira's wedding.' Feroze was no relation to 'Mahatma' Gandhi, but many Indians and not a few foreigners believed he was, an association that would do Indira no harm at all.

Indira and Feroze spent little time together once their sons Rajiv and Sanjay had been born in 1944 and 1946. When Jawaharlal, a widower, became prime minister in 1947 in newly independent India, he needed a consort and Indira—with Rajiv and Sanjay—moved in to the prime minister's residence, learning diplomacy at home and on foreign visits. It was here that Indira acquired the imperious attitude that the Nehrus were the ruling family.

When Indira became minister of information in the government formed by Lal Bahadur Shastri after her father's death in 1964, it was her first experience of government, though she was referred to as 'the only man in the cabinet' after she took decisive action during the war with Pakistan in 1965. Less than two years later Shastri died suddenly, and Indira Gandhi was called upon to take over as the only person who could hold the Congress Party together and unite the nation. In the election that followed, Indira declared that she would pursue policies in the interests of the country: 'the Congress is big, but India is bigger.' It was the true message of her campaign: to rely on her own popularity with the people, going over the heads of the party chiefs. It was during this election in 1967 that she was addressed as 'Mother Indira' for the first time.

Indira's imperious rule earned her enemies who finally caught up with her when she was taken to court on a charge of minor electoral irregularities in 1975. The court invalidated her election of 1971 and disbarred her from office for six years. Announcing that 'the security of India is threatened by internal disturbances', she therefore declared a state of emergency. Opposition leaders were arrested, the press controlled, and strikes banned. The state of emergency was not forced on Indira; insulated from reality by her hand-picked advisers and sycophants, she had projected her own fears and insecurities onto the nation. India was not 'in peril from both internal and external enemies', as she protested; but Indira herself was menaced by her enemies, and she so closely identified her fate with that of the nation that she was unable to distinguish that a threat to one was not necessarily a threat to both.

Meanwhile, Indira was grooming her younger son, Sanjay, to succeed her, but he was piling up enemies even in Nehru loyalist heartlands by a brutal policy of forced sterilizations to achieve lower population growth. When Indira finally permitted elections in 1977 (using the slogan 'Indira is India') she lost decisively and was expelled from parliament. For the first time since independence the Congress Party was not in power.

Indira fought back, a branch of Congress loyal to her alone. In the election of 1980, as if trying to out-perform her father, she travelled 40,000 miles, addressing twenty-two meetings a day with a combined audience of one hundred million. After she was returned to power a journalist asked her how it felt to be India's leader again. Indira responded ferociously, 'I have always been India's leader.'

Six months after the election Sanjay Gandhi was killed while performing aerobatic stunts in a private plane. Indira was devastated, but publicly remarked 'People come and go but the nation continues to live'—as usual, placing a family event in a national context. Sanjay's widow Maneka was ready to step into Sanjay's shoes, but Indira refused to endorse her and, in a public falling-out with her daughter-in-law, threw her out of the family home. Maneka, the only member of the younger generation who was a natural politician, subsequently became an MP and was a minister in four governments, all in opposition to Congress. Indira's elder son Rajiv, a quiet man who had a job he loved as an airline pilot, was conscripted to take over his brother's constituency and was made nominal head of Indira's Congress Party. He ingenuously confessed to reporters that he had entered politics 'to help mummy'.

On October 31st, 1984, Indira was assassinated by her Sikh bodyguards, enraged by her having ordered an attack on the Golden Temple in Amritsar, which Sikh terrorists had been using as a stronghold. Congress loyalists, thrown into confusion and lacking a procedure for selecting anyone but a Nehru to rule, reached for the next member of the dynasty. The official announcement of Indira's death was made at 6 P.M., nearly nine hours after she had been shot, and long after the BBC World Service had announced the news. At 6.20 Rajiv was sworn in. After only three years in parliament, with no cabinet, or even junior ministerial experience, Rajiv Gandhi became prime minister of the world's largest democracy. Two months later his Congress Party won 415 of 543 parliamentary seats, the largest electoral landslide in Indian history.

The inexperienced and reluctant politician lost the next election, in 1989, and became leader of the opposition, an unusual situation for a Nehru-Gandhi. When, during an election campaign in May 1991 Rajiv was blown to pieces by a Tamil suicide bomber, the tragedy of his death was compounded by the political turmoil caused by the absence of an obvious successor. In a gesture of exceptional bad taste, within four days of Rajiv's death Congress unanimously elected his Italian-born widow Sonia president. She declined the honour, and also refused to stand in an election later that year.

Throughout the early 1990s a barely competent minority Congress administration that felt it needed the Nehru magic continued to woo Sonia and her two children, Priyanka and Rahul. Sonia's position was impossible: she hated politics for having taken her beloved husband from her even before it had killed him. She had no political skill and did not speak any of the languages of India, except English. But only involvement in politics would guarantee her children the level of protection they needed if they were to escape the fate of their father and grandmother. Slowly, Sonia edged closer to the political centre, joining the party in 1997, becoming its president in 1999, and successfully standing for election in 1999. She then took office as leader of the opposition.

After the election of May 2004, won by Congress and its allies, Sonia was set to become the fourth prime minister of the Nehru-Gandhi dynasty, unanimously supported by the other parties in the coalition. Her enemies counted up the strikes against her: she was a Roman Catholic, Indian by neither birth nor blood, and with a poor command of Hindi. After a tense few days, Sonia judiciously listened to her 'inner voice' and recommended the respected economist Manmohan Singh as prime minister. She retained the post of chair of the Congress parliamentary party.

Rahul Gandhi successfully contested his father's former constituency in 2004. His sister Priyanka, considered the more charismatic of the younger Nehru-Gandhis, acted as a campaign manager and did constituency work but resolutely refused a formal political role. Supporters have established a site of martyrdom at the former family home in Delhi, now the Indira Gandhi Memorial Museum, where a path of shining, underlit crystal glass in the grounds shows the last walk Indira took to the spot where she was killed. Relics of the exalted ones are shown as if they were a holy family: the blood-stained sari Indira wore when she was gunned down; the shredded clothes in which Rajiv was dressed when he was blown up. With the fourth generation of Nehru-Gandhis in charge of Indian politics, and a fifth preparing for the future, the family's tryst with destiny seems to have many more years to run.

# The Roots of Chinese Xenophobia

**During most of the twentieth century, Chinese schools taught history as a series of *guo chi*, or national humiliations caused by foreign powers.**

DENNIS VAN VRANKEN HICKEY

In 1900, the American public reacted with horror to newspaper accounts describing a siege of hundreds of foreign diplomats and civilians who were trapped inside a diplomatic compound in Peking, China. The atrocities committed by some members of the Chinese population—in this instance instigated by a group known as the Boxers—seemed incomprehensible and barbaric to many in the international community.

Almost one century later—in 1999 to be exact—the American public once again expressed surprise and bewilderment as news stories depicted Chinese mobs attacking the U.S. Embassy in Beijing. In both cases, strong evidence suggested that the Chinese government tacitly condoned the sieges. At the same time, however, it appeared that the assaults enjoyed widespread popular approval.

When seeking to explain these and other ugly incidents, Western news reports traditionally dismissed them as symbols of Chinese irrationality and xenophobia. More recently, they are ascribed simply to a particularly virulent and nasty brand of nationalism. Unfortunately, little effort is directed toward uncovering the reasons *why* the Chinese sometimes seem xenophobic, angry, or irrational.

## The Chinese Paradigm

The concept of paradigms is borrowed from Thomas Kuhn, who employed them to describe advances in science. A paradigm may be defined as a basic assumption in a field of science. The acceptance of these assumptions is shared by practitioners in a given field and usually is not subject to widespread discussion or debate. Over time, paradigms may shift, but this change often comes very slowly.

Some scholars have suggested that the concept may be applied to the orientation of a nation and its population. A country's foreign policy paradigm is shaped by critical events. For example, the Japanese sneak attack on Pearl Harbor in 1941 culminated in a paradigm shift in American policy. Following the attack, the United States abandoned isolationism and adopted an interventionist and internationalist approach to foreign policy—an approach that many believe remains intact today.

A series of cataclysmic events led China to adopt a distinctly different outlook. Beijing eyes much of the global community with deep suspicion and distrust—particularly the most powerful states in the international system. When provided the opportunity, it believes, these governments will use their power to bully, dismember, and humiliate China.

The Chinese also suspect that many of the problems confronting their country—particularly troubles relating to territorial sovereignty and economic development—may be traced to the actions of foreign powers. It is noteworthy that the central tenets of this paradigm were shared by the governing elites in both the Republican and communist eras of China's modern history.

Why do the Chinese hold such a dark view of international politics? Why does the population sometimes appear xenophobic and paranoid to outside observers? Why does Beijing suspect that foreign powers work to keep the country divided and weak? This article seeks to address these questions.

## The National Humiliations

During most of the twentieth century, Chinese schools taught history as a series of *guo chi,* or national humiliations. Consequently, the Chinese tend to see numerous events—ranging from the accidental American bombing of the Chinese Embassy in Belgrade to the midair collision between a Chinese warplane and an American spy plane near Hainan Island—as major embarrassments.

Less dramatic incidents—ranging from trade disputes to quarrels over the location of the Olympic Games—are also considered prime examples of guo chi. To the Chinese, it's simply a matter of history repeating itself. A review of some of their country's major defeats and humiliations at the hands of foreign governments may help readers understand this perspective.

China's humiliations began in the nineteenth century, when the Western powers and Japan forced imperial China open and began to dismember it. One of the earliest (and worst) episodes involved the British and their determination to peddle opium to the Chinese population. Outraged by the Chinese government's

# A History of Foreign Intervention

China's humiliations began in the nineteenth century, when the Western powers and Japan forced it open and began to dismember it.

In 1898, Britain coerced China into leasing the New Territories—a large agricultural area that would help support Hong Kong—for 99 years.

Britain's encroachments encouraged other powers to follow its lead. France, Germany, Belgium, Sweden, Norway, Russia, and the United States all forced treaties on China that would provide their governments with special rights and privileges.

The actions of the foreign powers gave the Chinese ample reason to become xenophobic. These sentiments exploded in 1900 when a peasant movement known as the Boxer Rebellion sought to expel the imperialists from the country.

Throughout the first half of the twentieth century, foreigners continued to enjoy special privileges in China while the people suffered.

Matters took a dramatic turn for the worse when Japan occupied Manchuria and initiated a war that lasted from 1937 to 1945. According to some estimates, 13.5 million Chinese perished in the conflict.

attempts to ban the drug and punish opium traders, Great Britain declared war on China and defeated it in the so-called Opium War (1839–42).

The results of this conflict were disastrous. Millions of Chinese became drug addicts, and the imperial government was forced to pay Great Britain for the costs it had incurred during the war. Moreover, the resulting Treaty of Nanking—the first in a series of unequal treaties—provided the British with the right to trade with the Chinese at five ports and ceded the island of Hong Kong to the United Kingdom "in perpetuity."

Great Britain was not satisfied with the gains that it secured during the Opium War. After emerging victorious in a second conflict in 1860, the British obtained more indemnities from the Chinese government, secured 10 more treaty ports, and occupied the Kowloon Peninsula.

This prime piece of real estate, located directly across from the island of Hong Kong, was also ceded to the British in perpetuity. Then, in 1898, Great Britain coerced China into leasing the New Territories—a large agricultural area that would help support Hong Kong—for 99 years.

Great Britain's encroachments encouraged other powers to follow its lead. France, Germany, Belgium, Sweden, Norway, Russia, and the United States all forced treaties on China that would provide their respective governments with special rights and privileges.

For example, Germany obtained a 99-year lease on the tip of Shandong, France secured a 99-year lease on the Bay of Guanzhou, and Russia obtained a 25-year lease for a base in Dalian and Port Arthur. And after China's defeat in the Sino-Japanese War of 1895, the island province of Taiwan was formally incorporated into the Empire of Japan.

During the last years of the nineteenth century, some predicted that China, like Africa, might be carved up entirely by the world's most powerful imperialist powers. These fears prompted America to promote an "open door" policy, under which all countries would be permitted to trade in Chinese territories that were dominated by other powers. This was not an altruistic gesture. Rather, it was designed to prevent the weaker imperialist nations—like the United States—from being cut out of the lucrative China trade.

The actions of the foreign powers gave the Chinese ample reason to become xenophobic. These sentiments exploded in 1900 when a peasant movement known as the Boxer Rebellion sought to expel imperialists from the country. To many Chinese, the Boxers symbolized patriotism. To the imperialists, however, they were barbarians who unwittingly provided foreigners with another excuse to carve up China.

After the Boxers were defeated, the Chinese government was forced to pay massive indemnities to the victors and permit foreign troops to be stationed at key positions throughout the country. The defeat also served as a spark that helped fuel the flames of nationalism in China, paving the way for the overthrow of the Qing dynasty in 1911 and the establishment of the Republic of China.

Perhaps the most critical incident contributing to the rise of Chinese nationalism occurred after World War I. In 1919, the victorious Allied powers announced at the Paris Peace Conference that Germany's special rights in Shandong Province would be transferred to Japan. There was a strong feeling that China—which had supported the Allied cause during the war—had been betrayed. The news from Paris sparked massive student protests, widespread demonstrations, and a boycott of Japanese goods throughout the country.

The ensuing turmoil came to be known as the May Fourth Movement. It set the stage for the rise of both the Kuomintang (KMT) and the Chinese Communist Party (CCP) as mass movements dedicated to promoting nationalism, uniting the country, and ending the era of guo chi.

The May Fourth Movement did not put an immediate end to China's humiliations. Throughout the first half of the twentieth century, foreigners continued to enjoy special privileges while the Chinese people suffered. Matters took a dramatic turn for the worse when Japan occupied Manchuria in 1931. The war it initiated on July 7, 1937, would last until 1945. According to some estimates, 13.5 million Chinese perished in the conflict.

Following World War II, China descended into civil war. After several years of bitter fighting, the CCP emerged victorious and the KMT retreated to Taiwan (in keeping with wartime agreements, the island and other territories had been formally returned to China in 1945). When proclaiming the founding of the new People's Republic of China on October 1, 1949, Mao

Zedong declared proudly that the Chinese people had finally "stood up." The message was unmistakable: the era of guo chi would come to an end.

As Mao's troops swept into China's major cities, the foreigners abandoned their opulent enclaves. This time, the imperialist powers did not intervene. After expelling the imperialists, Mao set out to reassemble the Chinese empire that had crumbled during the waning years of the Qing dynasty.

Chinese authority was reestablished in the territories of Eastern Turkestan, Inner Mongolia, and Tibet. The fact that the minority populations occupying these regions had little, if anything, in common with Chinese culture meant nothing to the communist regime. The territories had once belonged to the Chinese empire, and they had been claimed by Chiang Kaishek's KMT. Consequently, they would now become part of the "New China."

Other territories proved more difficult to acquire. In 1954, Mao asked the Soviet Union to "return" Outer Mongolia, but Moscow refused. After years of prolonged negotiation, Deng Xiaoping, Mao's successor, engineered the return of the British colony of Hong Kong (all three parts of it) to China in 1997.

Shortly afterward, the Portuguese colony of Macao was returned. Most recently, Beijing's attention has shifted to Taiwan. China insists that the island, like all other "lost" or "stolen" territories, must be returned. The prospect of independence for Taiwan—a proposition embraced by a new generation of leadership in Taipei—is deemed out of the question. If Taiwan moves too close to de jure independence, Beijing has threatened to use force to unite it with the mainland.

## Conclusion

The foreign treaty ports, gunboats, and colonies that humiliated China for over 100 years are now part of history. Even the physical traces of this past are beginning to disappear. Many of the Western buildings that once characterized the international settlement in Shanghai are gone. The Victorian-era structures have been replaced by modern skyscrapers and shopping centers. Nevertheless, the psychological scars and pains of the era of guo chi linger and continue to influence relations with the outside world.

At present, China confronts massive corruption, unemployment, and other wrenching dislocations associated with its transition to a market-style economy. To be sure, the government sometimes seeks to use nationalism to deflect attention from its failures and shore up support for the regime.

---

## Many Chinese complain that the government is not forceful enough in the face of perceived foreign transgressions.

---

Nevertheless, it would be a mistake to assume that the population's nationalistic sentiment may be attributed solely to government propaganda or manipulation. In fact, many Chinese complain that the government is not forceful enough in the face of perceived foreign transgressions.

Nationalism has been a potent force in Chinese politics since the Boxer Rebellion. Increasingly, many Chinese at both the elite and popular levels perceive the United States as the sole remaining foreign power that is determined to keep the country divided, weak, and poor. This is a very troubling development. Ironically, however, America is still popular among many Chinese. It remains a chief destination for China's students, and its technology, business methods, and even political institutions are widely admired.

One of the greatest challenges for the United States will be to manage an increasingly complicated relationship with China. Given the unfortunate history of Beijing's ties with much of the international community, it is likely that this relationship will be characterized by a fairly consistent amount of tension. Consequently, both sides will have to work hard to promote harmony and avoid conflict.

---

**Dennis Van Vranken Hickey** is professor in the political science department at Southwest Missouri State University.

# Exposing the Rape of Nanking

**Exclusive excerpts from a Chinese-American author's unflinching re-examination of one of the most horrifying chapters of the second world war.**

IRIS CHANG

The chronicle of humankind's cruelty is a long and sorry tale. But if it is true that even in such horror tales there are degrees of ruthlessness, then few atrocities can compare in intensity and scale to the rape of Nanking during World War II.

The broad details of the rape are, except among the Japanese, not in dispute. In November 1937, after their successful invasion of Shanghai, the Japanese launched a massive attack on the newly established capital of the Republic of China. When the city fell on December 13, 1937, Japanese soldiers began an orgy of cruelty seldom if ever matched in world history. Tens of thousands of young men were rounded up and herded to the outer areas of the city, where they were mowed down by machine guns, used for bayonet practice, or soaked with gasoline and burned alive. By the end of the massacre an estimated 260,000 to 350,000 Chinese had been killed. Between 20,000 and 80,000 Chinese women were raped—and many soldiers went beyond rape to disembowel women, slice off their breasts, nail them alive to walls. So brutal were the Japanese in Nanking that even the Nazis in the city were shocked. John Rabe, a German businessman who led the local Nazi party, joined other foreigners in working tirelessly to save the innocent from slaughter by creating a safety zone where some 250,000 civilians found shelter.

Yet the Rape of Nanking remains an obscure incident. Although the death toll exceeds the immediate number of deaths from the atomic bombings of Hiroshima and Nagasaki (140,000 and 70,000 respectively, by the end of 1945) and even the total civilian casualties for several European countries during the entire war (Great Britain lost 61,000 civilians, France 108,000, Belgium 101,000, and the Netherlands 242,000), the horrors of the Nanking massacre remain virtually unknown to people outside Asia. The Rape of Nanking did not penetrate the world consciousness in the same manner as the Jewish Holocaust or Hiroshima because the victims themselves remained silent. The custodian of the curtain of silence was politics. The People's Republic of China, Taiwan, and even the United States all contributed to the historical neglect of this event for reasons deeply rooted in the cold war. After the 1949 Communist revolution in China, neither the People's Republic of China nor Taiwan demanded wartime reparations from Japan (as Israel had from Germany) because the two governments were competing for Japanese trade and political recognition. And even the United States, faced with the threat of communism in the Soviet Union and mainland China, sought to ensure the friendship and loyalty of its former enemy Japan. In this manner, cold-war tensions permitted Japan to escape much of the intense critical examination that its wartime ally was forced to undergo.

In trying to understand the actions of the Japanese, we must begin with a little history. To prepare for what it viewed as an inevitable war with China, Japan had spent decades training its men. The molding of young men to serve in the Japanese military began early: In the 1930s, toy shops became virtual shrines to war, selling arsenals of toy soldiers, tanks, rifles, antiaircraft guns, bugles, and howitzers. Japanese schools operated like miniature military units. Indeed, some of the teachers were military officers, who lectured students on their duty to help Japan fulfill its divine destiny of conquering Asia and being able to stand up to the world's nations as a people second to none. They taught young boys how to handle wooden models of guns, and older boys how to handle real ones. Textbooks became vehicles for military propaganda. Teachers also instilled in boys hatred and contempt for the Chinese people, preparing them psychologically for a future invasion of the Chinese mainland. One historian tells the story of a squeamish Japanese schoolboy in the 1930s who burst into tears when told to dissect a frog. His teacher slammed his knuckles against the boy's head and yelled, "Why are you crying about one lousy frog? When you grow up you'll have to kill one hundred, two hundred chinks!"

In the summer of 1937 Japan finally seized the opportunity to provoke a full-scale war with China. One night in July several shots were fired at members of a Japanese regiment, garrisoned by treaty in the Chinese city of Tientsin, and a Japanese soldier failed to appear during roll call after the maneuvers. Japanese troops advanced upon the nearby Chinese fort of Wanping and demanded that its gates be opened so that they could search for the soldier. When the Chinese commander refused, the Japanese shelled the fort. The confrontation escalated, and by August the Japanese had invaded Shanghai. Conquering China proved to be a more difficult task than the Japanese anticipated. In Shanghai alone Chinese forces outnumbered the Japanese marines ten to one, and Chiang Kai-shek, leader of the Nationalist government, had reserved his best troops for the battle. For months the Chinese defended the metropolis with extraordinary valor. To the chagrin of the Japanese, the battle of Shanghai proceeded slowly, street by street, barricade by barricade.

Little was spared on the path to Nanking. Japanese veterans remember raiding tiny farm communities, where they clubbed or bayoneted everyone in sight. Small villages were not the only casualties; entire cities were razed to the ground. Consider the example of Suchow, a city on the east bank of the Tai Hu Lake. One of the oldest cities of China, it was prized for its delicate silk embroidery, palaces, and temples. Its canals and ancient bridges had earned the city its Western nickname as "the Venice of China." On November 19, on a morning of pouring rain, a Japanese advance guard marched through the gates of Suchow, wearing hoods that prevented Chinese sentries from recognizing them. Once inside, the Japanese murdered and plundered the city for days, burning ancient landmarks, and abducting thousands of Chinese women for sexual slavery. The invasion, according to the *China Weekly Review,* caused the population of the city to drop from 250,000 to less than 500. By the time Japanese troops entered Nanking, an order to eliminate all Chinese captives had been not only committed to paper but distributed to lower-echelon officers. On December 13, 1937, the Japanese 66th Battalion received the following command:

"All prisoners of war are to be executed. Method of execution: divide the prisoners into groups of a dozen. Shoot to kill separately. Our intentions are absolutely not to be detected by the prisoners."

There was a ruthless logic to the order: the captives could not be fed, so they had to be destroyed. Killing them would not only eliminate the food problem but diminish the possibility of retaliation. Moreover, dead enemies could not form up into guerrilla forces.

## It would be disastrous if they were to make any trouble.

But executing the order was another matter. When the Japanese troops smashed through Nanking's walls in the early pre-dawn hours of December 13, they entered a city in which they were vastly outnumbered. Historians later estimated that more than half a million civilians and ninety thousand Chinese troops were trapped in Nanking, compared with the fifty thousand Japanese soldiers who assaulted the city. General Kesago Nakajima knew that killing tens of thousands of Chinese captives was a formidable task: "To deal with crowds of a thousand, five thousand, or ten thousand, it is tremendously difficult even just to disarm them. . . . It would be disastrous if they were to make any trouble."

Because of their limited manpower, the Japanese relied heavily on deception. The strategy for mass butchery involved several steps: promising the Chinese fair treatment in return for an end to resistance, coaxing them into surrendering themselves to their Japanese conquerors, dividing them into groups of one to two hundred men, and then luring them to different areas near Nanking to be killed. Nakajima hoped that faced with the impossibility of further resistance, most of the captives would lose heart and comply with whatever directions the Japanese gave them.

All this was easier to achieve than the Japanese had anticipated. Resistance was sporadic; indeed, it was practically non-existent. Having thrown away their arms when attempting to flee the city as the Japanese closed in, many Chinese soldiers simply turned themselves in, hoping for better treatment. Once the men surrendered and permitted their hands to be bound, the rest was easy.

After the soldiers surrendered en masse, there was virtually no one left to protect the citizens of the city. Knowing this, the Japanese poured into Nanking, occupying government buildings, banks, and warehouses, shooting people randomly in the streets, many of them in the back as they ran away. As victims toppled to the ground, moaning and screaming, the streets, alleys, and ditches of the fallen capital ran rivers of blood. During the last ten days of December, Japanese motorcycle brigades patrolled Nanking while Japanese soldiers shouldering loaded rifles guarded the entrances to all the streets, avenues, and alleys. Troops went from door to door, demanding that they be opened to welcome the victorious armies. The moment the shopkeepers complied, the Japanese opened fire on them. The imperial army massacred thousands of people in this manner and then systematically looted the stores and burned whatever they had no use for.

## The killing went on nonstop, from morning until night.

These atrocities shocked many of the Japanese correspondents who had followed the troops to Nanking. Even seasoned war correspondents recoiled at the orgy of violence, and their exclamations found their way into print. From the Japanese military correspondent Yukio Omata, who saw Chinese prisoners brought to Hsiakwan and lined up along the river: "Those in the first row were beheaded, those in the second row were forced to dump the severed bodies into the river before they themselves were beheaded. The killing went on nonstop, from morning until night, but they were only able to kill 2,000 persons in this way. The next day, tired of killing in this fashion, they set up machine guns. Two of them raked a cross-fire at the lined-up prisoners. Rat-tat-tat-tat. Triggers were pulled. The prisoners fled into the water, but no one was able to make it to the other shore."

## Even war correspondents recoiled at the violence.

Next, the Japanese turned their attention to the women. The rape of Nanking is considered the worst mass rape of world history with the sole exception of the treatment of Bengali women by Pakistani soldiers in 1971. Kozo Takokoro, a former soldier in the 114th Division of the Japanese army in Nanking, recalled, "No matter how young or old, they all could not escape the fate of being raped. We sent out coal trucks from Hsiakwan to the city streets and villages to seize a lot of women. And then each of them was allocated to 15 to 20 soldiers for sexual intercourse and abuse."

Surviving Japanese veterans claim that the army had officially outlawed the rape of enemy women. But rape remained so deeply embedded in Japanese military culture and superstition that no one took the rule seriously. Many believed that raping virgins would make them more powerful in battle. Soldiers were even known to wear amulets made from the pubic hair of such victims, believing that they possessed magical powers against injury.

The military policy forbidding rape only encouraged soldiers to kill their victims afterwards. Kozo Takokoro was blunt about this. "After raping, we would also kill them," he recalled. "Those women would start to flee once we let them go. Then we would bang! shoot them in the back to finish them up." According to surviving veterans, many of the soldiers felt remarkably little guilt about this. "Perhaps when we were raping her, we looked at her as a woman," Shiro Azuma, a former soldier in Nanking, wrote, "but when we killed her, we just thought of her as something like a pig."

One of the most bizarre consequences of the wholesale rape that took place at Nanking was the response of the Japanese government. The Japanese high command made plans to create a giant underground system of military prostitution—one that would draw into its web hundreds of thousands of women across Asia. The plan was straightforward. By luring, purchasing, or kidnapping between eighty thousand and two hundred thousand women—most of them from the Japanese colony of Korea but many also from China, Taiwan, the Philippines, and Indonesia—the Japanese military hoped to reduce the incidence of random rape of local women (thereby diminishing the opportunity for international criticism), to contain sexually transmitted diseases through the use of condoms, and to reward soldiers for fighting on the battlefront for long stretches of time. Later, of course, when the world learned of this plan, the Japanese government refused to acknowledge responsibility, insisting for decades afterwards that private entrepreneurs, not the imperial government, ran the wartime military brothels. But in 1991 Yoshiaki Yoshimi unearthed from the Japanese Defense Agency's archives a document entitled "Regarding the Recruitment of Women for Military Brothels." The document bore the personal stamps of leaders from the Japanese high command and contained orders for the immediate construction of "facilities of sexual comfort" to stop troops from raping women in regions they controlled in China.

The first official comfort house opened near Nanking in 1938. To use the word *comfort* in regard to either the women or the "houses" in which they lived is ludicrous, for it conjures up spa images of beautiful geisha girls strumming lutes, washing men, and giving them shiatsu massages. In reality, the conditions of these brothels were sordid beyond the imagination of most civilized people. Untold numbers of these women (whom the Japanese called "public toilets") took their own lives when they learned of their destiny; others died from disease or murder. Those who survived suffered a lifetime of shame and isolation, sterility, or ruined health.

In interview after interview, Japanese veterans from the Nanking massacre reported honestly that they experienced a complete lack of remorse or sense of wrongdoing, even when torturing helpless civilians. Hakudo Nagatomi spoke candidly about his emotions in the fallen capital: "I remember being driven in a truck along a path that had been cleared through piles of thousands and thousands of slaughtered bodies. Wild dogs were gnawing at the dead flesh as we stopped and pulled a group of Chinese prisoners out of the back. Then the Japanese officer proposed a test of my courage. He unsheathed his sword, spat on it, and with a sudden mighty swing he brought it down on the neck of a Chinese boy cowering before us. The head was cut clean off and tumbled away on the group as the body slumped forward, blood spurting in two great gushing fountains from the neck. The officer suggested I take the head home as a souvenir. I remember smiling proudly as I took his sword and began killing people."

After almost sixty years of soul-searching, Nagatomi is a changed man. A doctor in Japan, he has built a shrine of remorse in his waiting room. Patients can watch videotapes of his trial in Nanking and a full confession of his crimes. The gentle and hospitable demeanor of the doctor belies the horror of his past, making it almost impossible for one to imagine that he had once been a ruthless murderer. "Few know that soldiers impaled babies on bayonets and tossed them still alive into pots of boiling water," Nagatomi said. "They gang-raped women from the ages of twelve to eighty and then killed them when they could no longer satisfy sexual requirements. I beheaded people, starved them to death, burned them, and buried them alive, over two hundred in all. It is terrible that I could turn into an animal and do these things. There are really no words to explain what I was doing. I was truly a devil."

# Judgment at Nuremberg

**Fifty years ago the trial of Nazi war criminals ended: the world had witnessed the rule of law invoked to punish unspeakable atrocities.**

ROBERT SHNAYERSON

In the war-shattered city of Nuremberg, 51 years ago, an eloquent American prosecutor named Robert H. Jackson opened what he called "the first trial in history for crimes against the peace of the world." The setting was the once lovely Bavarian city's hastily refurbished Palace of Justice, an SS prison only eight months before. In the dock were 21 captured Nazi leaders, notably the fat, cunning drug addict Hermann Göring.

Their alleged crimes, the ultimate in 20th-century depravity, included the mass murders of some six million Jews and millions of other human beings deemed "undesirable" by Adolf Hitler. "The wrongs which we seek to condemn and punish," said Robert Jackson, "have been so calculated, so malignant and so devastating, that civilization cannot tolerate their being ignored because it cannot survive their being repeated."

Here were satanic men like Ernst Kaltenbrunner, the scar-faced functionary second only to Heinrich Himmler in overseeing the death camps and the Nazi police apparatus; Alfred Rosenberg, cofounder of the Nazi Party and chief theorist of anti-Semitism; and Hans Frank, the vicious and venal Nazi proconsul in Poland. At the time, many asked why such messengers of evil were to be allowed even one day in court, much less the 403 sessions they were about to undergo. It was a question that Jackson, on leave from his job as a Justice of the U.S. Supreme Court to prosecute this case, quickly addressed in his opening statement.

With the kind of moral clarity that marked American idealism at the time, Jackson declared, "That four great nations, flushed with victory and stung with injury stay the hand of vengeance and voluntarily submit their captive enemies to the judgment of the law is one of the most significant tributes that Power ever has paid to Reason. . . . The real complaining party at your bar is Civilization. . . . [It] asks whether law is so laggard as to be utterly helpless to deal with crimes of this magnitude."

So began, in November 1945, the century's most heroic attempt to achieve justice without vengeance—heroic because the victors of World War II had every reason to destroy the vanquished without pity. Heroic because they ultimately resisted the temptation to impose on the Germans what the Nazis had imposed on their victims—collective guilt. Instead, they granted their captives a presumption of innocence and conducted a ten-month trial to determine their personal responsibility.

Locked up in solitary cells each night, constantly guarded by American M.P.'s mindful of recent suicides among high-ranking Nazis, the defendants spent their days in a giant court-room built for 400 spectators, listening to evidence drawn from 300,000 affidavits and meticulous German documents so voluminous they filled six freight cars. Nearly all were ready to acknowledge the horrific facts while cravenly assigning blame to others. (Göring, who died unrepentant, was the exception.) When it was all over in October 1946, and ten defendants had been hanged messily in the Palace of Justice's gymnasium, this first Nuremberg trial stood as the judicial Everest of those who hoped, as Jackson did, that the rule of law could punish, if not prevent, the atrocities of war.

The exercise of justice at Nuremberg reverberates across this century. And next month, on November 13 and 14, scholars will ponder the lessons of history at an international conference on the trials, sponsored by the Library of Congress and the U.S. Holocaust Memorial Museum.

How this trial, and the 12 that followed, came to be held is a story in itself. In April 1944, two Jews who escaped the Auschwitz death camp described its horrors to the world. They detailed Germany's technology of genocide, such as the camp's four new gas-and-burn machines, each designed to kill 2,000 prisoners at a time. They pinpointed a huge slave-labor operation at nearby Birkenau, run by Germany's fine old industrial names (I. G. Farben and Siemens among others), where Allied prisoners and kidnapped foreign laborers were fed so little and worked so hard that as many as one-third died every week. Their testimony paved the way to Nuremberg.

The Allied leaders had little trouble agreeing that German war crimes must be punished. But punished how? Treasury Secretary Henry Morgenthau Jr. urged that all captured Nazi leaders be shot immediately, without trial, and that Germany be reduced to the status of an agricultural backwater. Secretary of War Henry Stimson thought dooming all Germans to a kind of national execution would not do. It violated the Allied (if not Soviet) belief in the rule of law. It would deny postwar Germany a working economy and perhaps, ultimately, breed another war.

Roosevelt, who wanted to bring G.I.s (and their votes) home promptly, sought a compromise between Morgenthau and Stimson. The man asked to find it was Murray Bernays, a 51-year-old lawyer turned wartime Army colonel in the Pentagon.

Immediately, a basic but legally complex question rose to the fore—what is a war crime, anyway? At the end of the 19th century, the increased killing power of modern weapons led to the various Hague and Geneva conventions, binding most great powers to treat civilians humanely, shun the killing of unarmed prisoners and avoid ultimate weapons, such as germ warfare, "calculated to cause unnecessary suffering." Such "laws of war" are quite frequently applied. They have saved thousands of lives. In combat the basic distinction between legitimate warfare and atrocities occurs when acts of violence exceed "military necessity."

Before Nuremberg, jurisdiction over war crimes was limited to each country's military courts. After World War I, when the victors accused 896 Germans of serious war crimes, demanding their surrender to Allied military courts, the Germans insisted on trying them and accepted a mere 12 cases. Three defendants never showed up; charges against three others were dropped; the remaining six got trivial sentences.

Bernays envisioned a different scenario: an international court that held individuals liable for crimes the world deemed crimes, even if their nation had approved or required those actions. The accused could not plead obedience to superiors. They would be held personally responsible.

Other big questions remained. One was how an international court trying war crimes could legally deal with crimes committed by the Nazis before the war. Another involved the sheer volume of guilt. The dreaded Schutzstaffel, or SS (in charge of intelligence, security and the extermination of undesirables), and other large Nazi organizations included hundreds of thousands of alleged war criminals. How could they possibly be tried individually? Bernays suggested putting Nazism and the entire Hitler era on trial as a giant criminal conspiracy. In a single stroke, this would create a kind of unified field theory of Nazi depravity, eliminating time constraints, allowing prosecution of war crimes and prewar crimes as well. He also suggested picking a handful of top Nazi defendants as representatives of key Nazi organizations like the SS. If the leaders were convicted, members of their organizations would automatically be deemed guilty. Result: few trials, many convictions and a devastating exposé of Nazi crimes.

Roosevelt promptly endorsed the plan, with one addition. The Nazis would be charged with the crime of waging "aggressive" war, or what the eventual indictments called "crimes against peace"—the first such charge in legal history.

Nobody was more enthusiastic about the strategy than Robert Jackson. Then 53, Jackson was a small-town lawyer from western New York with a gift for language. He had served in various posts in New Deal Washington before Roosevelt elevated him to the Supreme Court in 1941. By July 21, 1945, barely two months after Germany surrendered, Jackson had won President Truman's approval for a four-power International Military Tribunal and had persuaded the Allies to conduct it in Nuremberg.

A master list of 122 war criminals was put together, headed by Hermann Göring, the ranking Nazi survivor. (Hitler, Himmler and Goebbels were dead by their own hand. Martin Bormann, Hitler's secretary, had vanished, never to be found.) Reichsmarschall Göring, a daring World War I ace, had not allowed defeat to tarnish his reputation for candor, cunning and gluttony. He had turned himself in at a weight of 264 pounds (he was 5 feet 6 inches tall). His entourage included a nurse, four aides, two chauffeurs and five cooks. His fingernails and toenails were painted bright red. His 16 monogrammed suitcases contained rare jewels, a red hatbox, frilly nightclothes and 20,000 paracodeine pills, a painkiller he had taken at the rate of about 40 pills a day. He managed to charm some of his captors to the point of almost forgetting his diabolism.

On August 8, 1945, the Charter of the International Military Tribunal (IMT, unveiled by the victorious Allies in London, declared aggressive war and international crime. The IMT charter was grounded in the idea that Nazism was a 26-year-long criminal conspiracy. Its aim: to build a war machine, satisfy Hitler's psychopathic hatred of Jews and turn Europe into a German empire. Judges representing the four powers (the United States, Great Britain, France and the Soviet Union), plus four alternates, were named. They were to take jurisdiction over high-ranking Nazis deemed personally guilty of war crimes, conspiracy to commit war crimes, crimes against peace and crimes against humanity.

The 24 men named in the original indictment represented a wide spectrum of Germany's political-military-industrial complex. With Martin Bormann (tried in absentia), the list of those actually presented for trial was further reduced by two surprise events. Robert Ley, the alcoholic, Jew-baiting boss of the German Labor Front, which had governed the lives of 30 million German workers, hanged himself in his cell on the night of October 25. And, at the last moment, the prosecutors realized their key industrial defendant, the weapons maker Alfried Krupp, had not personally run his family's slave-labor factories until after the war began, giving him an easy defense against the prewar conspiracy charge. (Krupp was later sentenced to 12 years for war crimes, but he was released from prison in 1951.)

The trial of the remaining defendants began on the morning of November 20, 1945. In the refurbished courtroom, floodlights warmed the new green curtains and crimson chairs, illuminating the two rows of once fearsome Nazis sitting in the dock guarded by young American soldiers. Göring had shed 60 pounds during his six months of confinement, acquiring what novelist John Dos Passos, reporting for *Life,* called "that wizened look of a leaky balloon of a fat man who has lost a great deal of weight." Next to him in the front row were the ghostly Rudolf Hess, feigning amnesia; Joachim von Ribbentrop, Hitler's foreign minister; and Field Marshal Wilhelm Keitel, the Führer's Wehrmacht chief. Next in order of indictment came Ernst Kaltenbrunner (ill and absent for the first three weeks), Alfred Rosenberg and Hans Frank, who somehow thought his captors would spare his life when he handed over one of the trial's most damning documents—his 38-volume journal. (He would be sentenced to hang.)

Throughout that first day, as black-robed American, British and French judges and their two uniformed Soviet colleagues peered somberly from the bench, listening via earphones to translations in four languages, the prosecutors droned an almost boring litany of sickening crimes—shooting, torture, starvation, hanging—to which, in descending tones of indignation, from Göring downward, the accused each pleaded not guilty.

The next morning, Robert Jackson opened the prosecution case on Count One, conspiracy to commit war crimes. "This war did not just happen," Jackson told the judges. The defendants' seizure of the German state, he continued, "their subjugation of the German people, their terrorism and extermination of dissident elements, their planning and waging of war . . . , their deliberate and planned criminality toward conquered peoples—all these are ends for which they acted in concert."

"We will not ask you to convict these men on the testimony of their foes," Jackson told the court. There was no need. Allied agents had found 47 crates of Alfred Rosenberg's files hidden in a 16th-century castle, 485 tons of diplomatic papers secreted in the Harz Mountains, and Göring's art loot and Luftwaffe records stashed in a salt mine in Obersalzberg.

One especially incriminating find—indispensable to the conspiracy theory—was the notes of Hitler aide Col. Friedrich Hossbach from a meeting between Hitler, Göring and other Nazis in Berlin on November 5, 1937. Hossbach quoted Hitler insisting that, as Europe's racially "purest" stock, the Germans were entitled to "more living space" in neighboring countries, which he planned to seize, he said, "no later than 1943–45."

During the opening weeks, the pace of the trial was slow. Most of the American prosecution team neither read nor understood German. What with translation gaffes, repetitions and monotone readings, the documentary evidence—reams of it—at times had judges yawning and the defendants themselves dozing off.

Of course, the banality of overdocumented evil did not soften the prosecution's gruesome narrative. And a month into the recitation of Hitler's prewar aggressions from the Rhineland to Austria to Czechoslovakia, the Americans suddenly animated the documents by showing films of Nazi horrors. One German soldier's home movie depicted his comrades in Warsaw, clubbing and kicking naked Jews. In one scene, an officer helped a battered young woman to her feet so that she could be knocked down again.

An American movie documented the liberation of concentration camps at Bergen-Belson, Dachau and Buchenwald, filling the darkened courtroom with ghastly images of skeletal survivors, stacked cadavers and bulldozers shoveling victims into mass graves. In his cell that night, Hans Frank burst out: "To think we lived like kings and believed in that beast!" Göring was merely rueful. "It was such a good afternoon, too—" he

said, "and then they showed that awful film, and it just spoiled everything."

Even when badly translated, Jackson's documents made a mesmerizing record of Hitler's appalling acts on the road to Armageddon. They revisited his rise to power as the people's choice in the depression year 1932. Billing himself as Germany's economic savior, the Führer immediately began spending so much on weapons that in six years, the treasury was almost empty. A diversion was called for.

Thrilling his admirers—millions of still worshipful Germans—Hitler bullied British and French leaders into selling out Czechoslovakia at the pusillanimous Munich conference in 1938 (SMITHSONIAN, October 1988). Next, Nazi thugs were unleashed on *Kristallnacht,* the "Night of Broken Glass" (November 9)—a nationwide campaign of anti-Semitic violence. Huge chunks of Jewish wealth wound up in Nazi pockets. Göring, the biggest thief, further demeaned his victims by ordering German Jews to pay the regime a "fine" of one billion marks ($400 million). As he explained it, "The Jew being ejected from the economy transfers his property to the state."

Hjalmar Schacht, then head of the Reichsbank, warned Hitler in January 1939 that his arms race was fueling runaway inflation. Hitler immediately fired Schacht and ordered new currency, largely backed by stolen Jewish property. Schacht, long a Hitler apologist, then began working secretly for U.S. intelligence and wound up at Dachau. Now, to his disgust, he sat in the Nuremberg dock.

According to trial documents, Hitler's profligacy helped propel his aggressions. By 1941, Hitler had made his suicidal decision to renege on the nonaggression pact signed with Stalin in 1939 and invade the Soviet Union. "What one does not have, but needs," he said, "one must conquer."

It began well, on June 22, 1941, and ended badly. By late 1942, with German casualties soaring at Stalingrad, Hitler had lost so many soldiers in Russia that he had to keep drafting German workers into the army, replacing them with foreign laborers, mainly French and Russian prisoners. In early 1943, with more than five million industrial slaves already toiling in Germany, the surrender at Stalingrad forced Hitler's manpower boss, Nuremberg defendant Fritz Sauckel, to kidnap 10,000 Russian civilians per day for work in Germany. Few survived longer than 18 months—a powerful incentive for Russians still at home to flee the kidnappers and join Soviet guerrillas in killing German troops.

Hitler's campaign to "Aryanize" Germany began before the war with the deliberate poisoning of incurably sick people and retarded children—labeled "garbage children." The regime's contempt for non-Aryan life conditioned millions of Germans to turn a blind eye to more and more epidemic evils—the death camps, the ghastly medical experiments, the relentless massacres of those Hitler called "Jews, Poles, and similar trash."

Listening to the facts, the almost incomprehensible facts, even the defendants longed for some answer to the overpowering question—why? Why did one of the world's most advanced nations descend to such acts so easily? So swiftly? The trial provided few answers. Hitler's truly diabolic achievement, French prosecutor François de Menthon observed, was to revive "all the instincts of barbarism, repressed by centuries of civilization, but always present in men's innermost nature."

For weeks, the prosecution cited such acts as the use of Jewish prisoners as guinea pigs in military medical experiments to determine the limits of high-altitude flying by locking them in pressure chambers, slowly rupturing their lungs and skulls. How long downed German pilots could last in the ocean was determined by submerging prisoners in icy water until they died. To develop a blood-clotting chemical, the doctors shot and dismembered live prisoners to simulate battlefield injuries. Death did not end this abuse. A Czech doctor who spent four years imprisoned at Dachau, where he performed some 12,000 autopsies, told investigators that he was ordered to strip the skin off bodies. "It was cut into various sizes for use as saddles, riding breeches, gloves, house slippers, and ladies handbags. Tattooed skin was especially valued by SS men."

The scale of Hitler's madness was almost beyond imagination. The documents showed that after conquering Poland in 1939, he ordered the expulsion of nearly nine million Poles and Jews from Polish areas he annexed for his promised Nordic empire. The incoming colonists were "racially pure" ethnic Germans imported from places like the Italian Tirol. The SS duly began herding the exiles from their homes toward ethnic quarantine in a 39,000-square-mile cul-de-sac near Warsaw. Opposition grew; progress slowed. In righteous rage, the SS unleashed hundreds of *Einsatzgruppen*—killer packs assigned to spread terror by looting, shooting and slaughtering without restraint. Thereafter, the SS action groups murdered and plundered behind the German Army as it advanced eastward.

By January 1946, prosecutor Jackson was at last animating his documents with live witnesses. The first was a stunner. Otto Ohlendorf, blond and short, looked like the choirboy next door. In fact he was 38, a fanatic anti-Semite and the former commander of Einsatzgruppe D, the scourge of southern Russia. He testified with icy candor and not an iota of remorse.

How many persons were killed under your direction? asked Jackson. From June 1941 to June 1942, Ohlendorf flatly replied, "90,000 people."

Q. "Did that include men, women, and children?"

A. "Yes."

Rather proudly, Ohlendorf asserted that his 500-man unit killed civilians "in a military manner by firing squads under command." Asked if he had "scruples" about these murders, he said, "Yes, of course."

Q. "And how is it they were carried out regardless of these scruples?"

A. "Because to me it is inconceivable that a subordinate leader should not carry out orders given by the leaders of the state."

The prosecution rested after three months, capped off by another movie distilling still more Nazi horror, and displays of macabre human-skin lampshades and shrunken Jewish heads submitted as evidence.

German defense lawyers then spent five months trying to cope with major handicaps. Most had grown to abhor their clients. All were unfamiliar with adversarial cross-examinations used in the United States and Britain, to say nothing of key documents that the Americans tended to withhold before springing them in court.

They managed to outflank the court's ban on tu quoque evidence (meaning, "If I am guilty, you are, too")—a stricture aimed at keeping Allied excesses, notably the mass bombing of German cities, out of the trial. In the dock was Adm. Karl Dönitz, accused of ordering U-boats to sink merchantmen without warning and let the crews drown whenever a rescue attempt might jeopardize the Germans. Dönitz never denied the charge. Instead, his lawyer produced an affidavit from Adm. Chester Nimitz, commander of the wartime U.S. Pacific fleet, stating that American submariners had followed the same policy against Japanese ships. (In the end, he was sentenced to ten years; upon release in 1956, he lived 24 more years, to age 88.)

The prosecution had depicted a vast conspiracy to wage war and commit atrocities. But in choosing representative Nazis as defendants, it wound up with 21 men who, though all pleaded ignorance or powerlessness, were otherwise so different that many hated one another. Each tried to save himself by accusing others. As a result, the defense naturally failed to muster a united front, and the prosecution's conspiracy theory steadily unraveled.

The trial's highlight was the star turn of its one wholly unabashed defendant, Hermann Göring. In three days of direct examination, Göring sailed through an insider's history of Nazism, defending Germany's right to rearm and reoccupy territory lost by the Versailles treaty. He laughed off the notion that his fellow defendants were ever close enough to Hitler to be called conspirators. "At best," he said, "only the Führer and I could have conspired."

Jackson's cross-examination was a disaster. Göring understood English well; while questions were translated into German, he had time to improvise his answers. At one point, Jackson prodded Göring to admit that the Nazis' plan to occupy the Rhineland, enacted without warning in 1936, was a Nazi secret, hidden from other countries. Göring smoothly answered, "I do not believe I can recall reading beforehand the publication of the mobilization preparations of the United States."

Jackson conducted a bizarre cross-examination of Albert Speer, Hitler's personal architect of gigantic edifices and stage manager of the Nuremberg rallies. Smart, suave, handsome, not yet 40, the wellborn Speer ranked high among Hitler's few confidants and was chief of all Nazi war production for the regime's last three years. He oversaw 14 million workers; he could hardly claim ignorance of their condition or how they were recruited. In the spring of 1944, for example, he ordered 100,000 Jewish slave workers from Hungary as casually as if they were bags of cement.

On the witness stand, Speer said he had become totally disillusioned with Hitler when the Führer responded to Germany's inevitable defeat by ordering a nationwide scorched-earth policy: the total destruction of everything in the path of the

Allied armies. Rejecting Hitler's monomania, which he called a betrayal of ordinary Germans, Speer told the court, "It is my unquestionable duty to assume my share of responsibility for the disaster of the German people." And he revealed—offering no proof—that in February 1945 he had set out to assassinate Hitler by dropping poison gas through an air shaft in the Führer's bunker, only to find the shaft sealed off.

Speer, the most attractive defendant at Nuremberg, had been debriefed by interrogators avid for his special knowledge of how German war factories managed to keep humming despite immense Allied bombing. Some saw him as just the kind of man needed to rehabilitate postwar Germany. Under cross-examination, he got mostly easy questions, typically prefaced by Jackson's disclaimer, "I am not attempting to say that you were personally responsible for these conditions."

That Speer actually received a 20-year sentence seems remarkable, given his adroit performance. That his equally (or perhaps less) culpable colleague, Fritz Sauckel—brutal, low-born, ill spoken—was sentenced to death, seems as legally unfair as it was morally deserved.

After Robert Jackson's powerful summation of the trial's "mad and melancholy record," the case went to the trial judges, from whom no appeal was permitted. The great unspoken issue at Nuremberg was the question of collective guilt, and hindsight clarifies the extraordinary dilemma those eight judges faced 50 years ago. Collective guilt had tainted the Versailles treaty and helped ignite the Holocaust. It is the fuel of human barbarism, currently on display from Rwanda to Serbia. And though the Nuremberg judges were given every reason to savage the Nazi tyranny, they came to believe that justice could be served only by asserting the principle of individual responsibility. Justice required, in fact, a virtual rejection of the United States' whole grand conspiracy concept.

The Nazi Party founders had been charged with conspiring for 26 years (1919–45) to launch World War II and related atrocities. All 22 defendants (including Bormann) stood accused of planning aggressive war; 18 were charged with wartime crimes and crimes against humanity, such as genocide. If the court approved, seven Nazi organizations would also be convicted, rendering all their thousands of members guilty without trial.

The problem was that conspiracy is a crime of joint participation. Conviction required proof that two or more people knowingly agreed at a specific time and place to use criminal means to achieve criminal ends. But the distinguished French judge, Donnedieu de Vabres, urged his colleagues to observe that the defendants had seemed to act less in cahoots with, than in bondage to, a megalomaniac. Jackson's documents showed the "Führer Principle" in practice—the madness of Hitler's erratic orders, executed by lackeys too blind, venal or terrified to disobey. The evidence seemingly proved chaos, not organized conspiracy.

The judges, risking a backlash from Europe's Nazi victims by sharply limiting their verdicts to the hard evidence, ruled that the war conspiracy began not in 1919 but on November 5, 1937, at the "Hossbach conference" in which Hitler's aides heard his schemes for conquering Germany's neighbors.

The conspiracy charge (Count One) was restricted to eight defendants (led by Göring) who knowingly carried out Hitler's war plans from 1938 onward. In effect, the defendants were liable only for actual wartime crimes beginning September 1, 1939—a dizzying number of crimes but one that eliminated perhaps a third of the prosecution's evidence and produced three acquittals, including that of Schacht.

Under such an approach, guilt for simply belonging to the Nazi organizations was impossible. The court held that only the SS, the Gestapo-SD and the top Nazi leadership had been proved "criminal," meaning that their members had voluntarily joined in committing war crimes after 1939. That left several million potential defendants for lower courts to handle. But since the Nuremberg judges ruled them all innocent until proven guilty, relatively few were ever tried—the prosecutorial job was too formidable.

The trial removed 11 of the most despicable Nazis from life itself. In the early morning hours of Wednesday, October 16, 1946, ten men died in the courthouse gymnasium in a botched hanging that left several strangling to death for as long as 25 minutes. Ribbentrop departed with dignity, saying, "God protect Germany." Göring had cheated the hangman 2 1/2 hours earlier. He killed himself in his cell, using a cyanide capsule he had managed to hide until then. In one of four suicide notes, he wrote, "I would have consented anytime to be shot. But the Reichsmarschall of Germany cannot be hanged."

The Nuremberg trial never remotely enabled the world to outlaw war. By 1991, the wars of the 20th century had killed more than 107 million people. And given Nuremberg's uniqueness—winners in total control of losers—the court of 1945 may seem irrelevant to the wars of the 1990s, in which ethnic killers, such as Gen. Ratko Mladic, the Bosnian Serb implicated in the mass murder of unarmed prisoners, manage to avoid justice.

Yet the United Nations' seven "Nuremberg Principles" hold that no accused war criminal in any place or position is above the law. What the Nuremberg judges really achieved, in fact, has never been more relevant. By rejecting group guilt and mass purges, the 1945 judges defied hatred and struck a blow for peace that may yet, half a century later, help temper the madness of war.

---

*The author, formerly editor of* Harper's, *has written extensively on the U.S. Supreme Court and on legal matters.*

Originally appeared in *Smithsonian,* October 1996, pp. 124–126, 128–132, 134. Copyright © 1996 by Robert Shnayerson. Reprinted by permission of the author.

# Starting the Cold War

Geoffrey Roberts

## Historians and the Cold War

The term 'cold war' first came into currency in 1947. It was used to denote a sharp and unexpected deterioration in postwar relations between the Soviet Union and the United States. In 1945 the USA and the USSR—the two main victors of the Second World War—had proclaimed their commitment to postwar unity and co-operation. But by the end of 1947 this public harmony had been replaced by mutual recrimination about who was to blame for the postwar breakup of the allied coalition that had defeated Hitler, Each side blamed the other for generating the political, ideological, and military rivalry that divided Europe into competing blocs and spawned a dangerous global power struggle between communism and liberal democratic capitalism.

From the very beginning of the cold war there was a dispute about its origins—about when, why and how the conflict started and who was responsible. Among historians the cold war origins debate went through several main phases.

From the 1940s to the 1970s it centred on the contribution of American foreign policy. Some historians (often labelled 'traditionalists' by their opponents) endorsed the official US government view that the cold war started because America resisted a series of aggressive and expansionary moves by the Soviet Union. Other historians (called 'revisionists' because they sought to revise the semi-official views of the traditionalists) were much more critical of American policy, arguing that the US had acted in an aggressive and unreasonable manner after the war, provoking a Soviet counter-response.

By the end of the 1970s the debate between traditionalist and revisionists had exhausted itself. Most historians were prepared to settle for a 'post-revisionist' or 'post-traditionalist' compromise view—essentially the idea that neither the Americans nor the Russians were to blame and that both sides had pursued what they considered legitimate security and foreign policy interests. The historical consensus was that the cold war was the result of mutual misunderstandings and of unavoidable clashes between Soviet and American foreign interests.

By the 1980s, however, the historical debate had entered a new phase with the publication of a number of studies on the origins of the cold war which emphasised the role of the lesser players, in particular Britain, France and West Germany. The themes of this literature were the European origins of the cold war, the independent role of the West European states, and the influence of politicians such as Churchill, Bevin, Bidault and Adenauer on US foreign policy.

> **Each side blamed the other for generating the political, ideological, and military rivalry that divided Europe into competing blocs and spawned a dangerous global power struggle between communism and liberal democratic capitalism.**

Since the 1990s historical work on the cold war has been dominated by research on Soviet foreign policy. Following the fall of communism in the USSR and Eastern Europe, there was a significant opening up of Soviet bloc archives. Furthermore, the end of the cold war and the break-up of the Soviet Union facilitated more detached reflection on the roles and responsibilities of the different players. Broadly speaking, the post-revisionist consensus that nobody really wanted or was solely responsible for the cold war still holds. But it is a view that can now be validated from a multi-archival perspective.

## The Grand Alliance

When exactly did the cold war begin? The two main responses to this question in the historical literature are: (i) 1917 and (ii) 1947. The first school of thought sees the cold war as a phase in a long history of antagonistic relations between the Soviet Union and the west. This history, it is argued, started when the Bolsheviks seized power in 1917 and began the socialist experiment in Russia, thereby provoking the ideological animosity of western liberal capitalism.

The alternative viewpoint focuses on the post-Second World War period and on the intense character of the Soviet-Western clash from 1947 onwards: not only ideological rivalry and hostility, but the emergence of polarised military-political power blocs kept on a permanent war footing and engaged in nuclear competition with each other.

Historians who characterise Soviet-western relations in the interwar period as an 'early cold war' make an important point. The post-1945 suspicion and mistrust among the great powers did not come out of thin air. Yet they tend to skip over possibly the most important phase in Soviet-Western relations before the cold war—the Grand Alliance period of 1941–1947, a phase of co-operation not confrontation.

The 'Grand Alliance', a grandiose concept popularised by Winston Churchill in the 1950s, is the most common name for the wartime coalition of Britain, the United States and the Soviet Union. It was forced into being by Nazi Germany, which attacked Russia in June 1941 and declared war on the United States in December 1941. During the early period of its existence (1941–43) the alliance was primarily a war coalition, one dominated by military issues and priorities. However, with victory assured, decision-makers in London, Washington and Moscow began to turn their attention to the forthcoming peace settlement. From 1943 there were a series of tripartite negotiations and agreements concerning the postwar world. Of particular importance was a series of summits of the leaders of the Big Three at Teheran, Yalta and Potsdam. At these meetings Stalin, Churchill, Roosevelt, Truman and Attlee agreed on the need for a peacetime grand alliance. The governing concept was that the postwar world should be shaped by the Big Three to assure peace, security and prosperity for all nations.

The story of the origins of the cold war is fundamentally one of how and why the grand alliance disintegrated. There were, it is true, a number of general conditions and contexts that pointed in the direction of such a break-up. Ideological differences and a history of difficulties in Soviet-Western relations have already been mentioned. During the war a large measure of agreement on postwar issues had been achieved but important unresolved disputes remained. At the end of the war there emerged numerous practical problems of working together in liberated Europe, above all in Germany. The fact that the Americans had the atomic bomb and the Russians did not was also problematical, as was the extent of the Soviet need for human and material resources to rebuild their war-devastated economy. Some historians argue that these factors made some kind of cold war inevitable. At the time, however, none of these problems was seen as insurmountable, given mutual respect and good will.

---

## The story of the origins of the cold war is fundamentally one of how and why the grand alliance disintegrated.

---

When the war ended there was good will aplenty—at least on most people's part. But not for long. It soon became evident that there were fundamental differences of policy and perspective between the Soviet Union and its grand alliance partners. The three most important areas of dispute concerned Eastern Europe, Germany and the political and economic reconstruction of Europe.

# Eastern Europe

The dispute over Eastern Europe arose from the Soviet Union's determination to establish its domination of the region. Moscow saw control of the East European states—many of which

had fought on the side of Germany during the war—as essential to Soviet security. Hence it wanted a Soviet sphere of influence in Eastern Europe. This required the establishment of pro-Soviet governments and, so Stalin believed, the exclusion of western influence from the region. Since the Red Army had conquered most of Eastern Europe on its victorious march to Berlin the Soviets were in a strong position to get what they wanted. An additional factor in their favour was support from the East European communist parties, which wielded considerable political influence after the war. As a consequence Moscow pursued political as well as security goals in Eastern Europe—the strengthening of their communist allies and the sponsorship of radical, left-wing regimes.

The British and Americans opposed Soviet domination of Eastern Europe. They accepted that the Russians had legitimate security interests in the region but emphasised the commitment made in the Declaration on Liberated Europe, agreed at the Yalta conference in February 1945, that the peoples of Eastern Europe would be free to choose their own governments. London and Washington were also concerned about the exclusion of American and British influence from the region. Anglo-American sympathies lay with anti-Soviet and anti-communist politicians in Eastern Europe. Britain and the US argued that the Soviets and their communist allies were interfering with the democratic process in Eastern Europe, in particular by rigging ballots to ensure the election of pro-Moscow governments.

The main forum for the dispute over Eastern Europe was the Council of Foreign Ministers (CFM). Established by the Potsdam conference in August 1945, the CFM was an organisation of the foreign ministers of Britain, China, France, the Soviet Union and the United States charged with the negotiation of the postwar peace settlement. It held its first meeting in London in September 1945—a meeting which broke up in disarray when the western states refused to recognise the legitimacy of pro-Soviet governments in Bulgaria and Rumania. In due course that particular deadlock was resolved (the two governments were recognised) and the CFM resumed its meetings. Indeed, in 1945–47 the CFM successfully completed its main initial task of drawing up peace treaties for Italy, Rumania, Bulgaria, Finland and Hungary. However, the experience of these negotiations, which were exhausting and acrimonious, was none too edifying. Compounding the difficulties in the negotiations was the fact that much of the debate took place in public, in the press and elsewhere. Such public diplomacy resulted in the adoption of inflexible policy positions and often degenerated into purely propagandistic polemics.

The main problem in the negotiations was that the Soviets were unwilling to make any concessions that could undermine their position in Eastern Europe. Moscow also insisted on the principle of tripartism and co-decision-making, i.e. that everything should be decided by the Soviet Union, Britain and the US (the French and Chinese were considered, at best, as junior partners) and that within that tripartite arrangement each of the partners had a policy veto. For their part, the British and Americans sought to hold on to the positions they held—for example their influence in Italy and Greece—and to broaden out the process of decision and consultation on the postwar settlement.

Beyond the confines of the CFM the most important development in the Soviet-Western dispute over Eastern Europe was Churchill's 'Iron Curtain' speech in Fulton, Missouri, in March 1946. Churchill, in Fulton to receive an honorary degree, used the occasion to attack Soviet policy in Eastern Europe:

> 'From Stettin in the Baltic to Trieste in the Adriatic, an iron curtain has descended across the continent. Behind that line lie all the capitals of the ancient states of central and eastern Europe. Warsaw, Berlin, Prague, Vienna, Budapest, Belgrade, Bucharest and Sofia, all these famous cities and the populations around them lie in the Soviet sphere and all are subject . . . not only to Soviet influence but to a very high and increasing measure of control from Moscow.'

Churchill was no longer Prime Minister and his speech was not an official statement of British government policy. On the other hand, US President Harry Truman (who had succeeded Roosevelt in 1945) shared the platform with Churchill and the former PM's views could be taken as indicative of an influential strand in western policy and thinking. This was certainly how the Soviets interpreted the speech. Stalin himself publicly denounced Churchill as an anti-bolshevik warmonger. Privately, Moscow was becoming more and more concerned about the growth of anti-Soviet and anti-communist forces in the western states, worry which received ample confirmation with Truman's speech to the US Congress in March 1947:

> 'The peoples of a number of countries . . . have recently had totalitarian regimes forced upon them against their will. The Government of the United States has made frequent protests against coercion and intimidation . . . in Poland, Rumania, and Bulgaria . . . At the present moment in world history nearly every nation must choose between alternative ways of life . . . One way of life is based on the will of the majority . . . The second way of life is based upon the will of a minority forcibly imposed upon the majority . . . I believe it must the policy of the United States to support free peoples who are resisting attempted subjugation by armed minorities or by outside pressures.'

Truman's statement calling upon the United States to act in defence of the 'free world' subsequently became known as the Truman Doctrine. It signalled American determination to resist further Soviet expansion and to do so by the deployment of countervailing power, by what was called the policy of containment.

Truman's speech was delivered just as the CFM was convening in Moscow to consider the question of a peace treaty for Germany. His evident abandonment of diplomacy and adoption of a confrontational position did not auger well for its proceedings.

# Germany

Germany's future was the second important area of dispute between the erstwhile wartime allies. During the war it had been agreed that Germany would be jointly occupied by the

## timeLINE

| 1945 | February | The Yalta Conference |
|------|----------|---------------------|
|      | 7 May | Unconditional surrender of Germany |
|      | August | Potsdam Conference |
|      | 14 August | Unconditional surrender of Japan |
|      | 1 September | First meeting of the Council of Foreign Ministers |
| 1946 | 5 March | Churchill's 'Iron Curtain' speech |
| 1947 | March | The 'Truman Doctrine' announced |
|      | June | Marshall's speech on aid at Harvard |
|      | July | Paris conference on aid; USSR withdrew |
|      | September | Zhdanov's two camps' speech |
| 1948 | June | Soviets blockaded Berlin |
| 1949 | April | North Atlantic Treaty Organisation set up |
|      | August | Soviets tested Atomic bomb |

allies and then denazified, demilitarised and democratised. To this end Germany was divided into Soviet and western zones of military occupation. Berlin too was divided, despite the fact that it lay deep in the Soviet zone of occupation. During the war there had been much talk of dismembering Germany, but both the Soviets and their western allies had found it convenient to drop this idea. Instead, the political future of the German state would be subject to further allied negotiations.

On Soviet insistence detailed discussion of a peace settlement with Germany (and Austria) was deferred until the conclusion of the peace treaties with the minor axis states. However, by the time the CFM met to discuss Germany the supposedly temporary zones of occupation had begun to solidify into something much more permanent. The Anglo-Americans in their western zone (the British and American zones were merged economically at the end of 1946) and the Russians in their Eastern zone both pursued policies which indicated an East-West political and economic division of Germany.

At the Moscow conference of the CFM in March–April 1947 the Russians pressed strongly for a unified German administration to be established, but the British and Americans could not agree with Moscow the terms and conditions for the creation of a single German state. One particular sticking point was the issue of reparations. Moscow on wanted economic reparations from Germany to pay for Soviet war damage. The British and Americans accepted that the Russians could extract such reparations from the Eastern zone but not from their western zone. The western priority was postwar German economic recovery, seen as essential to a wider European economic revival. It was feared that reparations would cripple such a recovery—as had happened after the First World War.

Yet more important than economics was politics. By 1947 the British and American political priority was to retain political control of western Germany, a policy which was increasingly linked to a wider project of building a West European security bloc. The Soviets attempted to disrupt western political plans for Germany by insisting on the implementation of decisions taken at Yalta and Potsdam regarding the establishment of a central German administration. At the same time Moscow pursued a unilateral policy of consolidating the communist position in Eastern Germany. It was on this plane that Soviet policy converged with western. Insistence on continuing communist control of the Soviet zone could not but contribute to the eventual division of Germany.

Against this background, the CFM failed to reach any agreement on the future of Germany. Further attempts at negotiation proved equally forlorn. By the end of 1947 Soviet-Western negotiations on a German peace treaty had, to all intents and purposes, broken down.

# European Reconstruction

The third important postwar dispute within the grand alliance concerned European reconstruction. By mid-1947 the western states had more or less given up on the grand alliance. The Soviets were moving in that direction too, though in fact Stalin still clung to the possibility of striking a deal over Germany and other issues still in dispute. In May 1947 he gave an interview to a visiting American senator in which he stressed the desirability of continuing peaceful coexistence and co-operation with the west. In summer 1947, however, there was a decisive change in his outlook. The precipitating event was the launch of the so-called 'Marshall Plan'.

In June 1947 US Secretary of State, George C. Marshall, spoke at Harvard University on the need for a large-scale programme of American financial support to aid European economic recovery. Behind Marshall's proposal lay American fears of a communist take-over in Western Europe, which remained wartorn and impoverished. The communist parties of France, Italy and other countries had established a strong position for themselves after the war. Until May 1947 the French and Italian communist parties were members of ruling coalitions, and communists participated in the government of other West European states as well. In sponsoring a European economic recovery which would contribute to political stability, Marshall aimed to undermine support for the communist left and to strengthen the political position of anti-communist parties and movements.

Although the Americans were thinking mainly in terms of Western Europe, the Soviet Union and Eastern Europe were not excluded from the proposed aid programme. Indeed the British and French governments responded to Marshall's Harvard speech by inviting the Russians to a conference in Paris to discuss a European response to the plan. In Moscow, however, the Soviets were in two minds. On the one hand, they welcomed the possibility of American loans and grants, for themselves and for their East European allies. On the other, they feared that the Marshall Plan was an economic counterpart of the Truman Doctrine—a means of using American financial muscle to build an anti-Soviet alliance in Western Europe.

At the Paris conference in July 1947 Moscow's worst fears were realised. The British and French insisted (in accordance with Marshall's express wishes) that any American aid programme had to be co-ordinated and organised on a pan-European basis. This was seen by the Soviets as a western device for interference in the economic and political life of the East European countries. Such western involvement was completely unacceptable to Stalin. Consequently the USSR withdrew from all negotiations concerning the Marshall Plan and insisted its East European allies did not participate either.

**1947 was the year of the cold war. By the end of that year the break up of the grand alliance—signalled by the Truman Doctrine, Zhdanov's two-camps speech and the breakdown of Soviet-Western negotiations over the Germany and the Marshall Plan—was complete.**

The Soviet riposte to the Truman Doctrine and the Marshall Plan was not long in coming. In September 1947 politburo member A.A. Zhdanov delivered what became known as the 'two camps' speech to the founding conference of the Communist Information Bureau (Cominform), the successor to the Communist International or Comintern. Zhdanov's speech set out a new, cold war perspective for the European communist parties:

> 'The more the war recedes into the past, the more distinct become two major trends in post-war international policy, corresponding to the division of the political forces operating on international arena into two major camps: the imperialist and antidemocratic camp . . . and the anti-imperialist and democratic camp . . . The principal driving force of the imperialist camp is the USA . . . The cardinal purpose of the imperialist camp is to strengthen imperialism, to hatch a new imperialist war, to combat socialism and democracy, and to support reactionary and anti-democratic pro-fascist regimes and movements everywhere . . . The anti-fascist forces comprise the second camp. This camp is based on the USSR and the new democracies [of Eastern Europe] . . . The purpose of this camp is to resist the threat of new wars and imperialist expansion, to strengthen democracy and to extirpate the vestiges of fascism.'

While Truman had called for a defence of the free world against communist subversion and coercion, Zhdanov demanded action to defend postwar left-wing gains from imperialist threat and encroachmet.

# Conclusion: the Cold War Begins

1947 was the year of the cold war. By the end of that year the break up of the grand alliance—signalled by the Truman

Doctrine, Zhdanov's two-camps speech and the breakdown of Soviet-Western negotiations over Germany and the Marshall Plan—was complete. In Eastern Europe Moscow's communist allies proceeded to impose full-scale Soviet-style authoritarian regimes. Germany remained divided; indeed, by 1949 two separate German states had been established: the Federal Republic of Germany in the west and the German Democratic Republic in the east. 1948 witnessed the first of the great cold war crises when the Russians cut off land access to West Berlin and forced the western powers to mount a massive airlift to supply their sectors of the city. The military-political division of Europe further deepened with the setting up of NATO in April 1949. With the Soviet A-bomb test of August 1949 and the communist invasion of South Korea in June 1950 the cold war confrontation entered a new and even more dangerous phase.

# Further Reading

Caroline Lewis Gaddis, *We Now Know: Rethinking Cold War History* (Clarendon Press, 1997).

Martin McCauley, *The Origins of the Cold War* (Longman, 1990).

David S. Painter, *The Cold War: An International History* (Routledge, 1999).

Geoffrey Roberts, *The Soviet Union in World Politics: Coexistence, Revolution and the Cold War, 1945–1991* (Routledge, 1999).

Marc Trachtenberg, *A Constructed Peace: The Making of the European Settlement, 1945–1963* (Princeton University Press, 1999).

---

**GEOFFREY ROBERTS** is Statutory Lecturer in History at University College Cork. Among his books are *Unholy Alliance, Stalin's Pact with Hitler* (1989), *The Soviet Union and the* Origins of the Second World War (1995) and *The Soviet Union and the Grand Alliance* (forthcoming).

---

From *History Review*, December 2009, pp. 9–14. Copyright © 2009 by History Today, Ltd. Reprinted by permission.

# A Case of Courage

MICHAEL BESCHLOSS

As the Wednesday afternoon sun slanted through the tall windows of the Oval Office, Gen. George Marshall, Harry Truman's secretary of State and the architect of victory in World War II, took a chair beside the president's. Sitting in front of the president's desk, befitting his more junior position, was Truman's White House counsel, Clark Clifford. On Friday, May 14, 1948, at midnight, two days from now, the British would withdraw from Palestine. The United Nations had resolved to divide the region into one Jewish state and one Arab state, with ancient, holy Jerusalem as an international city. Despite the U.N. plan, five Arab armies were ready to kill the fledgling Jewish state.

Clifford implored Truman to recognize the new nation as soon as it was declared. If the U.S. granted legitimacy, so would its allies, allowing the Jewish state to survive. But Marshall advised Truman to keep his distance, warning that the Jews could never stave off Arab legions who far outnumbered them. If they came "running to us for help," the U.S. would have to say no. In what Clifford called "a righteous Goddamned Baptist tone," Marshall said, "If you follow Clifford's advice . . . I would vote against you." Shaken to be condemned by the national hero he called "the great one of the age," Truman later warned Clifford, "I can't afford to lose General Marshall!"

## For israel to survive, Clifford argued, the United States needed to grant legitimacy.

Truman's ultimate decision about a Jewish state—one of the most significant foreign-policy decisions in U.S. history— emerged from a storm of cross-pressures and motives. He was besieged by Zionists, anti-Zionists, Democratic politicians eager to court the Jewish vote in an election year and diplomats afraid to rile the Arabs. He felt compassion for the Holocaust survivors still in European camps and reverence for Biblical history. But he feared as well that the new state might require defense by U.S. troops and dreaded that respected leaders like Marshall would accuse him of warping American diplomacy to his own cheap political needs. Truman also had to rise above his own lingering small-town parlor anti-Semitism. Even as president, he privately said malicious things about American Jews to his wife, his friends and his diary that were unworthy of the towering leader he had become.

In April 1945, as Harry Truman became president and Allied soldiers liberated the death camps of Europe, Americans were learning about the terrible reach of the Holocaust. For many American Jews, the Holocaust showed that they must never again depend on the kindness of strangers: only a Jewish state could protect their people from another Hitler. They feared that the small-town Missouri Baptist in the White House could not possibly understand their predicament. They did not know that Truman had grown up knowing Jews or that he had studied their history since boyhood.

For two years in Independence, a Jewish family called the Viners lived next door to Truman's family. As Sarah Viner much later recalled, her brother Abe was "very close friends" with the future president: "Harry was always over at our house . . . I think this was his first contact with Jewish people." On the Sabbath, when observant Jews could not do household chores, Harry served as the Viners' "Shabbos goy."

While a 16-year-old student at Independence High School, young Truman was assigned to write about Shylock, Shakespeare's Jewish villain in "The Merchant of Venice," in an essay discovered in 2000. Given vast potential for indulging in anti-Semitism when writing of Shylock, Truman viewed the Jewish people with unexpected sympathy: "We cannot blame Shylock for getting money as a means for revenge upon those who persecuted him. He was not a miser, and if one of his own nation had been in trouble, he would have helped him as quickly as a Christian would help a Christian . . . I never saw Jew, Christian or any other man who, if he had the chance, wouldn't take revenge."

Truman went on to insist that no one "except the Hebrews" had "ruled" the world, then "when they fell," remained "a distinct people." He wrote that after 2,000 years, the Jews were "a nation apart from nations . . . persecuted for their religion," still "waiting for a leader" to gather their "scattered people."

In the wake of the holocaust, many American Jewish leaders blamed themselves for not having demanded that their government do more to stop it. Believing now that the survival of the European detainees and their entire people was at stake, they cast off the polite deference that leaders now derided as "court Jews" had once used around Franklin Roosevelt. In

July 1946, Rabbi Abba Hillel Silver pounded on Truman's desk and bellowed at him about an Anglo-American committee report that let Holocaust survivors into Palestine, but not with U.S. military support to protect them.

That same month, the two Democratic senators from New York and a pro-Zionist ex-diplomat, James McDonald, came to complain about the report. His back up, Truman told them he thought it was "marvelous." McDonald warned the president he was "scrapping" the Jewish cause in Palestine and would "go down in history as anathema." Truman erupted: "You cannot satisfy the Jews anyway . . . They are not interested in the United States. They are interested in Palestine and the Jews . . . The Jews aren't going to write the history of the United States—or my history!" Tactlessly, McDonald noted that FDR had understood the "imponderables" of the issue. "I am not Roosevelt!" cried Truman. "I am not from New York. I am from the Middle West. I must do what I think is right."

Truman had always been hypersensitive to any efforts to bulldoze him—and he was determined to show that it couldn't be done. With an eternal chip on his shoulder against the arrogant and powerful, Truman thus bridled at the intense, well-financed Zionist apparatus. He complained to Eleanor Roosevelt that "Jews are like all underdogs. When they get on top, they are just as intolerant and cruel as the people were to them when they were underneath." He banned Zionist leaders from the Oval Office. In a passage of his diary discovered in 2003, Truman wrote, "The Jews have no sense of proportion, nor do they have any judgment on world affairs . . . The Jews, I find, are very, very selfish."

Truman consulted his wife, Bess, almost every night about the issues he was dealing with. She was unlikely to have urged him to support a Jewish homeland. After Truman left office, the talk-show host David Susskind spent some time in Independence to interview the ex-president for a TV series. Susskind asked Truman why he never asked him inside his home. By Susskind's account, Truman replied, "You're a Jew, David, and no Jew has ever been in the house. Bess runs it, and there's never been a Jew inside the house in her or her mother's lifetime." (As late as 1957, long after his cardinal role in creating a Jewish homeland, Truman would still write to Bess that New York City was "the U.S. capital of Israel.")

Anxious about their exclusion, Jewish leaders searched for some new way to reach the president. A Kansas City attorney named A. J. Granoff got a call from a national official of the Jewish fraternal organization B'nai B'rith: "Do you know a man by the name of Jacobstein . . . who is supposed to be a very close friend of President Truman?" "You mean Eddie Jacobson," said Granoff. "Sure, I ought to! I'm his friend and lawyer."

In 1917, the genial, quiet Private Jacobson clerked in an Army canteen at Camp Doniphan, Oklahoma, under Lieutenant Harry Truman. Truman wrote his girlfriend, Bess Wallace, back in Independence, that he had a "Jew clerk" running his canteen and that Jacobson was "a crackerjack." After fighting the Germans in France, the two friends opened a men's store in Kansas City, with Harry as salesman-bookkeeper, Eddie as buyer and many old Battery D pals as customers. Then came the postwar depression. "I lost all I had and all I could borrow," said Truman. "Our creditors drove Eddie into bankruptcy, but I became a public official, and they couldn't do that to me."

The friendship survived. During senator Truman's visits to Kansas City, the ex-partners drank bourbon, played poker, told off-color stories and joked about "losing our asses in that store." But the friendship did not include their wives and families. Jacobson's wife, Bluma, recalled that Bess Truman's Wallace relatives were "aristocracy in those parts" and that "the Trumans couldn't afford to have Jews at their house."

In the summer of 1947, Jacobson sat down at Kansas City's Hotel Muehlebach with Granoff and Frank Goldman, the national president of B'nai B'rith. He told them he would never ask Truman for a personal favor, but would "always be glad" to discuss with him "my suffering people across the seas." He had endless faith in Harry's "kindly heart." Granoff said the problem was getting more Jewish refugees into Palestine. Eddie said, "Harry Truman will do what's right if he knows all the facts . . . But I'm no Zionist, so first I need the facts from you."

Arriving in Washington, Eddie called the president's appointments secretary, Matt Connelly, who gibed, "What the hell are you doing here without his permission?" When Jacobson and Granoff were ushered into the Oval Office, Truman said, "Sit down, you bastards!" As Eddie recalled, after Truman signed dollar bills for their children and asked about business in Kansas City, he and the president talked "takhles"—a Yiddish term that means "with serious purpose."

Making their case for a Jewish homeland, Granoff and Jacobson insisted they would never ask Truman to act against America's best interests. "You guys wouldn't get to the front gate if I thought any differently," said Truman. "You bastards are the only ones that never tried to embarrass me in any way."

Before retiring at night, Truman donned a green eyeshade and put his hawklike nose in a history book. He had "tried to increase my knowledge all my life by reading and reading and reading"—especially biography and history, insisting, "There's nothing new in human nature . . . The only thing new in the world is the history you don't know." As a nearsighted boy in Independence, Harry devoured a gold-trimmed, four-volume history called "Great Men and Famous Women—from Nebuchadnezzar to Sarah Bernhardt." From the tales he read, he always remembered Cyrus the Great, the Persian king of the sixth century B.C., who enabled the Jewish people to leave their exile and go back to Palestine.

In October 1947, Jacobson implored the president to back a U.N. committee's proposal for Jewish and Arab states in Palestine. He wrote, "Harry, my people need help and I am appealing on you to help them." Loy Henderson, assistant secretary of State, warned that if the U.S. had anything to do with founding a Jewish state, it would jeopardize oil supplies in Iraq and Saudi Arabia, and the "whole Arab world" would become the "enemy" of the United States.

The president endorsed Palestine's partition, but warned that the U.S. would not give money to a Jewish state, and that it lacked deployable forces to defend it from the Arab armies.

Furious that Truman had overruled him, Henderson tried to whittle down the territory allotted for the Jews. He argued that the town of Jaffa was "essentially Arab" and that Arab herdsmen required the Negev desert for "seasonal grazing." But after making it into the Oval Office, Chaim Weizmann, chief of the World Zionist Organization, unfolded maps and persuaded Truman that losing the Negev would undermine a Jewish state by blocking vital access to the Red Sea.

In late November 1947, at the U.N.'s temporary quarters in a converted skating rink at Flushing Meadows, Queens, Palestine's partition came up for a vote by the General Assembly. Arguing that U.S. prestige would suffer if allies like the Philippines and Haiti were seen voting against it, Clark Clifford persuaded Truman to let his aides lobby for partition. As Clifford recalled, "I kept the ramrod up the State Department's butt."

In January 1948, Truman's secretary of Defense, James Forrestal, told him that enforcing partition might require as many as 160,000 American ground troops. Loy Henderson proposed that since partition could not be imposed without a military commitment that Truman would not make, the U.N. should govern Palestine as a trustee when Britain withdrew in May. Horrified that Truman seemed to be wavering on a Jewish state, Chaim Weizmann rushed to New York, hoping to see the president. But Truman told his aides he had seen enough Zionists: "The Jews are so emotional, and the Arabs are so difficult to talk with that it is almost impossible to get anything done." B'nai B'rith's Frank Goldman called Eddie Jacobson in Kansas City. The president was "washing his hands" of Palestine: "You must help us, Eddie."

Jacobson wired Truman, "I have asked very little in the way of favors during all our years of friendship, but I am begging you to see Dr. Weizmann as soon as possible." Tired of what he called Zionist "badgering," the president wired Eddie that the Palestine problem was probably "not solvable." Refusing to give up, Jacobson flew to Washington in hopes of changing his mind, and when Matt Connelly let Jacobson into the Oval Office, Connelly warned him not to mention Palestine. Truman told his friend, "Eddie, I know what you are here for, and the answer is no."

Surprised at his own "nerve," Jacobson asked the president to reconsider, which touched off an explosion. Truman bellowed that the "Eastern Jews" had "slandered and libeled" him since the moment he became president. He didn't want to discuss "Palestine or the Jews or the Arabs or the British." Let the United Nations handle it. Tears rolled down Eddie's face. He felt "shocked" and "crushed" that his "dear friend" was "as close to being an anti-Semite as a man could possibly be."

---

## Surprised at his own 'nerve,' Jacobson got the president to listen to the Zionists' pleas.

---

Jacobson's eye caught a replica of the courthouse statue in Jackson County, Missouri, that Truman had worked so hard to build. Improvising, he said, "Harry, all your life, you have had a hero. You are probably the best-read man in America on the life of Andrew Jackson." He recalled Truman sitting in a corner of their failed store, "reading books and papers and pamphlets" on Old Hickory. "Well, Harry, I too have a hero—a man I never met, but who is, I think, the greatest Jew who ever lived . . . Chaim Weizmann. He is a very sick man . . . but he traveled thousands of miles just to see you . . . Now you refuse to see him just because you are insulted by some of our American Jewish leaders—even though you know that Weizmann had absolutely nothing to do with these insults . . . It doesn't sound like you, Harry . . . I thought you could take this stuff they have been handing out."

Deep in thought, Truman drummed his desktop, then swiveled in his chair to gaze at the South Grounds, turning green with spring. For what seemed "like centuries," Eddie held his breath. Then the president spun back around and uttered the most "endearing" words Jacobson had ever heard him speak: "You win, you bald-headed son-of-a-bitch! I will see him."

On Thursday, March 18, after dark, Chaim Weizmann was slipped into the Oval Office. The president could never pronounce Weizmann's first name, so he called him "Cham." Truman pledged to "press forward with partition." Worried about leaks, he did not even tell his secretary of State about Weizmann's visit.

The next day, Truman's U.N. ambassador, Warren Austin, seemed to reverse U.S. policy when he told the Security Council that since peaceful partition into Jewish and Arab states seemed impossible, the United States now believed that the U.N. should rule Palestine as the world's trustee. Informed that Austin had just trampled the president's private promise to Weizmann, Eddie Jacobson couldn't believe it: "I was as dazed as a man could be." Feeling "physically sick," he collapsed into bed for two days.

Unfolding his Saturday morning newspapers, Truman was incensed to read about his administration's "badly bungled" somersault on partition. "This morning I find that the State Dept. has reversed my Palestine policy," Truman told his diary. "The first I know about it is what I see in the papers! Isn't that hell? I'm now in the position of a liar and a double-crosser. I've never felt so in my life." Truman inveighed against the "people on the 3rd and 4th levels of the State Dept. who have always wanted to cut my throat." The president called in Clark Clifford: "How could this have happened? I assured Chaim Weizmann I would stick to it. He must think I am a s—t-ass . . . My God, how can I ever face Weizmann again?"

Recovering in Kansas City from what he called "Black Friday," Eddie Jacobson took a call from Chaim Weizmann, who told him not to "feel badly." Privately, Weizmann had been reassured that the president hadn't known of Ambassador Austin's speech in advance and that his commitment to partition still stood. Weizmann told Eddie he was now "the most important single man in the world. You have a job to do, so keep the White House doors open." Jacobson felt "encouraged" to "go on with the work which Fate put on my shoulders."

In April 1948, he eluded reporters by entering the White House through the East Gate, "something I had never done before." Briefed in advance by Weizmann, he informed Truman that a Jewish state would be declared as soon as the British left Palestine. It was "vital" for the U.S. to recognize it. As Eddie recalled, Truman "agreed with a whole heart," saying that "Henderson or a thousand Hendersons won't stop me." But he asked his friend not to mention this private pledge to anyone else.

By then, Truman had decided that the "striped-pants boys" at the State Department who put Jews "in the same category as Chinamen and Negroes" were trying to "put it over on me about Palestine." He wrote his brother he would now "do what I think is right and let them all go to hell."

On Friday, May 14, 1948, in Tel Aviv, the Jews were poised to declare their new nation at 6:00 p.m., Washington time. Truman and Clifford expected the new state to be called "Judea."

At 4 o'clock, Marshall's deputy, Robert Lovett, informed Clifford that the secretary of State would not publicly oppose recognition. Marshall had decided that he should not quit "when the man who has the Constitutional authority to make a decision makes one." Clifford told Lovett, "God, that's good news!"

In a heavily guarded art museum in Tel Aviv, David Ben-Gurion declared that after 20 centuries of wandering, there was now "a Jewish state in Palestine, to be called Israel." At 6:11 p.m. in the White House, Truman signed a document recognizing the Jewish state's "de facto authority," and scrawled the word "Approved." Thinking of Weizmann, he said, "The old doctor will believe me now!" Marshall kept his promised public silence about Truman's decision, but he never spoke to Clark Clifford again.

Chosen as first president of Israel, Chaim Weizmann invited Jacobson to New York, where the good doctor asked him to be "temporary spokesman for the baby state." Eddie wrote, "What a thrill that was! The Lord is sure good to me when He gives me these honors." Eddie flew to New York. When his airport limousine approached the Waldorf, he saw a huge crowd staring up at the new blue and white Star of David flag, flying "beside the stars and stripes of my own country." He wrote, "That was the payoff!" As Jacobson later recalled, "I stood on the sidewalk like a fool, and cried and cried and cried."

In late May, President Weizmann came to Washington, feeling like a "happy man" with a "light heart." Crowds sang the Israeli anthem "Hatikvah." In the White House Rose Garden, Weizmann gave the president a Torah. "Thanks," said Truman. "I've always wanted one of these!"

The presidential campaign of September 1948 found Truman running well behind Thomas Dewey, with Henry Wallace and Strom Thurmond siphoning normally Democratic votes from the left and the right. Clifford had expeced that if the president recognized Israel, Jewish donors would pony up for his campaign. But Truman had warned him that by fall, the Jews would say "we've done nothing for them recently." They would be "off and on" him "sixteen times by then."

When Truman won his surprise election victory in November 1948, he lost New York, New Jersey, Pennsylvania and Michigan, all abundant with Jewish voters. Much of the blame went to Wallace, who complained that Truman wasn't sufficiently pro-Israel. After his victory, Truman wrote Chaim Weizmann that his "elation" on being reelected must resemble Weizmann's when the Jews had proclaimed their state. The man who had once castigated what he called Jewish "underdogs" for being "intolerant" and "cruel" now told Weizmann that he and Israel were clearly both underdogs: "We had both been abandoned by the so-called realistic experts on our supposedly forlorn lost causes. Yet we both kept pressing for what we were sure was right—and we were both proven to be right."

## Truman said he and Israel had something in common: they'd fought as underdogs.

In the end, Truman recognized Israel for many different reasons. The Jews' display of military strength in Palestine had convinced him that U.S. troops would not be needed to defend them. He feared that letting the Russians recognize Israel first would give them a foothold in Palestine. Truman was also motivated by sheer politics. With a tough campaign ahead, he felt that if he did not recognize Israel, the backers of a Jewish state would make his life a living hell. For the hard-bitten Marshall, who operated from cold facts on the ground, Israel was chiefly a potential burden for an overstretched U.S. military. But Truman realized helping to found a Jewish state was a historic act that might qualify him for some future edition of "Great Men and Famous Women."

His favorite psalm had always been, "By the rivers of Babylon, there we sat down, yea, we wept, when we remembered Zion." By recognizing Israel, Truman knew he would be forever damned by people who did not want the Jews to have their own state—or who did not want it in Palestine. But as Truman always told himself, the ultimate test of any presidential decision was "not whether it's popular at the time, but whether it's right . . . If it's right, make it, and let the popular part take care of itself."

In 1949, wearing a lucky hat inscribed by Truman, Eddie Jacobson made a pilgrimage to Israel, where he was feted by President Weizmann and Prime Minister Ben-Gurion. A Kansas City rabbi told reporters that Jacobson should be president of Israel. Truman wrote his old friend that Israel "couldn't nominate a better man, but I sincerely hope you won't take it." Jacobson explained that it was just "a silly dream of a very emotional rabbi." He was "too proud of my American citizenship to trade it for any office in the world."

When Truman retired in 1953, Eddie wanted to be escort for the ex-president's first visit to the nation whose birth they had both midwived: "I sincerely hope my dream comes true." But in 1955, Eddie died of a massive heart attack. As a daughter remembered, when Truman called on the mourning family, he "put his head in his hands and started to sob," exclaiming, "I've lost my brother!"

In 1965, an Eddie Jacobson Auditorium was built in Tel Aviv. Truman hoped "at long last" to "make my journey" to Israel, but a bruising fall in the shower had made him old almost overnight. Instead he wrote a tribute to "my great and irreplaceable friend," saying that Eddie's name "should be forever enshrined in the history of the Jewish people." Interviewed by an Israeli reporter in Independence, Truman said, "Now remind me, how did Eddie use to say 'congratulations' in Hebrew—Mazel something? . . . Yeah, tov. Mazel tov!"

Truman once said that "a weeping man is an abomination." But with his reverence for the Bible and ancient history, Truman was profoundly moved to know he had helped regather the Jews in the Holy Land. Told that an Israeli village had been renamed "Kfar Truman," the stricken president had to cover his face with a handkerchief. Soon the president was proudly comparing himself to the ancient Persian king who had enabled the Jews to return to Zion. During a visit to the Jewish Theological Seminary in New York just after Truman left office, Eddie Jacobson introduced his old friend by saying, "This is the man who helped to create the state of Israel." The ex-president brought Eddie up short: "What do you mean 'helped create'? I am Cyrus! I am Cyrus!"

# UNIT 5

# The Era of the Cold War, 1950–1990

## Unit Selections

## Key Points to Consider

- Was the Marshall Plan an act of altruism or political realism? Make a case for both arguments.

- What circumstances produced the Korean War? What resulted from it?

- What effects did Mao Zedong have on China's twentieth century development? Was he a liberator? An oppressor? Or both?

- How has the last century been a troubling one for Iraq? Do you think the present one will be any better? Why or why not?

- Why has Japan refused to come to terms with its war crimes in the past? What has resulted from this refusal?

- What differences exist in the Balkans today? How can the area's problems be resolved?

- Who is responsible for the conditions that created governmental mass murders in Cambodia? What lessons could be learned from this calamity?

## Student Website

www.mhhe.com/cls

## Internet References

**The Marshall Plan**
www.marshallfoundation.org

**Russia on the Web**
www.valley.net/~transnat

**Vietnam Online**
www.pbs.org/wgbh/amex/vietnam

**WWW Virtual Library: Russian and East European Studies**
www.ucis.pitt.edu/reesweb

Since the end of World War II, Japan has, for the most part, refused to accept responsibility for aggressive actions against its Asian neighbors that many have labeled war crimes. With public attention on the "Rape of Nanking" and the use of Korean women as sex slaves, some in Japan have urged their country to own up to its wartime atrocities. Thus far, steps in this direction have been minimal.

Following World War II, Western leaders realized that they would have to confront the power of the Soviet Union. In 1946, Winston Churchill, the wartime prime minister of Great Britain, described the descent of an iron curtain across central Europe and warned about the spread of communism. American leaders calculated that the economic distress of war-torn Europe would provide fertile ground for communism. Congress, and Secretary of State George Marshall, sponsored an aid program to enable Western Europe to rebuild and restore its economic foundations. The Marshall Plan worked and is considered an unprecedented act of generosity.

In the struggle between the United States and the Soviet Union, the competition remained "cold," never resulting in direct conflict that heated up into open warfare. With the Cold War in the background, however, the United States fought against presumed communist aggression in both Korea and Vietnam, while the Soviet Union fought in Afghanistan. In Korea, the attempt by the North to subdue the South was blocked by a United Nations army, consisting mainly of U.S. troops. For the United States, which had prided itself on never having lost a war, the conflict ended frustratingly where it began, along the 38th parallel line. It was a limited war that resulted in an unstable conclusion.

Four consecutive U.S. presidents committed the country to the containment of communism. By the time Lyndon Johnson became president, after the assassination of John F. Kennedy in 1963, there were a half million U.S. troops in Vietnam, and the war ultimately widened to include Laos and Cambodia. After a decade, the U.S. withdrew. Defeat was bitter, and the war became a cautionary tale about the dangers of waging war against an elusive enemy. Some are beginning to call the U.S. war in Iraq a "quagmire," the same phrase used to describe Vietnam. Iraq began as a British protectorate, when European powers carved up the Middle East, after the first World War. Saddam Hussein's dictatorship began in 1979. The question today is whether U.S.-sponsored wars in Iraq and Afghanistan will have liberated those countries to unleash deadly factional violence.

© Library of Congress, Prints and Photographs Division [LC-USZ62-117122].

Some Americans have found the roots of their country's interventions in Afghanistan and Iraq in the United States's forceful subjugation of the Philippine Islands after the Spanish-American War. The jingoism, patriotism, and egocentrism that fueled that action seem to some a parallel with the attitudes that have created an Iraq quagmire today. In both Japan and the Balkans, we also find historical legacies that remain as troubling reminders. Conservative/nationalist governments in Japan have refused to acknowledge large-scale war crimes committed by their armed forces in World War II. However, War Crimes trials emanating from ethnic conflicts of the 1990s offer some hope that the Balkans can finally come to terms with the sectarianism that tore Yugoslavia apart.

# The Plan and the Man

**High vision and low politics: how George Marshall and a few good men led America to an extraordinary act of strategic generosity.**

EVAN THOMAS

During the winter of 1946–47, the worst in memory, Europe seemed on the verge of collapse. For the victors in World War II, there were no spoils. In London, coal shortages left only enough fuel to heat and light homes for a few hours a day. In Berlin, the vanquished were freezing and starving to death. On the walls of the bombed-out Reichstag, someone scrawled "Blessed are the dead, for their hands do not freeze." European cities were seas of rubble—500 million cubic yards of it in Germany alone. Bridges were broken, canals were choked, rails were twisted. Across the Continent, darkness was rising.

Americans, for the most part, were not paying much attention. Having won World War II, "most Americans just wanted to go to the movies and drink Coca-Cola," said Averell Harriman, who had been FDR's special envoy to London and Moscow during the second world war. But in Washington and New York, a small group of men feared the worst. Most of them were, like Harriman, Wall Street bankers and diplomats with close ties to Europe and a long view of America's role in the world. They suspected that in the Kremlin, Soviet dictator Joseph Stalin was waiting like a vulture. Only the United States, they believed, could save Europe from chaos and communism.

With sureness of purpose, some luck and not a little finagling, these men persuaded Congress to help rescue Europe with $13.3 billion in economic assistance over three years. That sum—more than $100 billion in today's dollars, or about six times what America now spends annually on foreign aid—seems unthinkable today. Announced 50 years ago next week, the European Recovery Program, better known as the Marshall Plan, was an extraordinary act of strategic generosity. How a few policymakers persuaded their countrymen to pony up for the sake of others is a tale of low politics and high vision.

Yet their achievement is recalled by many scholars as a historical blip, a moment of virtue before the cold war really locked in. A truer, if more grandiloquent, assessment was made by Winston Churchill. The Marshall Plan, said England's war leader from his retirement, was "the most unsordid act in history."

It was, at the time, a very hard sell. The men who wanted to save Europe—Harriman, Under Secretary of State Dean Acheson, diplomats like George Kennan—were unelected and for the

most part unknown. They needed a hero, a brand name respected by ordinary Americans. They turned to George C. Marshall.

His name would bring blank stares from schoolchildren today, but Marshall, the army's highest-ranking general in World War II, was widely regarded then as the Organizer of Victory. "He is the great one of the age," said President Harry Truman, who made Marshall secretary of state in January 1947. Upright, cool to the point of asperity ("I have no feelings," he said, "except those I reserve for Mrs. Marshall"), Marshall made worshipers of his followers. Dean Acheson described his boss walking into a room: "Everyone felt his presence. It was a striking and communicated force. His figure conveyed intensity, which his voice, low, staccato and incisive, reinforced. It compelled respect. It spread a sense of authority and calm." Though self-effacing and not prone to speechifying, Marshall used a few basic maxims. One was "Don't fight the problem. Decide it."

Without hesitation, Marshall gave his name and authority to the plan to rescue Europe. His only advice to the policymakers: "Avoid trivia." The unveiling came in a commencement speech at Harvard on June 5, 1947. Wearing a plain business suit amid the colorful academic robes, Marshall was typically plain-spoken and direct: "Our policy," he said, "is not directed against any country or doctrine, but against hunger, poverty, desperation and chaos."

The response in the American press was tepid, but the leaders of Europe were electrified. Listening to the address on the BBC, British Foreign Minister Ernest Bevin regarded Marshall's speech as a "lifeline to a sinking man." Bevin immediately headed for Paris to urge the French to join him in grabbing the rope.

Marshall did not want Washington to appear to be dictating to its allies. "The initiative, I think, must come from Europe," he had said at Harvard. But the Europeans fell to squabbling. The French, in particular, were wary of reviving Germany. "The Plan? There is no plan," grumbled George Kennan, the diplomat sent to Paris that summer of 1947 to monitor the talks. The Europeans were able to write shopping lists, but nothing resembling an overall program. In a cable to Marshall, Kennan predicted that

130

the United States would listen, "but in the end, we would not *ask* them, we would just *tell* them what they would get."

First, however, Marshall's men had to persuade Congress to provide the money. In October, President Truman tried to appeal to America's sense of sacrifice, urging Americans to eat less chicken and fewer eggs so there would be food for starving Europeans. Urged to "waste not," some schoolchildren formed "clean-plate clubs," but that was about as far as the sacrificial zeal went. Members of Congress were profoundly wary. Bob Lovett, another Wall Streeter who replaced Acheson in the summer of 1947 as under secretary, managed to win over Senate Foreign Relations Committee chairman Arthur Vandenberg, mostly by feeding him top-secret cables over martinis at cocktails every night. But many lawmakers regarded foreign aid as "Operation Rathole," and viewed the rescue plan slowly taking shape at the State Department as a "socialist blueprint." Said Charles Halleck, the Republican leader in the House: "I've been out on the hustings, and I know, the people don't like it."

Clearly appealing to good will was not going to suffice. It was necessary, then, to scare the voters and their elected representatives. As it happened, Russia growled at just the right moment. In the winter of 1948, Moscow cracked down on its new satellite state of Czechoslovakia. Jan Masaryk, the pro-Western foreign minister, fell—or was pushed—to his death from his office window in Prague. At the Pentagon, the generals worried that Soviet tanks could begin to roll into Western Europe at any moment. The atmosphere in Washington, wrote Joseph and Stewart Alsop, the hawkish establishment columnists, was no longer "post-war." It was now "pre-war."

In fact, the fears of Soviet invasion were exaggerated. We now know that after World War II the Red Army began tearing up railroad tracks in Eastern Europe because Stalin feared an attack by the West against the Soviet Union. Exhausted by a war that cost the lives of 20 million Russians, the Kremlin was not ready to wage another. Because of poor intelligence, Washington did not fully appreciate Russia's weakness. Top policymakers were aware, however, that the hysteria was exaggerated, that war was unlikely. Even so, they were not above using scare tactics in a good cause—like winning congressional approval of the Marshall Plan. Sometimes, said Acheson, "it is necessary to make things clearer than the truth."

Frightened by the talk of war, urged to recall that isolationism after World War I succeeded only in producing World War II, Congress waved through the European Recovery Plan that spring. In April the SS *John H. Quick* sailed from Galveston, Texas, with 19,000 tons of wheat. Before long, there were 150 ships every day carrying food and fuel to Europe. There were new nets for the fishermen of Norway, wheat for French bakers, tractors for Belgian farmers, a thousand baby chicks for the children of Vienna from 4-H Club members in America.

Politics, needless to say, sometimes interfered with altruism. Some congressmen tried to turn the Marshall Plan into a giant pork barrel, voting to send Europeans the fruits of their districts, needed or not. From Kentucky and North Carolina poured millions of cigarettes; from the Midwest arrived thousands of pounds of canned spaghetti, delivered to gagging Italians. In London drawing rooms, there was some resentment of the heavy American hand. "Our Uncle, who art in America, Sam be thy name/Thy Navy come, they will be done," went one ditty. In Paris, fearful for the purity of the culture (and the sale of wine), the French National Assembly banned the sale, manufacture and import of Coca-Cola.

American aid had a darker side. The Marshall Plan provided the CIA with a handy slush fund. To keep communists from taking over Italy (a genuine threat in 1948), the CIA began handing out money to Italian politicians. At first, the agency had so little money that America's gentlemen spooks had to pass the hat in New York men's clubs to raise cash for bribes. But with the Marshall Plan, there was suddenly plenty of "candy," as CIA official E. Howard Hunt called it, to tempt European politicians and labor leaders.

The CIA's meddling looks sinister in retrospect (though it seemed essential in 1948, when policymakers feared Stalin could start a revolution in Italy and France "just by picking up the phone"). The actual impact of the aid is also a source of dispute. Some economists have argued that the plan played only a superficial role in Europe's recovery. They point to Europe's pent-up innovation and restorative will. But the fact is that from 1938 to 1947 the standard of living in Europe had been declining by about 8 percent a year. After the arrival of the first Marshall aid, the arrows all turned up. Europe's per capita GNP rose by a third between 1948 and 1951. American technicians brought know-how to Europe and reaped enormous good will.

Perhaps America's best export was hope. The Marshall Plan arrived at a time of despondency as well as hardship. Forced to work together, Europeans overcame some historic enmities while America shed its tradition of peacetime isolationism. Ties strengthened by the Marshall Plan evolved into the Western Alliance that stood fast until communism crumbled of its own weight in the Soviet Union. Some of the men who made the Marshall Plan possible saw the romantic and epic quality of their task. It was "one of the greatest and most honorable adventures in history," wrote Dean Acheson. His friend and successor at State, Bob Lovett, had a more practical view: the Marshall Plan was that rare government program that came in on budget, accomplished its goal—and then ended.

The men who made the Marshall Plan were practical, and their motivations can be regarded coldly as a matter of economics and power. But they also wanted to act because they believed that saving Europe was the right and only thing to do. They achieved that rarity among nations—a bold act by one that benefited all.

---

*Newsweek* Assistant Managing Editor **EVAN THOMAS** is coauthor of *The Wise Men,* a history of six friends who shaped postwar American foreign policy.

---

# Korea: Echoes of a War

**After 50 years, is it time for real peace?**

STEVEN BUTLER

Big anniversaries rarely coincide with genuinely important events. Yet this week, the leaders of North and South Korea will meet for the first time ever, 50 years to the month after North Korean troops opened a massive artillery barrage and then stormed across the 38th parallel in a drive that nearly obliterated South Korea. The meeting is more than symbolic. For decades, North Korea refused to talk directly to South Korea because the Seoul government never signed the armistice that halted fighting between belligerents—United Nations forces led by the United States on one side, North Korean and Chinese forces on the other. When North Korean leader Kim Jong Il meets as an equal with South Korean President Kim Dae Jung, it will be an admission of sorts that war is finally over and that South Korea is a reality that can't be wished away.

Even so, 50 years of combat and military stalemate have left unsolved the main issue of the Korean War: how to restore unity to an ancient nation that was divided as a tragic afterthought at the end of World War II. As Japan prepared to surrender in August 1945, two American Army colonels, Dean Rusk (later President Kennedy's secretary of state) and Charles H. Bonesteel, were ordered to find a place to divide the Korean Peninsula. Within 30 minutes, they chose the 38th parallel as the spot where Soviet troops, coming south to accept the surrender of Japanese troops, would meet the American troops moving north. No one imagined it would become a permanent border. The Soviets helped establish a Stalinist-style dictatorship in Pyongyang under the leadership of Kim Il Sung.

Meanwhile, America struggled with only partial success to establish a democracy under Syngman Rhee in half a nation whose civil infrastructure and society were torn apart by 35 years of harsh Japanese colonial rule. In fact, America gave up the job as hopeless. America withdrew its occupation troops in 1949, and public and private statements by Secretary of State Acheson and military leaders suggested that the United States had resigned itself to watching all of Korea fall under Soviet influence. Who would have dreamed that a civil war launched by North Korea to reunify its homeland would have brought a massive response involving at its peak almost a quarter of a million U.S. troops and contributions from 19 other United Nations members? Certainly not Kim Il Sung nor Soviet dictator Joseph Stalin, who hesitantly gave the nod to Kim's war plans.

Collision course. America assumed—erroneously, historians say—that the invasion launched on June 25, 1950, was part of a communist master plan involving eventual expansion of communist China and a Soviet move into Western Europe. As a result, with little consideration for the consequences, President Truman ordered the 7th Fleet into the Taiwan Strait. That thwarted plans by Chinese communists to end the Chinese civil war by launching an amphibious assault against Taiwan, where remnants of Chiang Kai-shek's Nationalist Army had taken refuge. And it put China and America on a collision course from which they have yet to veer.

Of course, Truman also ordered U.S. troops into Korea, with approval from the U.N. Security Council after the Soviet delegate foolishly boycotted the proceedings. Inexperienced soldiers on soft duty in Japan were airlifted to Pusan, from where they formed Task Force Smith and raced north to block the southern advance of North Korean troops. They failed to halt the unexpectedly disciplined and well-equipped North Korean Army, and were forced into a chaotic retreat, sometimes dropping equipment on the run.

Yet Task Force Smith slowed the enemy's advance, giving America crucial extra days to move supplies and men through the port of Pusan. A wide defensive perimeter around the city held against repeated assaults from North Korean troops. Full relief came on September 15, when Gen. Douglas MacArthur launched a risky but technically brilliant assault at the port of Inchon, near Seoul, where tides as high as 30 feet seemed to make a big amphibious landing impossible. Military historians still debate whether the Inchon landing was actually necessary from a military standpoint or whether it was instead another example of MacArthurian showboating. But American troops succeeded in cutting supply and retreat lines of the overextended North Korean Army and broke the back of the invasion.

It was MacArthur's last triumph. The overconfident general sent U.S. troops north of the 38th parallel toward the Chinese

# View from Moscow

## Why Stalin thought the U.S. would stay out

The Korean War might never have happened—or might have turned out quite differently—if the Soviet Union and the West had accurately gauged each other's intentions.

President Truman and his advisers reacted to the North Korean invasion on June 25, 1950, as a direct challenge to the United States by Joseph Stalin. But in the post-Soviet 1990s, archives revealed that the push actually came from North Korean President Kim Il Sung, who pestered Stalin with 48 telegrams seeking approval for an attack. Stalin refused many times, then finally gave his assent in January 1950.

But why did he change his mind? Since the Soviet dictator didn't have to explain himself to anyone, historians could only guess. Now they know for sure: Stalin, who wanted anything but a head-on confrontation with Washington, believed the United States would not respond. "According to information coming from the United States, it is really so," he told Kim, during an April 1950 meeting in Moscow, where the plan took shape. "The prevailing mood is not to interfere." The U.S. mood was reinforced, Stalin said, by the Soviet Union's successful A-bomb test the previous August. One can only imagine what might have happened if Washington had warned in advance it would resist a thrust into South Korea, says historian Kathryn Weathersby, who has studied the new evidence for the Woodrow Wilson Center's Cold War International History Project.

**Miscalculation.** The summary of the critical Stalin-Kim talks, contained in documents from Moscow's tightly guarded Presidential Archive, may refuel an old controversy. Secretary of State Dean Acheson notably excluded South Korea from the U.S. "defense perimeter" in a National Press Club speech on Jan. 12, 1950. Redbaiters later accused him of helping precipitate the invasion. But Acheson was merely citing Truman's policy. And the "information" Stalin alluded to was apparently the U.S. Asia policy document itself, NSC 48. Moscow would have known about it thanks to British spy Donald Maclean. Stalin cited another reason why Korea could be unified by force: the Chinese Communists' victory over the Nationalists. It was a sign of Western weakness and freed Mao's revolutionaries to help in Korea if need be.

Stalin made another major blunder. The original war plan called for an advance on the Ongjin Peninsula, which would bring a response from the South. Claiming it had been attacked first, the North would then launch the full invasion. "The war should be quick. . . . Southerners and Americans should not have time to come to their senses," Stalin told Kim. The U.S.S.R. would not participate directly, he said. But on June 21, four days before the war was to start, Stalin received a telegram from his ambassador in Pyongyang, warning that the South had learned of the plan. Stalin replied the same day, agreeing to Kim's proposal for an all-out attack across the 38th parallel. The World War II-style blitzkrieg virtually ensured that the West would respond, Weathersby says. Respond it did. While that's history, it may hold a lesson for dealing with tomorrow's dictators.

—Warren P. Strobel

border, despite warnings from China that it would enter the war on the North's side. And he blundered tactically by allowing his forces to become separated by the mountain range running down the spine of Korea. Chinese "volunteers" began infiltrating the border in late October and moved down the center of the peninsula before launching a massive counterattack in November, forcing U.S. troops into yet another disorderly retreat at a huge cost of men and equipment. It was the longest U.S. military retreat in history.

**"American Caesar."** In less than six months, the city of Seoul had changed hands no less than three times. U.N. forces regrouped and charged north again, but on reaching the 38th parallel, few were willing to risk going farther north again. Few, that is, except MacArthur, who threatened China with attack in public defiance of Truman's policies. Truman fired MacArthur for insubordination, causing a political uproar at home, where MacArthur was revered as a World War II hero, an "American Caesar," as biographer William Manchester called him. The war ground on—World War I style—with huge, bloody battles from entrenched positions over relatively small tactical objectives, places dubbed Heartbreak Ridge and Pork Chop Hill.

Failure to bring the war to an early close may have cost the Democrats the presidential election in 1952, and President-elect Eisenhower made good his pledge to visit Korea. Eisenhower hinted he might expand the war, perhaps even using atomic weapons. Then Stalin died, and negotiators at last settled the final issue that had held up armistice for several years: whether prisoners of war could choose repatriation or not. A committee from neutral nations screened POWs, with 23 Americans and 14,704 Chinese choosing not to go home.

Americans were anxious to forget the war and to enjoy the long economic boom of the 1950s. Yet the war changed the world, and America, in ways that few people appreciate today. For one, it was America's first taste of military defeat, and its first experience of limited warfare, where outright victory was deemed too costly an objective. The wartime demand helped restore Japan's economy, devastated by its defeat in World War II, and made the former enemy into a strategic partner in Asia. It was the first of many military interventions under the United Nations flag. It also was the event that first turned the Cold War hot, swiftly reversing the cuts in U.S. military spending that had left U.S. forces unprepared to fight. An enormous military buildup followed: Military spending nearly quadrupled in three years, and the ranks of the armed forces more than doubled from 1.5 million to 3.5 million.

And yet, the war really settled nothing—36,516 Americans and millions of Koreans and Chinese dead just to agree on an existing demarcation line. North Korea survives as perhaps the most repressive government in the world, a lone Stalinist state that embraces central planning, threatening the world with long-range missiles while its own people starve in a horrendous famine. South Korea evolved tortuously into a proud and prosperous democracy. And Korea is still divided, with over a million heavily armed men on both sides of the 38th parallel. Taiwan, too, remains dangerously estranged from China. This week's Korean summit could prove a modest step to resolving a Cold War that has ended almost everywhere else in a victory for democracy and free-market capitalism.

# Mao Zedong: Liberator or Oppressor of China?

Michael Lynch

The setting is Tiananmen Square in Beijing, the capital of China. The date is August 1966. The Square is packed with a vast throng of young people. In unison, their faces a picture of ecstasy, they wave their little red books of the sayings of Chairman Mao and repeatedly scream and chant his name. The object of their adoration, who stands on the balcony of the South Gate overlooking the Square, is a drug addicted 73-year-old womaniser. He is also the ruler of a quarter of the world's population.

Such scenes remain one of the most powerful images of twentieth-century China. The worship of Chairman Mao Zedong was extreme, but it was not wholly irrational. It was a recognition of what he had achieved for China. Those many millions of Chinese who ritualistically intoned 'Mao, Mao, Mao Zedong' saw him as the supreme hero who had freed their country from a century of humiliation at the hands of the foreigner. One of the titles given him was 'the red sun rising in the east', an apt metaphor for the man who, having led a momentous social and political revolution in China, went on to make his country a nuclear Superpower, defying the USA, displacing the Soviet Union as the leader of international socialism, and becoming the model for the struggle against colonialism.

## Imperial China

The China into which Mao Zedong was born in 1893 was a deeply troubled land. For centuries it had believed itself to be superior to all other cultures and had deliberately avoided foreign contacts. But by the end of the nineteenth century its self-belief had been shattered. Since the 1840s a number of Western nations, principally Britain, Germany, France and the USA, had forced the Chinese to enter into a series of 'unequal treaties' which obliged them to surrender sovereign territory and accept trade on Western terms. By 1900 over 50 Chinese 'treaty ports' were in foreign possession. The people's bitterness at such humiliation created mounting dissatisfaction with the imperial government. The inability of the ruling Qing (Manchu) dynasty to protect China encouraged the growth of a revolutionary movement whose chief aim was to achieve 'a revolution against the world to join the world', to end China's subjection to the West by adopting progressive Western political and economic ways.

## Mao's Early Years

Mao was born into a relatively well-to-do landed family in Hunan province. He was what might be termed a 'natural rebel'. Doted on by his mother, he fell out with his father and refused to show him the respect traditionally expected of Chinese sons. As a teenager, Mao played a small role as a volunteer soldier in Changsha in the Chinese Revolution of 1911, which saw the collapse and abdication of the Qings. He then moved to Beijing where he furthered his education and in 1919 took up a post as librarian in Beijing University. It was there that he was introduced to Marxist ideas and developed the conviction that if China was to be truly regenerated it would have to undergo a profound social and political revolution.

His belief was strengthened by his awareness that the 1911 revolution had brought China little benefit. Although a republican government had replaced the imperial system, it exercised only nominal power. Throughout China local warlords and factions struggled to assert authority. Mao recorded the savagery that became commonplace:

> During my student days in Hunan, the city was overrun by the forces of rival warlords—not once but half a dozen times. Twice the school was occupied by troops and all the school funds confiscated. The brutal punishments inflicted on the peasants include such things as gouging out eyes, ripping out tongues, disembowelling and decapitation, slashing with knives and grinding with sand, burning with kerosene and branding with red hot irons. The situation was appalling. People had nothing to eat; families were split up.

The barbarity Mao witnessed greatly affected him. He concluded that the only way to gain power was through violence. This helps to explain why throughout his career he was so ready to use brutal means in crushing political opponents. One of his most revealing sayings was, 'All power grows out of the barrel of a gun'.

By the 1920s two main revolutionary parties were in contention in China: the Nationalists or Guomindang (GMD), created by Sun Yatsen and led after 1925 by Chiang Kaishek, and the Chinese Communist Party (CCP), which came into being in 1921 with Mao as one of its founder members. In 1924 the two parties formed a GMD-CCP united front against the warlords, but the unity was more apparent than real. The GMD's main aim under Chiang was to destroy the Communists. In 1927 it launched the 'White Terror' extermination campaign against them. Mao survived by taking his CCP forces to the mountains of Jiangxi province, where he organised guerrilla resistance, known as the Autumn Harvest Rising.

During the next seven years Mao helped to establish the Jiangxi Soviet, dedicated to the furtherance of peasant revolution. He showed himself unwilling to accept dictation from the Comintern, the USSR's organisation for fomenting international revolution. He frequently rejected orders from Moscow which instructed the CCP to base its activities in the towns rather than the countryside.

It was also during the Jiangxi period (1927–34) that Mao revealed an utter ruthlessness that characterised his whole career. In the notorious 'Futian incident' in 1930 he had no compunction in torturing and executing some 4,000 Red Army troops whom he regarded as rebels. Philip Short, Mao's most recent biographer, visited the site of the horrors:

> All along the two sides of the courtyard there are cells with thick wooden doors and lattice work, lattice struts going horizontally and vertically just like the bars of a cage. In here behind these wooden bars the prisoners were held; they were brought out to be tortured, women as well as men . . . They were tortured to make them speak and they tortured on Mao's orders. There is a document in the party archives which Mao approved which says, 'do not kill the important leaders too quickly, but squeeze out of them the maximum information; then from the clues they give, you can go on to unearth others'.

## The Long March, 1934–35

Although the GMD became the official government of China in the early 1930s, it was weakened by its halfhearted response to the Japanese military occupation, beginning in 1931, of many parts of the Chinese mainland. The fact was that Chiang Kaishek was still more intent on crushing his Communist enemies within China than resisting the Japanese invader. This was evident in 1934 when Chiang systematically encircled the CCP's base in Jiangxi with a view to destroying it altogether. Again Mao survived, this time by leading his followers on one of the great epics of Communist folklore—the Long March— a 6,000 mile odyssey which crossed 18 mountain ranges, 24 rivers and several deserts. Of the 100,000 who set out, scarcely 20,000 survived to reach their destination at Yanan. It was during the 18-month march that a critical CCP strategy meeting took place at Zunyi. Mao outmanoeuvred his opponents in the CCP and imposed on the Party his notion of a peasant-based revolution, as opposed to the urban-based campaigns that the pro-Soviet members had wanted.

## The Yanan Years, 1935–45

During the Yanan period Mao, by a combination of political and military skill, luck and utter ruthlessness, succeeded in imposing his personal authority on the CCP. In 1942 he launched a series of 'rectification of conduct' campaigns, which, in effect, were a set of purges by which he removed party opponents. It was also during this time that Mao led the CCP from its northern bases in a spirited resistance to the Japanese occupation. Mao's main strategy was to win over the peasants who made up 80 per cent of the Chinese population. His success in this had the double effect of providing military recruits for the anti-Japanese struggle and political supporters for the CCP in its campaign against the urban-based GMD.

## The Defeat of the GMD

With the defeat of Japan at the end of the Second World War, the CCP turned on the GMD in a renewal of the civil war that had lasted intermittently since the late 1920s. A fierce four-year struggle for supremacy ended with the complete victory of the Communists. By 1949 Chiang and the Guomindang had been driven from the Chinese mainland; their one remaining stronghold was the offshore island of Taiwan. Mao and the CCP were now in a position to establish Communist rule over the whole of mainland China.

## Creating the People's Republic of China

In Beijing on 1 October 1949, Mao formally declared the People's Republic of China (PRC) to have come into being. Between then and his death in 1976, Mao Zedong was revered by the mass of the Chinese people as a living god. But he faced huge problems as leader of the new China. His most demanding task was to bring stability to a nation that had been riven by decades of turmoil. Mao's political approach was a simple one: he would tolerate no opposition to the CCP. All other parties were outlawed and the total obedience of the nation to the new government was demanded.

Mao and the CCP leaders organised campaigns of vilification against anyone in public life who opposed official policy. An atmosphere of fear and uncertainty was systematically created by a series of 'anti-movements', launched against those whom the CCP regarded as socially or politically suspect. The Chinese people were urged to expose all who had cooperated with the former GMD government. China became a nation of informers. The vengeful atmosphere was intensified by Mao's decision to enter the Korean War (1950–53) in support of the North Koreans. This struggle placed great demands on the new regime and provided further pretexts for the government to harry the population. Some of the worst excesses occurred in the countryside where the landlords were brutally dispossessed of their properties.

Purges were also carried out within the CCP. Members suspected of not totally following the party line were condemned as 'rightists' who were opposed to the progress of the PRC. Purges alternated with periods when party members were encouraged to criticise current policies. This apparent liberalising was invariably followed by the imposition of even tougher restrictions on freedom of expression. A striking example occurred in 1957 when Mao, using the slogan 'Let a hundred flowers bloom; let a hundred schools of thought contend', called on members to air their grievances. Those who were rash enough to do so were then attacked as 'rightists'. Such purges were to become a recurrent feature of Chinese politics down to Mao's death in 1976.

# Great Leap Forward and Famine, 1958–66

In economic matters Mao's basic aim was to industrialise China. He hoped that within a short period the new China would be able to match both the Soviet Union and the capitalist West in industrial output. To achieve this, he copied the Stalinist model of a series of five-year plans. These involved prodigious physical efforts by the Chinese workers; but, since Mao deliberately chose to place his faith in mass labour rather than in modern technology, the plans were only partially successful. The limitations of Mao's approach were particularly evident during the Second Five-Year Plan (1958–62). Intended to be 'the Great Leap Forward', the Plan fell far short of its production targets. The extent of the failure was hidden from the people, but what the authorities could not conceal was the widespread famine that accompanied the Plan. The land which had been given to the peasants after its seizure from the landlords had to be forfeited in a mass collectivisation programme which ended private ownership. The dislocation this caused produced a national catastrophe. Between 1958 and 1962, 30 million Chinese died from starvation.

Mao did not openly accept responsibility for the famine, but in the early 1960s he withdrew into the political background, leaving two prominent party figures, Deng Xiaoping and Liu Shaoqi, to tackle the problem of food shortages. Their attempts to do so led them to abandon collectivisation. Mao, however, saw this as an undermining of the socialist principles on which China's 1949 revolution rested. In a series of dramatic gestures, which included his swimming in the Yangzi river, the ageing Chairman reappeared in public and reasserted his dominance in Chinese politics. What prompted him to return was the fear that had always moved him, and which increased as he grew older, that the revolution he had led might not survive his death. To prevent this he was determined to impose a political and social structure on China that would permanently define its character as a nation. This was the intention behind his introduction in 1966 of the great Cultural Revolution, an extraordinary movement that plunged China into a decade of deliberately engineered turmoil.

# The Cultural Revolution 1966–76

Mao's objective in unleashing the Cultural Revolution was to oblige the Party to acknowledge its errors and purge itself of all possible rivals to his authority. His chosen instrument

for achieving this was the youth of China. In 1966 he called upon the young to set themselves up in judgement over their elders. He urged them to form a mass movement to destroy the 'four olds' that were threatening China's revolution—'old culture, old thoughts, old customs and old habits'. The young people responded with an idealistic enthusiasm that soon degenerated into a brutal fanaticism. Squads of teenagers, known as Red Guards, rampaged through China's cities and towns, assaulting those whom they regarded as the 'bad elements' representing China's corrupt past. No part of China's antique culture was sacred. Buildings—whether universities, libraries, museums or temples—which in the eyes of the Red Guards stood as memorials to Chinese decadence were smashed or burned.

The violence was part of a wholesale attack upon China's traditional culture. All forms of artistic expression were subjected to crippling censorship. They had to pass the test of 'socialist value' imposed by Mao's fourth wife, Jiang Qing, who was entrusted with responsibility for recreating Chinese culture. In the event she achieved the reverse. Her demand that all forms of creativity must conform absolutely with her notions of true socialist culture meant that nothing of real worth was produced or presented. China became an artistic wilderness.

The Cultural Revolution was an act of madness but there was method in it. The Red Guards were a highly visible and terrifying feature of the movement but they were essentially a front. Mao was using the apparent anarchy to enforce his will upon the CCP and the nation. It was a means of fulfilling his concept of 'continuing revolution', the belief that unless the Communist Party was regularly purified it would cease to be a revolutionary force and China would cease to be truly socialist. For ten years after 1966 the Cultural Revolution distorted China both internally and in its relations with the outside world.

In foreign affairs a particularly significant development was the PRC's deepening estrangement from the USSR. In its early years the PRC had looked upon the Soviet Union as its mentor and had sided with it as a natural ally in the Cold War. But China's belief that it was being financially and commercially exploited by the Soviet Union, which refused to accept her as an equal partner in the international revolutionary movement, led to profound mutual hostility in the 1960s. The Cultural Revolution was confirmation that China under Mao would follow its own path, regardless of Soviet opinion. For a time there was a real possibility that a nuclear war might break out between China and the Soviet Union.

The deterioration in Sino-Soviet relations was balanced by an improvement in China's relations with the West. Largely as the result of the skillful diplomacy of the PRC's foreign minister, Zhou Enlai, there was a break in 'the bamboo curtain' and in 1972 Mao received Richard Nixon in Beijing, the first US president to visit Communist China.

By 1976, after a decade of Cultural Revolution, there were signs that even Mao himself considered that the social and political extremism had gone too far. Yet what he finally thought of the Cultural Revolution is not easy to judge since in the last two years of his life his physical decline and increasing dependence on drugs reduced him to a shambling, incoherent wreck.

# Mao's Achievements

Mao Zedong stands with Lenin, Stalin and Hitler as one of 'the makers of the twentieth-century'. Beginning in the 1920s, he created a peasant movement which carried him and his Chinese Communist Party to power in 1949. It was an extraordinary accomplishment which both complemented and contradicted the Russian revolution of 1917. Between the founding of the People's Republic of China in 1949 and Mao's death in 1976, Maoism became the inspiration and hope of a range of anti-colonial movements worldwide and was taken up enthusiastically by many revolutionary hopefuls in the Western world. The subsequent abandonment of Maoism in China and its decline as an inspirational force internationally does not lessen the magnitude of Mao's achievement in having led to victory the century's largest popular movement.

Historical controversy still surrounds Mao Zedong. Was it international Marxism or Chinese nationalism that inspired him and characterised the Chinese revolution of 1949? Was Maoism essentially a continuation of the Chinese imperial tradition or was it an entirely new brand of politics? Was Mao the new red emperor or the last great Marxist leader? Was Maoism a genuine development of Marxism-Leninism or a form of heretical socialism whose main purpose was to reassert traditional notions of Chinese cultural supremacy? Such are the questions with which historians continue to grapple.

# Iraq's Unruly Century

Ever since Britain carved the nation out of the Ottoman Empire after World War I, the land long known as Mesopotamia has been wracked by instability.

JONATHAN KANDELL

On a July morning in Baghdad in 1958, Iraq's constitutional monarchy came to a brutal end when an army faction led by Iraqi Gen. Abdul Karim Qassem stormed the royal palace. In the courtyard, rebel troops killed King Faisal II, the 23-year-old grandson of the first monarch, and a score of men, women and children. Faisal's body was removed to a secret burial place. But no such respect was accorded his uncle and former regent, Abdul Ilah, whom the plotters blamed for the monarchy's pro-British slant; his corpse was thrown to a mob outside the palace gates, dragged around the city and displayed for two days in a public square.

The 1958 coup d'état was not the first upheaval in Iraq's modern political history, which has been marked by nationalist fervor, ethnic uprisings, tribal conflicts, palace treacheries, warfare and deadly oppression. In the monarchy's 37 years, the government cabinet was shuffled more than 50 times. Scholars have offered a catalog of reasons why antiquity's "cradle of civilization" has been so unstable. Some blame geography, pointing out that Iraq, which covers some 168,000 square miles, has a mere 12 miles of shoreline, on the Persian Gulf, making it the most land-locked—and culturally isolated—nation in the Middle East. Others tie Iraq's "bloody history," as many have described it, to the preponderance of groups vying for power. The rivalry goes deeper than Arab versus British, however, or Sunni versus Shiite versus Kurd. As the Kurdish analyst Siyamend Othman said this past November, the "history of Iraq has been conditioned, if not determined, by the conflict between city and countryside," meaning the conflict between an emerging educated class around major urban areas and the old semi-literate rural sheikhdoms.

Britain's experiment in nation-building failed partly because it did not unify the disparate factions, says Charles Tripp, a British citizen and author of the 2000 book, *A History of Iraq.* Instead, Britain seeded unrest by relying on the Sunni minority to run the military and civil service and also by subordinating the northern, Kurdish territory. In addition, he says, Britain's decision to allow tribal sheikhs to maintain order in rural areas heightened tensions by "treating Iraqi society as a collection of groups rather than individuals."

But Adeed Dawisha, an Iraq-born historian and author of *Arab Nationalism in the Twentieth Century,* suggests that Britain failed mainly because it granted Iraq too little autonomy. "From the establishment of the constitutional monarchy in 1921 all the way to its fall in 1958," Dawisha says, "it was very clear that none of the Iraqi governments could carry out any policy against British opposition. And I would put oil [policies] at the top of the list. Oil sales served the interests of Britain, not Iraq."

It was at the start of World War I that Britain first occupied Mesopotamia, then part of the Ottoman Empire. The Ottomans had allied with Germany, and Britain justified its 1914 invasion as a move to protect its oil fields in neighboring Iran and its access to Persian Gulf shipping lanes to India. Many Iraqis welcomed the British troops with open arms. The 1916–1918 Arab Revolt against the Ottoman Turks, encouraged by the British military liaison officer T. E. Lawrence (better known as Lawrence of Arabia), raised nationalist Arab expectations in the region. And to court Arabs throughout the Middle East, the British vowed to end three centuries of Ottoman rule, which had grown corrupt, repressive and economically stifling. "Our armies do not come into your cities and lands as conquerors or enemies but as liberators," proclaimed Gen. Stanley Maude, commander of the British forces, as his troops marched into Baghdad in 1917.

In 1920, the newly formed League of Nations granted Britain a "mandate" over Iraq—a kind of pre-independence trusteeship. It gave Britain the right to raise and spend revenues, to appoint officials and to make and enforce laws. (Britain was also mandated to govern Palestine. Another mandate put Syria and Lebanon under French jurisdiction.) Though the mandate approach was flawed, says historian David Fromkin, it appealed to League members because it gave the Allied powers control over territories without endorsing imperialism outright. "The mandate system responded to people who were idealistic and anti-imperialistic and others who felt it was a useful disguise to maintain the old colonial system in place," says Fromkin, author of *A Peace to End All Peace.*

In the end, the boundaries of the new Iraq—a seventh-century name meaning "well-rooted country"—largely mirrored the boundaries of three Ottoman provinces, though that was not the original plan. In 1915 the British had wanted the northernmost province around Mosul to go to France, to serve as a buffer between British holdings and possible Russian expansion. But Britain changed its stance in 1918 in part because of growing appreciation for the importance of oil, believed to be abundant in the Mosul area. (So it is. A well first struck oil in Kirkuk in 1927.) As for Kuwait, it had been virtually a separate British protectorate since 1899 and by World War I was already splitting from the Ottoman province of Basra that would become part of Iraq.

By the time of the 1920 mandate, Iraqi nationalism outweighed pro-British feeling. British officials differed over how to deal with the threat. "There were people like Gertrude Bell," says Phebe Marr, a Washington, D.C.-based historian, "who came to believe in the need for some sort of self-government as soon as possible, and conservatives like Arnold Wilson [Bell's chief], who thought that the local folk weren't capable of running their own show and had to be tutored for a long time."

For a while, Wilson's arguments held sway—to the frustration of Bell and most Iraqis. When an Iraqi delegation met with Wilson, a forceful imperialist then in his 30s, he brushed them off as "ungrateful politicians." He proceeded to turn Iraq into a virtual appendage of Britain's colonial rule in India, bringing troops and administrators over from the subcontinent. Nationalist protests increased, and in the summer of 1920, one leader, Imam Shirazi of Karbala, issued a fatwa, or religious decree, that British rule violated Islamic law. He called for a jihad, or holy war, against the British—and for once Sunnis, Shiites and rival sheikhdoms united in a common cause. The armed rebellion spread from Karbala and Najaf, in the center, to the south of the country, with uprisings by Kurds in the north as well.

Wilson came down hard, ordering aerial bombardments, the machine-gunning of rebels and the destruction of whole towns. "The British overreaction made things much worse," says Janet Wallach, author of a biography of Bell, *Desert Queen*. An aghast Bell wrote to her mother, "We have underestimated the fact that this country is really an inchoate mass of tribes which can't as yet be reduced to any system. The Turks didn't govern and we have tried to govern—and failed." Some 6,000 Iraqis and 500 British and Indian soldiers perished before the revolt was finally put down in October. By then, the British press and public had turned against Colonial Office plans to run Iraq. As *The Times* of London had put it three months earlier, "How much longer are valuable lives to be sacrificed in the vain endeavour to impose upon the Arab population an elaborate and expensive administration which they never asked for and do not want?"

The following year, a conference in Cairo presided over by Winston Churchill, then colonial secretary for Iraq affairs, determined that a constitutional monarchy was the surest path toward a stable, prosperous Iraq. At first glance, Faisal seemed an unlikely choice as ruler. The 35-year-old prince, son of the Sharif Hussein of Mecca (now part of Saudi Arabia), had never set foot in Iraq and spoke an Arabic dialect that was barely intelligible to many of his future subjects. "He had no knowledge of the Iraqi tribes, no friendships with their sheikhs, no familiarity with the terrain—the marshes in the south, the mountains in the north, the grain fields, the river life—and no sense of connection with its ancient past," Wallach writes.

But Bell and other Arabists in the Colonial Office believed that Faisal, who had fought with Lawrence against the Turks, had the charisma to hold the new country together. Also, he traced his lineage to Muhammad, and to emphasize that claim he set out for his new kingdom from Mecca, birthplace of the Prophet. Along his route, chieftains tried to rally crowds—"For the sake of Allah, cheer!"—but most spectators remained unmoved. In a national referendum on his monarchy, Faisal was officially declared to have won 96 percent of the vote, prompting charges that the election was rigged. Still, a relieved Bell wrote in another letter: "We've got our King crowned."

The Oxford-educated Bell served as Faisal's adviser and confidante. During afternoon teas at the palace, she reeled out her vision of a progressive Iraq that could become a beacon for the Middle East. "When we have made Mesopotamia a model state, there is not an Arab of Syria and Palestine who wouldn't want to be part of it," she told the king, adding that she hoped to see Faisal "ruling from the Persian frontier to the Mediterranean."

But Faisal wasn't looking beyond his borders. Ruling his subjects—divided by ethnicity, religion and geography—was trouble enough. Like the Ottomans before them, the British and Faisal, himself a Sunni, found it expedient to favor the more pro-Western Sunni Arabs of Baghdad and the central region, though they accounted for barely 20 percent of the population. More than half of Iraqis were Shiite Arabs, concentrated in the south. Close to 20 percent were Kurds, living mostly in the north. The remainder included Jews, Assyrians and other minorities. "The British turned to the same educated elite—mostly Sunni—who had been trained and used by the Ottomans," says historian Marr. "But a number of them soon proved to be ornery and nationalistic."

It was left to Faisal to deal with the Iraqi nationalists. The British-designed constitution gave him the power to select the prime minister, dissolve parliament and issue decrees when parliament wasn't in session. And no law could be passed without his assent. But Faisal struggled to balance British and Iraqi demands. One moment, he was beseeching British officials not to withdraw from Iraq. Days later, he was refusing to suppress anti-British demonstrations in Baghdad and Basra. "There's always this problem of needing the support of the West and at the same time bowing to the will of the people for independence," says Wallach.

The most insistent issue that the king faced was a new Anglo-Iraq treaty, which would provide for the maintenance of British military bases, give British officials a veto over legislation and perpetuate British influence over financial and international matters for 20 years. Faisal equivocated. In private, he assured Bell that he favored the treaty. But in public speeches, he criticized it for stopping short of removing the mandate.

"Gertrude was livid at his double-dealing," Wallach writes. A special Iraqi assembly ratified the treaty in 1924, with Faisal's tacit support. But he had demonstrated that the British could not take him for granted.

Faisal ruled long enough to see the mandate end, in 1932, when Iraq was admitted to the League of Nations as an independent state. (Though Britain's direct participation in local government ended in 1930, pro-British elements would exercise influence until 1958.) Faisal died of a heart attack at age 48 in 1933 while seeing physicians in Switzerland. "He made himself a buffer between Iraqi nationalists and the British," says Tripp, the British historian. "Before he died, he reached out beyond that small Sunni circle he had inherited from the Ottomans and built ties with the Shiites and Kurds."

Today, scholars debate the extent of British influence on Iraq after the mandate. "If Faisal had lived ten more years, the history of Iraq would have been very different," says Edmund Ghareeb, an Iraq-born historian at Georgetown University. "After his death, the British were able to undermine the government and the monarchy by constantly putting pressure on them to serve Britain's interests—involving oil, foreign affairs in the gulf region and other issues."

But Reeva S. Simon, a Columbia University historian, says Iraq achieved a measure of independence: "It joined the League of Nations. It had a press that was open and critical of the British. In foreign policy, it did not simply follow the British lead but showed itself to be increasingly pro-German during the 1930s, and invited to Baghdad people who opposed British rule in the Middle East."

In any event, Marr says, Britain's imprint was profound. "Even after the mandate ended, the British presence focused Iraqis constantly on independence. Not on developing the country, not on how to make the constitutional system work better, not on how to integrate Kurds, Shiites and Sunnis. Instead, the question that was always asked was, how can we get rid of the British? As a result, there is even to this day an obsession that there be no foreign control." As Fromkin says, "We tend to overlook a basic rule: that people prefer bad rule by their own kind to good rule by somebody else."

Britain's presence in Iraq was not the only thing that aroused Iraqi anger. By the 1930s, Arab leaders were also angered by the growing numbers of European Jews migrating to Palestine, a British mandate until 1948. When the British suppressed a revolt by Palestinian Arabs in 1939, Iraqi Army officers invited the defeated leader, the Mufti of Jerusalem, to live in Baghdad. Then, as World War II began, Iraqi antipathy to Britain turned into support for Hitler. "It was widely acknowledged that most of the junior officers in the Iraqi army are pro-German and anti-British," Paul Knabenshue, a U.S. diplomat in Baghdad, wrote in May 1940. Iraq attempted to ally itself with Germany and in 1941 threatened to fire on British planes at an airfield near Baghdad.

In April 1941, Rashid Ali, a civilian figurehead for an Iraqi Army faction led by four colonels staged a coup d'état. British Royal Air Force troops stationed on the outskirts of Baghdad held the Iraqi Army at bay while British reinforcements from India landed in Basra and marched north.

In Baghdad, some 400 British nationals and their Iraqi sympathizers sought refuge in the British Embassy. The last person admitted into the compound was Freya Stark. Previously disdained by many compatriots, she was now hailed as a savior. "With her fluent local Arabic and her aplomb and bonhomie, she became our most useful contact at our gates with the Iraqi police posted here, and helped us to buy fresh meat and vegetables to leaven our Spartan fare," one observer recalled. Her good relations with the guards may have saved the embassy from mobs. "We could see the crowds from the upper town, incited by speeches of the Mufti and their own radio, advancing with banners and drums and dancing figures silhouetted against the sky, towards our gates," Stark wrote.

By early June, British forces had taken control of Baghdad. Rashid Ali's two-month rule ended when he fled to Berlin. The four Iraqi colonels behind his coup were captured and hanged. In retaliation, outraged Iraqi mobs stormed the Jewish quarter, presumed to be pro-British, and killed 179 men, women and children, injuring hundreds more.

Saddam Hussein, a child at the time, would later say that Rashid Ali's rise and fall affected him deeply because the uncle who raised him was an army officer whose career ended when the coup was crushed.

Anti-British passions were further inflamed by the outbreak, in 1948, of war in Palestine, where Iraqi troops fought on the Arab side against the Israelis, whose ultimate victory, most Iraqis believed, could not have been achieved without British (and American) assistance. They were inflamed again in 1956 by the British role in wresting the Suez Canal back from Egyptian president Gamal Abdel Nasser. Then, the Qassem coup d'état in 1958 destroyed the monarchy once and for all. Ilah, the former regent, and Prime Minister Nuri Said were killed because they were felt to have been too eager to please the British by executing the plotters of Rashid Ali's coup 17 years earlier.

The massacre of the Iraqi royal family left two major legacies of Great Britain's four-decades-long involvement in Iraq: the nation retained essentially the same boundaries that Britain had traced in the early 1920s, and the Sunni minority held on to power.

The monarchy's collapse was followed by a decade of even greater instability, ending with a coup in 1968 by army officers linked to the Baathists, a pan-Arab socialist movement that opponents have described as neo-Fascist. A jubilant Saddam Hussein, 31, rode through Baghdad atop a tank. His kinsman, Gen. Ahmad Hassan al-Bakr, had led the coup and became president. Like Bakr, Hussein was from Tikrit, a Sunni town north of Baghdad that historically had fielded a disproportionate share of army officers. But Hussein did not come up through the military ranks in the usual way. After high school in Baghdad, he earned a living as a street tough for politicians, organizing gangs that disrupted opponents' political rallies and beating up shopkeepers whose stores remained open during strikes. Hussein graduated to assassin and spent almost two years in prison and in exile for political murders or attempted killings.

But his ferocity and cunning had impressed General Bakr, who, as president, appointed him to run the national security apparatus. In that capacity he set out to eliminate his main rivals, and he placed relatives and fellow Tikritis in positions of power and influence in the Baath Party, the armed forces and the government. As Bakr's power broker, Hussein nationalized foreign oil holdings in 1972, then accepted acclaim as Iraq's annual oil revenues rose eight-fold, to $8 million over the next three years, then tripled over the next five. Hussein then oversaw state investments in education, health, transportation, agriculture and industry, drawing praise as a model for the Middle East.

When, in 1979, Hussein became president following Bakr's "resignation"—Hussein almost certainly engineered it—many Iraqis thought he would lead them into prosperity. (Bakr died in 1982.) Instead, Hussein, after having his rivals killed, ruled despotically for nearly a quarter of a century, waging war on Iran (with American backing) and killing many thousands of Iraqis, including thousands of Kurds killed by chemical weapons. Hussein dragged his oil-rich, once-ascendent nation into poverty, and his pursuit of weapons of mass destruction put him on a collision course with the world's lone superpower.

JONATHAN KANDELL, a former foreign correspondent for the *New York Times,* wrote last for these pages about "Boss" Tweed.

# Remembering the War—Japanese Style

Kiichi Fujiwara

The recent conflict over historical issues between Japan and its neighbors is hardly unprecedented—similar outbursts have occurred at almost regular intervals in the past. But this time around, there are some disturbing new factors which make the situation more problematic than ever before. Further, the recent deterioration in relations couldn't happen at a worse time, as Japan attempts to develop policies to guide it's future relationship with the Asian region. To avoid a major policy failure, Japan must re-examine its articulation of war memory, which is the major impediment to forging closer ties with Asia.

Before discussing war memory in depth, it is worth examining some of these new realities Tokyo faces as certain Japanese politicians become more vocal in their defense of visits to Yasukuni Shrine and become more assertive about Japan's war-time past. Last spring China and South Korea were rocked by nationalistic demonstrations, with protestors demanding the Japanese retreat from "occupied" territories. South Korea demanded that Japan drop its claim to the Takeshima or Dokdo IslaDd, and China demanded the same regarding the Senkaku or Diaoyu Islands. This was the first time that the contending memories over the war past have been connected to a territorial dispute in the present. Although there have been numerous territorial spats before, never have they been inflamed by acts which provoke historical acrimony, such as Yasukuni Shrine visits by political leaders, to the extent to which they are nowadays.

In the face of such hostility, Japan has evinced a stronger resistance—or consistency, depending on your point of view—on the issue. This has only served to exacerbatq the current problem. In the good old days, whenever Beijing or Seoul issued strong statement about war crimes, the Japanese leaders would say: "We're sorry. We have apologized,and we will apologize again." The South Korean or the Chinese government would nominally accept the apology. This is no longer the case under the Koizumi administration.

In April this year, at the Asian-African summit in Jakarta, Mr. Koizumi offered an apology. However, Mr. Koizumi's apology was a word-for-word repetition of the one made by then Prime Minister Tomoiichi Murayama in 1995 on the occasion of the 50th anniversary of the end of World War II. This fact gave Mr. Koizumi's words a hollow ring. It was as if he was merely stating a memorized mantra. Five months after the Jakarta apology, Prime Minister Koizumi had the nerve to visit the Yasukuni Shrine again. Given subsequent statements and actions by Mr. Koizumi and his close political allies on the issue of Yasukuni, we can expect Tokyo to maintain this tough stance in the future.

Another difference in this latest conflict over history is that it is playing out amid a broader regional conflict. Anti-Japanese sentiment in China and South Korea reached a zenith just as Tokyo sought to gain a permanent seat on the United Nations Security Council. In the end, this bid turned out to be a total fiasco. Not only did Japan meet resistance from Beijing and Seoul, but also from the Association of Southeast Asian Nations (Asean), with not one of its member states supporting Tokyo's bid. This was a major defeat for Japanese diplomacy in the Asian region. Mr. Koizuffii, however, does not seem too bothered, given that the Security Council permanent seat bid was derived more from the Ministry of Foreign Affairs' agenda than Mr. Koizumi's. In fact, it could be argued that the prime minister was never really interested in the bid, and its failure was never really considered a defeat in his mind. Similarly, Japan's Foreign Ministry is also keen to expand the proposed East Asian Community to include India and Australia, if only because Tokyo wants to contain Chinese influence in the community. China, not surprisingly, wants a smaller East Asian Community maintaining the existing Asean Plus Three arrangement. The trouble, however, is that China is gaining the upper hand in these talks and, yet again, the Koizumi administration does not seem to be bothered.

Mr. Koizumi's lack of interest in genuinely engaging in Asian diplomacy should not come as a surprise. The origins of his administration's stance can be traced to the Liberal Democratic Party's political factions.

Mr. Koizumi belongs to the Mori faction, which derived from the Fukuda faction, which in turn came from the Kishi faction. These factions were all conservative and nationalistic. This is in contrast to the once-powerful Tanaka faction, which has all but collapsed. The demise of the Tanaka faction is tragic in a way because it was this faction that was most interested in Asian diplomacy. In its place, more conservative and right-wing politicians dominate today's political picture in Japan.

Beneath the Ruling faction's diplomatically tone-deaf policies, however, runs a much deeper current, and that concerns how the Japanese people "remember" World War II. I use the word "remember" but actually, when people think of any conflict, they do not remember it as such, but rather reconstitute the past in a way that suits our needs today. We imagine the future in away that suits our known experiences, so we remember the future. We are supposed to remember the past, but we are not really interested in objectively studying the past. Rather, we extract useful bits of the past in order to prove in the present that something "actually happened before." Thus, we imagine the past and remember the future. In many ways, this framework applies to wartime memories of Japan.

The Japanese remember the war and wartime atrocities, but they remember it in their own way-in a way which is totally different from how the war is remembered in China or South Korea.

After the war, in Japan, virtually all war remembrance was directed toward the memory of the suffering of civilian Japanese. Of course, it is true that World War II inflicted great calamity and suffering to ordinary Japanese civilians. How could anyone not feel sympathy with this, because civilians were indeed the victims of the war. Yet it is quite a different matter to use this sympathy for civilian casualties to substantiate Japan's constant postwar assertions that it would never wage war again.

There is a universalist element, and also a very particularist, narrow element in this approach. On the one hand, this justification for pacifism is a broad, noble idea, affirming that no nation should engage in war and that Japan will drop all its weapons in accordance with Article 9 of its constitution At the same time, it is extremely narrow and limited, because the only kind of death that is being discussed in this narrative is the death of Japanese civilians. Non-Japanese victims, who died during the war because of Japanese aggression, are seldom considered. Similarly, Japanese soldiers who fought in the Chinese theater and the Pacific theater were also seldom addressed.

Japanese war memories run as a narrative of a victimized nation. The easiest way to convey this paradigm of victimization is to recall the film *Godzilla*. Godzilla is a superficial and imaginary creature, but especially in the older versions of the movie, one can see an antinuke, antimilitary ideology at work. Godzilla was a dinosaur that resurfaced to wreak havoc on Tokyo because of nuclear experimentation. This film was released into theaters right after the nuclear testing in the Bikini Atoll, which elicited an enormous reaction from the Japanese public. That Hiroshima was not over, that the world may be foolish enough to use nuclear weapons again—these were the attitudes feeding the outcry over nuclear testing.

A narrative with Hiroshima at the center became the key interpretation of war memory in Japan. A visit to Japan reveals this kind of story everywhere, especially at the Hiroshima Peace Memorial Museum. Ian Buruma was upset about this museum and argued that it is a symbol of "Japanese victimhood." I consider Mr. Buruma to be a bit unfair, because tens of thousands of people did indeed suffer in Hiroshima and Nagasaki. However, the museum does represent Japan's tendency to be highly selective in acknowledging only Japanese victims from among all the victims of World War II.

During the 1970s, this mainstream discourse began to be challenged. One challenge came with China's call for normalization of ties between Tokyo and Beijing. Many voices from mainland China began to be heard in Tokyo, whereas Chinese perspectives were almost never broadcasted or printed before then. Japanese reporters took up this issue, and Katsuichi Honda, one of the well known reporters from the *Asahi Shimbun* newspaper, ran a series in the *Asahi* called "Journey to China."

In the series he discussed the Nanjing Massacre of 1937–38, or the so-called "Rape of Nanking." The Nanjing Massacre was widely publicized at the time it took place, but it was later somehow forgotten. One reason for this was that the Chinese Communist government was not really interested in publicizing the massacre in Nanjing-there were other massacres in other regions which were under Communist Party control. Nanjing was the Kuomintang capital, and this was a period when suffering under KMT control was not met with a sympathetic eye in Beijing.

Japanese people reacted strongly and divisively to Mr. Honda's coverage of the massacre. On the one hand, there were those who argued that Japan should pay more attention to criminal atrocities in Nanjing—and other World War II atrocities for that matter. The story drew a more amazing reaction from the conservatives in Japan. They argued that there was not really a Nanjing Massacre, or that the numbers were wrong, and other claims along these lines. The *Asahi* series represented the first time that discussion of the war touched on the suffering of non-Japanese casualties.

Interestingly, with coverage of the suffering of non-Japanese, the discussion of the war became very divisive. When the Japanese were talking only about their own civilian dead, the victims of nuclear war, it never really was divisive. When it came to Japanese aggression it was different.

As long as Japan's leaders hold firm to a line of exceptionalism, informed by victimization, that somehow excuses them from acts that offend their neighbors—and as long as China inevitably reacts with its own expression of nationalism—then hostilities between the countries will persist. Reading the newspaper in Tokyo, one would get the impression that the Chinese government is manipulating the Chinese people to rally against the Japanese. In contrast, in Chinese papers, one might surmise that the Japanese government is somehow prodding its people into supporting provocative acts that implicate the war, and is withholding real evidence about the war. Both sides are accusing the other government of manipulating the evidence. How do we find a way out of this situation?

One first step is to recognize that the hostility on both sides is not as bad as the newspapers would have one believe. There are surely people in Beijing who were using the opportunity of nationalist demonstration for their own wishes, but the Chinese Communist Party is basically uninterested in using the history cause to mobilize the masses against the Japanese. In fact many people—especially the technocrats under Hu Jintao—believe that runs against their own best interests.

In Japan, there are many politicians who are counting on anti-Chinese nationalism for popular support. Nevertheless' there is not yet widespread public support for Prime Minister Koizumi's stance. A case in point would be that Mr. Koizumi chose not to visit Yasukuni Shrine before the election—he only visited it afterward. The September lower house elections were not about diplomacy. In fact, there was very little discussion about ties with Asian neighbors since such a debate would be against Mr. Koizumi's interests.

Although there are strong feelings against the Japanese in China, and many people in Japan are agitated by their own prejudiced nationalist feelings, this is not the whole society. Solutions to the historically ensnared Sino-Japanese conflict are possible, and they can be found among people in both societies who are quietly thinking about the conflict along lines more profound than government propaganda.

One possible answer is already on the table. A proposal has come from the Japanese government—with support from the Komeito, the Buddhist party—to build a new national monument that would commemorate all wartime deaths. This proposal needs to move forward now. In Okinawa, there is a wonderful peace memorial, *Heiwa no Ishiji* (Cornerstone of Peace), which recalls all people, regardless of nationalities, who died in the battle of Okinawa in 1945. In addition to Japanese soldiers, the memorial remembers Korean civilians and Korean soldiers who were forced to join the Imperial Army, as well as Chinese, and American civilians and soldiers who died in Okinawa.

If Mr. Koizumi wishes to talk about Japanese culture in visiting Yasukuni Shrine, he may do well to remember that an ecumenical approach to the commemoration of the war dead has been an Okinawa and a Japanese tradition. Further, in Kamakura, an ancient capital not far from the city of Yokohama, there is a small temple which commemorates Mongolian soldiers and Chinese soldiers who invaded Japan. This was, of course, during the Middle Ages, so no one really remembers it. But the point is that this temple is not dedicated to Japanese *samurai* but to Mongolians and Chinese, based on the Buddhist belief that all who died in a war have the right to be remembered.

These are the only two cases that show Japanese culture is not as simple as Prime Minister Koizumi seems to want to believe and demonstrate. And if our narrow minded, universalist pacificism is to result in anything constructive, then the proposal for a new national monument would be the kind of memorial that should be constructed in Japan: a memorial that all Chinese and Japanese and Germans and Filipinos could visit without thinking that they are aiding some narrow-minded political philosophy.

**KIICHI FUJIWARA** is a professor of international politics at the University of Tokyo.

# Coming to Terms with the Past: Former Yugoslavia

DEJAN DJOKIC

An Extraordinary Exchange occurred in early October 2002 at the trial of Slobodan Miloševic, indicted for war crimes, crimes against humanity and genocide, at the International Criminal Tribunal at The Hague. Miloševic, the ex-president of the latest former Yugoslavia (replaced in 2003 by the State Union of Serbia and Montenegro), who is conducting his own defence, was cross-examining Stjepan Mesic, the president of Croatia and the last president of socialist Yugoslavia. Mesic had been called by the prosecution to testify about Miloševic's role in the break-up of Yugoslavia and specifically in the war in Croatia of 1991–92.

Although most of the cross-examination centred on the role of Mesic and his then party, the Croatian Democratic Union (HDZ), in the disintegration of Yugoslavia, on several occasions the two old rivals clashed over their interpretation of the history of Serb-Croat relations during the last two centuries. Particularly heated was their dispute over the ideologies of Ante Starcevic, the leader of a nationalist and anti-Serb Croatian Party of Right, founded in the 1860s, and Vuk Stefanovic Karadžic, a nineteenth-century Serb linguistic reformer.

Miloševic claimed that the HDZ based its programme on the teachings of Starcevic, whose ideology inspired the Ustašas, the Croat Fascists who ruled over a Greater Croatia in the Second World War and who were responsible for the death of hundreds of thousands of Serbs as well as thousands of Jews, Roma and anti-Fascist Croats. Mesic responded by arguing that Starcevic had merely advocated an independent Croatia, then part of the Habsburg Monarchy, and that it was that aspect of his ideology that the HDZ emphasised. In addition, he pointed out that the HDZ's programme also derived from the ideology of the centrist Croatian Peasant Party, the largest Croat party during the interwar period, and from the Second World War communist Partisan tradition. On the other hand, Mesic retaliated, contemporary Serb nationalism draws inspiration from Vuk Karadžic, Starcevic's contemporary, who believed that all Bosnian Muslims and most Croats were in fact Serbs. Perhaps not surprisingly, Richard May, the Presiding Judge, interrupted the debate, arguing that it was irrelevant: 'The Trial Chamber is not assisted by the exchange of abuse, particularly abuse [originating] a hundred years ago'.    .

Yet conflicting Serb and Croat interpretations of their common history have played an important role in the break-up of Yugoslavia. The debate over Starcevic and Karadžic was more relevant than Judge May realised, not least because the HDZ programme is partly based on Starcevic's ideology. The importance of history, or rather its misuse and misinterpretation, was tacitly acknowledged by the prosecution, led by Carla Del Ponte. In addition to witnesses such as Mesic and other leading Yugoslav politicians, and numerous 'ordinary', mostly non-Serb, victims of the Miloševic régime, last year the prosecution asked a Harvard-based scholar to produce a report tracing the development of Serbian nationalism from the nineteenth century anti-Ottoman uprisings to the rise of Miloševic in the late 1980s.

## Conflicting Serb and Croat interpretations of their history played an important role in the break-up of Yugoslavia.

The reason why Miloševic and Mesic hold opposing historical views not that they are uniquely biased and nationalist. Their opinions reflect the views of most of their co-nationals, including many historians. Both Starcevic and Karadžic were more complex figures than the former official Yugoslav or present-day Croatian and Serbian historiographies have acknowledged, and therefore it is possible to interpret their ideologies in starkly contrasting fashions.

Starcevic was in his youth a supporter of a pan-Yugoslav group of mostly Croat intellectuals, known as Illyrians, but he grew disillusioned with Yugoslavism and turned into an extreme Croat nationalist. He denied the existence of the Serbs, arguing that they were in fact 'Orthodox Croats'. (Unlike Croats, who are predominantly Roman Catholic, most Serbs are Eastern Orthodox.) At the same time, somewhat self-contradictorily, he regarded them as sub-human. However, towards the end of his life Starcevic returned to his earlier views and supported a faction of his party which called for a Serb-Croat cooperation. Karadžic, on the other hand, was not a politician but a linguist, language reformer and an oral historian. Influenced by the then-liberal view of the nation as a community defined above all by language, Karadžic regarded as Serbs all South Slav speakers of the štokavian dialect, spoken by Serbs. Although this meant that the Muslim Slavs of Bosnia-Herzegovina and the Salad ak and many Croats were thus turned into 'Serbs,' Karadžic's view was shared by most leading European scholars at the time. However, Karadžic collaborated with the Illyrians and was instrumental in the creation of the modern Serbo-Croat. Even more than Starcevic in the case of Croats, Karadžic can thus be seen as both an early proponent of Yugoslavism and as a more narrow Serb nationalist. Indeed, both men were considered as proto-Yugoslavs by the official historiography in royal and socialist Yugoslavia. Starcevic was also regarded as the progenitor of the Croatian nationalism by the Ustašas and is held as such, albeit in a different way, by most Croats today.

Disagreements between former Yugoslavs over their nineteenth-century history, although deep, pale into insignificance when compared to different interpretations of more contentious subjects, such as the Second World War in Yugoslavia (1941–45). Because the wars of the 1990s have finished so recently it is too early to predict how the former Yugoslavs will come to terms with the country's final disintegration and the brutal wars that followed (although one may safely assume that it will not be an easy and straightforward process). However, the precedent provided by the Second World War and its aftermath might offer an instructive example.

In 1941 Yugoslavia was invaded and partitioned by the Axis powers. Resistance and collaboration went hand in hand with a series of civil wars. Two resistance movements emerged soon after the occupation: the Cetniks, led by Colonel (later General) Mihailovic, whose predominantly Serb forces were joined, overtaken and eventually defeated by the Partisans, skilfully organised by Josip Broz Tito, the Communist Party's General Secretary. Both movements sought to restore a Yugoslavia and they also both fought against the Ustašas. But the Cetniks' fear and hatred of Communism sometimes surpassed their hatred of the occupying forces—so much so that they were prepared to join the Germans and Italians in order to fight the Partisans. The Partisans, for their part, considered Mihailovic their most dangerous internal enemy and in 1943 even proposed a cease-fire to the Germans so that they could engage Cetnik forces (a proposal that was rejected). The Partisans were well organised, while the Cetnik 'movement' consisted of groups of loosely connected, dispersed forces who often recognised Mihailovic's leadership only nominally. The main difference between the two groups, however, apart from their ideology and tactics, was that the Partisans were able to attract followers among all Yugoslavs, despite initially being mostly a Serb force. The Cetniks remained almost exclusively Serb.

How did the new Communist régime, established after 1945 by the victorious Partisans and enjoying considerable popularity among 'ordinary' Yugoslavs, overcome four years of violent war to reunite Yugoslavia? The answer lies partly in the official interpretation of the 1941–45 period.

This can be summarised as follows: the victorious Partisans, composed of and supported by all Yugoslav nations, fought and won a liberation war, which was at the same time a socialist revolution, against German, Italian, Bulgarian and Hungarian occupiers as well as the domestic collaborators, represented by the pre-war bourgeoisie. The atrocities that were committed and the very large number of war dead (around one million in a country of 16 million) were blamed solely on the Partisans' opponents. While all Yugoslav nations officially received equal recognition for liberating the country, the blame was also equally distributed—among the quislings and other anticommunists from all nations, but above all the Croatian Ustašas and Serbian Cetniks, between whom there was said to be little difference. Only the Communist Party of Yugoslavia and its undisputed leader, Tito, were portrayed in a positive light, as the sole resistance movement that eventually liberated and re-unified the country and its citizens.

One of the founding myths of socialist Yugoslavia and of Titoism was the concept of 'brotherhood and unity'. It was, it may be argued, the communists' way of reconciling the Yugoslavs, particularly Serbs and Croats. The new régime, unlike its royalist predecessor, did not claim that all South Slavs living in Yugoslavia were a single ethnic nation; they were now free and indeed encouraged to declare their particular national identities, whether as Serb, Croat, Slovene, Macedonian, Montenegrin and, from the 1960s, Muslim (but not 'Bosnian'). Therefore, the 1941–45 revolution was also a national liberation. However, Yugoslavia still meant 'South Slavia', remaining above all the state of the South Slavs. Others, such as the ethnic Albanians and Hungarians, were considered minorities regardless of their size. Thus, Yugoslavia was, certainly up until the mid-1960s, when important constitutional reforms began, something between a nation-state and a multi-national state.

Contrary to popular belief, the ideology of 'brotherhood and unity' was not based on a total forgetting of what happened in the Second World War. It rested on what the German historian Wolfgang Hoepken has called 'fragmented memory': instead of recognising that the Second World War in Yugoslavia was also an inter-ethnic and even intra-ethnic war, only one dimension existed in the official memory: the war was a 'national liberation war and a socialist revolution'. Fratricidal war between Yugoslavs, which probably led to more victims than the armed resistance against the occupiers, was not to be publicly debated and if possible forgotten. Numerous monuments to the 'victims of fascism' were erected throughout the former Yugoslavia, presenting a painful reminder to those who survived. Yet, in the words of another historian, Stevan K. Pavlowitch, the régime had 'drawn a veil over the details so as not to open up incompletely-healed wartime wounds, and inflame intercommunal relations.'

As Yugoslavia entered the post-Tito era, there were increasing calls for the pursuit of the Rankean ideal of finding what really happened in Yugoslavia in the Second World War. The official history was bound to be challenged in the more relaxed political atmosphere which eventually emerged following the death of Tito in 1980, when the so-called 'hidden', unofficial, accounts of the war years began to appear. During what one Serbian weekly described as 'the burst of history', the official interpretation of Yugoslavia's recent past was questioned by every engaged intellectual. To many observers in the late 1980s, it must have seened that the Second World War had broken out for the second time in Yugoslavia—verbally, for the time being.

Initially, attempts to question the official interpretation of Yugoslavia's past were not necessarily motivated by nationalism or anti-Yugoslavism. For instance, Emir Kusturica's internationally acclaimed film *When father Was Away on Business,* winner of the Palm d'Or at Cannes in 1986, dealt with the taboo of Goli Otok—a Yugoslav gulag where a large number of Yugoslavs, accused of siding with Stalin, ended up after the 1948 conflict between Belgrade and Moscow. Similarly, books and interviews by Milovan Djilas, Yugoslavia's most important dissident, began to be published in the late 1980s. However, as the official historiography began to disintegrate together with the state, historical revisionism became increasingly nationalist and anti-Yugoslav.

The most controversial and most debated issue was that of Croatian genocide against Serbs during the Second World War. Both the Ustaša-directed project to rid the Independent State of Croatia of its almost two million Serbs (and also Jews and Roma) and the nature and scope of the genocide have been the subject of scholarly works. The issue remains a bone of contention between Serbs and Croats, with the former exaggerating the number of Serbs killed and the latter minimising it. Moreover, some Serbs argue that anti-Serbianism has always been present among Croats and that the Ustaša genocide was merely the last phase of a long process. (Similar arguments were later put forward by some Croat—and also Western—authors in relation to the wars of the 1990s. It has been suggested that there is a long history of Serbian aggression and even genocide, so that what happened in the last decade was historically predetermined.)

The nationalist discourse in Yugoslavia, but especially in Serbia and Croatia in the late 1980s and early 1990s, sought a reconciliation between victors and losers of the Second World War who belonged to the same nation; between Partisans and Cetniks in the case of Serbs, and Partisans and Ustašas in the case of Croats. In Yugoslavia at the time 'reconciliation' meant a homogenisation of the nation by reconciling ideological differences within the nation. Attempts to achieve the intra-ethnic reconciliation among Serbs and Croats were closely linked to the break-up of Yugoslavia. Yet intra-ethnic, ideological differences still remain, nearly sixty years since the end of the Second World War, although these are usually ignored by authors who concentrate exclusively on inter-ethnic conflicts.

A scholarly and public debate between historians from across former Yugoslavia will be essential if the Yugoslavs are to come to terms with their most recent and therefore most painful past. Currently, state borders are not easy to bridge, but lack of dialogue is obvious even among historians belonging to the same nation. Nevertheless, the picture is not as bleak as it may first appear, despite the recent resurgence of nationalist parties in both Serbia and Croatia.

When the 600th anniversary of the Kosovo battle was celebrated on June 28th, 1989, the event was used to 'crown' Miloševic as the undisputed leader of all Serbs—a leader they had allegedly long lacked due to historical circumstances. The myth of the Serbian Prince Lazar, who in 1389 chose a 'heavenly kingdom' (i.e. certain death at the hands of a superior Ottoman army), forms the central part of the much-written-about Serbian Kosovo myth. The loss of medieval statehood and several centuries of Ottoman rule, which ended during the long liberation struggle of the nineteenth century, were symbolised by the 'defeat' at Kosovo (which was actually a draw, with heavy Ottoman casualties). Miloševic, who in 1989 flew to the site of the battle in a helicopter, was greeted by a crowd of around one million people, as a resurrected Lazar(us). The 'Ottomans' were now predominantly Muslim Albanians, who formed an absolute majority in the region. This (mis)use of the anniversary and myth had a potentially explosive effect at a time of high ethnic tensions.

In February 2004, post-Miloševic Serbia marked the 200th anniversary of the First Serbian Uprising against the Ottoman rule. Although the event was wrongly dubbed as 'the 200th anniversary of the modern Serbian state', the tone of the official celebration was more moderate than that of the 1989 event. The government-sponsored commemoration, held in a small town in central Serbia where the Uprising began, was relatively modest and even moderate, despite the presence of Church representatives and other 'patriotic' voices. The official programme even included a play directed by a young man well known for his opposition to the former régime. The director's post-modern approach is a far cry from the 'national-realism' preferred by organisers of the 1989 celebration, or the 'social-realism' of the Tito-era anniversaries. (An alternative anniversary, organised by a group of 'patriotic' intellectuals who felt the official programme was not 'Serbian' and 'national' enough, attracted little popular support.)

Was this a sign that Serbia is getting tired of its past? It is too early to say, but the answer is probably yes. As for the Hague Tribunal, however long, contentious and wearying its trials may be, they will not rewrite the pre-1980s past. Yet the Tribunal's proceedings will undoubtedly provide invaluable primary sources on the Yugoslav wars of the 1990s, which await their historians.

**DEJAN DJOKIC** is Lecturer in Serbian and Croatian Studies at the University of Nottingham and a Postdoctoral Fellow at Columbia University, New York for the Spring semester 2004. He is the editor of *Yugoslavism: Histories of a Failed Idea, 1918–1992* (Hurst and University).

# Coming to Terms with the Past: Cambodia

## Ben Kieman

Half a millennium of civil conflict, foreign invasions, and even genocide not only devastated Cambodia, but "also prevented the Khmer people from weighing their experiences in historical perspective. Hindu, Buddhist, royalist, republican, colonial and communist regimes came and went. Five relocations of the Khmer capital preceded the three foreign occupations and seven regime changes of the past sixty years alone. Officials abandoned archives, rulers erased rivals from the record, international leaders denied Cambodia's history or blocked its documentation. Yet recent events offer some hope of an accounting for the Khmer Rouge genocide of 1975–79.

A substantial corpus of inscriptions and archaeological sites like the twelfth-century Hindu temple of Angkor War testify to Cambodia's medieval glory. Then, around 1432, the Khmer court moved downriver, founding a new capital, Lovek. Buddhist monks maintained Angkor, but its perishable palm-leaf records vanished. In 1594, a Thai army sacked Lovek. Within two years, Iberian conquistadores razed its successor. Later royal attempts to chronicle Cambodia's fifteenth and sixteenth centuries were, as Michael Vickery shows, 'composed artificially' from Thai court chronicles for, lack of Khmer sources. Cambodian events stayed in shadow.

Civil wars also wracked the country, leaving little record. A rare inscription carved at Angkor in 1747 celebrates the Khmer king's defeat of an unnamed rebel princess. Tracking down her tortes by 'blocking and searching every road', the royal army 'drove out, pursued and scattered' (kchat kchay) the rebels. The king was presented with 'many of the slaves and possessions of the princess' and all her 'commanders, troops, and goods'.

Ethnic violence followed. A French missionary wrote in 1751 that the new Khmer king, Ang Snguon,

> gave orders or permission to massacre all the Cochinchi-
> nese [Vietnamese] who could be found, and this order was
> executed very precisely and very cruelly; this massacre
> lasted a month and a half; only about twenty women and
> children were spared; no one knows the number of deaths,
> and it would be very difficult to find out, for the massacre
> was general from Cahon to Ha-tien.

No survivors were found of the numerous Vietnamese resident in Cambodia. Nor do other records of that pogrom survive.

Better-documented conflicts raged for a century. From the west, Thailand seized the Angkor region. Vietnam encroached from the east. Then France colonised Vietnam and, in 1863, imposed a Protectorate on Cambodia. The French moved the capital from Oudong to Phnom Penh, retook Angkor from Thailand, and restored its archaeological sites. But the colonialists neglected Khmer schools. Pagoda schools declined; literacy rates fell. Ninety years of colonial rule produced only 144 Khmer Baccalaureats.

While history publishing flourished in colonial Vietnam, even educated Cambodians lacked Khmer-language historical sources, which French and royal officials often suppressed to monopolise state legitimacy. After Cambodia's independence, the regime of Prince Norodom Sihanouk (1954–70) greatly expanded education. But, as Sihanouk's adviser Charles Meyer later recalled with near accuracy, the kingdom permitted publication in Khmer of 'no serious work of history'.

In the 1960s, as US forces intervened in neighbouring Vietnam, Sihanouk tried to keep Cambodia neutral. His ouster in 1970 brought the contending armies crashing over the border. Cambodia became a theatre of the Vietnam War. 'That damned Mr Force can do more about hitting Cambodia with their bombing attacks,' President Nixon told Henry Kissinger on December 9th, 1970; 'I want a plan where every goddamn thing that can fly goes into Cambodia and hits every target that is open . . . I want them to use the big planes, the small planes, everything they can.' Kissinger ordered 'a massive bombing campaign in Cambodia. Anything that flies on anything that moves.' By 1973, half a million tons of US bombs had killed 100,000 peasants and devastated the countryside. The destruction helped Pol Pot's Khmer Rouge guerrillas recruit vengeful survivors, whom they misled, claiming that 'The killing birds came from Phnom Penh.' The guerrilla army expanded, and shelled the capitol, diverting history against the innocent.

The Khmer Rouge won the war in April 1975, and emptied Cambodia's cities into the countryside, persecuting and murdering the deported townspeople. Pol Pot's new communist regime, called Democratic Kampuchea (DK), also committed genocide against the Khmer Buddhist monkhood, the traditional bearers of cultural literacy. DK expelled 150,000 Vietnamese residents from Cambodia, killed all 10,000 who stayed, and carried out larger, less systematic genocide against the country's Chinese and Muslim minorities. In all, 1.7 million people died in four years. Upgrading the traditional term for routing enemies, DK's slogan became *kchat kchay os roling* ('scatter to the last'). Targeting history too, the Khmer Rouge scattered libraries, burned books, closed schools, and murdered schoolteachers. Three-quarters of Cambodia's 20,000 teachers perished, or fled abroad.

As the genocide progressed, for geopolitical reasons Washington, Beijing, and Bangkok all supported the continued independent existence of the Khmer Rouge regime. When President Gerald Ford visited Indonesian president Suharto on December 6th, 1975, the transcript reveals that Ford deplored the recent US defeat in Vietnam and then told Suharto: 'There is, however, resistance in Cambodia to the influence of Hanoi. We are willing to move slowly in our relations with Cambodia, hoping perhaps to slow down the North Vietnamese influence although we find the Cambodian government very difficult.' Kissinger explained Beijing's similar strategy: 'the Chinese want to use Cambodia to balance off Vietnam . . . We don't like Cambodia, for the government in many ways is worse than Vietnam, but we would like it to be independent. We don't discourage Thailand or China from drawing closer to Cambodia.'

When the Vietnamese communist army overthrew the Khmer Rouge in January 1979, the new People's Republic of Kampuchea (PRK) reopened cities and schools but faced an international embargo led by China and the USA. A Cambodian education official recalled starting from nothing. A UN consultant found a school 'surrounded by mines and graveyards'. Another possessed eight pens per class of fifty pupils. One class meeting under a tree had to stop for the rainy season. Some pupils went 'completely naked'.

With Vietnamese aid the PRK reopened the Teachers' College, and printed forty school textbooks by 1980. But for a decade, Cambodian schools offered no history subjects, only classes on 'Political Morality' and folk tales. DK destruction of books was not the sole reason for this curriculum gap. Vietnamese advisors at the new Education Ministry planned a new, revolutionary history syllabus, but the PRK dragged its feet. One official explained that the country's history had yet to be written. Yet from 1985 to 1987, the PRK banned as 'incorrect' even a new 584-page Khmer-language history of Cambodia, published in the USSR. In 1986 the Ministry published, but withheld from schools, a new fifth-grade history textbook. Some suspected that Cambodian history would be 'approved' only when defined in terms of Vietnamese history.

None of Cambodia's pre-1975 professors or lecturers who had remained in the country survived the genocide. But from 1979 the PRK trained a hundred new tertiary educators. In 1988, after thirteen years, Phnom Penh University re-opened its doors, with 2,000 students. Seventy studied History. The new History Department comprised two former graduates with *licences es lettres* from the pre-1975 Faculty of Arts, and three post-1980 Teachers' College graduates. They had already co-authored new history

school texts, including the 1986 book, which now went into use, accompanied by three new texts for higher grades. At each level, pupils began to study Cambodian History and World History.

Classes addressed some symbolic issues. For instance, the fifth-grade text tried to assess Vietnam's nineteenth-century interventions in Cambodia. In that era, the Vietnamese court at Hue had vied with Thailand for dominance there. The textbook informed pupils that, to escape Bangkok's control, 'our Khmer kings ran to rely on the feudalists in the east, that is, the Vietnamese kingdom'. Hue's intervention 'became steadily more active', especially in the court of King Ang Chan II (1794–1834). Thailand, too, 'used force to pressure King Ang Chan II and to encourage him to accept absolute Thai sovereignty. Worried by such pressure, King Ang Chan II requested help from the Hue court'. Vietnamese troops invaded, defeating the Thai. However, the King died in 1834 leaving no male heir. The Hue court 'began to use manoeuvres to enthrone Princess Ang Mey, who was a daughter of King Ang Chart II, as ruler of the kingdom. In order to strengthen its own influence and eliminate Thai influence, the Hue court intervened in the internal affairs of the Oudong court with increasing power.'

This fairly frank discussion of past Vietnamese interventions was not matched by lessons on the Khmer Rouge genocide. After Hanoi's forces left Cambodia in 1989, few students gained access to primary documents or secondary accounts of the recent past. Crowds thronged the museum that had been DK's notorious Tuol Sleng prison. Western scholars perused its archives of torture and murder Cambodian governments, excluded from the United Nations, protested at the exiled DK regime's presence there. An official eleventh-grade 1991 political education text lamented: 'During the Pol Pot regime, the Cambodian people lived in hopelessness, without meaning, and in constant fear; in addition they suffered every kind of oppression [by] those violent savage murderers, and were transformed into the slaves of that gang.' Yet school history classes omitted the Khmer Rouge period altogether.

The vacuum fostered an uneasy relationship with Cambodia's past. In January 2003, a Thai TV star reportedly asserted that Angkor belonged to Thailand. Khmer protesters sacked the Thai embassy, Phnom Penh. Gangs torched a Thai airline office, hotels, and restaurants. Yet Cambodian schoolteachers still have to skirt the Khmer Rouge genocide. In 2001 the Education Ministry published new history texts, which finally included sections on DK, but recalled them in 2003 after a semester of use.

International actors also fostered a lack of accountability. Behind the scenes, the ousted Khmer Rouge received US support from the Carter, Reagan and first Bush administrations. Carter's national security advisor Zbigniew Brzezinski echoed Kissinger's earlier policy when he revealed that in 1979: 'I encouraged the Chinese to support Pol Pot. Pol Pot was an abomination. We could never support him, but China could.' Washington 'winked, semi-publicly' at Chinese and Thai aid to the Khmer Rouge. In 1982 the US and China encouraged Sihanouk to join a DK coalition-in-exile. Secretary of State George Schultz refused to support a proposed international genocide tribunal. In 1989 his successor James A. Baker even urged that the Khmer Rouge be included in the Cambodian government.

Twenty years of UN silence on the Khmer Rouge genocide further encouraged Cambodians to ignore the past. After a meeting of the Southeast Asian countries in 1988, the Indonesian chairman noted a consensus opposing any return to 'the genocidal policies and practices of the Pol Pot regime'. Yet in 1989 the UN General Assembly declined to identify the perpetrators of 'the universally condemned policies and practices of the recent past'. The Security Council's live permanent members deplored only unspecified, unauthored, undated 'policies and practices of the past'. During the 1991–93 UN operation in Cambodia, Pol Pot would enjoy 'the same rights, freedoms, and opportunities to participate in the electoral process' as others.

In 1990 the UN Human Rights Sub-commission considered condemning the 'genocide committed in particular during the period of Khmer Rouge rule' and urging states to 'bring to trial those who had been responsible for crimes against humanity committed in Cambodia, and prevent the return to governmental positions of those who were responsible.' However, the Sub-commission deleted this agenda item after speakers denounced its 'disservice' to the UN. Only in 1991 did it urge 'the international community to prevent the recurrence of genocide in Cambodia'. Washington now pledged cooperation in bringing the Khmer Rouge to justice. But the next year the director of the UN's Human Rights Component in Cambodia deplored its 'complete inability to work in one of the zones', a feeble criticism of Khmer Rouge obstruction, and he assimilated the 1975–79 genocide into what be called 'decades of conflict, upheaval and confrontation'. This obfuscation made it harder to blame Cambodians for failing to face their past.

Yet they had no choice. From jungle bases, the Khmer Rouge boycotted the UN-organised 1993 elections, and kept killing Cambodian troops and civilians. Bringing them to justice became US law under President Clinton in 1994. Two years later, Yale University's Cambodian Genocide Program uncovered 100,000 pages of secret DK documents revealing the role of top Khmer Rouge leaders in the 1975–79 mass killings, and began posting their contents on the internet (at www.yale.edu/cgp). In 1997, Cambodia's rival Prime Ministers, Hun Sen and Sihanouk's son Norodom Ranariddh, jointly requested UN aid to prosecute DK leaders for their past crimes. The UN Secretary-General appointed a 'Group of Experts' to examine the case.

As the international lawyers worked, defections and mutinies wracked the Khmer Rouge army. Pol Pot died in 1998, and was cremated in the jungle, and his former deputy, Nuon Chea, and the DK head of state, Khieu Samphan, surrendered. The Khmer Rouge were defeated. Within months, Cambodian troops captured former DK military commander Chhit Choeun (alias Mok) and arrested the former commandant of Tuol Sleng prison, Deuch. Both went to jail pending trial.

In early 1999, the UN Experts recommended charging the surviving DK leaders 'for crimes against humanity and genocide' perpetrated in 1975–79. As well as committing 'war crimes' against Vietnam and Thailand, DK had 'subjected the people of Cambodia to almost all of the acts' listed in the 1948 UN Genocide Convention: 'Evidence also suggests the need led prosecutors to investigate the commission of genocide against the Chain, Vietnamese and other minority groups, and the Buddhist monkhood.'

The UN began negotiations with Hun Sen's government for a mixed national/international trial of senior Khmer Rouge leaders. Cambodia's National Assembly passed a 'Law on the Establishment of the Extraordinary Chambers in the Courts of Cambodia for the Prosecution of Crimes Committed during the Period of Democratic Kampuchea'. On June 6th, 2003, Cambodia and the UN signed their cooperation Agreement, which awaits ratification by Ranariddh's royalist party and the Assembly.

Under President George W. Bush, it is unclear whether Washington will fulfil its commitments to justice for Cambodians, especially as American leaders ignore the earlier US contribution to Cambodia's tragedy. But in 2004, seventeen members of Congress co-sponsored a resolution in support of the Khmer Rouge tribunal.

Twenty-five years after the genocide, Cambodia's tourism ministry plans to commercialise the jungle site of Pol Pot's cremation, complete with a local Khmer Rouge guide. But UN-Cambodian cooperation on a tribunal brings legal accountability within reach. On April 9th, 2004, Cambodia's General Prosecutor asked local officers 'to lay charges, and ask the magistrate to issue warrants' for the arrests of former DK leaders Khieu Samphan, Nuon Chea, and Ieng Sary.

A legal accounting of the crimes of the Khmer Rouge era cannot restore to Cambodians their lost loved ones, but it could give them back their history. If at last the tribunal goes ahead, Cambodian pupils may one day have textbooks to study the tragedy. Pol Pot's ashes are 'scattered to the last', but the growing documentation of his genocide cannot be lost like so much of Cambodia's earlier history.

This article first appeared in *History Today,* September 2004. Copyright © 2004 by History Today, Ltd. Reprinted by permission.

# UNIT 6

# Global Problems, Global Interdependence

## Unit Selections

## Key Points to Consider

- Is global warming a serious problem? Is there any historical precedent that is informative?

- How serious is Africa's AIDS crisis today? What will be its impact on human history?

- What were the similarities and differences between the Rwandan genocide of 1994 and the Nazi-inspired Jewish Holocaust of World War II? What role did religion play in both atrocities?

- What strategies are Afghan women employing in their fight for equality in their country? Are their efforts likely to produce positive results?

- Has the war against the Jihadis been won? What proof is offered to support that position?

- What paths did India and China take in their quest for status as economic superpowers? Which one will eventually emerge as the continent's leading giant?

- What factors make it possible for terrible leaders to rule countries today? Can anything be done to stop this trend?

- What major problems face nations as they search for a new and just world order? How can these be overcome to produce the desired result?

## Student Website

www.mhhe.com/cls

## Internet References

**Africa News Website: Crisis in the Great Lakes Region**
www.africanews.org/greatlakes.html
**Africa Notes**
www.csis.org/html/2africa.html
**Amnesty International**
www.amnesty.org
**Reliefweb**
www.reliefweb.int
**Target America**
www.pbs.org/wgbh/pages/frontline/shows/target

The cold war and its aftermath left many unresolved problems for a world in which every nation is linked with the welfare of others. As the Soviet Union collapsed, the landscape was revealed as an environmental shambles, with polluted air, food, and water. The countries abandoned by the former Soviet bloc are too poor to repair the damage and their recovery will probably take decades. There has also been a proliferation of knowledge about methods of mass destruction, not only nuclear weapons, but also poison gases and infectious diseases.

Almost any determined nation can manufacture these weapons, as recent threats from Iraq, Iran, and North Korea confirm. Ironically, we may look back on the cold war, when two superpowers controlled most of the weaponry, as a time of desirable simplicity.

In the background of contemporary concerns is a rapidly increasing world population that will soon reach 6.5 billion people. Will the planet be able to sustain the projected population of 9 billion in 2050? The population of democratic India is projected to surpass that of communist China in the near future—mainly because China strictly enforces a one-child policy. Is China right to restrict its own population growth? No one knows the capacity of the planet, but shortages seem likely to occur in many areas as the world's population grows. It seems clear that all the world's peoples will share a common fate.

Population, moreover, is moving from the countryside to the cities and from farming into manufacturing and information technology. Air pollution has increased, and scientists are in agreement that we are experiencing a rise in temperature that is known as global warming. Consequences are somewhat difficult to pinpoint, but the increase in violent storms as well as earthquakes and volcanic eruptions have many concerned. Some ancient conflicts remain.

One example is the conflict in Sudan, where civil war has raged for 20 years. In the Middle East, terrorism keeps the flames of hatred going between Israelis and Palestinians. In Central Africa, Uganda and Rwanda fell into warfare over which side to support in the Congo; tribal hatreds and ethnic cleansing have been the devastating results. Problems in Africa are compounded by disease, particularly HIV/AIDS, which has created more than 10 million orphans—an unprecedented humanitarian crisis.

Recent events suggest that the twenty-first century may be at least as challenging as the twentieth century was. Some have compared the Rwandan genocide with the Nazi-perpetrated holocaust of the Jews. Large numbers of Christians were

© Library of Congress Prints and Phoographs Division [LC-DIG-ggbain-34899]

complicit in both genocides. Contemporary warfare is justified by evoking a cosmic struggle of good vs. evil, and some Islamist terrorism has its roots in an anti-secular, anti-globalism worldview that "satanizes" enemies and has infinite patience.

Moderate Muslims hold the key to the future of Islamic/Western relations. As the United States shifts its military and intelligence efforts into discrete places, so-called failed nations become key battlegrounds. The absence of government leadership or the presence of corrupt leaders creates a breeding ground for radical ideologies.

# The Weather Turns Wild

**Global warming could cause droughts, disease, and political upheaval.**

NANCY SHUTE

The people of Atlanta can be forgiven for not worrying about global warming as they shivered in the dark last January, their city crippled by a monster ice storm that hit just before the Super Bowl. So can the 15 families in Hilo, Hawaii, whose houses were washed away by the 27 inches of rain that fell in 24 hours last November. And the FBI agents who searched for evidence blown out of their downtown Fort Worth office building, which was destroyed by a tornado last March. Not to mention the baffled residents of Barrow, Alaska, who flooded the local weather office with calls on June 19, as rumbling black clouds descended—a rare Arctic thunderstorm.

But such bizarre weather could soon become more common, and the consequences far more dire, according to a United Nations scientific panel. Last week, the Intergovernmental Panel on Climate Change met in Shanghai and officially released the most definitive—and scary—report yet, declaring that global warming is not only real but man-made. The decade of the '90s was the warmest on record, and most of the rise was likely caused by the burning of oil, coal, and other fuels that release carbon dioxide, as well as other so-called greenhouse gases. What's more, future changes will be twice as severe as predicted just five years ago, the group says. Over the next 100 years, temperatures are projected to rise by 2.5 to 10.4 degrees worldwide, enough to spark floods, epidemics, and millions of "environmental refugees."

By midcentury, the chic Art Deco hotels that now line Miami's South Beach could stand waterlogged and abandoned. Malaria could be a public health threat in Vermont. Nebraska farmers could abandon their fields for lack of water. Outside the United States, the impact would be much more severe. Rising sea levels could contaminate the aquifers that supply drinking water for Caribbean islands, while entire Pacific island nations could simply disappear under the sea. Perhaps the hardest-hit country would be Bangladesh, where thousands of people already die from floods each year. Increased snowmelt in the Himalayas could combine with rising seas to make at least 10 percent of the country uninhabitable. The water level of most of Africa's largest rivers, including the Nile, could plunge, triggering widespread crop failure and idling hydroelectric plants. Higher temperatures and lower rainfall could stunt food production in Mexico and other parts of Latin America.

No more words. "The debate is over," says Peter Gleick, president of the Pacific Institute for Studies in Development, Environment, and Security, in Oakland, Calif. "No matter what we do to reduce greenhouse-gas emissions, we will not be able to avoid some impacts of climate change."

This newest global-warming forecast is backed by data from myriad satellites, weather balloons, ships at sea, and weather stations, and by immense computer models of the global climate system. As scientists have moved toward consensus on warming's inevitability, there has been growing movement to come up with realistic adaptations to blunt the expected effects. Instead of casting blame at polluting SUV drivers, environmentalists and businesses alike are working to create feasible solutions. These range from measures as complex as global carbon-dioxide-emissions taxes to ones as simple as caulking leaks in Russian and Chinese natural gas pipelines. The take-home message: Change is difficult but not impossible, and the sooner we start, the easier it will be. Civilization has adjusted to drastic weather changes in the past (see box, "Weathering the storms" on p. 160) and is well positioned to do so again. Indeed, while governments squabble over what is to be done, major corporations such as BP Amoco and DuPont are retooling operations to reduce greenhouse gases. "I am very, very optimistic," says Robert Watson, an atmospheric scientist, World Bank official, and leader of the IPCC panel that created the report.

Concern about greenhouse gases is hardly new; as early as the 1700s, scientists were wondering whether atmospheric gases could transmit light but trap heat, much like glass in a greenhouse. By 1860, Irish physicist John Tyndall (the first man to explain why the sky is blue) suggested that ice ages follow a decrease in carbon dioxide. In 1957, Roger Revelle, a researcher at the Scripps Institution of Oceanography in California, declared that human alteration of the climate amounted to a "large-scale geophysical experiment" with potentially vast consequences.

Such dire predictions had been made before and not come true, and this environmental hysteria emboldened skeptics. But by 1988, the evidence was hard to rebut; when NASA atmospheric scientist James Hansen told a congressional hearing that global warming had arrived, climate change became a hot political topic. At the 1992 Rio de Janeiro Earth Summit, 155 nations, including the United States, signed a treaty to control

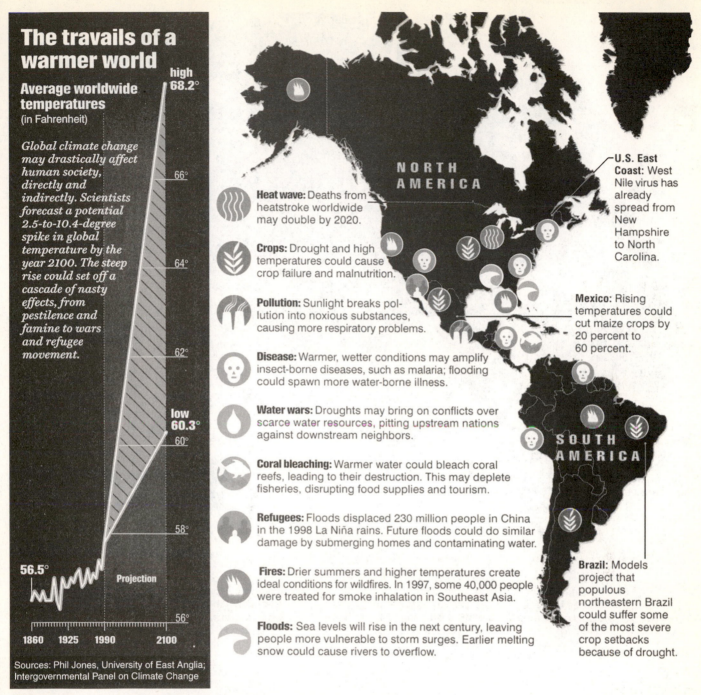

## The travails of a warmer world

### Average worldwide temperatures
(in Fahrenheit)

high 68.2°

*Global climate change may drastically affect human society, directly and indirectly. Scientists forecast a potential 2.5-to-10.4-degree spike in global temperature by the year 2100. The steep rise could set off a cascade of nasty effects, from pestilence and famine to wars and refugee movement.*

66°

64°

62°

low 60.3°

60°

58°

56.5°  Projection

56°

1860  1925  1990  2100

Sources: Phil Jones, University of East Anglia; Intergovernmental Panel on Climate Change

**Heat wave:** Deaths from heatstroke worldwide may double by 2020.

**Crops:** Drought and high temperatures could cause crop failure and malnutrition.

**Pollution:** Sunlight breaks pollution into noxious substances, causing more respiratory problems.

**Disease:** Warmer, wetter conditions may amplify insect-borne diseases, such as malaria; flooding could spawn more water-borne illness.

**Water wars:** Droughts may bring on conflicts over scarce water resources, pitting upstream nations against downstream neighbors.

**Coral bleaching:** Warmer water could bleach coral reefs, leading to their destruction. This may deplete fisheries, disrupting food supplies and tourism.

**Refugees:** Floods displaced 230 million people in China in the 1998 La Niña rains. Future floods could do similar damage by submerging homes and contaminating water.

**Fires:** Drier summers and higher temperatures create ideal conditions for wildfires. In 1997, some 40,000 people were treated for smoke inhalation in Southeast Asia.

**Floods:** Sea levels will rise in the next century, leaving people more vulnerable to storm surges. Earlier melting snow could cause rivers to overflow.

**NORTH AMERICA**

**SOUTH AMERICA**

**U.S. East Coast:** West Nile virus has already spread from New Hampshire to North Carolina.

**Mexico:** Rising temperatures could cut maize crops by 20 percent to 60 percent.

**Brazil:** Models project that populous northeastern Brazil could suffer some of the most severe crop setbacks because of drought.

**Figure 1** Reporting by Rachel K. Sobel and Kevin Whitelaw.

*(Graphic continued next page)*

Sources: National Center for Atmospheric Research, University of Virginia, Worldwatch Institute, National Climatic Data Center, World Meteorological Organization, and staff reports

Note: Rod Little, Rob Cady, and Stephen Rountree—*USN&WR.*

greenhouse emissions, which also include other gases such as methane. That accord led to the 1997 Kyoto protocol calling for reducing emissions of developed nations below 1990 levels but placing no emissions restrictions on China and other developing nations. In November, talks over the treaty broke down over the issue of how to measure nations' progress in reducing emissions. They are set to resume by midyear, after the Bush administration has formulated its position.

Doubters remain. Some argue that climate is too chaotic and complex to trust to any computerized prediction, or that Earth's climate is too stable to be greatly upset by a little more $CO_2$. "I don't see how the IPCC can say it's going to warm for sure," says Craig Idso, a climatologist and vice president of the Center for the Study of Carbon Dioxide and Global Change in Tempe, Ariz. He calls predictions of drastic warming "a sheer guess" and says that extra carbon dioxide "is going to be nothing but a boon for the biosphere. Plants will grow like gangbusters."

But these skeptics appear to be losing ground. "There are fewer and fewer of them every year," says William Kellogg, former president of the American Meteorological Society and

**Marshall Islands, Tuvalu, Kiribati:** Swelling oceans could cover these islands, forcing residents to evacuate.

**Bangladesh:** Faster melting snowpacks in the Himalayas, rising sea levels, and cholera outbreaks could force millions from their homes.

**Nigeria:** A 3-foot rise in sea level could displace almost 4 million people and leave parts of the capital city, Lagos, underwater.

**South Africa:** Malaria may surge in areas previously too cold for mosquitoes to inhabit.

**Zimbabwe:** River flow along the Zambezi could fall steeply, disrupting crop production and possibly producing refugees.

**Australia:** The Great Barrier Reef could be ruined as a tourist attraction if the water temperature increases by a mere 3.6 degrees.

**Figure 1**  *(continued)*

a retired senior scientist at the National Center for Atmospheric Research. "There are very few people in the serious meteorological community who doubt that the warming is taking place."

If the majority view holds up and temperatures keep rising, over the next century global weather patterns will shift enough to affect everyday life on every continent. The effects would vary wildly from one place to the next; what might be good news for one region (warmer winters in Fairbanks, Alaska) would be bad news for another (more avalanches in the Alps). Weather would become more unpredictable and violent, with thunderstorms sparking increased tornadoes and lightning, a major cause of fires. The effects of El Niño, the atmospheric oscillation that causes flooding and mudslides in California

and the tropics, would become more severe. Natural disasters already cost plenty; in the 1990s the tab was $608 billion, more than the four previous decades combined, according to Worldwatch Institute. The IPCC will release its tally of anticipated effects on climate and societies on February 19 in Geneva. Key climate scientists say that major points include:

Death and pestilence. Cities in the Northern Hemisphere would very likely become hotter, prompting more deaths from heatstroke in cities such as Chicago and Shanghai. Deaths would also increase from natural disasters, and warmer weather would affect transmission of insect-borne diseases such as malaria and West Nile virus, which made a surprise arrival in the United States in 1999. "We don't know exactly how West Nile was

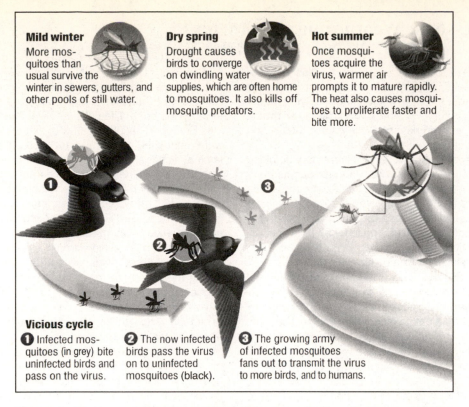

**Mild winter** More mosquitoes than usual survive the winter in sewers, gutters, and other pools of still water.

**Dry spring** Drought causes birds to converge on dwindling water supplies, which are often home to mosquitoes. It also kills off mosquito predators.

**Hot summer** Once mosquitoes acquire the virus, warmer air prompts it to mature rapidly. The heat also causes mosquitoes to proliferate faster and bite more.

**Vicious cycle**
❶ Infected mosquitoes (in grey) bite uninfected birds and pass on the virus.
❷ The now infected birds pass the virus on to uninfected mosquitoes (black).
❸ The growing army of infected mosquitoes fans out to transmit the virus to more birds, and to humans.

**Figure 2  Mercury rising: droughts and fevers.**  Cycles of extreme weather, likely caused by global warming, may have helped fuel the spread of West Nile virus in North America by boosting the mosquito population.

Source: Robert Kemp—*USN&WR.*.

introduced to the U.S., but we do know that drought, warm winter, and heat waves are the conditions that help amplify it," says Paul Epstein, a researcher at Harvard's School of Public Health (see box, "Mercury Rising").

Wildfires. Rising temperatures and declining rainfall would dry out vegetation, making wildfires like last summer's—which burned nearly 7 million acres in the West and cost $1.65 billion—more common, especially in California, New Mexico, and Florida.

Rain and flooding. Rain would become more frequent and intense in the Northern Hemisphere. Snow would melt faster and earlier in the Rockies and the Himalayas, exacerbating spring flooding and leaving summers drier. "This is the opposite of what we want," says Gleick. "We want to be able to save that water for dry periods."

Rising sea levels. Sea level worldwide has risen 9 inches in the last century, and 46 million people live at risk of flooding due to storm surges. That figure would double if oceans rise 20 inches. The IPCC predicts that seas will rise anywhere from 3.5 inches to 34.6 inches by 2010, largely because of "thermal expansion" (warmer water takes up more space), but also because of melting glaciers and ice caps. A 3-foot rise, at the top range of the forecast, would swamp parts of major cities and islands, including the Marshall Islands in the South Pacific and the Florida Keys.

Water wars. Drought—and an accompanying lack of water—would be the most obvious consequence of warmer temperatures.

By 2015, 3 billion people will be living in areas without enough water. The already water-starved Middle East could become the center of conflicts, even war, over water access. Turkey has already diverted water from the Tigris and Euphrates rivers with dams and irrigation systems, leaving downstream countries like Iraq and Syria complaining about low river levels. By 2050, such downstream nations could be left without enough water for drinking and irrigation.

Refugees. The United States is the single largest generator of greenhouse gases, contributing one quarter of the global total. But it, and other higher-latitude countries, would be affected less by climate change than would more tropical nations. The developing world will be hit hardest—and least able to cope. "Bangladesh has no prayer," says Stephen Schneider, a climatologist at Stanford University, noting that flooding there, and in Southeast Asia and China, could dislocate millions of people. "The rich will get richer, and the poor will get poorer. That's not a stable situation for the world."

Those daunted by this roster of afflictions will be cheered, a bit, by the United Nations group's report on how to fend off these perils, which will be released March 5 in Ghana. Not only is humanity not helpless in the face of global warming, but we may not even have to give up all the trappings of a First World lifestyle in order to survive—and prosper.

The first question is whether it's possible to slow, or even halt, the rise in greenhouse gases in the atmosphere. Scientists and energy policy experts say yes, unequivocally. Much of the

# History Lessons: Weathering the Storms

It was a pretty good run as societies go: over a millennium with all the material wealth, political organization, and advanced arts and learning that the word *society* implies. Then, at the dawn of the 10th century A.D., the Classic Maya civilization abruptly imploded, leaving deserted cities, trade routes, and pyramids throughout the southern Yucatán.

Three hundred years later, a very different story unfolded on California's Channel Islands. The Chumash people there rapidly transformed themselves from scattered populations of hunter-gatherers into a sophisticated trading culture with clear political leadership and an areawide monopoly on the production of trading beads. The connection? Both groups, climate reconstructions show, were confronted with sudden, dramatic, and long-lasting climate change.

It may be our fault this time around, but climate swings have always affected human societies. Writing in the current issue of the journal *Science,* Yale archaeologist Harvey Weiss cites more than a dozen examples of ancient cultures collapsing in the face of rapidly altered weather. Bad news for a society facing massive global change. But perhaps we can learn something from the Chumash, who, says University of California–Los Angeles archaeologist Jeanne Arnold, "came up with creative political and economic responses to their changing environment." Prospective survivors of climate upheaval, in other words, should be flexible and must be wary of leaders who are overly occupied with building monuments, getting re-elected, and other such trivialities.

**Choices.** "Different cultures have different philosophies about things like making changes," says Brian Fagan, a University of California–Santa Barbara archaeologist. In his forthcoming book, *The Little Ice Age,* Fagan details how various European nations dealt with that unusually cool period, which stretched from 1300 to 1850. The French endured famine, disease, and general wretchedness when cold, wet weather spoiled their traditional cereal crops year after year. The Dutch suffered the same miserable weather but were quicker to adopt new crops and intensive farming methods, perhaps, suggests Fagan, sparking the development of mature market economies.

Confronting massive climate change is never easy—excavations show evidence of dislocation and violence during the Chumash restructuring. But the record at least suggests that climate is not necessarily destiny. Fast-forward to 2001. Scientists tell us we have the technology to adapt, and unlike the Akkadians of Mesopotamia (done in by drought, circa 2290 B.C.) or the Peruvian Moche civilization (drought backed by floods some three millenniums later), we have advance notice that trouble's coming. All we need then is the flexibility of the Dutch and the political will of the Chumash. Will we find them? That's one for the historians in a couple of hundred years. If there are any of them left.

—Thomas Hayden

needed technology either has already been developed or is in the works. The first step is so simple it's known to every third grader: Conserve energy. Over the past few decades, innovations from higher gas mileage to more efficient refrigerators to compact fluorescent lights have saved billions of kilowatts of energy. The second step is to use less oil and coal, which produce greenhouse gases, and rely more on cleaner energy sources such as natural gas and wind, and later on, solar and hydrogen. In Denmark, 13 percent of electricity now comes from wind power, probably the most economical alternative source. In Britain, a company called Wavegen recently activated the first commercial ocean-wave-energy generator, making enough electricity to power about 400 homes.

Taxing ideas. But despite such promising experiments, fossil fuels remain far cheaper than the alternatives. To reduce this cost advantage, most Western European countries, including Sweden, Norway, the Netherlands, Austria, and Italy, have levied taxes on carbon emissions or fossil fuels. The taxes also are intended to nudge utilities toward technologies, like coal gasification, that burn fossil fuels more cleanly. In Germany, where "eco-taxes" are being phased in on most fossil fuels, a new carbon levy will add almost 11 cents to the price of a gallon of gasoline.

But the United States has always shunned a carbon tax. John Holdren, a professor of environmental policy at Harvard's Kennedy School of Government, says such a tax could stimulate economic growth and help position the United States as a leader in energy technology. "The energy technology sector

is worth $300 billion a year, and it'll be $500 to $600 billion by 2010," Holdren says. "The companies and countries that get the biggest chunk of that will be the ones that deliver efficient, clean, inexpensive energy."

A growing number of companies have already figured that out. One of the most advanced large corporations is chemical giant DuPont, which first acknowledged the problem of climate change in 1991. Throughout the past decade, the company worked to cut its carbon dioxide emissions 45 percent from 1990 levels. Last year, it pledged to find at least 10 percent of its energy from renewable sources.

Even more surprising was the dramatic announcement by oil giant BP in 1997 agreeing that climate change was indeed occurring. Even with other oil firms protesting that the evidence was too thin, BP pledged to reduce its greenhouse-gas emissions by 10 percent from 1990 levels by 2010. At the same time, BP Amoco is pouring money into natural gas exploration and investing in renewable energy like solar power and hydrogen.

Even America's largest coal-burning utility company is experimenting. American Electric Power of Columbus, Ohio, is testing "carbon capture," which would separate out carbon dioxide emissions and dispose of them in deep underground saline aquifers, effectively creating carbon-emission-free coal power. Application is at least a decade away. "If we're able to find creative solutions, they're going to place us at a competitive advantage in our industry," says Dale Heydlauff, AEP's senior vice president for environmental affairs.

In automobile manufacturing, there is already a race on for alternatives to fossil fuels. Several automakers like Ford, DaimlerChrysler, and Volkswagen have developed prototypes of cars run by hydrogen fuel cells rather than gasoline. The performance is very similar to that of today's cars, but the cost remains, for now, prohibitive. Fuel-cell vehicles are unlikely to be mass-produced until after 2010, and even then, people will need a push to make the switch. "Climate change is too diffuse to focus people's attention," says C. E. Thomas, a vice president at Directed Technologies, an Arlington, Va., engineering firm working on fuel cells. "But if we have another war in the Middle East or gasoline lines, that will get their attention."

Even with these efforts, and many more, climatologists point out that turning the atmosphere around is much harder than turning a supertanker. Indeed, atmospheric changes already underway may take hundreds of years to change. As a result, some vulnerable countries are already taking preventive, if costly, measures. More than half of the Netherlands lies below sea level and would be threatened by increased storm surges.

Last December, the Dutch government outlined an ambitious plan to bolster the sea defenses. Over the next decade, the Netherlands will spend more than $1 billion to build new dikes, bolster the natural sand dunes, and widen and deepen rivers enough to protect the country against a 3-foot rise in ocean levels.

Some of the most successful adaptations to climate change probably won't involve high-tech gizmos or global taxes. They'll be as simple as the strips of cloth distributed to women in Bangladesh, which they use to screen cholera-causing microbes from water. Villages where women strained water have reduced cholera cases by 50 percent.

"Society is more robust than we give it credit for," says Michael Glantz, a political scientist at the National Center for Atmospheric Research. Like farmers who gradually change to new crops as wells grow dry, people may learn to live comfortably in a new, warmer world.

---

With reporting by Thomas Hayden, Charles W. Petit, Rachel K. Sobel, Kevin Whitelaw, and David Whitman.

# 10 Million Orphans

**For the children who have lost their parents to AIDS, grief is only the beginning of their troubles. The disease's lasting victims.**

TOM MASLAND AND ROD NORDLAND

Even on the mean streets of Homa Bay, a fishing center of 750,000 on Lake Victoria, the children stand out: Kenya has 350,000 AIDS orphans, and 35,000 of them live here. Many of those who have not been forcibly removed to the orphanage are street children—pickpockets and beggars, prostitutes and thieves. To Hamis Otieno, 14, and his brother, Rashid Faraji, 10, the streets of Homa Bay were their last, best hope. Their father had died of AIDS in 1995; their mother turned to prostitution and abandoned them soon after. Relatives, unable to provide for the boys, cast them out. The brothers made their way by bus to Nairobi, 150 miles away, where they stole, begged and worked as drug couriers. But after a year, hungry and alone, the boys went home; hustling promised to be easier on the less competitive streets of Homa Bay. Soon after their arrival, however, they caught what in their world counts as a break: they were picked up and taken by force to an orphanage. There, every one of the children is an AIDS orphan. But then, that is hardly surprising: in Homa Bay, some 50 to 70 percent of the adults are HIV-positive. "So many have died," says Hamis, "so many."

In the nations south of the Sahara, almost two decades of AIDS deaths—2.2 million in 1998 alone, and a still untallied but certainly greater number in 1999—is leaving a sea of orphans in its wake. By the end of this year, 10.4 million of the children under 15 will have lost their mothers or both parents to AIDS. Before the current epidemic, the perennial cataclysms of war and famine orphaned 2 percent of the region's children; AIDS makes that figure look benign. A generation of orphans threatens to undermine economic development, for children without parents can seldom afford education. And many AIDS orphans end up "roaming the streets, prime targets for gangs [and] militia and creating more child armies like those that participated in massacres in West Africa," says Dr. Peter Piot, executive director of UNAIDS. But worse lies ahead. The number of AIDS orphans in the region is projected to double or triple by 2010.

It is not only the raw numbers that make this orphan crisis unlike any ever seen. The children, who have often watched their parents die alone and in pain, are left in a world where AIDS has unraveled such traditional safety nets as the extended family, and in households where not a single adult is able to earn a living. Josephine Ssenyonga, 69, lives on a small farm in the Rakai district of Uganda, where AIDS has been cutting through the population like a malevolent scythe for 14 years: 32 percent of the under-15 population, a total of 75,000 children, have been orphaned in Rakai. Of the four daughters and nine sons Ssenyonga raised, 11 are dead. Her son Joseph left her with eight children; Francis left four; Peter left three. "At first there were 22, living in that small hut over there," she says. "My children did not leave me any means to look after these young ones. All they had was sold to help treat them." Overwhelmed, she took the children to the hut one day. "I told them to shut the door so we could all starve to death inside and join the others," Ssenyonga says. She changed her mind when a daughter returned home to help, and World Vision provided a three-room house for them all.

Bernadette Nakayima, 70, lives in Uganda's Masaka district, where 110,000 of the 342,000 children are orphans. Nakayima lost every one of her 11 children to AIDS. "All these left me with 35 grandchildren to look after," she says. "I was a woman struck with sorrow beyond tears." But she is not alone: one out of every four families in Uganda is now caring for an AIDS orphan, says Pelucy Ntambirweki of the Ugandan Women's Effort to Save Orphans (UWESO).

When AIDS takes a parent, it usually takes a childhood, too, for if no other relative steps in, the oldest child becomes the head of a household. Yuda Sanyu Kitali was 10 in 1992 when his mother died of AIDS; the disease had killed his father in 1986. Sanyu had to drop out of school, of course, as did his younger brother, Emmanuel Kulabigwo, now 16, and sister, Margaret Nalubega, 15: when their parents died, so did any hope of affording academic fees. "No one came to claim us or to offer help," says Sanyu. A year after the children were orphaned, the grass-thatched house their father had built in the Rakai district collapsed in a heavy rain. "Since I was the oldest, I had to build another house," Sanyu says. He did his best with mud, poles, reeds and banana fiber. The children grew cassavas and greens on the land their parents left them, but they still went to sleep hungry many nights. As Sanyu tells his story Emmanuel nods silently. Margaret sits on a papyrus mat in the corner, staring at a wall and hiding a tear in her dirty brown dress.

---

## The number of people who have gone into the coffin-making business—that is something you can see without being an epidemiologist.

—G. Sikipa, *Unaids*

---

Most orphans are taken in by their extended families, if they are taken in by anyone, but the sheer number of these lost children fills orphanages, too. Ethembeni House, run by the Salvation Army in downtown Johannesburg, has 38 children 5 or younger. All of them have tested HIV-positive. All were abandoned: a vagrant found the newborn Moses, now 3, in a dumpster; a woman handed days-old Simon, now 2, to a street vendor and never returned. The rooms in Ethembeni, lined with cribs, are clean and decorated with pictures of clowns and dolls. Other pictures, of children who died here, line the mantel. Moses points to one: "He's gone," he says. When a stranger enters the room, the children turn expectant faces to her: "Mama, mama," they cry.

In times past it was usually war or neglect or famine or poverty that brought abandoned or orphaned children to the Sanyu Babies Home in Kampala. Now the caseload of 26 is almost entirely AIDS orphans, many of whom have lost not only parents but all their other adult relatives, too. Patricia Namutebi, 3, was brought in as a 1-year-old by a thin, sickly man who said he was her neighbor and that her mother had died of AIDS. Patricia has been sick with one opportunistic infection after another; today she restlessly drags a chair to and fro and swings on the curtains, apart from the other children. Workers at the Babies Home suspect that the man was her father, but it hardly mattered. When they trace abandoned children back to their families, says Joyce Lolindya, administrator of the home, the survivors seem to feel that "it is hard to look after an AIDS victim, and then also the children of that victim, when you know they will all die." Especially when AIDS carries with it such a social stigma. Unless abandoned AIDS orphans reach an institution like hers, they risk getting sucked into what Godfrey Sikipa of UNAIDS calls "a vicious circle." He adds: "In many cases the orphans, unless we prevent them from going into deeper poverty, will become prostitutes." The fortunate ones become child brides, or the plaything of a sugar-daddy. They can only hope that the men will not be among the millions who believe that sex with a virgin cures AIDS.

When an extended family cannot afford to educate all the children in its care—virtually everywhere in Africa governments charge school fees—it is the orphan who is the likeliest dropout. In Zambia, a study cited by the UNAIDS report found, one third of urban children with parents enroll in school, but only one quarter of orphans do. "I wish I could go all the time," says Ben Sengazi, 13, one of Ssenyonga's grandsons. But when the family cannot scrape up the fees, the school turns him away.

Compared with children with parents, AIDS orphans are at far greater risk of malnutrition and of not receiving the health care they need. The little girl named Forget was 4 when her mother died of AIDS last November and she went to live with her grandmother in a village southeast of Harare. Her small body has recently developed ugly lesions, which she scratches constantly. Her grandmother says the causes of the plague are a mystery to her. Although she is doing what she can for Forget, the assumption by many caregivers is that the orphan, too, is infected with HIV, and that her illness is untreatable. Perhaps that explains one of the puzzles of the AIDS orphans. In 1995 Uganda had 1.2 million of them; based on the number of AIDS deaths and other factors, there should be 1.5 million now, but there are "only" 1.1 million. That is, Uganda is missing 400,000 AIDS orphans. "Either the babies were born [HIV-] positive, or they died from a lack of care," says UWESO's Ntambirweki.

Government and private programs do what they can for AIDS orphans. In Botswana, nongovernmental and community-based organizations provide services ranging from day care to food, clothing and bus fare to and from school. Villages in Malawi have organized communal gardens. Charity groups and orphanages teach the older children AIDS prevention, hoping that the cataclysm that befell the parents will not be visited on the children. World Vision built Sanyu's family a four-room house, paid for his sister and brother's schooling and trained Sanyu in bicycle repair. And after Harriett Namayanja, now 17, lost her parents to AIDS, a loan from a private agency saved her and her eight brothers and sisters. Harriett used the money for sisal grass, from which she weaves doormats. She sells them in Kampala, and with the money, she says, "I am able to look after my younger siblings" and even pay school fees for her brothers. But she and Sanyu are exceptions. Funding has not kept up with the needs of so many orphans, and institutions are stretched almost to the breaking point.

Some 6,000 men and women in sub-Saharan Africa will die of AIDS today. Six thousand more will die tomorrow, and the next day. For the children they leave behind, the tragedy is only beginning.

---

With Simon Kaheru in Kampala, Lara Santoro in Homa Bay, Vera Haller in Johannesburg and Sharon Begley

# In God's Name: Genocide and Religion in the Twentieth Century

STEPHEN R. HAYNES

I vividly remember riding in a car during the summer of 1994 and listening with rapt attention to an account of the tragedy in Rwanda. In just 100 days, following a government coup in early April, some 800,000 Rwandans were ruthlessly murdered by their countrymen. When I arrived home, I located Rwanda on a map. For several weeks I paid close attention to reports of the refugee crisis that followed the slaughter. But then the genocide and its aftermath were mentioned less and less frequently by the news media and, like most Westerners, I stopped thinking about it. Later, when Rwanda did enter my mind, I had difficulty remembering who had killed whom. Had Tutsis been the victims of Hutus? Or was it the other way around?

While popular interest in Rwanda has waned in the years since the genocide, the literature of description and analysis continues to grow. Mahmood Mamdani's *When Victims Become Killers* is a detailed account of the political conditions underlying the Rwandan tragedy. While it devotes little attention to the killing per se or to the individuals who committed it, it sheds a great deal of light on Rwandan history and political institutions—precolonial, colonial and revolutionary. One notable feature of Mamdani's analysis is his recurrent mention of parallels between Rwanda and the Holocaust.

In fact, most studies of the Rwandan slaughter refer to the Nazi Final Solution. Apparently, the landscape of contemporary genocide is so dominated by the Holocaust that other tragedies remain invisible unless they are compared to it. As arguments for the uniqueness of the Jewish experience have multiplied over the past decade, students of genocide in other places—in Armenia, the Americas, the Balkans—have combated that argument with attention to understudied cases of genocide.

Philip Gourevitch introduces his riveting account of the Rwandan crisis and its aftermath (*We Wish to Inform You . . .*) with the observation that "the dead of Rwanda accumulated at nearly three times the rate of Jewish dead during the Holocaust. It was the most efficient killing since the atomic bombings of Hiroshima and Nagasaki." One of the first books on the subject, Alain Destexhe's *Rwanda and Genocide in the Twentieth Century,* begins with a quote from Holocaust survivor Primo Levi: "It has happened once, and it could all happen again."

But references to the Holocaust reflect more than competition for the attention of atrocity-numbed readers. The two tragedies share quite a few formal similarities. There are analogous stories of unprovoked cruelty and betrayal, of rescue and gratuitous kindness, of hiding, passing and surviving. There are similar rationalizations on the part of perpetrators and by-standers—self-exculpating images of entrapment, of killers having no choice but to act as they did. There is similar evidence of complicit Christian leaders and institutions, evidence that poses a challenge to the credibility of faith.

There are the same pregenocidal legal persecutions used to identify and stigmatize an ethnic minority (including quotas and identity cards); the same essentializing of "race" that casts one group as a threat to the other's survival; the same mystification of a minority as a strangely powerful entity against whom the majority must defend itself; the same dehumanizing of the victims through images ("rats" in Germany; "cockroaches" in Rwanda) that makes elimination easier once the genocide begins. And there are the same painstaking attempts afterwards to discover why some people killed their neighbors while others protected them, along with the same amazement at the latter's refusal to consider their behavior extraordinary.

Like Nazi Germany, genocidal Rwanda is an exceedingly unattractive venue for Christian self-examination. Much of the evidence indicates that "blood" proved thicker than baptismal water, that faith was powerless to overcome the interests of class or ethnicity. And Rwanda has provided few stories designed to restore our trust in humankind or the role of faith in confronting evil. So far, we know of no Rwandan Bonhoeffers with whom mainline Protestants can identify; no Hutu Corrie ten Booms to sustain evangelicals' belief that God protects the righteous; no Catholic bishops who risked their lives to speak out against the violence; no Le Chambon-sur-Lignons where the persecuted were sheltered by simple Christians in a "conspiracy of goodness."

Yet precisely because so little good news can be gleaned from the Rwandan genocide, Christians must not ignore it. One pressing issue raised by Rwanda is human nature, what theologians have traditionally called anthropology. Although scholars of the genocide assiduously avoid theological questions,

Christians must ask what this and other episodes of mass killing reveal about the essence and extent of our fallenness.

Reinhold Niebuhr reportedly said that the doctrine of original sin is the only doctrine for which Christians have any empirical evidence. If Niebuhr is correct, certainly the most compelling evidence for original sin is to be found in the study of mass murder. Considering this evidence theologically does not require that we ignore the communal and systemic dimensions of evil highlighted by social scientists, but it does help explain how easily human beings become complicit in the destruction of others—through abhorrence of difference, self-deception and the idolatry of race and nation.

Even more than the Holocaust, Rwanda pushes us to ask what adaptations or situational factors exacerbate the genocidal tendencies in human nature. Because it was extraordinarily low-tech, the Rwandan genocide does not allow us to take refuge in impersonal categories such as "bureaucratization" or "modernity." The killing was perpetrated not anonymously in gas chambers, but face to face with machetes, knives, guns and grenades. It was carried out not by a class of professional killers "doing their duty," but by bands of ordinary people that included women and children.

Rwanda also presents us with a stark reminder of the narrowness of national interests and the hollowness of official commitments to moral actions when they conflict with those interests. Both Gourevitch's book and the television documentary "The Triumph of Evil" argue that the Rwandan genocide might well have been averted if the UN or its member nations had acted on information received in January 1994 from a UNAMIR (United Nations Mission in Rwanda) field commander.

An informant close to Hutu Power extremists in the Rwandan government revealed that the militias he was charged with training had been formed not for protection from the RPF (a guerrilla army of Rwandan exiles) but for the extermination of Tutsis. UNAMIR's message to New York detailed his account of the Rwandan government's plans: "He has been ordered to register all Tutsi in Kigali. He suspects it's for their extermination. Example he gave was that in 20 minutes his personnel could kill up to 1,000 Tutsis."

Since the Hutu informant revealed the location of arms to be used for this grisly task, the UNAMIR commander requested permission to seize the weapons and protect the informant and his family. The information and request were discussed by key members of the UN staff and then ignored. Motivated by the desire to avoid "another Somalia," the commander's superiors prohibited him from taking any action.

Three months later, events in Rwanda unfolded just as the informant had predicted. The morning after President Juvenal Habyarimana's plane was shot down under suspicious circumstances, ten Belgian peacekeepers were kidnapped, tortured and mutilated as a warning to the Western democracies. Then the genocide was on: roadblocks were set up and marauding death squads (interahamwe) took the streets, encouraged and directed by broadcasts on national radio; educated professionals massacred their colleagues in churches and hospitals; Tutsis and moderate Hutus attempted to flee or cowered in embassies and hotels protected by foreign interests; white citizens of Western nations were evacuated amid heart-wrenching pleas for help by desperate Africans; and UNAMIR troops ignominiously withdrew from their compounds, leaving those who had sought their protection to be hacked to death.

As corpses began to rot in the streets and clog the rivers, the Western response to this maelstrom of genocidal evil was precisely what Hutu Power extremists had hoped for. Under pressure from Belgium and the United States, the UN Security Council voted to terminate its mission in Rwanda. While American and UN representatives steadfastly refused to utter the word "genocide," the Czech Republic's ambassador to the UN spoke to the point: "When you come from Central Europe, [you have] a sense of what holocausts are about; you recognize one when you see one."

All of which leads to a troubling question: If one of the Nazi leaders present at the Wannsee Conference in Berlin in January 1942 had—in a fit of conscience—leaked plans for the "Final Solution of the Jewish Question in Europe" to the Allies, would this information have altered the fate of Jews under Nazi control?

The Western response to the genocidal crisis in Rwanda suggests that the answer is no. There is every reason to believe that Allied government officials would have treated a leaked Wannsee protocol as irrelevant to their strategic interests. And recall that in 1942 Western democracies had neither the experience of the Holocaust to reflect on nor a political obligation under the UN's Genocide Convention to prevent genocide.

Thus, while our consciousness of mass death and our use of the word "genocide" have been thoroughly conditioned by the Holocaust, it is not at all clear that Holocaust awareness has made Western democracies or their citizens more sensitive to mass death, or more committed to incurring personal risk to stop it. This despite the fact that "never again"—the ubiquitous mantra of Holocaust remembrance—indicates a commitment on the part of the powerful and morally aware "never again" to stand by while a nation destroys those it deems a threat to its survival.

As the documentary "The Triumph of Evil" so poignantly demonstrates, it was only a few months after ceremonies marking the opening of the U.S. Holocaust Memorial Museum—ceremonies at which President Clinton vowed on behalf of all Americans "to preserve this shared history of anguish, to keep it vivid and real so that evil can be combated and contained"—that warnings of the Rwandan tragedy reached the White House. In April 1994, just a few weeks after *Schindler's List* claimed the Oscar for best picture, Vice President Al Gore proclaimed that Washington's Holocaust memorial was needed "to remind those who make the agonizing decisions of foreign policy of the consequences of those decisions." Meanwhile, his government was rejecting State Department proposals to impede the genocide and worrying about whether its refusal to act might hurt the party in upcoming mid-term elections. It is difficult to imagine a more dramatic example of the yawning gap between rhetoric and reality in contemporary politics.

While our culture is awash in images of a genocide that ended over 50 years ago, we have trouble remembering the victims of a genocidal assault that occurred within the past decade. Is it simply the passage of time that fixes international tragedies in our consciousness? More likely it is a function of what Richard L. Rubenstein has identified as a fundamental dimension of the Holocaust's "uniqueness"—its resonance with the biblical and theological motifs that animate Judeo-Christian civilization.

Yet perhaps the failure of Rwanda's tragedy to penetrate the Western mind has to do with geography and race as well. Perhaps Westerners perceive the Holocaust not only through a religious grid, but through the prism of color. Ironically, given the explicit racial dimensions of Nazi ideology, both perpetrator and victim in the Holocaust are perceived as vaguely "white." Even in the Balkans, the difficult-to-pronounce names and unfamiliar traditions notwithstanding, we perceive victims who "look like us."

Rwanda, however, is a different story. The mental maps of most Americans simply do not include East Africa. The crises there—even when they reach the threshold of media consciousness—seem far away, the historical and political contexts unfamiliar, the "tribes" involved indistinguishable. Unless a conflict pits "white" against "black," as in South Africa or Zimbabwe, it does not hold our attention for long. Is it possible that we find it difficult to forge a connection with victims of genocide unless we can identify with them on the level of ethnicity, religious affiliation or color? If so, herein lies another grim lesson regarding human nature.

What can Christians who want to remember Rwanda learn from this genocide? Most scholarly analyses ignore the religious dimensions of the tragedy, portraying the Hutu extermination campaign as an indictment of European colonialism or a metaphor for the dilemmas of post-cold-war foreign policy. But there are important exceptions. For instance, Timothy Longman's contribution to *In God's Name: Genocide and Religion in the Twentieth Century* documents the active involvement of church personnel and institutions in the genocide: "Numerous priests, pastors, nuns, brothers, catechists, and Catholic and Protestant lay leaders supported, participated in, or helped to organize the killings," Longman writes. And he remarks that more people may have been killed in church buildings than anywhere else.

In the same volume, Charles de Lespinay charges the Rwandan clergy of being "propagators of false information tending to maintain a climate of fear, suspicion and hatred." Prominent clergy refused to condemn the killing (characterizing it as wartime self-defense or "double genocide"), and even excused the murders as a sort of delayed justice for past wrongs. In Rwanda, Lespinay concludes, "the exacerbation of past and present rivalries is entirely the fault of the missionary-educated intellectual 'elites.'"

But the religious lessons from Rwanda transcend the genocidal behavior of believers in one of Africa's most Christianized societies (90 percent Christian and 63 percent Roman Catholic, according to a 1991 census). Rwanda also reminds us of the way biblical myths of origin can exercise a pernicious influence in history. As almost every commentator on the genocide has noted, the antagonism between Hutu and Tutsi is based on presumed racial distinctions constructed from a quasi-biblical

ideology introduced by 19th-century white explorers and reiterated by European colonialists who benefited from inter-African antagonism.

The intellectual foundation for the construction of racial difference in Rwanda is John Hanning Speke's *Journal of the Discovery of the Source of the Nile* (1863, reprinted in 1996). Like other 19th-century Westerners, the English explorer assumed that Africans were descendants of "our poor elder brother Ham [who] was cursed by his father, and condemned to be the slave of both Shem and Japheth." Speke's contribution to white perceptions of Africa was a theory of ethnology "founded on the traditions of the several nations, as checked by [his] own observation of what [he] saw when passing through them."

The distinctive physical appearance of the Wahuma (Tutsis) led Speke to surmise that they were descended from "the semi-Shem-Hamitic of Ethiopia," cattle-herding "Asiatic" invaders who moved south, lost their original language and religion, and darkened through inter-marriage. According to his journal, Speke elaborated his ethnological theory for a Tutsi king using the Book of Genesis "to explain all [he] fancied [he] knew about the origin and present condition of the Wahuma branch of the Ethiopians, beginning with Adam, to show how it was the king had heard by tradition that at one time the people of his race were half white and half black."

In the western mind this so-called Hamitic Hypothesis evolved to become an explanation for the arrival of "civilization" in Africa. Inside Rwanda, it was adopted as the basis for colonial theories of Tutsi superiority, for missionary education that placed ethnic diversity in a European class perspective, and for the Hutu revolutionary image of Tutsis as nonindigenous invaders from the north. While this "biblical" dimension of Rwandan history is rarely reported, it was well known to both the perpetrators and the victims of the genocide.

Rwanda also presents us with compelling evidence for the ineptitude of Christian leaders and institutions in resisting genocidal evil. Even as we struggle to understand the failure of Christian witness and action during the Holocaust, Rwanda raises new specters: of churches becoming killing sites, of parishioners murdering each other, of pastors being sought as war criminals, and of priests denying or excusing mass murder.

As Longman argues, one reason Christians failed to resist the forces that led to genocide was the Rwandan church's close relationship with the Habyarimana government and the refusal of church leaders to support groups and individuals advocating reform. The church's commitment to preserving the status quo helps explain its "resounding silence" in the wake of sporadic persecutions during the early 1990s, and all-out genocide in 1994.

Stories from Rwanda—like so many stories from the Holocaust—force us to ask how we would have behaved in a similar situation, whether we are different from the perpetrators and bystanders who became agents of genocide. These questions are faced with disturbing honesty in James Waller's forthcoming book *Children of Cain: How Ordinary People Commit Extraordinary Evil*. The book's title is taken from Gourevitch's application of Genesis 4 to the Rwandan tragedy: "In the famous story, the older brother, Cain, was a cultivator, and Abel, the younger, was a herdsman. They made their offerings to God—Cain from his crops, Abel from his herds. Abel's portion won God's regard; Cain's did not. So Cain killed Abel." In offering a unified theory of perpetrator behavior, Waller discredits the various psychological mechanisms we rely upon to distance ourselves from those who commit or countenance genocide.

Finally, because it reveals how the world's leading democracy conspired to ignore and deny an ongoing genocide at the very moment when American consciousness of the Holocaust was at its height, Rwanda forces Christians to ask precisely how Holocaust awareness contributes to antigenocidal thought and action. When we say "never again," we must pledge to remember Rwanda.

**Stephen R. Haynes** is associate professor of religious studies at Rhodes College and a member of the Church Relations Committee of the United States Holocaust Memorial Council.

# Women, Citizens, Muslims

AMY ZALMAN

On December 13, 2003, 502 members of Afghanistan's constitutional Grand Council, or loya jirga, met in the capital, Kabul, to begin writing the document that would henceforth shape governance of an Islamic, representative democracy. Three weeks later, after at least two rocket attacks near the council's meeting place and even more explosive politicking among the council's members, the council emerged with a new constitution.

Among those who watched the process with attention were Afghan women and their activist partisans in other parts of the world, who wanted the new constitution explicitly to reflect the rights and needs of women. They had particular reason to worry that the assembly gathered in Kabul would be hijacked by conservative extremists who would interpret women's rights narrowly using religion as an excuse, or who might eliminate mentions of women's human rights altogether.

The Grand Council met just two years after the United States toppled the Taliban, the extremist party that had been in control of Afghanistan's capital since 1996. The American objective was to destabilize a regime that had given refuge to Osama bin Laden and the leaders of Al Qaeda, whose bases were in Afghanistan. At that time, the United States linked its military agenda in Afghanistan with the need to liberate Afghan women from oppression. As First Lady Laura Bush put the matter in a national radio address in November 2001, "The brutal oppression of women is a central goal of the terrorists. Long before the current war began, the Taliban and its terrorist allies were making the lives of children and women in Afghanistan miserable." The first lady went on to assert that the removal of the Taliban from power would mean the liberation of Afghan women. For the next year, Afghan women were big news: There were books and reports, and pictures on the front pages of newspapers showing formerly illiterate women learning to read. Women began the work of reconstructing their lives by returning to the streets, to school, to work. Then the war in Iraq began, and Afghan women, and Afghanistan's reconstruction, became old news.

By the beginning of 2003, warlords in provinces who had been allies of the United States when it went to war against the Taliban were instituting measures themselves that were reminiscent of the Taliban era. Human Rights Watch reported in January 2003 that in the Western province of Herat, girls and boys would no longer be permitted to go to school together. Because most teachers are men, the ruling effectively shut girls and women out of an education. Other restrictions against interactions between the sexes were imposed; girls or women seen in public with a male might be taken against their will to a hospital to check for their "chastity." These alarming trends coincided with a sharp drop in international scrutiny, although Afghan women themselves continued to seek access to good health, higher education, and equal pay for their work.

Their experience in the last two years has made it clear that simply removing a dictatorial regime and installing a democracy does not automatically guarantee women's rights. Indeed, the challenges facing women's effort to make sure their rights are legally enforceable in the future highlight broad conflicts in Afghanistan between conservative and liberalizing factions of the future government and between forces competing to control interpretations of Islam in the public sphere. Islam is the prism through which human rights are articulated in Afghanistan, and it is it is therefore crucial for women that their rights to education, work, and freely chosen marriages be articulated in its terms. The importance of the relationship between Islam and rights is one supported by women. Indeed, "Ninety-nine percent of Afghan women are Muslims, and their faith is extremely important to them. Most feel their rights are available to them through Islam," says Masuda Sultan, the spokesperson for Women for Afghan Women (WAW), a New York City-based grassroots organization of Afghan women and their supporters. Sultan explains that the number of women who frame their rights in secular terms is much smaller.

The process of shaping a new women's rights doctrine that would take Islam into account was in evidence in the making of the "Women's Bill of Rights," authored in September 2003 by a representative group of 45 women who found ways to interpret relevant Islamic edicts in ways that amplified their human rights. The bill of rights was the achievement of a unique conference on women and the constitution sponsored by WAW. Organized with the help of the Afghan Women's Network and Afghans for Civil Society, the Kandahar conference brought women together to deliberate over how their rights could best be reflected in the constitution. Kandahar, unlike the more liberal capital, is one of Afghanistan's most conservative provinces, and it was unclear until the day of the conference whether it would be secure enough for the gathering to take place. It was, but only under heavily armed guard. The conference participants comprised elite female decision-makers as well as largely illiterate everyday women from all over the country. For some, simply completing the trip, whether alone or in the company of a male relative, was itself a triumph.

Over the course of three days, these women reviewed the 1964 constitution on which the 2003 draft was based and began composing the 16-point bill of rights, framed by the demand that the rights be not simply "secured in the constitution but implemented." Some of the demands are basics on the menu of modern human rights: women require mandatory education, equal pay for equal work, freedom of speech, and the freedom to vote and run for office and to be represented equally in Parliament and the judiciary.

But other points are specific to the situation of Afghan Muslim women and responsive to the recent forms of deprivation imposed by the Taliban and long-standing excesses based on tribal convention. There is, for example, the demand that women and children be protected against sexual abuse, domestic violence, and bad-blood price—when one family compensates a second for a crime by giving them one of the family's women. There is a request for "the provision of up-to-date heath services for women with special attention to reproductive rights." Under the Taliban women were denied healthcare by male doctors, who were not allowed to touch the bodies of women to whom they were not related, and severe restrictions on women's movements made it difficult for female doctors to supply healthcare. Women made it clear they wanted the right to marry and divorce according to Islamic law.

At the end of the conference, the document was presented publicly to President Hamed Karzai, and women were promised that their rights would be incorporated explicitly into the new constitution. However, when the draft constitution was released in November 2003, there was no explicit mention of women's rights. Instead, the constitution granted rights to all Afghan citizens. As Rim Sharma, the co-founder and executive director of the Women's Edge Coalition and Afifa Azim, the director of the Afghan Women's Network, argued in a joint editorial on the eve of the council's meeting, lumping together men and women in the text of the constitution, rather than clearly designating rights for women as well as men is "an important distinction because Afghan women are not issued the identification cards given to men. Therefore, some men argue, women are not citizens and entitled to equality." A crucial question at the Grand Council was whether women would be identified separately from men in the final constitution. It was a triumph when the constitution that was released contained an article stating that "The citizens of Afghanistan—whether man or woman—have equal rights and duties before the law."

At the same time, other challenges remain. The introduction of women's rights to the national political agenda cannot itself be taken for granted while control of the country is still in question. Although it is true that on paper, the government of Afghanistan is headed by President Karzai and moving toward democracy along well established lines such as the creation of a constitution, the actual situation in many parts of the country do not reflect this shift in power. The Taliban have reasserted power in Southern and Eastern parts of the country. Indeed, in the few days leading up to the meeting of the constitutional Grand Council, coalition forces waged their largest attacks to date on Taliban members who threatened violence against the proceedings. As a recent Amnesty International report also noted, Northern Alliance commanders who committed human rights abuses under the Taliban government now hold government positions themselves (the October 2003 report, Afghanistan: "No one listens to us and no one treats us as human beings" Justice denied to women, can be found at www.web.amnesty.org/library/index/engasa110232003). Where these commanders govern, women's movements remain as restricted, or nearly as restricted, as they did before they were "liberated."

So, one of the threats to women's rights is related to the ongoing danger to the entire nation's stability as well as to the ability of the most conservative or militant actors in Afghanistan to influence the political process. Extremists exploit claims to Islam to intimidate women. This means that although women themselves frame their rights in terms of Islam, they can also be intimidated into making claims for interpretations that don't serve their needs at all. Sultan explains:

> Security is still a huge issue, and regional warlords and extremists are around. A woman who doesn't speak in terms that acknowledge Islam will face trouble. The affirmation of being Muslim is important because otherwise they'll be called infidels or be threatened or seen as secular or non-Muslim.

The proper response to this situation, in the view of Sultan and others who work closely with Afghan women, is to promote the education of women in Islamic law and history so that they can express their own rights as well as refute interpretations that do not serve them. As the legal system begins to hammer out laws that confirm the bases of the constitution, such knowledge will be increasingly important. Jurists are qualified in Afghanistan through higher education or training in Islamic law. As Sultan notes, these qualifications "leave open the door" for those trained informally by radical Islamist clerics to shape law. Women's education in the language, tradition, and law through which they understand their rights and themselves is a practical and necessary step in this context. This may appear counterintuitive to onlookers in the United States and Europe, whose recent revolutions in rights have often taken place in social and political contexts that opposed democracy to religion. Enhancing the rights of women by encouraging their access to religious education may also seem counterintuitive in the present media environment, which is saturated by the idea that Islam is inherently undemocratic. But women working for their rights in Afghanistan make it clear that both Islam and democracy are evolving practices that permit competing interpretations. It is their right to shape both in ways that confirm their identities as women, Afghan citizens, and Muslims.

---

# The Jihad against the Jihadis: How Moderate Muslim Leaders Waged War on Extremists—and Won

Fareed Zakaria

September 11, 2001, was gruesome enough on its own terms, but for many of us, the real fear was of what might follow. Not only had al-Qaeda shown it was capable of sophisticated and ruthless attacks, but a far greater concern was that the group had or could establish a powerful hold on the hearts and minds of Muslims. And if Muslims sympathized with al-Qaeda's cause, we were in for a herculean struggle. There are more than 1.5 billion Muslims living in more than 150 countries across the world. If jihadist ideology became attractive to a significant part of this population, the West faced a clash of civilizations without end, one marked by blood and tears.

These fears were well founded. The 9/11 attacks opened the curtain on a world of radical and violent Islam that had been festering in the Arab lands and had been exported across the globe, from London to Jakarta. Polls all over the Muslim world revealed deep anger against America and the West and a surprising degree of support for Osama bin Laden. Governments in most of these countries were ambivalent about this phenomenon, assuming that the Islamists' wrath would focus on the United States and not themselves. Large, important countries like Saudi Arabia and Indonesia seemed vulnerable.

More than eight eventful years have passed, but in some ways it still feels like 2001. Republicans have clearly decided that fanning the public's fears of rampant jihadism continues to be a winning strategy. Commentators furnish examples of backwardness and brutality from various parts of the Muslim world—and there are many—to highlight the grave threat we face.

But, in fact, the entire terrain of the war on terror has evolved dramatically. Put simply, the moderates are fighting back and the tide is turning. We no longer fear the possibility of a major country succumbing to jihadist ideology. In most Muslim nations, mainstream rulers have stabilized their regimes and their societies, and extremists have been isolated. This has not led to the flowering of Jeffersonian democracy or liberalism. But modern, somewhat secular forces are clearly in control and widely supported across the Muslim world. Polls, elections, and in-depth studies all confirm this trend.

The focus of our concern now is not a broad political movement but a handful of fanatics scattered across the globe. Yet Washington's vast nation-building machinery continues to spend tens of billions of dollars in Iraq and Afghanistan, and there are calls to do more in Yemen and Somalia. What we have to ask ourselves is whether any of that really will deter these small bands of extremists. Some of them come out of the established democracies of the West, hardly places where nation building will help. We have to understand the changes in the landscape of Islam if we are going to effectively fight the enemy on the ground, rather than the enemy in our minds.

Once, no country was more worrying than bin Laden's homeland. The Kingdom of Saudi Arabia, steward of the holy cities of Mecca and Medina, had surpassed Egypt as the de facto leader of the Arab world because of the vast sums of money it doled out to Islamic causes—usually those consonant with its puritanical Wahhabi doctrines. Since 1979 the Saudi regime had openly appeased its homegrown Islamists, handing over key ministries and funds to reactionary mullahs. Visitors to Saudi Arabia after 9/11 were shocked by what they heard there. Educated Saudis—including senior members of the government—publicly endorsed wild conspiracy theories and denied that any Saudis had been involved in the 9/11 attacks. Even those who accepted reality argued that the fury of some Arabs was inevitable, given America's one-sided foreign policy on the Arab-Israeli issue.

America's initial reaction to 9/11 was to focus on al-Qaeda. The group was driven out of its base in Afghanistan and was pursued wherever it went. Its money was tracked and blocked, its fighters arrested and killed. Many other nations joined in, from France to Malaysia. After all, no government wanted to let terrorists run loose in its land.

But a broader conversation also began, one that asked, "Why is this happening, and what can we do about it?" The most influential statement on Islam to come out of the post-9/11 era was not a presidential speech or an intellectual's essay. It was, believe it or not, a United Nations report. In 2002 the U.N. Development Program published a detailed study of the Arab world. The paper made plain that in an era of globalization, openness, diversity, and tolerance, the Arabs were the world's great laggards. Using hard data, the report painted a picture of political, social, and intellectual stagnation in countries from the Maghreb to the Gulf. And it was written by a team of Arab scholars. This was not paternalism or imperialism. It was truth.

The report, and many essays and speeches by political figures and intellectuals in the West, launched a process of reflection in the Arab world. The debate did not take the form that many in the West wanted—no one said, "You're right, we are backward." But still, leaders in Arab countries were forced to advocate modernity and moderation openly rather than hoping that they could quietly reap its fruits by day while palling around with the mullahs at night. The Bush administration launched a series of programs across the Muslim world to strengthen moderates, shore up civil society, and build forces of tolerance and pluralism. All this has had an effect. From Dubai to Amman to Cairo, in some form or another, authorities have begun opening up economic and political systems that had been tightly closed. The changes have sometimes been small, but the arrows are finally moving in the right direction.

Ultimately, the catalyst for change was something more lethal than a report. After 9/11, al-Qaeda was full of bluster: recall the videotapes of bin Laden and his deputy, Ayman al-Zawahiri, boasting of their plans. Yet they confronted a far less permissive environment. Moving money, people, and materials had all become much more difficult. So they, and local groups inspired by them, began attacking where they could—striking local targets rather than global ones, including a nightclub and hotel in Indonesia, a wedding party in Jordan, cafés in Casablanca and Istanbul, and resorts in Egypt. They threatened the regimes that, either by accident or design, had allowed them to live and breathe.

Over the course of 2003 and 2004, Saudi Arabia was rocked by a series of such terrorist attacks, some directed against foreigners, but others at the heart of the Saudi regime—the Ministry of the Interior and compounds within the oil industry. The monarchy recognized that it had spawned dark forces that were now endangering its very existence. In 2005 a man of wisdom and moderation, King Abdullah, formally ascended to the throne and inaugurated a large-scale political and intellectual effort aimed at discrediting the ideology of jihadism. Mullahs were ordered to denounce suicide bombings and violence more generally. Education was pried out of the hands of the clerics. Terrorists and terror suspects were "rehabilitated" through extensive programs of education, job training, and counseling. Central Command chief Gen. David Petraeus said to me, "The Saudi role in taking on al-Qaeda, both by force but also using political, social, religious, and educational tools, is one of the most important, least reported positive developments in the war on terror."

Perhaps the most successful country to combat jihadism has been the world's most populous Muslim nation, Indonesia. In 2002 that country seemed destined for a long and painful struggle with the forces of radical Islam. The nation was rocked by terror attacks, and a local Qaeda affiliate, Jemaah Islamiah, appeared to be gaining strength. But eight years later, JI has

been marginalized and mainstream political parties have gained ground, all while a young democracy has flowered after the collapse of the Suharto dictatorship.

Magnus Ranstorp of Stockholm's Center for Asymmetric Threat Studies recently published a careful study examining Indonesia's success in beating back extremism. The main lesson, he writes, is to involve not just government but civil society as a whole, including media and cultural figures who can act as counterforces to terrorism. (That approach obviously has greater potential in regions and countries with open and vibrant political systems—Southeast Asia, Turkey, and India—than in the Arab world.)

Iraq occupies an odd place in this narrative. While the invasion of Iraq inflamed the Muslim world and the series of blunders during the initial occupation period created dangerous chaos at the heart of the Middle East, Iraq also became a stage on which al-Qaeda played a deadly hand, and lost. As al-Qaeda in Iraq gained militarily, it began losing politically. It turned from its broader global ideology to focus on a narrow sectarian agenda, killing Shias and fueling a Sunni-Shia civil war. In doing so, the group also employed a level of brutality and violence that shocked most Iraqis. Where the group gained control, even pious people were repulsed by its reactionary behavior. In Anbar province, the heart of the Sunni insurgency, al-Qaeda in Iraq would routinely cut off the fingers of smokers. Even those Sunnis who feared the new Iraq began to prefer Shia rule to such medievalism.

Since 9/11, Western commentators have been calling on moderate Muslim leaders to condemn jihadist ideology, issue *fatwas* against suicide bombing, and denounce al-Qaeda. Since about 2006, they've begun to do so in significant numbers. In 2007 one of bin Laden's most prominent Saudi mentors, the preacher and scholar Salman al-Odah, wrote an open letter criticizing him for "fostering a culture of suicide bombings that has caused bloodshed and suffering, and brought ruin to entire Muslim communities and families." That same year Abdulaziz al ash-Sheikh, the grand mufti of Saudi Arabia, issued a *fatwa* prohibiting Saudis from engaging in jihad abroad and accused both bin Laden and Arab regimes of "transforming our youth into walking bombs to accomplish their own political and military aims." One of al-Qaeda's own top theorists, Abdul-Aziz el-Sherif, renounced its extremism, including the killing of civilians and the choosing of targets based on religion and nationality. Sherif—a longtime associate of Zawahiri who crafted what became known as al-Qaeda's guide to jihad—has called on militants to desist from terrorism, and authored a rebuttal of his former cohorts.

Al-Azhar University in Cairo, the oldest and most prestigious school of Islamic learning, now routinely condemns jihadism. The Darul Uloom Deoband movement in India, home to the original radicalism that influenced al-Qaeda, has inveighed against suicide bombing since 2008. None of these groups or people have become pro-American or liberal, but they have become anti-jihadist.

This might seem like an esoteric debate. But consider: the most important moderates to denounce militants have been the families of radicals. In the case of both the five young

American Muslims from Virginia arrested in Pakistan last year and Christmas bomber Umar Farouk Abdulmutallab, parents were the ones to report their worries about their own children to the U.S. government—an act so stunning that it requires far more examination, and praise, than it has gotten. This is where soft power becomes critical. Were the fathers of these boys convinced that the United States would torture, maim, and execute their children without any sense of justice, they would not have come forward. I doubt that any Chechen father has turned his child over to Vladimir Putin's regime.

The data on public opinion in the Muslim world are now overwhelming. London School of Economics professor Fawaz Gerges has analyzed polls from dozens of Muslim countries over the past few years. He notes that in a range of places—Jordan, Pakistan, Indonesia, Lebanon, and Bangladesh—there have been substantial declines in the number of people who say suicide bombing and other forms of violence against civilian targets can be justified to defend Islam. Wide majorities say such attacks are, at most, rarely acceptable.

The shift has been especially dramatic in Jordan, where only 12 percent of Jordanians view suicide attacks as "often or sometimes justified" (down from 57 percent in 2005). In Indonesia, 85 percent of respondents agree that terrorist attacks are "rarely/never justified" (in 2002, by contrast, only 70 percent opposed such attacks). In Pakistan, that figure is 90 percent, up from 43 percent in 2002. Gerges points out that, by comparison, only 46 percent of Americans say that "bombing and other attacks intentionally aimed at civilians" are "never justified," while 24 percent believe these attacks are "often or sometimes justified."

This shift does not reflect a turn away from religiosity or even from a backward conception of Islam. That ideological struggle persists and will take decades, not years, to resolve itself. But the battle against jihadism has fared much better, much sooner, than anyone could have imagined.

The exceptions to this picture readily spring to mind—Afghanistan, Pakistan, Yemen. But consider the conditions in those countries. In Afghanistan, jihadist ideology has wrapped itself around a genuine ethnic struggle in which Pashtuns feel that they are being dispossessed by rival groups. In Pakistan, the regime is still where Saudi Arabia was in 2003 and 2004: slowly coming to realize that the extremism it had fostered has now become a threat to its own survival. In Yemen, the state simply lacks the basic capacity to fight back. So the rule might simply be that in those places where a government lacks the desire, will, or capacity to fight jihadism, al-Qaeda can continue to thrive.

But the nature of the enemy is now quite different. It is not a movement capable of winning over the Arab street. Its political appeal does not make rulers tremble. The video messages of bin Laden and Zawahiri once unsettled moderate regimes. Now they are mostly dismissed as almost comical attempts to find popular causes to latch onto. (After the financial crash, bin Laden tried his hand at bashing greedy bankers.)

This is not an argument to relax our efforts to hunt down militants. Al-Qaeda remains a group of relentless, ruthless killers who are trying to recruit other fanatics to carry out hideous attacks that would do terrible damage to civilized society. But the group's aura is gone, its political influence limited. Its few remaining fighters are spread thinly throughout the world and face hostile environments almost everywhere.

America is no longer engaged in a civilizational struggle throughout the Muslim world, but a military and intelligence campaign in a set of discrete places. Now, that latter struggle might well require politics, diplomacy, and development assistance—in the manner that good foreign policy always does (Petraeus calls this a "whole-of-government strategy"). We have allies; we need to support them. But the target is only a handful of extremist organizations that have found a small group of fanatics to carry out their plans. To put it another way, even if the United States pursues a broad and successful effort at nation building in Afghanistan and Yemen, does anyone really think that will deter the next Nigerian misfit—or fanatic from Detroit—from getting on a plane with chemicals in his underwear? Such people cannot be won over. They cannot be reasoned with; they can only be captured or killed.

The enemy is not vast; the swamp is being drained. Al-Qaeda has already lost in the realm of ideology. What remains is the battle to defeat it in the nooks, crannies, and crevices of the real world.

# The Next Asian Miracle

**Democracies are peaceful, representative—and terrible at boosting an economy. Or at least that's the conventional wisdom in Asia, where for years growth in India's sprawling democracy has been humbled by China's efficient, state-led boom. But India's newfound economic success flips that notion on its head. Could it be that democracy is good for growth after all? If so, China better watch its back.**

YASHENG HUANG

Consider the experiences of the following two Asian countries. In 1990, Country A had a per capita GDP of $317; Country B's stood at $461. By 2006, Country A, though 31 percent poorer than Country B only 16 years earlier, had caught up: It enjoyed a per capita GDP of $634, compared with Country B's $635. So, if you had to guess, which of these two Asian countries would you assume is a democracy?

You might be tempted to conclude that the better-performing country is authoritarian China and the laggard is democratic India. In reality, the faster-growing country is India, and the laggard is the occasionally autocratic Pakistan. This fact certainly belies the commonly held notion that—especially among Asian countries—authoritarian states have an advantage in growing an economy compared with their democratic counterparts, who are forced to reckon with such pesky trappings as labor standards and political compromises.

But surely, the familiar China-India comparison would support an authoritarian edge, right? The conclusion seems so obvious: China is authoritarian, and it has grown faster; India is democratic, and it has grown more slowly. For years, Indians have defended their democracy with a sheepish apology—"Yes, our growth rate is terrible, but low growth rates are an acceptable price to pay to govern a democracy as large and as diverse as India."

There is no need to apologize now. India has ended the infamous 2 to 3 percent annual "Hindu rate" of growth and begun its own economic takeoff. Recent Indian success is not only impressive in terms of its speed—growing at the "East Asian rate" of 8 to 9 percent a year—but also in terms of its depth and breadth. The Indian miracle is no longer confined to the much vaunted information-technology sector; its manufacturing is taking off. Even the historically lackluster agricultural sector is beginning to grow.

So where does this leave the "authoritarian edge" that China's economy has supposedly enjoyed for years? The emerging Indian miracle should debunk—hopefully permanently—the entirely specious notion that democracy is bad for growth. And the emerging Indian miracle holds substantial implications for China's political future. As Chinese political elites mark the 30th anniversary of economic reforms this year, they should reflect on the Indian experience deeply and absorb the real reason behind their own miracle.

The idea that there is a trade-off between economics and politics is ingrained in the minds of many policymakers and business executives in Asia, as well as the West. But that idea has never been systematically proven. If India, with its noisy, chaotic, and lumbering political arrangements, can grow, then no other poor country must face a Faustian choice between growth and democracy. A deeper look at the two countries shows that they have succeeded and failed at different times for remarkably similar reasons. Their economies performed when their politics turned liberal; their performances faltered when their politics slid backward. Now, as many poor countries grapple with similar political and economic choices, we must understand this dynamic. It is high time to get the China-India story right.

**If India can grow, then no other poor country must face a Faustian choice between growth and democracy.**

## India's Untold History

That story doesn't begin in 2008. It's a horse race that goes back decades, and one that tells us much about the relationship between democracy and growth, governance and prosperity. From an economic perspective, it is not the static state of a political system that matters, but how it has evolved. The growth

India enjoys today sped up in the 1990s as the country privatized TV stations, introduced political decentralization, and improved governance. And contrary to the conventional wisdom, India stagnated historically not because it was a democracy, but because, in the 1970s and 1980s, it was less democratic than it appeared. To understand just what is happening in India's economy today—and how it relates to the country's political system—we must travel as far back as the 1950s.

Many scholars blame India's first prime minister, Jawaharlal Nehru, for adopting a development strategy that caused India to stagnate from 1950 to 1990. But this view is unfair to Nehru, and it shifts the blame from the real culprit—Indira Gandhi, Nehru's daughter and prime minister during much of the period from 1966 to 1984. Nehru's commanding-heights approach was the reigning ideology in many developing countries, some of which, like South Korea, were quite successful. The issue is not how harmful Nehru's economic policies were, but why India intensified and persisted in this model when it was clearly not working. To answer this question we have to understand the lasting damage that Indira Gandhi inflicted on Indian democracy.

Patronage became her electoral strategy as she undermined a vital institution in a functioning democracy—the party system. Gandhi weakened the Congress Party, once a proud catalyst of the independence movement, by sidestepping many of its well-established procedures, reducing its grass-roots reach in the states, and appointing party officials rather than allowing rank-and-file members to elect them. The shriveling of the Congress Party meant that Gandhi had to use other means to get reelected: crushing political opposition, pandering to special interests, or offering political handouts.

Or cancellations of elections altogether. Indira Gandhi imposed emergency rule in June 1975 and cancelled the general election scheduled for the following year. It was no isolated event. As early as 1970, she postponed or cancelled Congress Party elections. In addition, she moved very far to replace federalism with her own centralized rule. One telling statistic, as shown by political scientists Amal Ray and John Kincaid, is that between 1966 and 1976 the Gandhi government invoked Article 356 of the constitution—which empowers the federal government to take over the functions of state governments in emergency situations—36 times. The government of Nehru and his successor (1950–65) resorted to this measure only nine times. From 1980 to 1984, she invoked this power an additional 13 times. The misuse of the extraordinary power vested in the executive damaged an important institution of Indian democracy.

The cumulative effect of Gandhi's actions is that the Indian political system, though still retaining some essential features of a democracy, became unaccountable, corrupt, and unhinged from the normal bench marks voters use to assess their leaders. In a functioning democracy, voters punish those politicians who fail to deliver at the ballot box. Not in India. Both the 1967 and 1971 reelections of the Congress Party followed a decline of per capita GDP the year before. It was not democracy that failed India; it was India that failed democracy.

The economic consequences of this period of illiberalism were long lasting. Because Gandhi's political fortunes depended on patronage, she felt no compulsion to invest in real drivers of economic growth—education and health. The ratio of teachers to primary-school students throughout the long Gandhi years stubbornly hovered around 2 percent. After her rule, in 1985, only 18 percent of Indian children were immunized against diphtheria, pertussis, and tetanus (DPT), and only 1 percent were immunized against measles. Even today, India is still paying for her neglect. The low level of human capital remains the single largest obstacle to that country's developmental prospects.

The good news is that India is shedding this harmful legacy. As Indian politics became more open and accountable, the post-Gandhi governments began to put welfare of the people at the top of the policy agenda. For example, the adult literacy rate increased from 49 percent in 1990 to 61 percent in 2006. In due time, these social investments will translate into real dividends.

## China's Great Reversal

The story of China's rise seems, on the surface, quite different. A communist and closed regime undertakes an efficient, massive, and rapid embrace of the global economy—and sends its country into overdrive. It appears to be a far cry from the common understanding that democracy promotes growth because it imposes constraints on rulers and reassures private entrepreneurs of the safety of their assets and fruits of their labor. The idea that China grew because of its one-party rule stems from a mistaken focus on a single snapshot in time at the expense of an understanding of shifting trends. China did not take off because it was authoritarian. Rather, it took off because the liberal political reforms of the 1980s made the country less authoritarian. Like India, when China reversed its political reforms and saw governance worsen in the 1990s, citizens' well-being declined. Household income growth slowed, especially in the rural areas; inequality rose to an alarming level; and the gains of economic growth accruing to ordinary people fell sharply. China even underperformed in its traditional areas of strength: education and health. Adult illiteracy rose. Immunizations fell. The country's GDP might have been booming, but it was also hazardous to your health.

The real Chinese miracle began back in the 1980s—when Chinese politics was most liberal. Personal income growth outpaced GDP growth; the labor share of GDP was rising; and income distribution initially improved. China accomplished far more in poverty reduction in the 1980s without any of the factors (such as foreign direct investment) now viewed as essential elements of the China model. In four short years (1980–84), China lifted more of its rural population out of poverty than in the 15 years from 1990 to 2005 combined. If India became less democratic under Indira Gandhi, China became less authoritarian under the troika rule of Deng Xiaoping, Hu Yaobang, and Zhao Ziyang in the 1980s. Therein lies the key insight into China's economic takeoff.

One of the first acts by the reformist leaders was to signal an improving environment for private property. In marked contrast to today's massive land grabs, the Chinese government in 1979 returned confiscated bank deposits, bonds, gold, and private homes to those former "capitalists" the regime had persecuted. The number of people affected by this policy was not large, around 700,000. But symbolism mattered for a country still reeling from the Cultural Revolution. There were also other symbolic acts designed to elicit the confidence of private entrepreneurs in the new political environment of a post-Mao era. In 1979, two vice premiers visited and personally congratulated an entrepreneur who was granted the first license to operate a private restaurant in Beijing. As early as 1981, a Communist Party document signaled a willingness to recruit its members from the private sector, a well-publicized gesture. The widely held view that the party only began to recruit capitalists late in the Jiang Zemin era is simply incorrect.

The reformist leaders also began to embark on meaningful political changes. As scholar Minxin Pei has noted, every single important political reform—such as the mandatory retirement of government officials, the strengthening of the National People's Congress, legal reforms, experiments in rural selfgovernment, and loosening control of civil society groups—was instituted in the 1980s. The Chinese media became freer in the early reform era. The timing here is critical. This "directional liberalism" of China's politics either preceded or accompanied China's economic growth. It was not a result of economic success.

This liberalism mattered the most for growth in rural China, where the majority of Chinese citizens live. Private access to capital eased in the 1980s. Private entrepreneurship and even some privatization became widespread, especially in poorer parts of the country that needed them most. Of 12 million rural businesses classified as township and village enterprises, 10 million were completely private. The change in direction of China's politics was sufficiently credible to encourage millions of entrepreneurs to go into business for themselves.

But in the 1990s, the Chinese state completely reversed the gradualist political reforms that the leadership began in the 1980s. This assessment comes from a well-placed insider, Wu Min, a professor at the Party School under the Shanxi Provincial Party Committee. In a 2007 article, Wu revealed that the political reform program adopted at the 13th Party Congress in 1987 implemented some substantial changes. The congress abolished the party committees in many government agencies and explicitly delineated the functions of the party and the state. After 1989, there was no progress on the political reform front, especially in reducing and streamlining the power of the Communist Party.

The political reforms of the 1980s were designed to enhance the accountability of the government by creating some checks and balances over the power of the party and by fostering intraparty democracy. Wu cites one specific measure in the 1990s to derail the reforms of the 1980s. According to Wu, in the 1990s China instituted explicit provisions prohibiting the National People's Congress (NPC) from conducting evaluations of officials in the executive branch and the courts. Wu comments, "This is obviously a step backward."

Just how far did this step set back China? How about nearly 30 years? Consider China's track record when it comes to industrial fatalities. In 1979, in the aftermath of the capsizing of an oil rig that resulted in 72 deaths, the NPC held hearings at which officials in the Ministry of Petroleum Industry were called to testify. The minister was determined to have been negligent and was sacked. But since the mid-1990s, there have been hundreds of explosions and industrial accidents in China's coal mines. Thousands of people have lost their lives. No hearings have been held, and not a single official at the rank of minister or provincial governor has ever been held explicitly responsible.

Like Indira Gandhi in the 1970s and 1980s, the Chinese state greatly centralized its economic management in the 1990s. It was another reversal from the promising reforms of a decade earlier, the gist of which was delegating decision-making to those best informed about local situations. In 1994, the central government increased substantially the shares of tax revenues going to the central coffers and abolished one of the most innovative Chinese reforms—fiscal federalism. A less well-known development in the 1990s was that the Chinese state centralized the budgetary and other functions of villages. So, even though people were voting in village elections, the officials elected exercised very little power.

The economic consequences of these reversals were substantial. The 1990s saw depressed growth in household incomes relative to GDP, which means that the average Chinese person was losing ground. The employee share of GDP—the income going to the general population—peaked in 1990, at 53.5 percent. By 2002, it had declined to 45 percent of GDP. At 45 percent, the Chinese economy in 2002 was benefiting its people less than it was in 1978, when its employee share of GDP stood at 48 percent. Similarly threatening for the poorest Chinese is a development that has garnered almost no attention: The country is backsliding on literacy. On April 2, 2007, the state-run China Daily published an article with an unusually frank title, "The ghost of illiteracy returns to haunt the country." It reported that the number of illiterate Chinese adults increased by 30 million between 2000 and 2005. In 2005, there were 115.7 million illiterate Chinese adults, compared with 85 million in 2000. The roots of the problem began in the 1990s. Consider how literacy is defined—the ability to identify 1,500 Chinese characters by the age of 7 to 9. An adult reaching into the illiterate group by 2005 received all his or her primary education in the mid-1990s. In addition, immunization rates against DPT and measles—rising throughout the 1980s—began to decline in the 1990s. In time, China will pay dearly for these colossal failures.

In the 1990s, the nature of China's growth was fundamentally altered. In the 1980s, growth was broad-based and positive for the poor; since then, the percentage of people benefiting from growth has narrowed, and social performance has deteriorated. The impact of this great reversal is strongest in the silent and less visible rural areas of China.

## The Way to Reform

Of course, understanding the origins of India's and China's separate paths to development is just half the story. What's more telling is how these two countries enacted and reacted to reforms—and what that says about the relationship between political liberalization and economic growth.

After the Soviet collapse, Chinese political elites converged on the view that China avoided the same fate because China had not reformed its politics. The truth is precisely the opposite. The single most important reason why China survived the 1989 Tiananmen crisis is because its rural population was content. In the 1980s, rural China experienced the most radical economic and political reforms. It was reform that saved the Chinese Communist Party.

Political reforms contributed to Indian growth as well. Take the media. During the long Gandhi era, though the print media were free, the government controlled the TV stations—a more important source of information for a country with high illiteracy. The privatization of the stations in the 1990s not only enriched the quality of entertainment for the average Indian but also added transparency to Indian politics. Many corruption and bribery scandals were first exposed on TV, the effects of the exposures being magnified by the vivid images of politicians receiving cash in shady hotel rooms. That is the right way to fight corruption.

As China tightened its political grip on rural affairs in the wake of the Soviet collapse, India moved in the opposite direction. In 1992, India amended its constitution to strengthen a reform with long and deep implications—village self-government. This *panchayati raj* phenomenon promises to transform an urban-centered, elitist system to one that is Tocquevillian in character and is empowering women along the way. The auxiliary institutions of Indian democracy, so atrophied under Indira Gandhi, have been renewed. World Bank indicators show a notable improvement in key areas of Indian governance during the period of high growth since the mid-1990s.

In fact, India leads China in a number of important areas of reform. Throughout the 1990s, India reduced state controls on the banking sector, allowed the entry of private domestic and foreign banks, and abolished government interference in setting the equity pricing of initial public offerings on the stock exchange. China is nowhere near India in terms of pace and depth of financial reforms.

Would democracy galvanize opposition to reforms? Many progressive reformers in China hold this view, but this is a hypothesis long on fear and short on facts. Consider the following fact about Indian politics: All the reforms have been carried out by a coalition of multiple parties rather than by a single majority ruling party. This is true of the Congress Party in the early 1990s, the Bharatiya Janata Party between 1998 and 2004, and the Congress Party today.

What about building infrastructure? Even liberals in India sometimes wish for a dose of authoritarianism here. A powerful government in China is able to sidestep all the political and legal complications and build world-class railroads, highways, water systems, and other networks overnight. Surely, authoritarianism has an edge when it comes to public works projects. But no. Building infrastructure has followed—not preceded—Chinese growth. In 1988, China had roughly 91 miles of expressway.

That did not begin to change until the late 1990s, when the country poured massive resources into infrastructure. Only in the past eight to 10 years could the country claim to have infrastructure rivaling that of developed countries.

Many foreign investors think that infrastructure explains the different pace of growth between China and India. No such evidence exists. In the 1980s, India started with some infrastructural advantages over China. It had a longer system of railways, for example. Although we can debate today which country is performing better, there is no doubt that China outperformed India in the 1980s. It was reforms and social investments that propelled Chinese growth, not fancy airports and skyscrapers.

One justification for building those massive infrastructure networks is to attract FDI. For years, Western economists and business analysts have chided India for not following China's lead in this area. But that criticism puts the cart before the horse. Like infrastructure, FDI follows GDP growth rather than precedes it. In the 1980s, China received very little FDI, and yet the country grew faster and more virtuously than its later growth. FDI is a result of growth, and the first order of the policy business is how to grow the economy—not how to attract FDI. As long as India can grow in the 8 to 9 percent range, even without superior infrastructure, it can easily triple or even quadruple its FDI inflows from its current level of $7 billion a year. Growth can self-finance the infrastructure truly needed for business and economic development.

China has built critical networks, such as power stations and transportation links, but since the mid-1990s, unconstrained by public voice, media scrutiny, and private land rights, Chinese leaders have wasted massive resources on urban skyscrapers that have no economic benefits. Many of them are government buildings and are extraordinarily expensive, costing more than $100 million in some cases. And the financial costs of these projects do not even begin to approach their opportunity costs—those investments in education and health China has failed to make. That a country constructed nearly 3,000 skyscrapers in Shanghai and added 30 million illiterate Chinese during the same decade is truly remarkable.

The economic dividends of political reform don't appear overnight, which skews the timeline and confuses the cause. But by using nearly every metric, political liberalization has spurred rather than stunted growth in both China and India.

## That China built nearly 3,000 skyscrapers and added 30 million illiterate people in the same decade is remarkable.

After a long hiatus, China's leadership has rhetorically returned to a vision of the 1980s—that political reforms should be a priority. Rural China has begun to recover from the neglect of the 1990s, and rural income has grown the fastest since 1989. All this is good news. But consolidating these achievements will require a more substantial undoing of the illiberal policies of the 1990s. How India managed to emerge from its own long shadow of illiberalism offers some valuable lessons. In the past, China taught India the importance of social investments and economic opening. It is time for today's China to take a page from India—and from the China of the 1980s—that political reforms are not antithetical to growth. They are the keys to a healthier and more sustainable foundation for the future.

**PROFESSOR YASHENG HUANG,** of the Sloan School of Management at MIT, is author of *Capitalism with Chinese Characteristics* (New York: Cambridge University Press, 2008). He is writing a book on how politics shapes business, education, and entrepreneurship in China and India.

# Bad Guys Matter

**They put the failed in failed states.**

PAUL COLLIER

There are bad leaders, good leaders, and great leaders. Let's start with one very bad one.

When I met Sani Abacha in 1997, the Nigerian dictator struck me as uninterested in matters economic, his eyes glazing over as I sketched Nigeria's untapped opportunities. But I later realized how badly I had misjudged him: In his short five years in office, he reportedly succeeded in amassing some $4 billion in private bank accounts overseas. It was only his country's economy that bored him. Good thing for Nigeria that he passed away when he did, in 1998. During the subsequent oil boom, more scrupulous leaders enabled Nigeria to accumulate $70 billion in reserves. Just think how much of that Abacha would have squirreled away.

Leaders matter, for better or, more likely, for worse. Sure, some of Asia's "benign" autocrats have turned their ambitions to building strong national economies. But not in Africa and many of the other countries that I call the bottom billion—quite a number of which crowd the upper reaches of the Failed States Index. There, the most common form of autocracy is anything but benign. These leaders not only neglect to build the economy, they actively avoid doing so. The best-known instance is President Mobutu Sese Seko's order to "build no roads" in the vast country then known as Zaire. Why? Because without roads, it was harder for opponents to organize a rebellion against him.

The world, unfortunately, has many Mobutus. When I asked Kenya's autocratic president, Daniel arap Moi, why he had banned food imports from neighboring Uganda, his answer so tortured common sense that one of his aides had to take me aside and tell me the real story: Some of the president's businessman friends had stocks of food warehoused and wanted prices to rise. In Angola, I once asked a finance minister why, in defiance of economic logic, his country operated multiple exchange rates. The president used the dual system to siphon off money, he whispered. Until last year, Zimbabwe's Robert Mugabe did the same.

Bad guys matter, and when they rule, they make weak states weaker. And the countless anecdotes are backed up by numbers: In a celebrated study, economists Benjamin Jones and Benjamin Olken looked at whether the death of a country's leader altered economic growth. It did, sometimes for better and sometimes for worse. Recently, an Oxford colleague, Anke Hoeffler, and I sifted through their results again, distinguishing this time between democrats and autocrats. We found that in democracies, changing the leader does not change growth—all leaders are disciplined to perform tolerably. But in autocracies, the growth rates are as unpredictably varied as the leaders' personalities. Here lies the difference between good leaders and great ones: Good leaders put right the policy catastrophes of bad leaders; great leaders, like the men who shaped the U.S. Constitution, build the democratic checks and balances that make good leaders redundant.

So much for the good and the great—now back to the bad. Like Tolstoy's unhappy families, leaders can be bad in many different ways, and the extremes of their badness matter out of all proportion to their frequency in the population. At the extreme of greed are kleptocrats. At the extreme of insensitivity to the pain of others are psychopaths. At the extreme of preference for getting their own way are tyrants. Although people with such characteristics are rare, they have a knack for getting themselves into precisely those positions where their traits are most damaging. Kleptocrats do not aspire to become monks; they want to be bankers. Psychopaths do not dream of being nurses; they strive to be soldiers. Tyrants do not plead to be social workers; they scheme to become politicians.

At the core of all successful societies are procedures for blocking the advancement of such men. The safety mechanisms are often rather mundane. Britain, for example, transformed the 19th-century civil service from corruption to efficiency by replacing promotion by patronage with competitive examinations.

The weakest states utterly lack such defenses. There, as extremely bad people of all three varieties infiltrate a wide range of key positions, countries are brought to their knees—and not just by politicians. Banks are routinely run by thieves who bankrupt them by "lending" the deposits to themselves. Rebel armies are led not by liberators, but by people more suited for a mental hospital. Take Liberian commander Prince

# The Worst of the Worst
# Bad Dude Dictators and General Coconut Heads

A continent away from Kyrgyzstan, Africans like myself cheered this spring as a coalition of opposition groups ousted the country's dictator, President Kurmanbek Bakiyev. "One coconut down, 39 more to harvest!" we shouted. There are at least 40 dictators around the world today, and approximately 1.9 billion people live under the grip of the 23 autocrats on this list alone. There are plenty of coconuts to go around.

The cost of all that despotism has been stultifying. Millions of lives have been lost, economies have collapsed, and whole states have failed under brutal repression. And what has made it worse is that the world is in denial. The end of the Cold War was also supposed to be the "End of History"—when democracy swept the world and repression went the way of the dinosaurs. Instead, Freedom House reports that only 60 percent of the world's countries are democratic—far more than the 28 percent in 1950, but still not much more than a majority. And many of those aren't real democracies at all, ruled instead by despots in disguise while the world takes their freedom for granted. As for the rest, they're just left to languish.

Although all dictators are bad in their own way, there's one insidious aspect of despotism that is most infuriating and galling to me: the disturbing frequency with which many despots, as in Kyrgyzstan, began their careers as erstwhile "freedom fighters" who were supposed to have liberated their people. Back in 2005, Bakiyev rode the crest of the so-called Tulip Revolution to oust the previous dictator. So familiar are Africans with this phenomenon that we have another saying: "We struggle very hard to remove one cockroach from power, and the next rat comes to do the same thing. Haba!" Darn!

I call these revolutionaries-turned-tyrants "crocodile liberators," joining the ranks of other fine specimens: the Swiss bank socialists who force the people to pay for economic losses while stashing personal gains abroad, the quack revolutionaries who betray the ideals that brought them to power, and the briefcase bandits who simply pillage and steal. Here's my list of the world's worst dictators. I have ranked them based on ignoble qualities of perfidy, cultural betrayal, and economic devastation. If this account of their evils makes you cringe, just imagine living under their rule.

## 1. Kim Jong Il of North Korea

A personality-cult-cultivating isolationist with a taste for fine French cognac, Kim has pauperized his people, allowed famine to run rampant, and thrown hundreds of thousands in prison camps (where as many as 200,000 languish today)—all while spending his country's precious few resources on a nuclear program.
  Years in Power: 16

## 2. Robert Mugabe of Zimbabwe

A liberation "hero" in the struggle for independence who has since transformed himself into a murderous despot, Mugabe has arrested and tortured the opposition, squeezed his economy into astounding negative growth and billion-percent inflation, and funneled off a juicy cut for himself using currency manipulation and offshore accounts.
  Years in Power: 30

## 3. Than Shwe of Burma

A heartless military coconut head whose sole consuming preoccupation is power, Shwe has decimated the opposition with arrests and detentions, denied humanitarian aid to his people after 2008's devastating Cyclone Nargis, and thrived off a black market economy of natural gas exports. This vainglorious general bubbling with swagger sports a uniform festooned with self-awarded medals, but he is too cowardly to face an honest ballot box.
  Years in Power: 18

## 4. Omar Hassan Al-Bashir of Sudan

A megalomaniac zealot who has quashed all opposition, Bashir is responsible for the deaths of millions of Sudanese and has been indicted by the International Criminal Court for war crimes. Bashir's Arab militias, the *janjaweed*, may have halted their massacres in Darfur, but they continue to traffic black Sudanese as slaves (Bashir himself has been accused of having had several at one point).
  Years in Power: 21

## 5. Gurbanguly Berdimuhamedov of Turkmenistan

Succeeding the eccentric tyrant Saparmurat Niyazov (who even renamed the months of the year after himself and his family), this obscure dentist has kept on keeping on with his late predecessor's repressive policies, explaining that, after all, he bears an "uncanny resemblance to Niyazov."
  Years in Power: 4

## 6. Isaias Afwerki of Eritrea

A crocodile liberator, Afwerki has turned his country into a national prison in which independent media are shut down, elections are categorically rejected, indefinite military service is mandatory, and the government would rather support Somali militants than its own people.
  Years in Power: 17

## 7. Islam Karimov of Uzbekistan

A ruthless thug ruling since Soviet times, Karimov has banned opposition parties, tossed as many as 6,500 political prisoners into jail, and labels anyone who challenges him an "Islamic terrorist." What does he do with "terrorists" once they are in his hands? Torture them: Karimov's regime earned notoriety for boiling two people alive and torturing many others. Outside the prisons, the president's troops are equally indiscriminate, massacring hundreds of peaceful

*(continued)*

*(continued)*

demonstrators in 2005 after a minor uprising in the city of Andijan.

Years in Power: 20

## 8. Mahmoud Ahmadinejad of Iran

Inflammatory, obstinate, and a traitor to the liberation philosophy of the Islamic Revolution, Ahmadinejad has pursued a nuclear program in defiance of international law and the West. Responsible for countless injustices during his five years in Power, the president's latest egregious offense was leading his paramilitary goons, the Basij, to violently repress protesters after June 2009's disputed presidential election, which many believe he firmly lost.

Years in Power: 5

## 9. Meles Zenawi of Ethiopia

Worse than the former Marxist dictator he ousted nearly two decades ago, Zenawi has clamped down on the opposition, stifled all dissent, and rigged elections. Like a true Marxist revolutionary, Zenawi has stashed millions in foreign banks and acquired mansions in Maryland and London in his wife's name, according to the opposition—even as his barbaric regime collects a whopping $1 billion in foreign aid each year.

Years in Power: 19

## 10. Hu Jintao of China

A chameleon despot who beguiles foreign investors with a smile and a bow, but ferociously crushes political dissent with brutal abandon, Hu has an iron grip on Tibet and is now seeking what can only be described as new colonies in Africa from which to extract the natural resources his growing economy craves.

Years in Power: 7

## 11. Muammar Al-Qaddafi of Libya

An eccentric egoist infamous for his indecipherably flamboyant speeches and equally erratic politics, Qaddafi runs a police state based on his version of Mao's Red Book—the Green Book—which includes a solution to "the Problem of Democracy." Repressive at home, Qaddafi masquerades as Africa's king of kings abroad (the African Union had to politely insist that he step down as its rotating head).

Years in Power: 41

## 12. Bashar Al-Assad of Syria

A pretentious despot trying to fit into his father's shoes (they're too big for him), Assad has squandered billions on foreign misadventures in such places as Lebanon and Iraq while neglecting the needs of the Syrian people. His extensive security apparatus ensures that the population doesn't complain.

Years in Power: 10

## 13. Idriss Déby of Chad

Having led a rebel insurgency against a former dictator, Déby today faces a similar challenge—from one of his own former cabinet officials, among others. To repel would-be coup leaders, Déby has drained social spending accounts to equip the military, co-opted opposition-leader foes, and is now building a moat around the capital, N'Djamena.

Years in Power: 20

## 14. Teodoro Obiang Nguema Mbasogo of Equatorial Guinea

Obiang and his family literally own the economy, having reportedly amassed a fortune exceeding $600 million while the masses are left in desperate poverty. Equatorial Guinea's extraordinary oil wealth puts its GDP per capita on par with many European states—if only it were evenly shared. Instead, revenues remain a "state secret."

Years in Power: 31

## 15. Hosni Mubarak of Egypt

A senile and paranoid autocrat whose sole preoccupation is self-perpetuation in office, Mubarak is suspicious of even his own shadow. He keeps a 30-year-old emergency law in place to squelch any opposition activity and has groomed his son, Gamal, to succeed him. (No wonder only 23 percent of Egyptians bothered to vote in the 2005 presidential election.)

Years in Power: 29

## 16. Yahya Jammeh of Gambia

This eccentric military buffoon has vowed to rule for 40 years and claims to have discovered the cure for HIV/AIDS. (Jammeh also claims he has mystic powers and will turn Gambia into an oil-producing country; no luck yet.) A narcissist at heart, the dictator insists on being addressed as His Excellency Sheikh Professor Alhaji Dr. Yahya Abdul-Azziz Jemus Junkung Jammeh.

Years in Power: 16

## 17. Hugo Chávez of Venezuela

The quack leader of the Bolivarian Revolution, Chávez promotes a doctrine of participatory democracy in which he is the sole participant, having jailed opposition leaders, extended term limits indefinitely, and closed independent media.

Years in Power: 11

## 18. Blaise Compaoré of Burkina Faso

A tin-pot despot with no vision and no agenda, save self-perpetuation in power by liquidating opponents and stifling dissent, Compaoré has lived up to the low standards of his own rise to power, after murdering his predecessor, Thomas Sankara, in a 1987 coup.

Years in Power: 23

## 19. Yoweri Museveni of Uganda

After leading a rebel insurgency that took over Uganda in 1986, Museveni declared: "No African head of state should be in power for more than 10 years." But 24 years later, he is still here, winning one "coconut election" after another in which other political parties are technically legal but a political rally of more than a handful of people is not.

Years in Power: 24

## 20. Paul Kagame of Rwanda

A liberator who saved the Tutsis from complete extermination in 1994, Kagame now practices the same ethnic apartheid he sought to end. His Rwandan Patriotic Front dominates all levers of power: the security forces, the civil service, the judiciary, banks, universities, and state-owned corporations. Those who challenge the president are accused of being a hatemonger or divisionist and arrested.

Years in Power: 10

## 21. Raúl Castro of Cuba

Afflicted with intellectual astigmatism, the second brother Castro is pitifully unaware that the revolution he leads is obsolete, an abysmal failure, and totally irrelevant to the aspirations of the Cuban people. He blames the failure of the revolution on foreign conspiracies—which he then uses to justify even more brutal clampdowns.

Years in Power: 2

## 22. Aleksandr Lukashenko of Belarus

An autocrat and former collective farm chairman, Lukashenko maintains an iron grip on his country, monitoring opposition movements with a secret police distastefully called the KGB. His brutal style of governance has earned him the title "Europe's last dictator"; he even gave safe haven to Kyrgyzstan's toppled leader when that country rose up this spring.

Years in Power: 16

## 23. Paul Biya of Cameroon

A suave bandit who has reportedly amassed a personal fortune of more than $200 million and the mansions to go with it, Biya has co-opted the opposition into complete submission. Not that he's worried about elections; he has rigged the term limit laws twice to make sure the party doesn't end anytime soon.

Years in Power: 28

—George B. N. Ayittey

Johnson, who filmed himself calmly sipping a beer while his captive, President Samuel Doe, was tortured to death.

But among the many varieties of badness, political tyranny is surely the most destructive. Politically ambitious crooks do not just fritter away the money they make from corruption; they invest it in future power. And that should frighten us most of all.

PAUL COLLIER is professor of economics at Oxford University and author of the recently published *The Plundered Planet.*Article 46. Why Bad Guys Matter, GEORGE B. N. AYITTEY, a native of Ghana, is president of the Free Africa Foundation in Washington. His book, *The March of Freedom: Defeating Dictators in Africa and Around the World,* will be published in 2011.

# A User's Guide to the Century

Jeffrey D. Sachs

The "new world order" of the twenty-first century holds the promise of shared prosperity . . . and also the risk of global conflict. This is the paradox of our time. The scale of human society—in population, level of economic production and resource use, and global reach of production networks—gives rise to enormous hopes and equally momentous challenges. Old models of statecraft and economics won't suffice. Solutions to our generation's challenges will require an unprecedented degree of global cooperation, though the need for such cooperation is still poorly perceived and highly contested by political elites and intellectuals in the United States and elsewhere.

Our world is characterized by three dominant patterns: rapid technological diffusion, which creates strong tendencies toward technological and economic convergence among major regions of the world; extensive environmental threats resulting from the unprecedented scale of global economic activity and population; and vast current inequalities of income and power, both between and within countries, resulting from highly diverse patterns of demography, regional endowments of natural resources, and vulnerabilities to natural and societal disruptions. These characteristics hold the possibilities of rapid and equalizing economic growth, but also of regional and global instability and conflict.

The era of modern economic growth is two centuries old. For the first one hundred years, this was a strong *divergence* in economic growth, meaning a widening gap in production and income between the richest regions and the rest of the world. The dramatic divergence of per capita output, industrial production and living standards during the nineteenth century between the North Atlantic (that is, Western Europe and the United States) and the rest of the world was accentuated by several factors. The combination of first-mover industrialization, access to extensive coal deposits, early development of market-based institutions, military dominance resulting from vast industrial power, and then colonial dominance over Africa and Asia all contributed to a century of *economic divergence,* in which the North Atlantic greatly expanded its technological lead (and also military advantage) vis-à-vis the rest of the world. The apogee of "Western" relative dominance was roughly the year 1910. Until the start of World War I, this economic and technological dominance was nearly overpowering.

The period 1910–1950 marked a transition from global economic divergence to economic convergence. Most importantly, of course, was Europe's self-inflicted disaster of two world wars and an intervening Great Depression, which dramatically weakened Europe and proved to be the downfall of the continent's vast overseas empires. Below the surface, longer-term forces of convergence were also stirring. These deeper forces included the global spread of literacy, Western science, the modern technologies of transport and communications, and the political ideas of self-determination and economic development as core national objectives.

Since 1950, we have entered into an era of global convergence, in which much of the non-Western world is gradually catching up, technologically, economically, geopolitically and militarily. The North Atlantic is losing its uniquely dominant position in the world economy. The technological and economic catching-up, most notable of course in Asia, is facilitated by several factors—the spread of national sovereignty following European colonialism; vastly improved transport and communications technologies; the spread of infectious-disease control, mass literacy and public education; the dissemination of global scientific and engineering knowledge; and the broad adoption of a valid "catch-up model" of economic development based on technology imports within a mixed public-private system. The system was modeled heavily on the state-led market development of Japan, the only non-Western country to succeed in achieving modern industrialization during the nineteenth century. Japan's economic development following the Meiji Restoration in 1868 can indeed be viewed as the invention of "catch-up growth."

The modern age of convergence, begun with Japan's rapid rebuilding after World War II, was extended in the 1950s and 1960s by the rise of Korea, Taiwan, Hong Kong and Singapore, all built on an export-led growth model using U.S. and Japanese technologies and institutions. Convergent economic growth then spread through Southeast Asia (notably Indonesia, Malaysia and Thailand) in the 1970s and 1980s, again supported by Japanese and U.S. technologies, and Japanese aid and development concepts. The convergence patterns were greatly expanded with the initiation of rapid market-based growth in China after 1978 (which imitated strategies in East and Southeast Asia) and then India in the 1980s (and especially after market-based reforms initiated in 1991). In the early twenty-first century, both Brazil and Mexico are similarly experiencing rapid technological catch-up.

In economic terms, the share of global income in the North Atlantic is now declining quickly as the emerging economies of Asia, the Middle East and Latin America grow rapidly. This is, of course, especially true when output and income are measured in purchasing-power-adjusted terms, thereby adding weight to the share of the emerging economies. By 2050, Asia will be home to more than half of global production, up from around 20 percent as of 1970. In geopolitical terms, the unipolar world of the North Atlantic is over. China, India, Brazil and other regional powers now fundamentally constrain the actions of the United States and Western Europe. This shift to multipolarity in geopolitics is bound to accelerate in the coming decades.

Modern economic growth did not end humans' dependence on their physical environment, contrary to the false impressions sometimes given by modern urban life. Our food still comes from farms, not from supermarkets and bakeries. Our crops still demand land and water, not simply microwaves and gas grills. Our industrial prowess has been built mainly on fossil fuels (first coal, then oil and natural gas), not merely on cleverness and efficiency. Our food production demands enormous inputs of energy and water, not only high-yield seeds. The bottom line is that the growth of the world economy has meant a roughly commensurate growth in human impacts on the physical world, not an escape from such impacts. These anthropogenic impacts are now so significant, and indeed threatening to the sustainable well-being of humans and other species, that Nobel Laureate Paul Crutzen (a codiscoverer of the human-induced loss of stratospheric ozone) has termed our age the Anthropocene, meaning the geological epoch when human activity dominates or deranges the earth's major biogeophysical fluxes (including the carbon, nitrogen and water cycles, among others).

The world economy is now characterized by 6.7 billion people—roughly ten times more than in 1750—producing output at a rate of roughly $10,000 per person per year in purchasing-power-adjusted prices. The resulting $67 trillion annual output (in approximate terms, as precision here should not be pretended) is at least one hundredfold larger than at the start of the industrial era. The human extent of natural-resource use is unprecedented—indeed utterly unrecognizable—in historical perspective, and is now dangerous to long-term well-being. While the typical economist's lighthearted gloss is that Malthusian resource pessimism was utterly and fully debunked generations ago—overcome by human ingenuity and technical know-how—it is more correct to say that the unprecedented level of global human output has been achieved not by overcoming resource constraints, but by an unprecedented appropriation of the earth's natural resources.

In fact, the current rate of resource use, if technologies remain constant, is literally unsustainable. Current fossil-fuel use would lead to the imminent peak of oil and gas production within years or decades, and of conventional coal deposits within decades or a century or two. We would see dangerous human impacts on the global climate system, and hence regional climates in all parts of the world, through greenhouse-gas emissions. The appropriation of up to half of the earth's photosynthetic potential, at the cost of other species, would occur. There would be massive deforestation and land degradation as a result of the increasing spatial range and the intensification of farming and pasture use; massive appropriation of freshwater resources, through depletion of fossil aquifers, diversion of rivers, melting of glaciers, drainage of wetlands, destruction of mangroves and estuaries, and other processes. And, an introduction of invasive species, pests and pathogens through a variety of human-induced changes.

The mistaken belief that we've overcome "similar" resource constraints in the past is no proof that global society will do it again, or at least do it successfully without massive economic and social upheavals, especially in view of the fact that our earlier "solutions" were rarely based on resource-saving technologies. Indeed, most earlier "solutions" to resource constraints typically involved new ways to "mine" the natural environment, not to conserve it. This time around, human societies will have to shift from resource-using technologies to resource-saving technologies. Some of the needed technologies are already known but often not widely used, while others will still have to be developed, demonstrated and diffused on a global scale.

Human pressures on the earth's ecological systems are bound to increase markedly in the years ahead. The global economy has been growing between 3 and 5 percent per year, meaning the economy will take fourteen to twenty-three years to double. Thus, the intense environmental and resource pressures now occurring will increase markedly and in short order. The catch-up growth of the largest emerging markets—Brazil, China and India, with around 40 percent of the world's population—is based squarely on the adoption and diffusion of resource-intensive technologies, such as coal-fired power plants and standard internal-combustion-engine vehicles.

The age of convergence offers the realistic possibility of ending extreme poverty and narrowing the vast inequalities within and between countries. The catching-up of China and India, for example, is rapidly reducing the national poverty rates in both countries. Other regions will also experience rapid declines in poverty rates. Yet the actual record of poverty reduction and trends in inequality leave major gaps in success. There are many parts of the planet where the numbers, and sometimes even proportions, of people in extreme poverty are rising rather than falling. Even more generally, the gaps between the rich and poor within nations seem to be widening markedly in most parts of the world.

Significant regions of the world—including sub-Saharan Africa, Central Asia, and parts of the Andean and Central American highlands—have experienced increasing poverty during the past generation. These places left behind by global economic growth tend to display some common infirmities. For example: long distances from major global trade routes, landlocked populations, heavy burdens of tropical diseases, great vulnerabilities to natural hazards (such as earthquakes, tropical storms and the like), lack of nonbiomass energy resources, lack of low-cost access to irrigation, difficult topography (e.g., high elevations and steep slopes), widespread illiteracy and a rapid growth of population due to consistently high fertility rates.

These conditions tend to perpetuate extreme poverty, and often lead to a vicious circle in which poverty contributes to further environmental degradation, persistence of high fertility rates, and social conflicts and violence, which in turn perpetuate or intensify the extreme poverty. These vicious circles (or "poverty traps") can be broken, but to succeed often requires external financial and technological assistance. Assistance like building infrastructure raises productivity and thereby controls the interlocking problems of transport costs, disease, illiteracy, vulnerability to hazards and high fertility. Without the external assistance, a continuing downward spiral becomes much more likely. The adverse consequences can then include war, the spread of epidemic diseases, displaced populations and mass illegal migration. On top of this can be the spread of illicit activities (drug trafficking, smuggling, kidnapping and piracy) and continued serious environmental degradation with large-scale poaching, land degradation and rampant deforestation, to name a few.

The global forces of demographic change, economic convergence and global production systems are also apparently contributing to rising inequalities within societies. Technological advances favor educated workers and leave uneducated workers behind. The entry of China and India into the global trading and production system, similarly, has pushed down the relative wages of unskilled workers in all parts of the world. Geography has played a key role, favoring those regions and parts of countries which are most easily incorporated into global production systems and which are well endowed with energy, fertile land, water and climate conducive to food production. Rapid population growth in rural and poverty-stricken regions (sub-Saharan Africa) has dramatically lowered well-being in these places. In general, urban dwellers have done better than rural dwellers in the past twenty years in almost all parts of the world.

Even relatively homogenous societies are facing major challenges of social stability as a result of massive changes in demographic patterns and economic trends across ethnic, linguistic and religious communities. By 2050, roughly half of the U.S. population will be "white, non-Hispanic," down from around 80 percent as of 1950. This trend reflects both the differential fertility rates across different subpopulations as well as the continued rapid in-migration of Hispanics into the United States. Such large demographic changes can potentially create major fissures in society, especially when there have been long histories of intercommunal strife and suspicion.

T he new world order is therefore crisis prone. The existence of rapidly emerging regional powers, including Brazil, China and India, can potentially give rise to conflicts with the United States and Europe.

The combination of rapid technological diffusion and therefore convergent economic growth, coupled with the natural-resource constraints of the Anthropocene, could trigger regional-scale or global-scale tensions and conflicts. China's rapid economic growth could turn into a strenuous, even hot, competition with the United States over increasingly scarce hydrocarbons in the Middle East, Africa and Central Asia. Conflicts over water flow in major and already-contested watersheds (among India, Bangladesh and Pakistan; China and Southeast Asia; Turkey, Israel, Iraq and Jordan; the countries of the Nile basin; and many others) could erupt into regional conflicts. Disagreements over management of the global commons—including ocean fisheries, greenhouse gases, the Arctic's newly accessible resources, species extinctions and much more—could also be grounds for conflict.

The continuation of extreme poverty, and the adverse spillovers from laggard regions, could trigger mass violence. Local conflicts can draw in major powers, which then threaten expanded wars—as in Afghanistan, Somalia and Sudan. When poverty is combined with rapid population growth and major environmental shocks (such as prolonged droughts in the Sahel and the Horn of Africa) there is a distinct likelihood of mass population movements, such as large-scale illegal migrations of populations escaping hunger and destitution. Such movements in the past have contributed to local violence, as in South Africa of late, and even to war, as in Darfur.

These intersecting challenges of our crowded world, multipolarity, unprecedented demographic and environmental stresses, and the growing inequalities both within and between countries, can trigger spirals of conflict and instability—disease, migration, state failure and more—and yet are generally overlooked by the broad public and even by many, if not most, foreign-policy analysts. The instability of the Horn of Africa, the Middle East and Central Asia has been viewed wrongly by many in the U.S. public and foreign-policy community mainly as the battleground over Islamic extremism and fundamentalism, with little reflection on the fact that the extremism and fundamentalism is often secondary to illiteracy, youth unemployment, poverty, indignation, economic hopelessness and hunger, rather than religion per se. The swath of "Islamic" extremist violence across the African Sahel, Horn of Africa, and into the Middle East and Central Asia lies in the world's major dryland region, characterized by massive demographic, environmental and economic crises.

The security institutions—such as ministries of defense—of the major powers are trained to see these crises through a military lens, and to look for military responses, rather than see the underlying demographic, environmental and economic drivers—and the corresponding developmental options to address them. Genuine global security in the next quarter century will depend on the ability of governments to understand the true interconnected nature of these crises, and to master the scientific and technological knowledge needed to find solutions.

I n the United States, I propose a new Department for International Sustainable Development, which would oversee U.S. foreign assistance and initiatives related to sustainable development in low-income countries, including water, food production, disease control and climate-change adaptation and mitigation.

I propose five major guideposts for a more-functional foreign policy in the coming years. First, we will need, on a global scale, to develop and diffuse new sustainable technologies so that the global economy can continue to support broad-based economic growth. If we remain stuck with our current technologies, the world will face a zero-sum struggle for increasingly scarce resources across competing regions. The new sustainable technologies will not arise from market forces alone. All major technological advances, such as the introduction of large-scale solar or nuclear power, will require massive public-sector investments (in basic science, demonstration projects, diffusion of proven technologies and regulatory framework) alongside the R&D of private markets. These public investments will be global-scale, internationally cooperative efforts.

Free-market ideologues who are convinced that technologies emerge from market forces alone should think again. They might compare the successful government-led promotion of nuclear power in France with the failure of the private-sector-led nuclear-power industry in the United States, which failed because of a collapse in U.S. public confidence in the safety of the technology. Similarly, they can examine the highly successful public-private partnerships linking the public-sector National Institutes of Health with the private-sector pharmaceutical industry, or the public-sector investments that underpinned the start-up of computer and Internet technologies.

Second, we will need to address the still-rapid rise of the world's population, heavily centered in the world's poorest countries. Sub-Saharan Africa is on a trajectory that will expand its population from around 800 million to 1.8 billion by 2050, according to the medium-fertility forecast of the United Nations Population Division. Yet that extent of population increase, an added 1 billion people, resulting from Africa's very high fertility rates, would actually be a grave threat to Africa's economy, political stability and environment, and would inevitably spill over adversely into the rest of the world. Rapid and voluntary fertility reduction in Africa is possible, if girls can be encouraged to stay in school through the secondary level; if family planning and contraception are made widely available; if child mortality is reduced (giving confidence to parents to reduce fertility rates); and if women are economically empowered.

Third, the world will need to address critical failings in the management of the global commons, most importantly, by restricting greenhouse-gas emissions, protecting the oceans and biodiversity, and managing transnational water resources sustainably at the regional level. Of course several global treaties have committed the world's nations to do just this, but these treaties have yet to be implemented. Three treaties of overriding importance are the UN Framework Convention on Climate Change, the UN Convention on Biological Diversity and the UN Convention to Combat Desertification. If these treaties are honored, the global commons can be sustainably managed.

Fourth, we will need to take seriously the risks of impoverished "failed states," to themselves, to their neighborhoods and to the world. The poorest and least-stable countries are rife with risks to peace and avoidable human tragedies like the 10 million children each year who die tragically and unnecessarily before their fifth birthday, largely the result of extreme poverty. Darfur, the Horn of Africa, Yemen, Afghanistan, Pakistan, Sri Lanka and elsewhere are places trapped in vicious cycles of extreme violence and poverty. These poverty-conflict traps can be broken, most importantly if the donors of the G-8, the oil-rich states in the Middle East, and the new donors in Latin America and Asia will pool their efforts to ensure the success of the Millennium Development Goals in today's impoverished and fragile regions.

Fifth, and finally, we require a new analytical framework for addressing our generation's challenges, and a new governmental machinery to apply that framework. Traditional problems of statecraft—the balance of power, alliances, arms control and credible deterrence—certainly will continue to play a role, but we need to move beyond these traditional concepts to face the challenges of sustainable development ahead. Will our era be a time of wondrous advances, based on our unprecedented scientific and technological know-how, or will we succumb to a nightmare of spreading violence and conflict? We face world-shaping choices. Our global challenges are unique to our generation, in scale and character. Vision, leadership and global cooperation will be our most-important resources for ensuring our future well-being.

---

**JEFFREY D. SACHS** is the director of the Earth Institute at Columbia University and author of *Common Wealth: Economics for a Crowded Planet* (Penguin, 2008).

# Test-Your-Knowledge Form

We encourage you to photocopy and use this page as a tool to assess how the articles in *Annual Editions* expand on the information in your textbook. By reflecting on the articles you will gain enhanced text information. You can also access this useful form on a product's book support website at www.mhhe.com/cls.

NAME:                                                                                          DATE:

_____

TITLE AND NUMBER OF ARTICLE:

_____

BRIEFLY STATE THE MAIN IDEA OF THIS ARTICLE:


_____

LIST THREE IMPORTANT FACTS THAT THE AUTHOR USES TO SUPPORT THE MAIN IDEA:




_____

WHAT INFORMATION OR IDEAS DISCUSSED IN THIS ARTICLE ARE ALSO DISCUSSED IN YOUR TEXTBOOK OR OTHER READINGS THAT YOU HAVE DONE? LIST THE TEXTBOOK CHAPTERS AND PAGE NUMBERS:




_____

LIST ANY EXAMPLES OF BIAS OR FAULTY REASONING THAT YOU FOUND IN THE ARTICLE:




_____

LIST ANY NEW TERMS/CONCEPTS THAT WERE DISCUSSED IN THE ARTICLE, AND WRITE A SHORT DEFINITION:

# We Want Your Advice

ANNUAL EDITIONS revisions depend on two major opinion sources: one is our Advisory Board, listed in the front of this volume, which works with us in scanning the thousands of articles published in the public press each year; the other is you—the person actually using the book. Please help us and the users of the next edition by completing the prepaid article rating form on this page and returning it to us. Thank you for your help!

## ANNUAL EDITIONS: World History Vol. 2, 11/e

### ARTICLE RATING FORM

Here is an opportunity for you to have direct input into the next revision of this volume.
We would like you to rate each of the articles listed below, using the following scale:

1. **Excellent: should definitely be retained**
2. **Above average: should probably be retained**
3. **Below average: should probably be deleted**
4. **Poor: should definitely be deleted**

Your ratings will play a vital part in the next revision.
Please mail this prepaid form to us as soon as possible.
Thanks for your help!

| RATING | ARTICLE | RATING | ARTICLE |
|---|---|---|---|
| | 1. Aztecs: A New Perspective | | 25. Two Cheers for Versailles |
| | 2. The Mughal Dynasties | | 26. One Family's Tryst with Destiny |
| | 3. The Peopling of Canada | | 27. The Roots of Chinese Xenophobia |
| | 4. The *Real* First World War and the Making of America | | 28. Exposing the Rape of Nanking |
| | 5. The Ottomans in Europe | | 29. Judgment at Nuremberg |
| | 6. How American Slavery Led to the Birth of Liberia | | 30. Starting the Cold War |
| | 7. Fighting the Afghans in the 19th Century | | 31. A Case of Courage |
| | 8. New Light on the 'Heart of Darkness' | | 32. The Plan and the Man |
| | 9. The World, the Flesh and the Devil | | 33. Korea: Echoes of a War |
| | 10. The Luther Legacy | | 34. Mao Zedong: Liberator or Oppressor of China? |
| | 11. Elizabeth I: Gender, Power and Politics | | 35. Iraq's Unruly Century |
| | 12. The Return of Catherine the Great | | 36. Remembering the War–Japanese Style |
| | 13. From Mercantilism to the 'Wealth of Nations' | | 37. Coming to Terms with the Past: Former Yugoslavia |
| | 14. A Woman Writ Large in Our History and Hearts | | 38. Coming to Terms with the Past: Cambodia |
| | 15. A Disquieting Sense of Deja Vu | | 39. The Weather Turns Wild |
| | 16. The Paris Commune | | 40. 10 Million Orphans |
| | 17. In God's Place | | 41. In God's Name: Genocide and Religion in the Twentieth Century |
| | 18. John Locke: Icon of Liberty | | 42. Women, Citizens, Muslims |
| | 19. The Workshop of a New Society | | 43. The Jihad against the Jihadis: How Moderate Muslim Leaders Waged War on Extremists—and Won |
| | 20. Slavery and the British | | 44. The Next Asian Miracle |
| | 21. Samurai, Shoguns and the Age of Steam | | 45. Bad Guys Matter |
| | 22. No Marx without Engels | | 46. A User's Guide to the Century |
| | 23. Sputnik + 50: Remembering the Dawn of the Space Age | | |
| | 24. From Boer War to Timor: Warfare in the Twentieth Century | | |

# ABOUT YOU

Name                                                                      Date

Are you a teacher? ❏ A student? ❏
Your school's name

Department

Address                                          City              State              Zip

School telephone #

# YOUR COMMENTS ARE IMPORTANT TO US!

Please fill in the following information:
For which course did you use this book?

Did you use a text with this ANNUAL EDITION?  ❏ yes ❏ no
What was the title of the text?

What are your general reactions to the Annual Editions concept?

Have you read any pertinent articles recently that you think should be included in the next edition? Explain.

Are there any articles that you feel should be replaced in the next edition? Why?

Are there any World Wide Websites that you feel should be included in the next edition? Please annotate.

May we contact you for editorial input? ❏ yes ❏ no
May we quote your comments? ❏ yes ❏ no

# NOTES

# NOTES

# NOTES

# NOTES

# NOTES

# NOTES